ADPOOL VOL. 2: SOUL HUNTER. Contains material originally published in magazine form as DEADPOOL #7-12. Third printing 2015. ISBN# 978-0-7851-6681-8. Published by MARVEL WORLDWIDE, INC., a subsidiary MARVEL ENTERTAINMENT, LLC. OFFICE OF PUBLICATION: 135 West 50th Street, New York, NY 10020. Copyright © 2013 MARVEL No similarity between any of the names, characters, persons, and/or institutions in s magazine with those of any living or dead person or institution is intended, and any such similarity which may exist is purely coincidental. **Printed in Canada.** ALAN FINE, President, Marvel Entertainment; DAN CKLEY, President, TV, Publishing and Brand Management; JOE QUESADA, Chief Creative Officer; TOM BREVOORT, SVP of Publishing; DAVID BOGART, SVP of Operations & Procurement, Publishing; C.B. CEBULSKI, VP of rnational Development & Brand Management; DAVID GABRIEL, SVP Print, Sales & Marketing; JIM O'KEEFE, VP of Operations & Logistics; DAN CARR, Executive Director of Publishing Technology; SUSAN CRESPI, Editorial rations Manager; ALEX MORALES, Publishing Operations Manager; STAN LEE, Chairman Emeritus. For information regarding advertising in Marvel Comics or on Marvel.com, please contact Jonathan Rheingold, VP of tom Solutions & Ad Sales, at jrheingold@marvel.com. For Marvel subscription inquiries, please call 800-217-9158. **Manufactured between 4/15/2015 and 5/18/2015 by SOLISCO PRINTERS, SCOTT, QC, CANADA.**

# DEADPOOL

**WRITERS**
**GERRY DUGGAN** & **BRIAN POSEHN**

**ARTISTS**
**SCOTT KOBLISH** (#7) & **MIKE HAWTHORNE** (#8-12)

**ADDITIONAL INKS, #12**
**JOHN LUCAS**

**COLOR ARTIST**
**VAL STAPLES**

**COVER ART**
**KEVIN MAGUIRE & ROSEMARY CHEETHAM** (#7), **ARTHUR ADAMS & PETER STEIGERWALD** (#8-9), **TRADD MOORE & EDGAR DELGADO** (#10-11) AND **TRADD MOORE & MARTE GRACIA** (#12)

**LETTERER**
**VC´S JOE SABINO**

**EDITOR**
**JORDAN D. WHITE**

**DEADPOOL CREATED BY ROB LIEFELD & FABIAN NICIEZA**

Collection Editor: Jennifer Grünwald • Assistant Editor: Sarah Brunstad • Associate Managing Editor: Alex Starbuck
Editor, Special Projects: Mark D. Beazley • Senior Editor, Special Projects: Jeff Youngquist
SVP Print, Sales & Marketing: David Gabriel • Book Design:Jeff Powell

Editor in Chief: Axel Alonso • Chief Creative Officer: Joe Quesada • Publisher: Dan Buckley • Executive Producer: Alan Fine

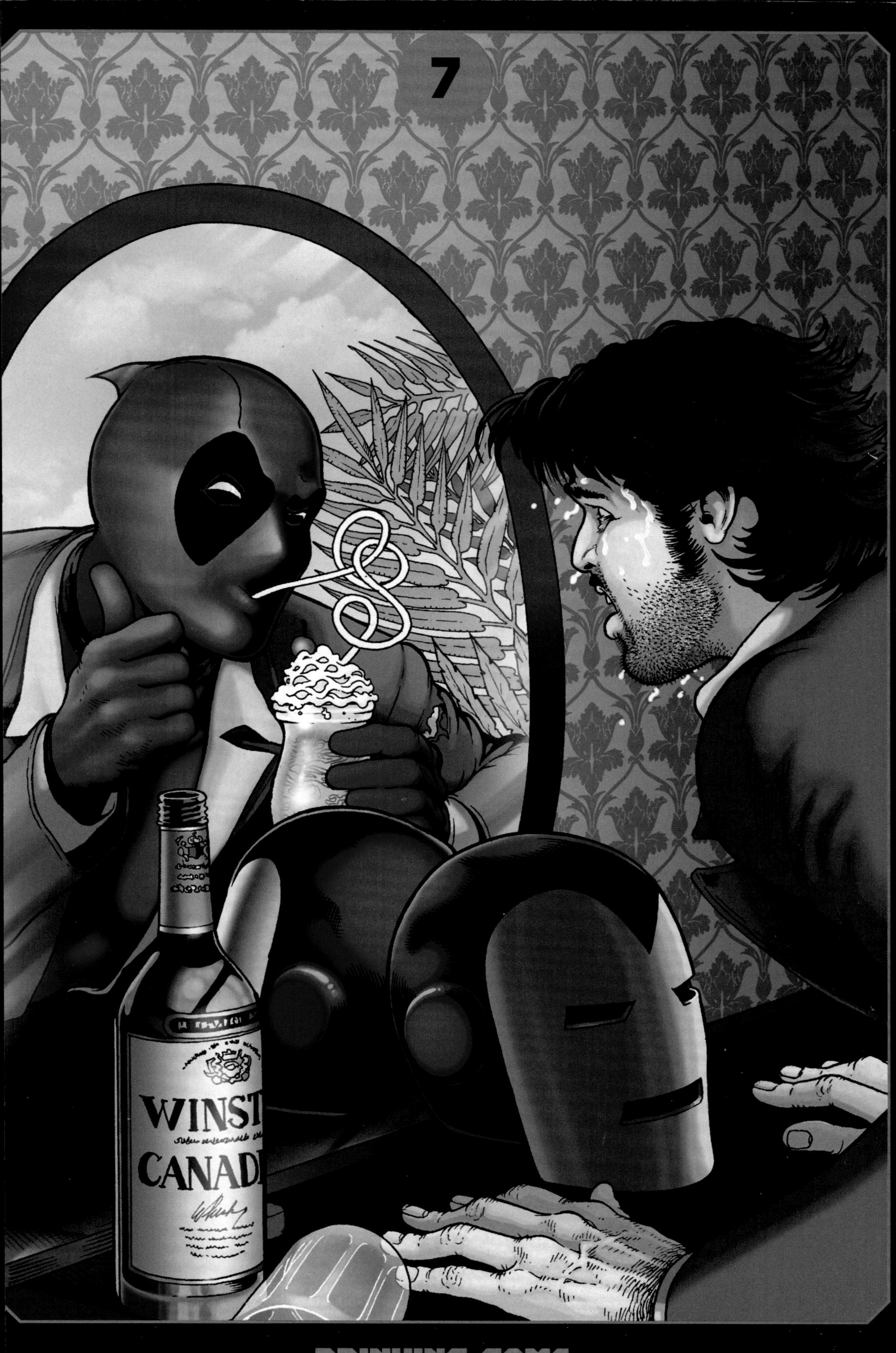
7
WINST
CANADI

DRINKING GAME

**Possibly the world's most skilled mercenary, definitely the world's most annoying, Wade Wilson was chosen for a top-secret government program that gave him a healing factor allowing him to heal from any wound. Now, Wade makes his way as a gun for hire, shooting his prey's faces off while talking his friends' ears off. Call him the Merc with the Mouth…call him the Regeneratin' Degenerate…call him…DEADPOOL.**

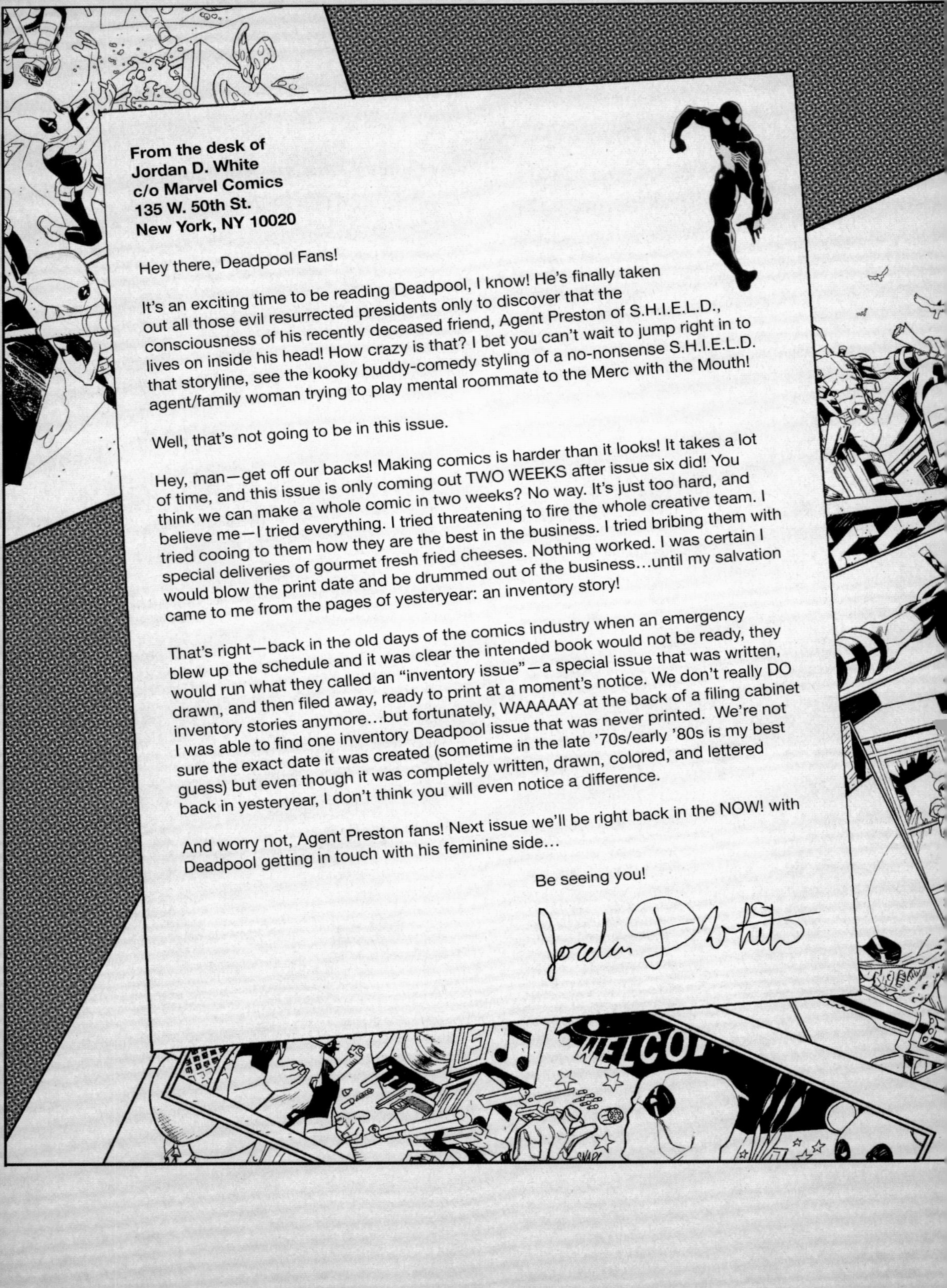

**From the desk of**
**Jordan D. White**
**c/o Marvel Comics**
**135 W. 50th St.**
**New York, NY 10020**

Hey there, Deadpool Fans!

It's an exciting time to be reading Deadpool, I know! He's finally taken out all those evil resurrected presidents only to discover that the consciousness of his recently deceased friend, Agent Preston of S.H.I.E.L.D., lives on inside his head! How crazy is that? I bet you can't wait to jump right in to that storyline, see the kooky buddy-comedy styling of a no-nonsense S.H.I.E.L.D. agent/family woman trying to play mental roommate to the Merc with the Mouth!

Well, that's not going to be in this issue.

Hey, man—get off our backs! Making comics is harder than it looks! It takes a lot of time, and this issue is only coming out TWO WEEKS after issue six did! You think we can make a whole comic in two weeks? No way. It's just too hard, and believe me—I tried everything. I tried threatening to fire the whole creative team. I tried cooing to them how they are the best in the business. I tried bribing them with special deliveries of gourmet fresh fried cheeses. Nothing worked. I was certain I would blow the print date and be drummed out of the business…until my salvation came to me from the pages of yesteryear: an inventory story!

That's right—back in the old days of the comics industry when an emergency blew up the schedule and it was clear the intended book would not be ready, they would run what they called an "inventory issue"—a special issue that was written, drawn, and then filed away, ready to print at a moment's notice. We don't really DO inventory stories anymore…but fortunately, WAAAAAY at the back of a filing cabinet I was able to find one inventory Deadpool issue that was never printed. We're not sure the exact date it was created (sometime in the late '70s/early '80s is my best guess) but even though it was completely written, drawn, colored, and lettered back in yesteryear, I don't think you will even notice a difference.

And worry not, Agent Preston fans! Next issue we'll be right back in the NOW! with Deadpool getting in touch with his feminine side…

Be seeing you!

Jordan D. White

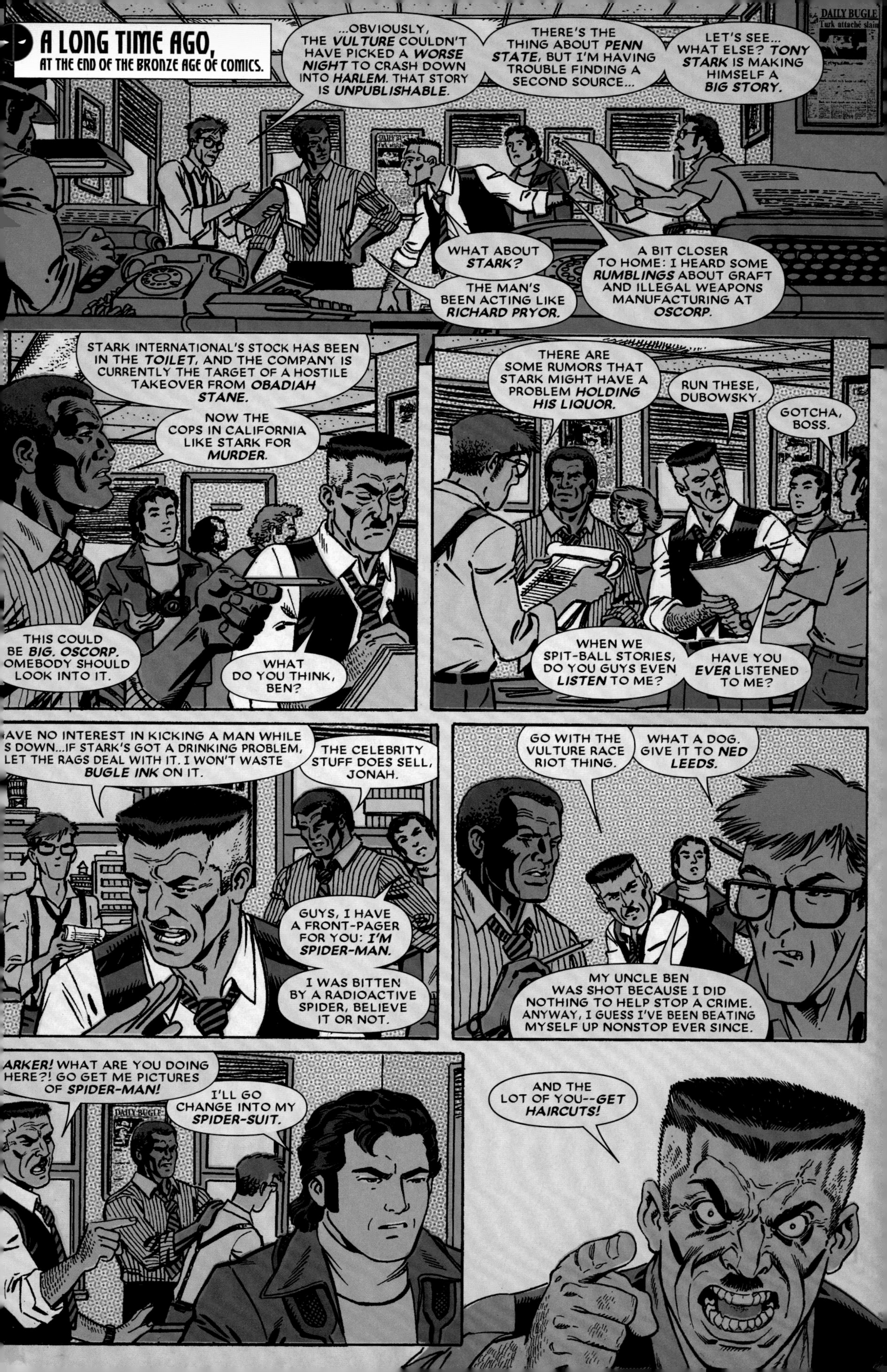

A LONG TIME AGO,
AT THE END OF THE BRONZE AGE OF COMICS.
...OBVIOUSLY, THE VULTURE COULDN'T HAVE PICKED A WORSE NIGHT TO CRASH DOWN INTO HARLEM. THAT STORY IS UNPUBLISHABLE.
THERE'S THE THING ABOUT PENN STATE, BUT I'M HAVING TROUBLE FINDING A SECOND SOURCE...
LET'S SEE... WHAT ELSE?... TONY STARK IS MAKING HIMSELF A BIG STORY.
WHAT ABOUT STARK?
THE MAN'S BEEN ACTING LIKE RICHARD PRYOR.
A BIT CLOSER TO HOME: I HEARD SOME RUMBLINGS ABOUT GRAFT AND ILLEGAL WEAPONS MANUFACTURING AT OSCORP.
STARK INTERNATIONAL'S STOCK HAS BEEN IN THE TOILET, AND THE COMPANY IS CURRENTLY THE TARGET OF A HOSTILE TAKEOVER FROM OBADIAH STANE.
NOW THE COPS IN CALIFORNIA LIKE STARK FOR MURDER.
THIS COULD BE BIG. OSCORP. OMEBODY SHOULD LOOK INTO IT.
WHAT DO YOU THINK, BEN?
THERE ARE SOME RUMORS THAT STARK MIGHT HAVE A PROBLEM HOLDING HIS LIQUOR.
RUN THESE, DUBOWSKY.
GOTCHA, BOSS.
WHEN WE SPIT-BALL STORIES, DO YOU GUYS EVEN LISTEN TO ME?
HAVE YOU EVER LISTENED TO ME?
AVE NO INTEREST IN KICKING A MAN WHILE S DOWN...IF STARK'S GOT A DRINKING PROBLEM, LET THE RAGS DEAL WITH IT. I WON'T WASTE BUGLE INK ON IT.
THE CELEBRITY STUFF DOES SELL, JONAH.
GUYS, I HAVE A FRONT-PAGER FOR YOU: I'M SPIDER-MAN.
I WAS BITTEN BY A RADIOACTIVE SPIDER, BELIEVE IT OR NOT.
GO WITH THE VULTURE RACE RIOT THING.
WHAT A DOG. GIVE IT TO NED LEEDS.
MY UNCLE BEN WAS SHOT BECAUSE I DID NOTHING TO HELP STOP A CRIME. ANYWAY, I GUESS I'VE BEEN BEATING MYSELF UP NONSTOP EVER SINCE.
ARKER! WHAT ARE YOU DOING HERE?! GO GET ME PICTURES OF SPIDER-MAN!
I'LL GO CHANGE INTO MY SPIDER-SUIT.
AND THE LOT OF YOU--GET HAIRCUTS!

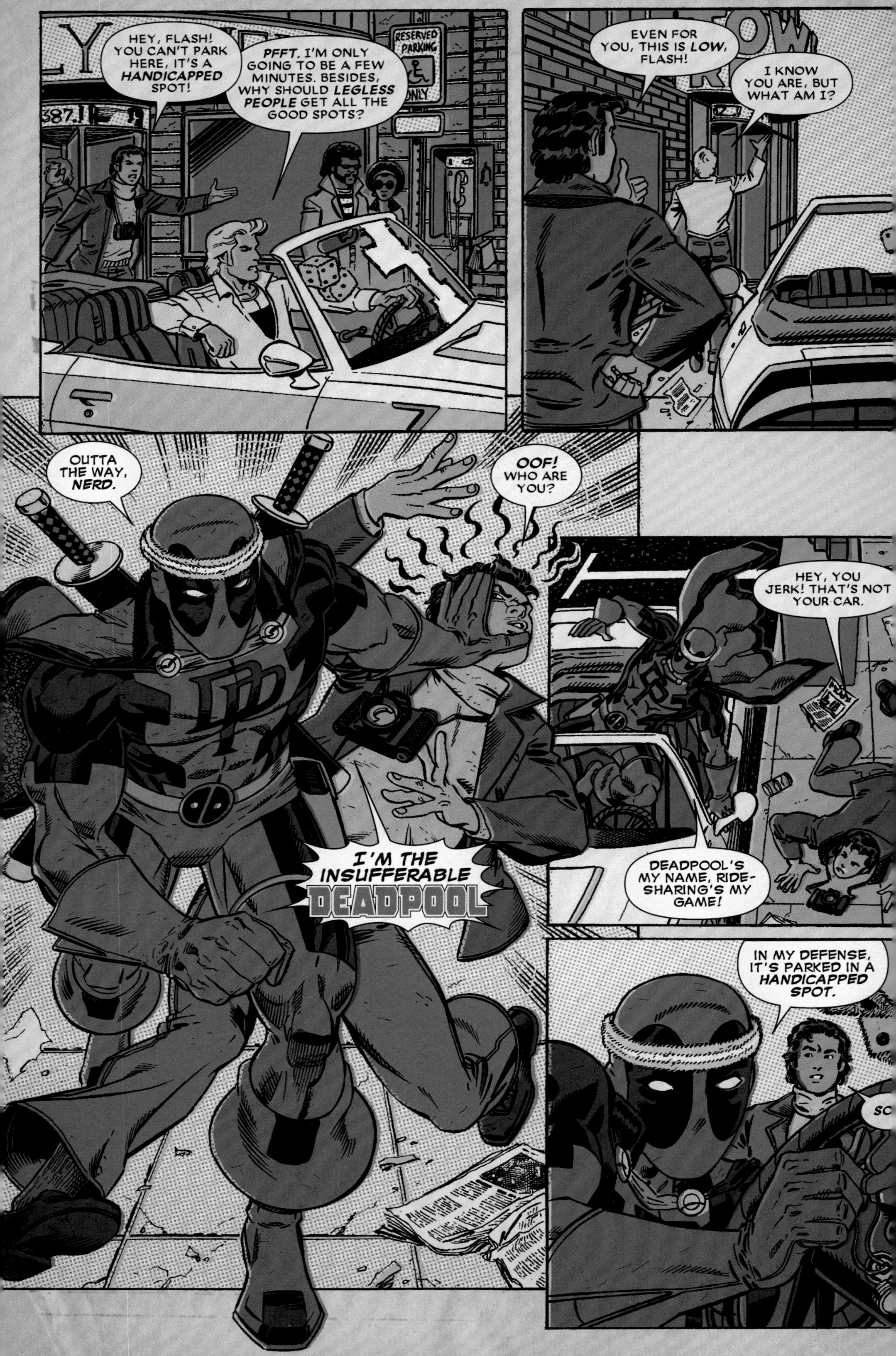

HEY, FLASH! YOU CAN'T PARK HERE, IT'S A HANDICAPPED SPOT!
PFFT. I'M ONLY GOING TO BE A FEW MINUTES. BESIDES, WHY SHOULD LEGLESS PEOPLE GET ALL THE GOOD SPOTS?
RESERVED PARKING ONLY
EVEN FOR YOU, THIS IS LOW, FLASH!
I KNOW YOU ARE, BUT WHAT AM I?
OUTTA THE WAY, NERD.
OOF! WHO ARE YOU?
I'M THE INSUFFERABLE DEADPOOL
HEY, YOU JERK! THAT'S NOT YOUR CAR.
DEADPOOL'S MY NAME, RIDE-SHARING'S MY GAME!
IN MY DEFENSE, IT'S PARKED IN A HANDICAPPED SPOT.

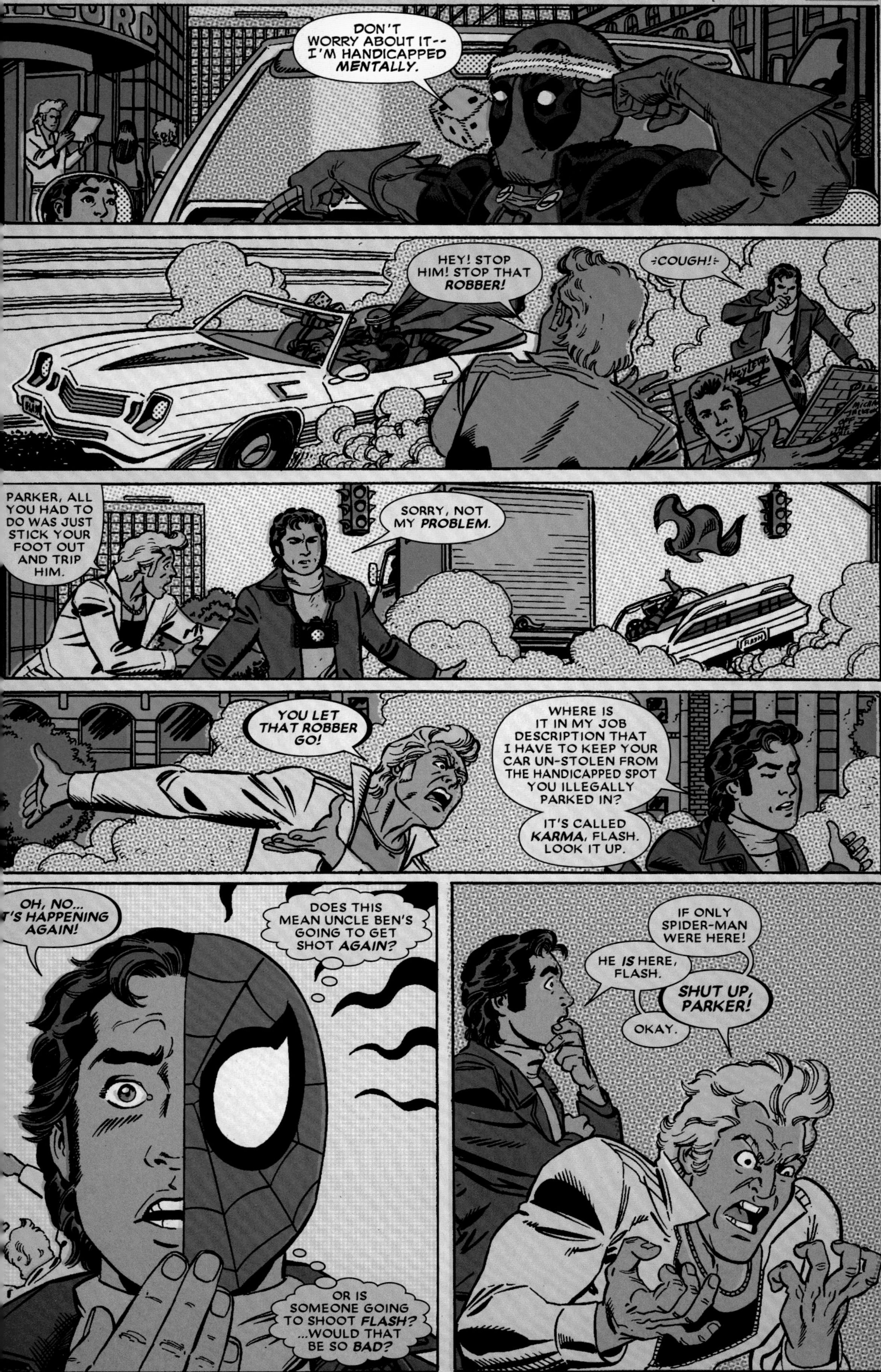
DON'T WORRY ABOUT IT-- I'M HANDICAPPED *MENTALLY.*
HEY! STOP HIM! STOP THAT *ROBBER!*
COUGH!
PARKER, ALL YOU HAD TO DO WAS JUST STICK YOUR FOOT OUT AND TRIP HIM.
SORRY, NOT MY *PROBLEM.*
*YOU LET THAT ROBBER GO!*
WHERE IS IT IN MY JOB DESCRIPTION THAT I HAVE TO KEEP YOUR CAR UN-STOLEN FROM THE HANDICAPPED SPOT YOU ILLEGALLY PARKED IN?
IT'S CALLED *KARMA*, FLASH. LOOK IT UP.
*OH, NO... IT'S HAPPENING AGAIN!*
DOES THIS MEAN UNCLE BEN'S GOING TO GET SHOT *AGAIN?*
OR IS SOMEONE GOING TO SHOOT *FLASH?* ...WOULD THAT BE SO *BAD?*
IF ONLY SPIDER-MAN WERE HERE!
HE *IS* HERE, FLASH.
**SHUT UP, PARKER!**
OKAY.

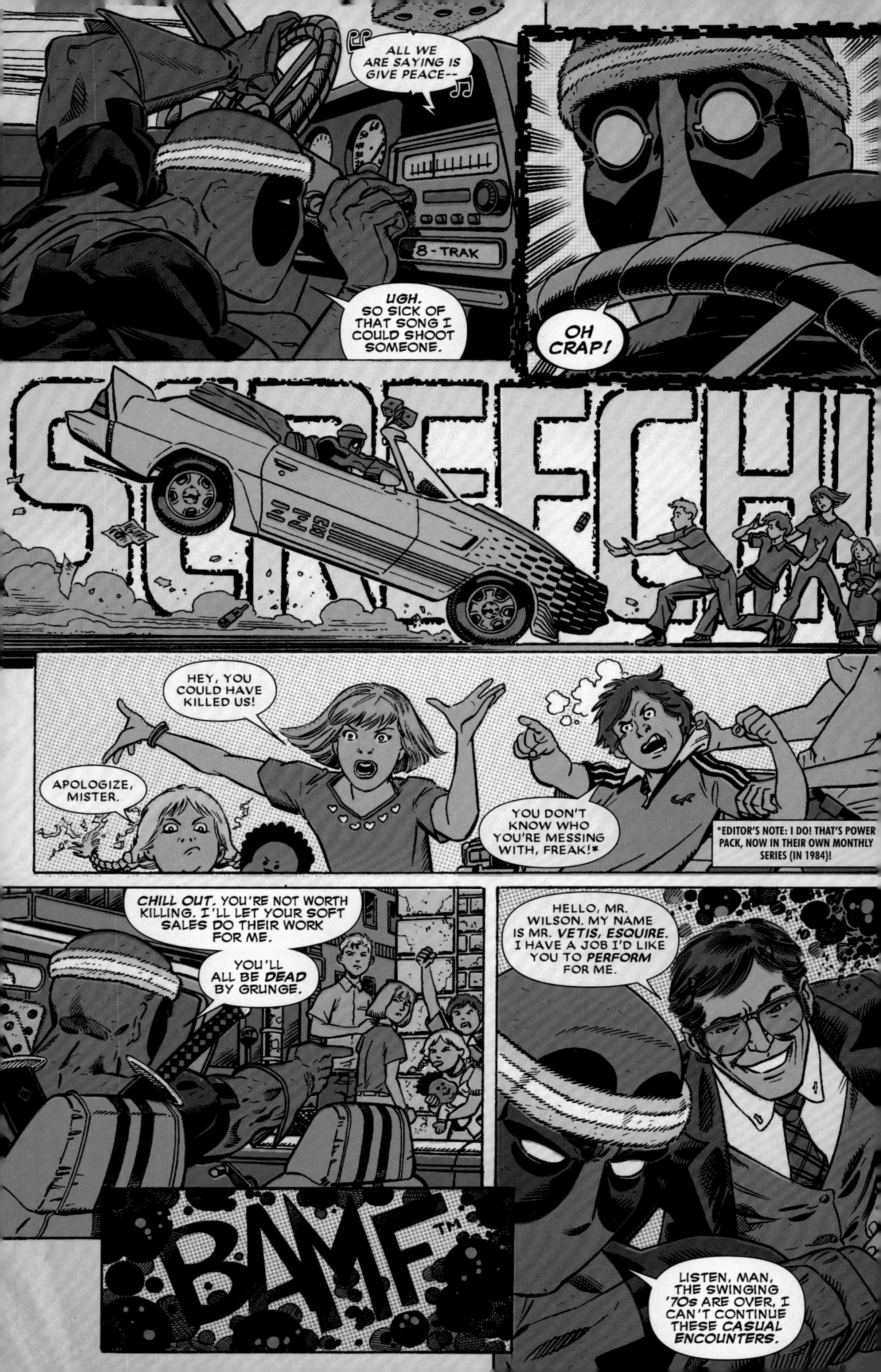

ALL WE ARE SAYING IS GIVE PEACE--
8-TRAK
UGH. SO SICK OF THAT SONG I COULD SHOOT SOMEONE.
OH CRAP!
SCREECH
HEY, YOU COULD HAVE KILLED US!
APOLOGIZE, MISTER.
YOU DON'T KNOW WHO YOU'RE MESSING WITH, FREAK!*
*EDITOR'S NOTE: I DO! THAT'S POWER PACK, NOW IN THEIR OWN MONTHLY SERIES (IN 1984)!
CHILL OUT. YOU'RE NOT WORTH KILLING. I'LL LET YOUR SOFT SALES DO THEIR WORK FOR ME.
YOU'LL ALL BE DEAD BY GRUNGE.
BAMF™
HELLO, MR. WILSON. MY NAME IS MR. VETIS, ESQUIRE. I HAVE A JOB I'D LIKE YOU TO PERFORM FOR ME.
LISTEN, MAN, THE SWINGING '70s ARE OVER, I CAN'T CONTINUE THESE CASUAL ENCOUNTERS.

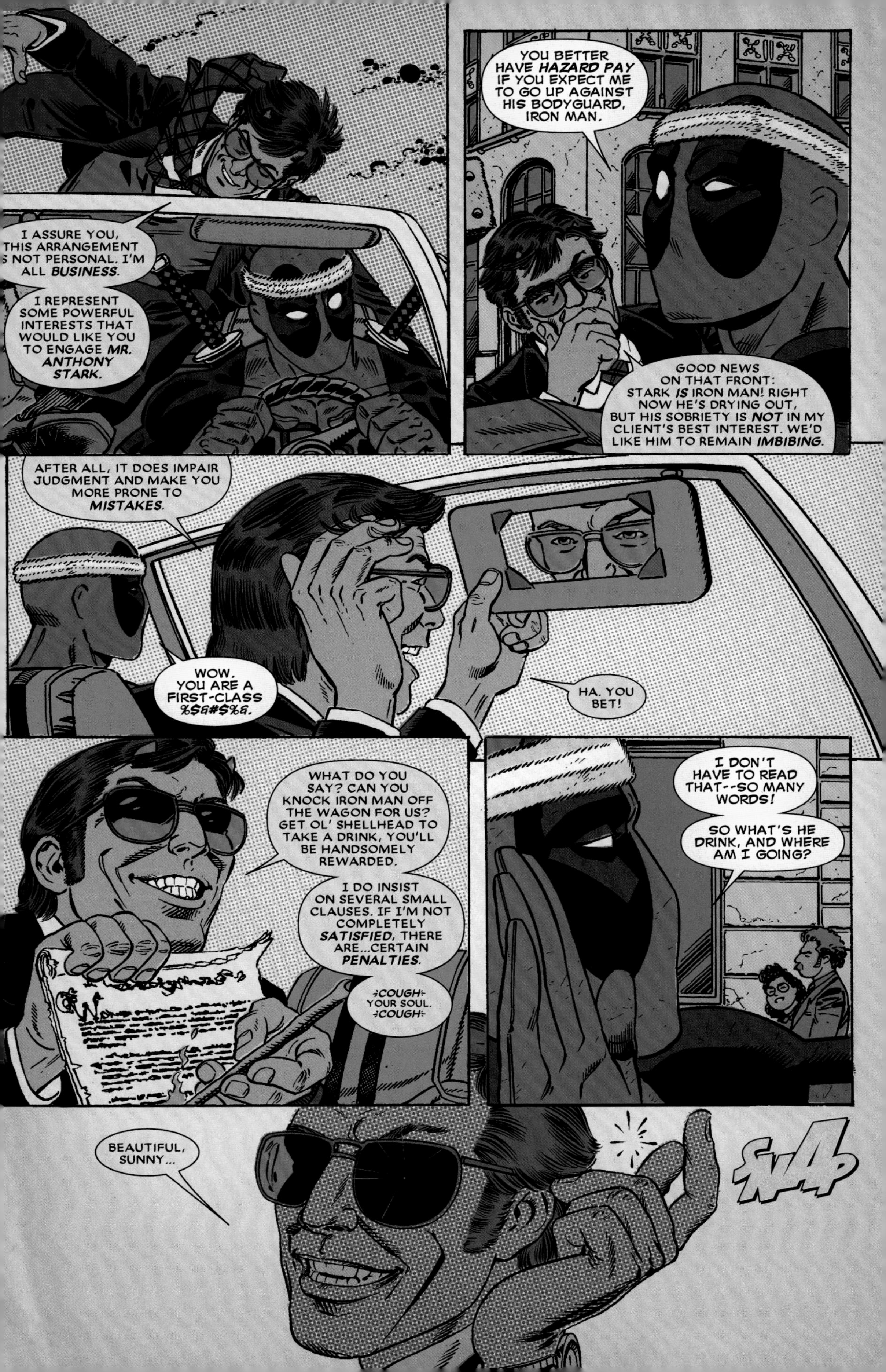
YOU BETTER HAVE HAZARD PAY IF YOU EXPECT ME TO GO UP AGAINST HIS BODYGUARD, IRON MAN.
I ASSURE YOU, THIS ARRANGEMENT IS NOT PERSONAL. I'M ALL BUSINESS.
I REPRESENT SOME POWERFUL INTERESTS THAT WOULD LIKE YOU TO ENGAGE MR. ANTHONY STARK.
GOOD NEWS ON THAT FRONT: STARK IS IRON MAN! RIGHT NOW HE'S DRYING OUT, BUT HIS SOBRIETY IS NOT IN MY CLIENT'S BEST INTEREST. WE'D LIKE HIM TO REMAIN IMBIBING.
AFTER ALL, IT DOES IMPAIR JUDGMENT AND MAKE YOU MORE PRONE TO MISTAKES.
WOW. YOU ARE A FIRST-CLASS %$@#$%@.
HA. YOU BET!
WHAT DO YOU SAY? CAN YOU KNOCK IRON MAN OFF THE WAGON FOR US? GET OL' SHELLHEAD TO TAKE A DRINK, YOU'LL BE HANDSOMELY REWARDED.
I DO INSIST ON SEVERAL SMALL CLAUSES. IF I'M NOT COMPLETELY SATISFIED, THERE ARE...CERTAIN PENALTIES.
COUGH YOUR SOUL. COUGH
I DON'T HAVE TO READ THAT--SO MANY WORDS!
SO WHAT'S HE DRINK, AND WHERE AM I GOING?
BEAUTIFUL, SUNNY...
SNAP

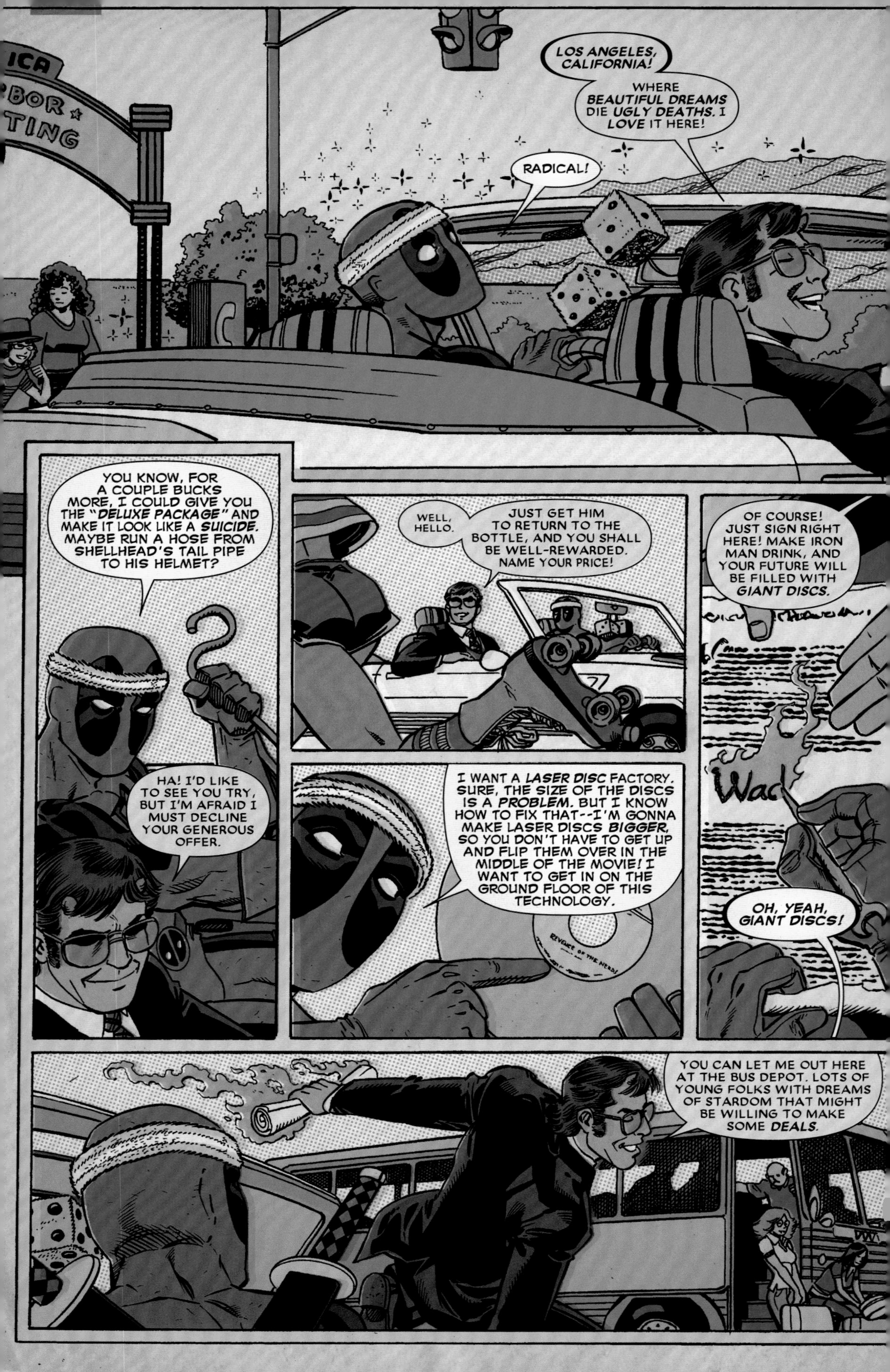
LOS ANGELES, CALIFORNIA!
WHERE BEAUTIFUL DREAMS DIE UGLY DEATHS. I LOVE IT HERE!
RADICAL!
YOU KNOW, FOR A COUPLE BUCKS MORE, I COULD GIVE YOU THE "DELUXE PACKAGE" AND MAKE IT LOOK LIKE A SUICIDE. MAYBE RUN A HOSE FROM SHELLHEAD'S TAIL PIPE TO HIS HELMET?
HA! I'D LIKE TO SEE YOU TRY, BUT I'M AFRAID I MUST DECLINE YOUR GENEROUS OFFER.
WELL, HELLO.
JUST GET HIM TO RETURN TO THE BOTTLE, AND YOU SHALL BE WELL-REWARDED. NAME YOUR PRICE!
I WANT A LASER DISC FACTORY. SURE, THE SIZE OF THE DISCS IS A PROBLEM. BUT I KNOW HOW TO FIX THAT--I'M GONNA MAKE LASER DISCS BIGGER, SO YOU DON'T HAVE TO GET UP AND FLIP THEM OVER IN THE MIDDLE OF THE MOVIE! I WANT TO GET IN ON THE GROUND FLOOR OF THIS TECHNOLOGY.
REVENGE OF THE NERDS
OF COURSE! JUST SIGN RIGHT HERE! MAKE IRON MAN DRINK, AND YOUR FUTURE WILL BE FILLED WITH GIANT DISCS.
OH, YEAH, GIANT DISCS!
YOU CAN LET ME OUT HERE AT THE BUS DEPOT. LOTS OF YOUNG FOLKS WITH DREAMS OF STARDOM THAT MIGHT BE WILLING TO MAKE SOME DEALS.

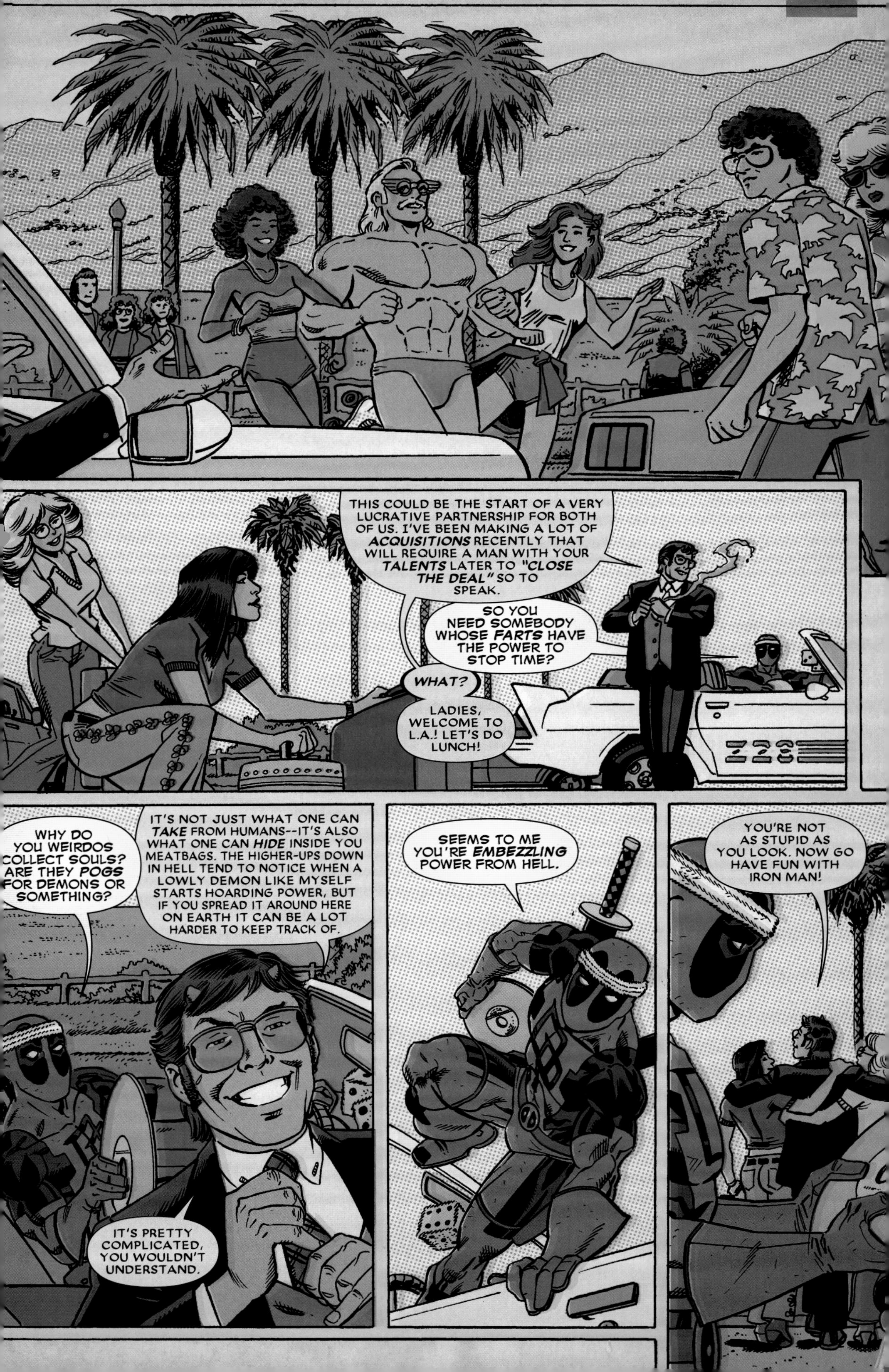
THIS COULD BE THE START OF A VERY LUCRATIVE PARTNERSHIP FOR BOTH OF US. I'VE BEEN MAKING A LOT OF ACQUISITIONS RECENTLY THAT WILL REQUIRE A MAN WITH YOUR TALENTS LATER TO "CLOSE THE DEAL" SO TO SPEAK.
SO YOU NEED SOMEBODY WHOSE FARTS HAVE THE POWER TO STOP TIME?
WHAT?
LADIES, WELCOME TO L.A.! LET'S DO LUNCH!
WHY DO YOU WEIRDOS COLLECT SOULS? ARE THEY POGS FOR DEMONS OR SOMETHING?
IT'S NOT JUST WHAT ONE CAN TAKE FROM HUMANS--IT'S ALSO WHAT ONE CAN HIDE INSIDE YOU MEATBAGS. THE HIGHER-UPS DOWN IN HELL TEND TO NOTICE WHEN A LOWLY DEMON LIKE MYSELF STARTS HOARDING POWER, BUT IF YOU SPREAD IT AROUND HERE ON EARTH IT CAN BE A LOT HARDER TO KEEP TRACK OF.
IT'S PRETTY COMPLICATED, YOU WOULDN'T UNDERSTAND.
SEEMS TO ME YOU'RE EMBEZZLING POWER FROM HELL.
YOU'RE NOT AS STUPID AS YOU LOOK. NOW GO HAVE FUN WITH IRON MAN!
Z28

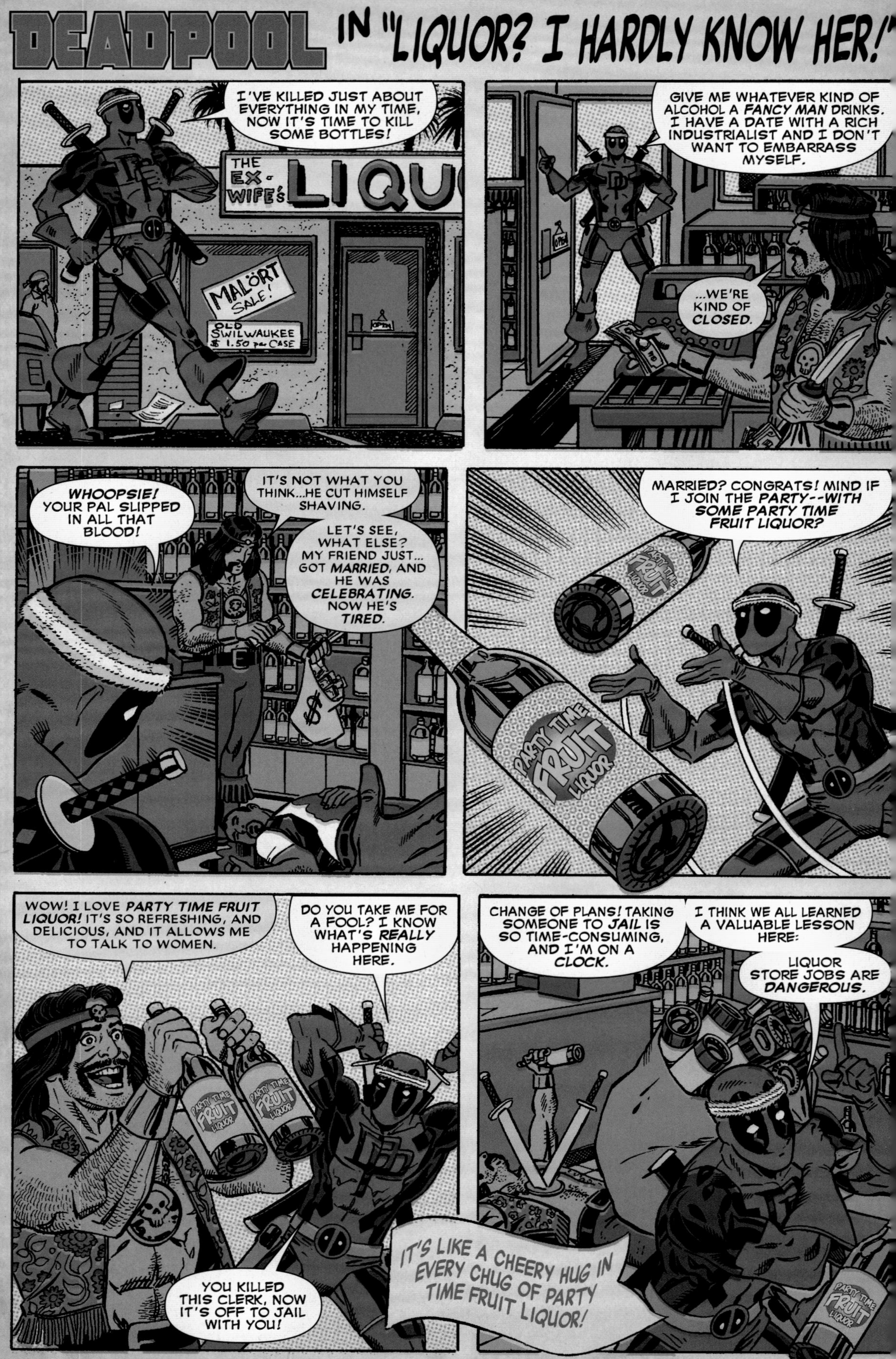
DEADPOOL IN "LIQUOR? I HARDLY KNOW HER!"
I'VE KILLED JUST ABOUT EVERYTHING IN MY TIME, NOW IT'S TIME TO KILL SOME BOTTLES!
THE EX-WIFE'S LIQU
MALÖRT SALE!
OLD SWILWAUKEE $1.50 per CASE
GIVE ME WHATEVER KIND OF ALCOHOL A FANCY MAN DRINKS. I HAVE A DATE WITH A RICH INDUSTRIALIST AND I DON'T WANT TO EMBARRASS MYSELF.
...WE'RE KIND OF CLOSED.
WHOOPSIE! YOUR PAL SLIPPED IN ALL THAT BLOOD!
IT'S NOT WHAT YOU THINK...HE CUT HIMSELF SHAVING.
LET'S SEE, WHAT ELSE? MY FRIEND JUST... GOT MARRIED, AND HE WAS CELEBRATING. NOW HE'S TIRED.
MARRIED? CONGRATS! MIND IF I JOIN THE PARTY--WITH SOME PARTY TIME FRUIT LIQUOR?
PARTY TIME FRUIT LIQUOR
WOW! I LOVE PARTY TIME FRUIT LIQUOR! IT'S SO REFRESHING, AND DELICIOUS, AND IT ALLOWS ME TO TALK TO WOMEN.
DO YOU TAKE ME FOR A FOOL? I KNOW WHAT'S REALLY HAPPENING HERE.
YOU KILLED THIS CLERK, NOW IT'S OFF TO JAIL WITH YOU!
CHANGE OF PLANS! TAKING SOMEONE TO JAIL IS SO TIME-CONSUMING, AND I'M ON A CLOCK.
I THINK WE ALL LEARNED A VALUABLE LESSON HERE:
LIQUOR STORE JOBS ARE DANGEROUS.
IT'S LIKE A CHEERY HUG IN EVERY CHUG OF PARTY TIME FRUIT LIQUOR!

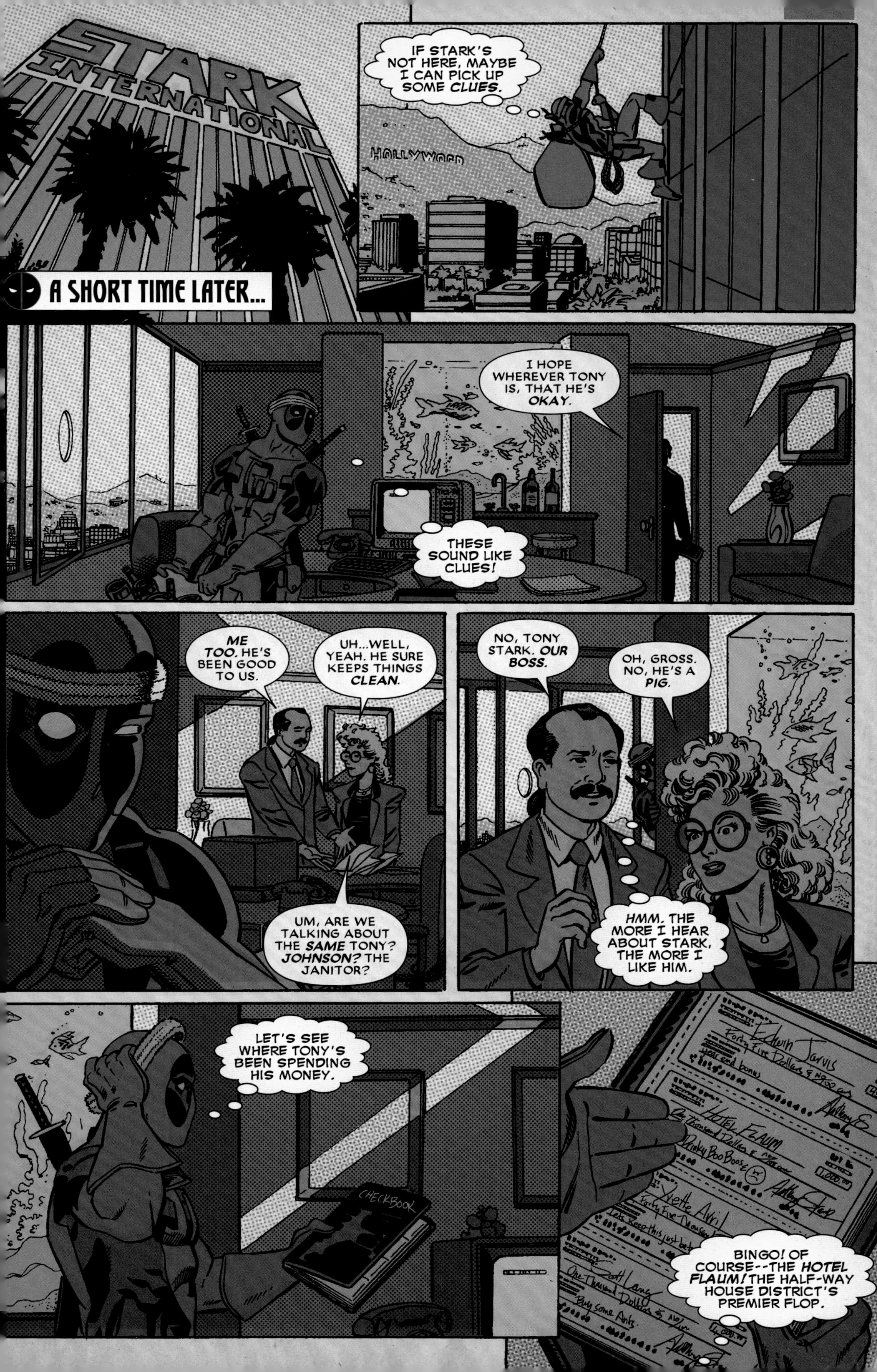
STARK INTERNATIONAL
HOLLYWOOD
IF STARK'S NOT HERE, MAYBE I CAN PICK UP SOME CLUES.
A SHORT TIME LATER...
I HOPE WHEREVER TONY IS, THAT HE'S OKAY.
THESE SOUND LIKE CLUES!
ME TOO. HE'S BEEN GOOD TO US.
UH...WELL, YEAH. HE SURE KEEPS THINGS CLEAN.
UM, ARE WE TALKING ABOUT THE SAME TONY? JOHNSON? THE JANITOR?
NO, TONY STARK. OUR BOSS.
OH, GROSS. NO, HE'S A PIG.
HMM. THE MORE I HEAR ABOUT STARK, THE MORE I LIKE HIM.
LET'S SEE WHERE TONY'S BEEN SPENDING HIS MONEY.
CHECKBOOK
Edwin Jarvis
Forty Five Dollars & no/100
year end bonus
Hotel Flaum
One Thousand Dollars & no/100
Drinky Boo Booze
1,000.00
Yvette Avril
Scott Lang
Buy some Ants.
BINGO! OF COURSE--THE HOTEL FLAUM! THE HALF-WAY HOUSE DISTRICT'S PREMIER FLOP.

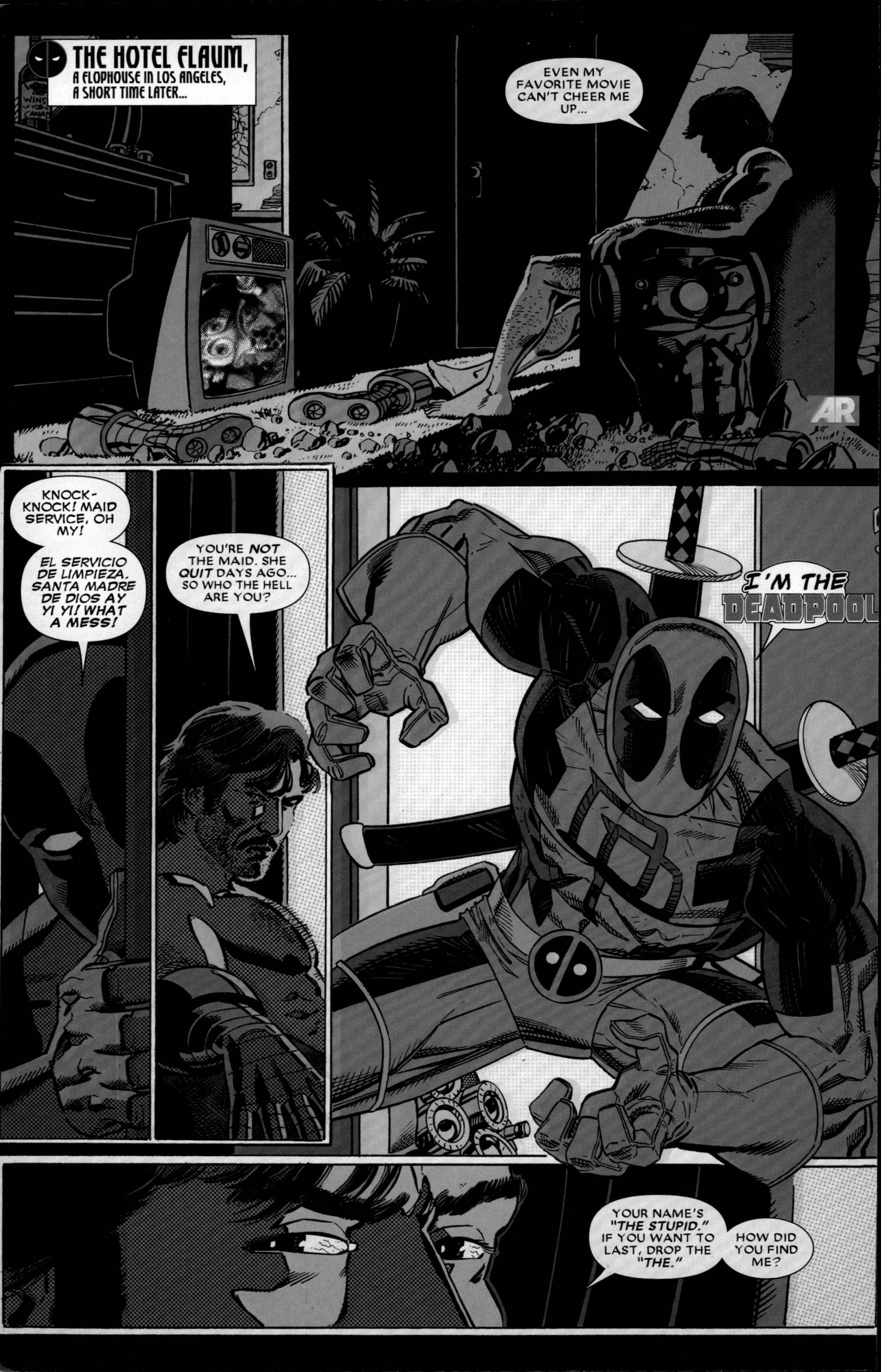
THE HOTEL FLAUM, A FLOPHOUSE IN LOS ANGELES, A SHORT TIME LATER...
EVEN MY FAVORITE MOVIE CAN'T CHEER ME UP...
KNOCK-KNOCK! MAID SERVICE, OH MY!
EL SERVICIO DE LIMPIEZA, SANTA MADRE DE DIOS AY YI YI! WHAT A MESS!
YOU'RE NOT THE MAID. SHE QUIT DAYS AGO... SO WHO THE HELL ARE YOU?
I'M THE DEADPOOL
YOUR NAME'S "THE STUPID." IF YOU WANT TO LAST, DROP THE "THE."
HOW DID YOU FIND ME?

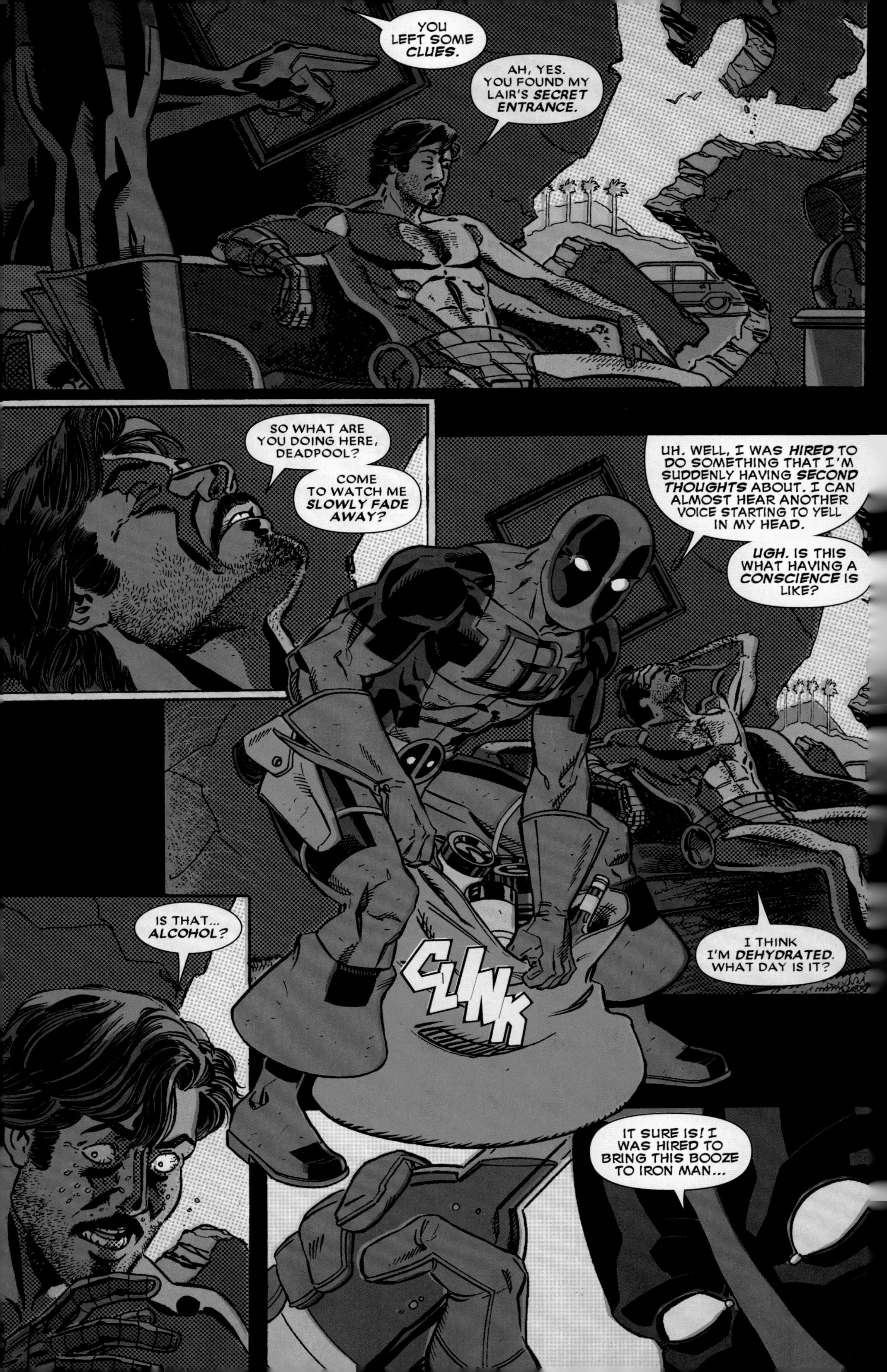
YOU LEFT SOME CLUES.
AH, YES. YOU FOUND MY LAIR'S SECRET ENTRANCE.
SO WHAT ARE YOU DOING HERE, DEADPOOL?
COME TO WATCH ME SLOWLY FADE AWAY?
UH. WELL, I WAS HIRED TO DO SOMETHING THAT I'M SUDDENLY HAVING SECOND THOUGHTS ABOUT. I CAN ALMOST HEAR ANOTHER VOICE STARTING TO YELL IN MY HEAD.
UGH. IS THIS WHAT HAVING A CONSCIENCE IS LIKE?
I THINK I'M DEHYDRATED. WHAT DAY IS IT?
CLINK
IS THAT... ALCOHOL?
IT SURE IS! I WAS HIRED TO BRING THIS BOOZE TO IRON MAN...

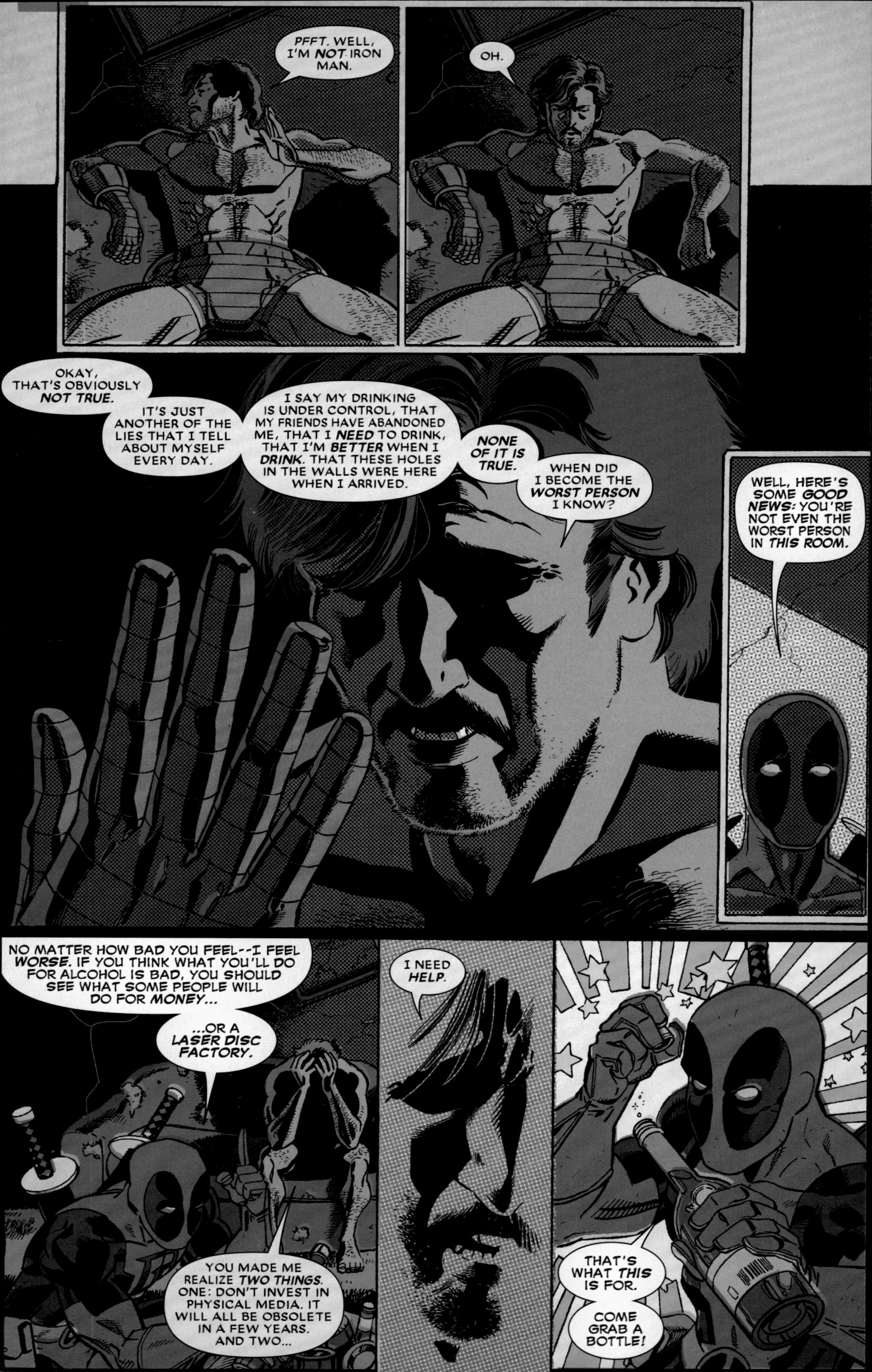
PFFT. WELL, I'M NOT IRON MAN.
OH.
OKAY, THAT'S OBVIOUSLY NOT TRUE.
IT'S JUST ANOTHER OF THE LIES THAT I TELL ABOUT MYSELF EVERY DAY.
I SAY MY DRINKING IS UNDER CONTROL, THAT MY FRIENDS HAVE ABANDONED ME, THAT I NEED TO DRINK, THAT I'M BETTER WHEN I DRINK. THAT THESE HOLES IN THE WALLS WERE HERE WHEN I ARRIVED.
NONE OF IT IS TRUE.
WHEN DID I BECOME THE WORST PERSON I KNOW?
WELL, HERE'S SOME GOOD NEWS: YOU'RE NOT EVEN THE WORST PERSON IN THIS ROOM.
NO MATTER HOW BAD YOU FEEL--I FEEL WORSE. IF YOU THINK WHAT YOU'LL DO FOR ALCOHOL IS BAD, YOU SHOULD SEE WHAT SOME PEOPLE WILL DO FOR MONEY...
...OR A LASER DISC FACTORY.
YOU MADE ME REALIZE TWO THINGS. ONE: DON'T INVEST IN PHYSICAL MEDIA. IT WILL ALL BE OBSOLETE IN A FEW YEARS. AND TWO...
I NEED HELP.
THAT'S WHAT THIS IS FOR.
COME GRAB A BOTTLE!

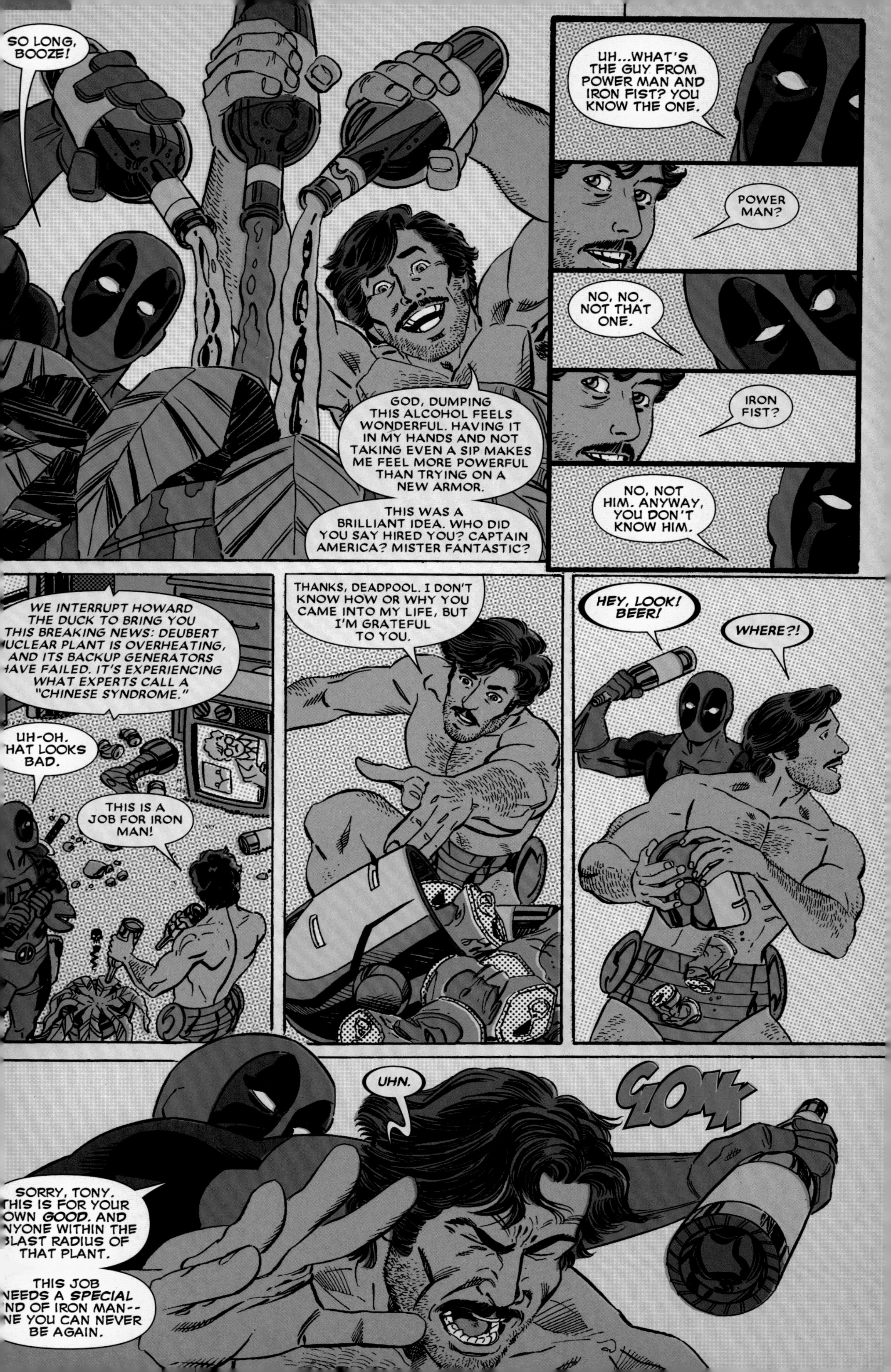
SO LONG, BOOZE!
UH...WHAT'S THE GUY FROM POWER MAN AND IRON FIST? YOU KNOW THE ONE.
POWER MAN?
NO, NO. NOT THAT ONE.
IRON FIST?
NO, NOT HIM. ANYWAY, YOU DON'T KNOW HIM.
GOD, DUMPING THIS ALCOHOL FEELS WONDERFUL. HAVING IT IN MY HANDS AND NOT TAKING EVEN A SIP MAKES ME FEEL MORE POWERFUL THAN TRYING ON A NEW ARMOR.
THIS WAS A BRILLIANT IDEA. WHO DID YOU SAY HIRED YOU? CAPTAIN AMERICA? MISTER FANTASTIC?
WE INTERRUPT HOWARD THE DUCK TO BRING YOU THIS BREAKING NEWS: DEUBERT NUCLEAR PLANT IS OVERHEATING, AND ITS BACKUP GENERATORS HAVE FAILED. IT'S EXPERIENCING WHAT EXPERTS CALL A "CHINESE SYNDROME."
UH-OH. THAT LOOKS BAD.
THIS IS A JOB FOR IRON MAN!
THANKS, DEADPOOL. I DON'T KNOW HOW OR WHY YOU CAME INTO MY LIFE, BUT I'M GRATEFUL TO YOU.
HEY, LOOK! BEER!
WHERE?!
UHN.
GONK
SORRY, TONY. THIS IS FOR YOUR OWN GOOD. AND ANYONE WITHIN THE BLAST RADIUS OF THAT PLANT.
THIS JOB NEEDS A SPECIAL KIND OF IRON MAN-- ONE YOU CAN NEVER BE AGAIN.

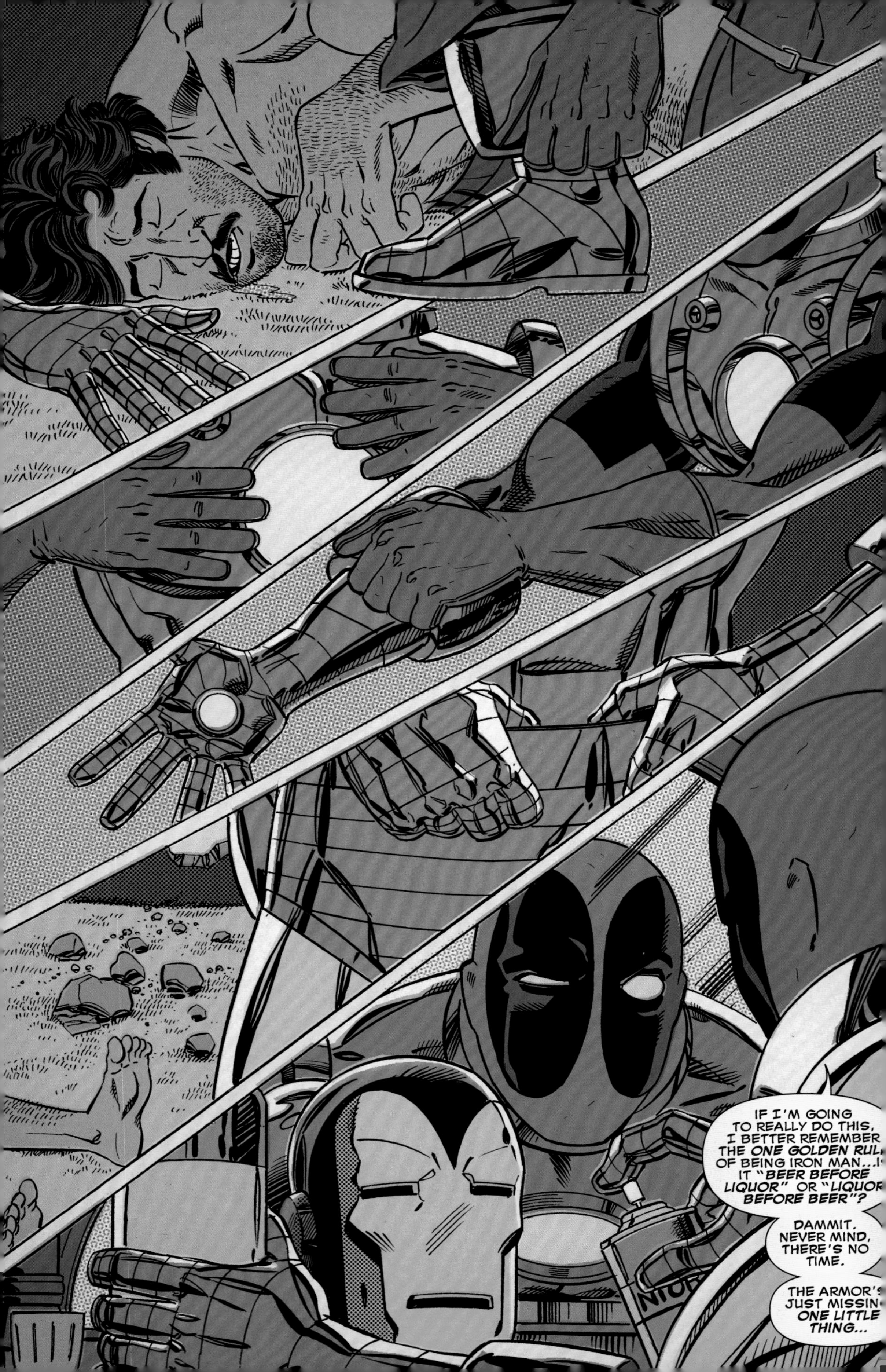

IF I'M GOING TO REALLY DO THIS, I BETTER REMEMBER THE ONE GOLDEN RUL OF BEING IRON MAN...I IT "BEER BEFORE LIQUOR" OR "LIQUOR BEFORE BEER"?
DAMMIT. NEVER MIND, THERE'S NO TIME.
THE ARMOR'S JUST MISSIN ONE LITTLE THING...

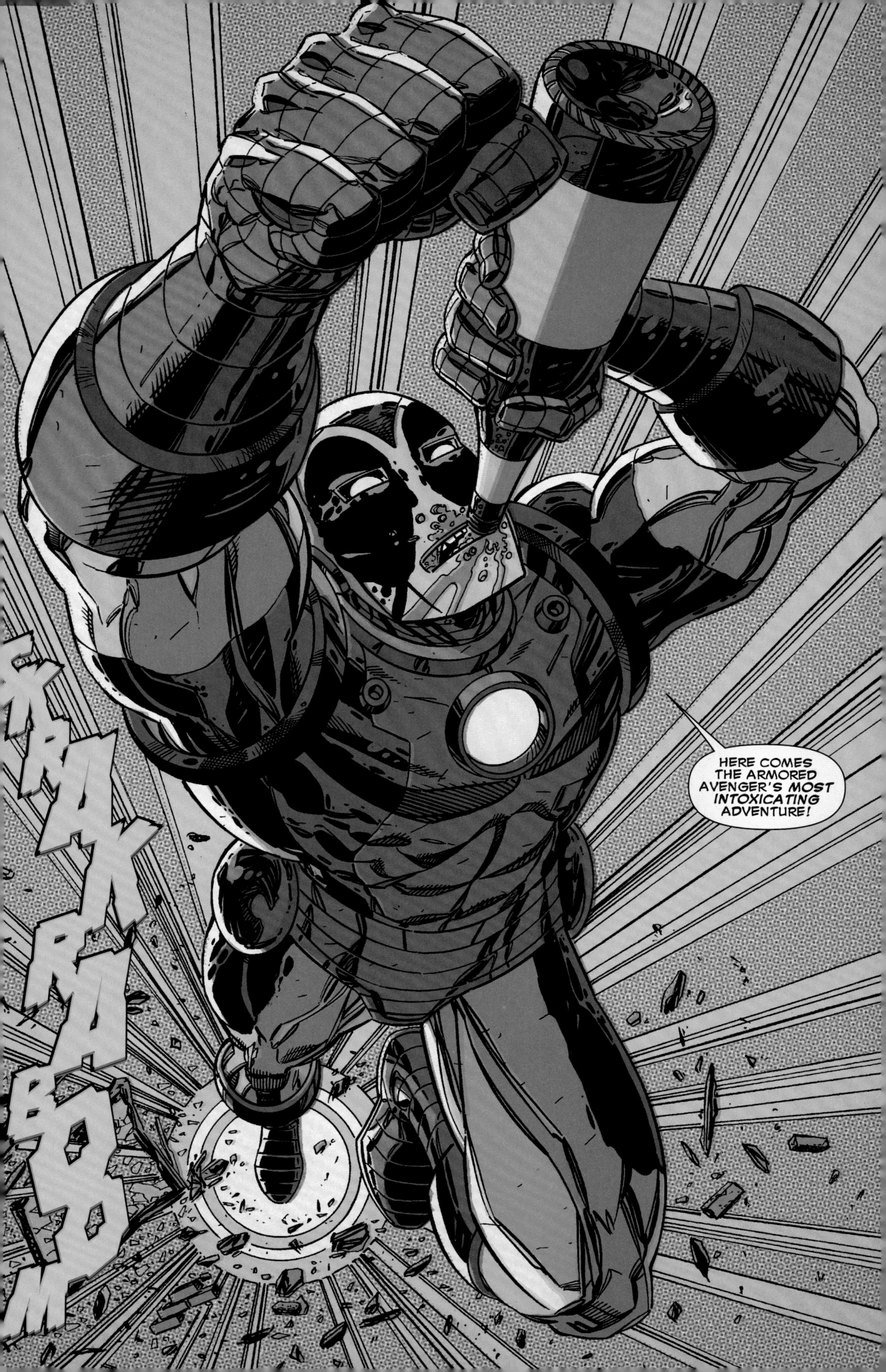
HERE COMES THE ARMORED AVENGER'S *MOST INTOXICATING* ADVENTURE!

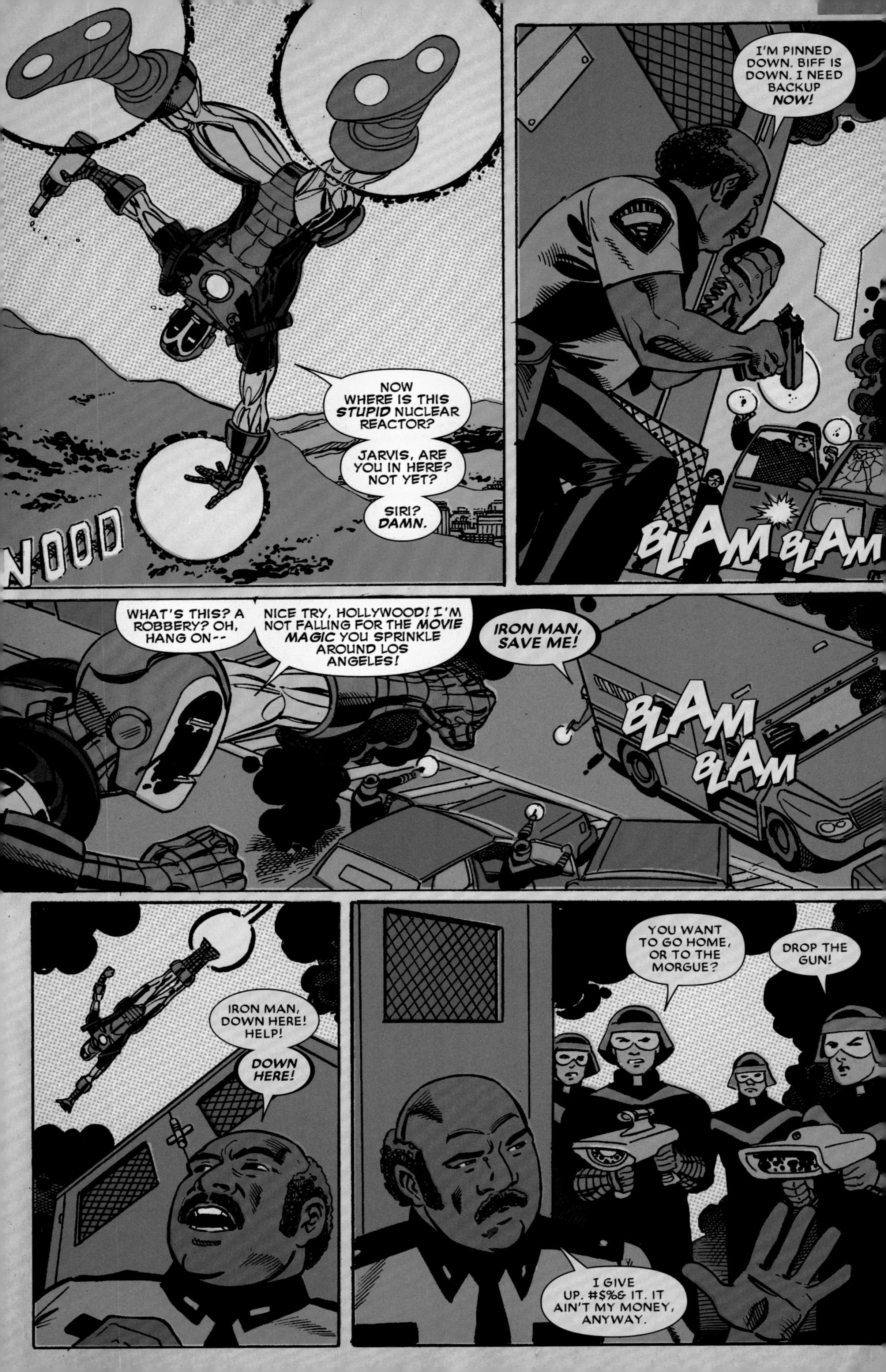
NOOD
NOW WHERE IS THIS STUPID NUCLEAR REACTOR?
JARVIS, ARE YOU IN HERE? NOT YET?
SIRI? DAMN.
I'M PINNED DOWN. BIFF IS DOWN. I NEED BACKUP NOW!
BLAM BLAM
WHAT'S THIS? A ROBBERY? OH, HANG ON--
NICE TRY, HOLLYWOOD! I'M NOT FALLING FOR THE MOVIE MAGIC YOU SPRINKLE AROUND LOS ANGELES!
IRON MAN, SAVE ME!
BLAM BLAM
IRON MAN, DOWN HERE! HELP!
DOWN HERE!
YOU WANT TO GO HOME, OR TO THE MORGUE?
DROP THE GUN!
I GIVE UP. #$%& IT. IT AIN'T MY MONEY, ANYWAY.

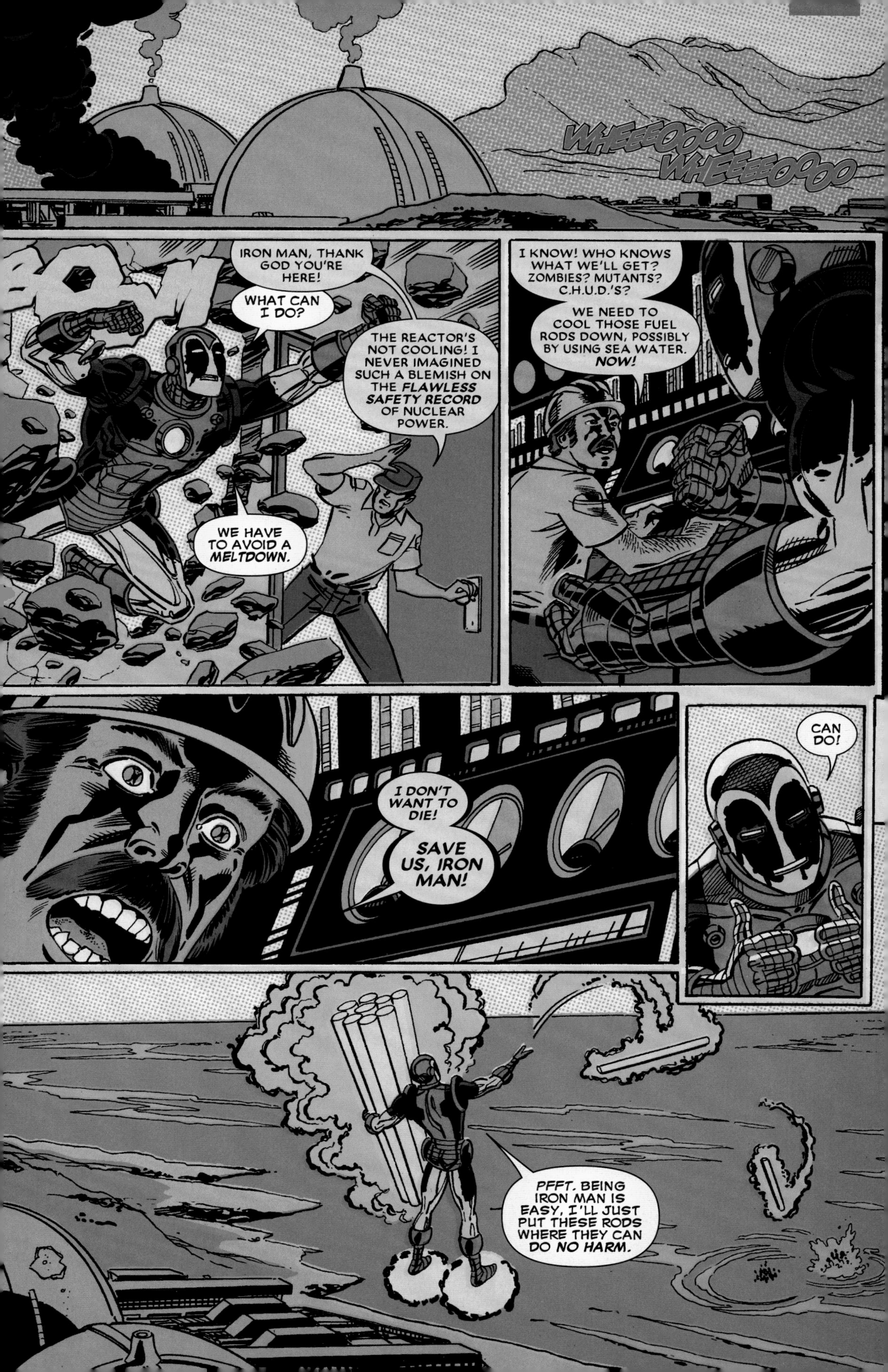
WHEEEOOOO WHEEEEOOOO
BOOM
IRON MAN, THANK GOD YOU'RE HERE!
WHAT CAN I DO?
THE REACTOR'S NOT COOLING! I NEVER IMAGINED SUCH A BLEMISH ON THE FLAWLESS SAFETY RECORD OF NUCLEAR POWER.
WE HAVE TO AVOID A MELTDOWN.
I KNOW! WHO KNOWS WHAT WE'LL GET? ZOMBIES? MUTANTS? C.H.U.D.'S?
WE NEED TO COOL THOSE FUEL RODS DOWN, POSSIBLY BY USING SEA WATER. NOW!
I DON'T WANT TO DIE!
SAVE US, IRON MAN!
CAN DO!
PFFT. BEING IRON MAN IS EASY, I'LL JUST PUT THESE RODS WHERE THEY CAN DO NO HARM.

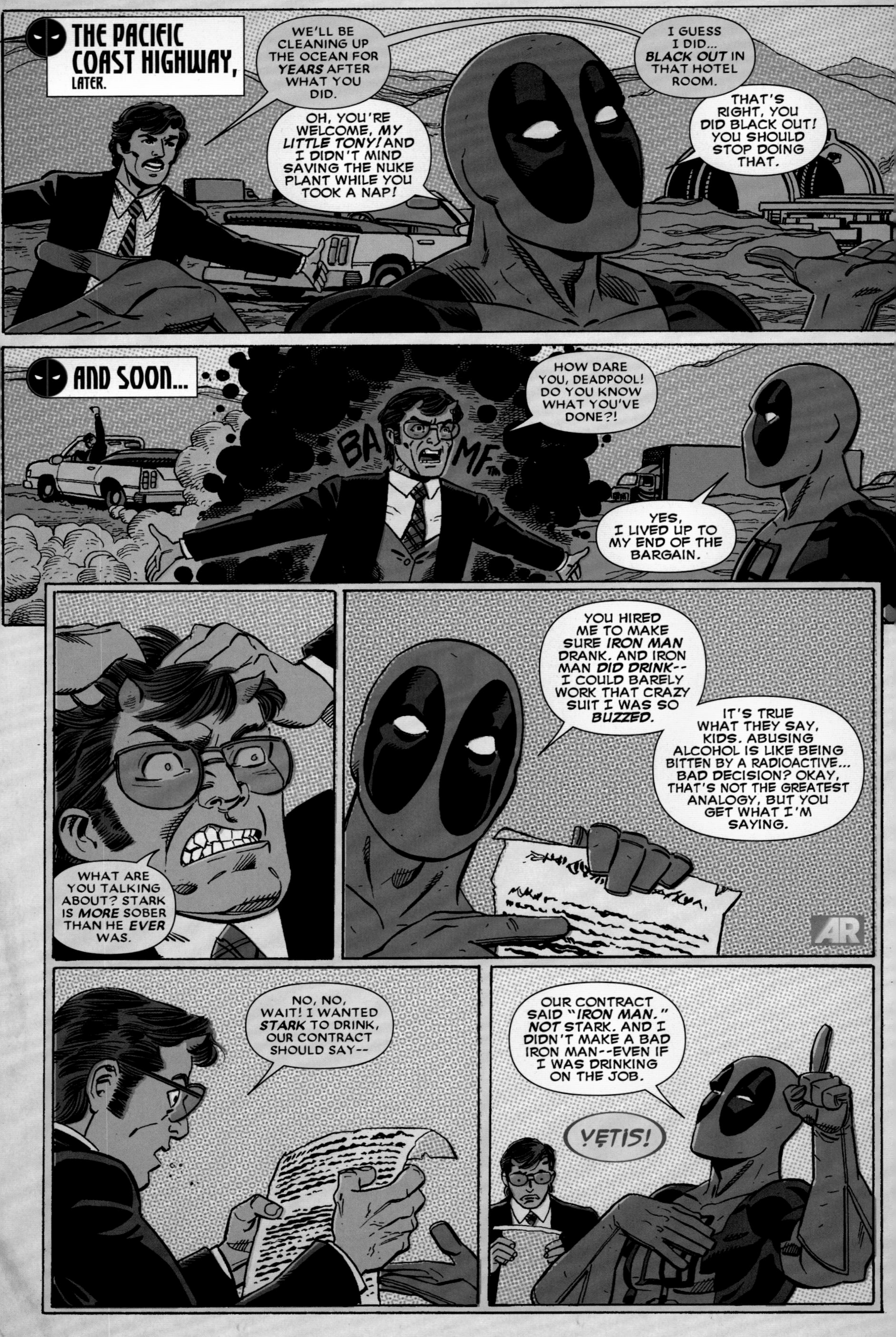
THE PACIFIC COAST HIGHWAY, LATER.
WE'LL BE CLEANING UP THE OCEAN FOR YEARS AFTER WHAT YOU DID.
OH, YOU'RE WELCOME, MY LITTLE TONY! AND I DIDN'T MIND SAVING THE NUKE PLANT WHILE YOU TOOK A NAP!
I GUESS I DID... BLACK OUT IN THAT HOTEL ROOM.
THAT'S RIGHT, YOU DID BLACK OUT! YOU SHOULD STOP DOING THAT.
AND SOON...
BAMF
HOW DARE YOU, DEADPOOL! DO YOU KNOW WHAT YOU'VE DONE?!
YES, I LIVED UP TO MY END OF THE BARGAIN.
WHAT ARE YOU TALKING ABOUT? STARK IS MORE SOBER THAN HE EVER WAS.
YOU HIRED ME TO MAKE SURE IRON MAN DRANK. AND IRON MAN DID DRINK-- I COULD BARELY WORK THAT CRAZY SUIT I WAS SO BUZZED.
IT'S TRUE WHAT THEY SAY, KIDS. ABUSING ALCOHOL IS LIKE BEING BITTEN BY A RADIOACTIVE... BAD DECISION? OKAY, THAT'S NOT THE GREATEST ANALOGY, BUT YOU GET WHAT I'M SAYING.
AR
NO, NO, WAIT! I WANTED STARK TO DRINK, OUR CONTRACT SHOULD SAY--
OUR CONTRACT SAID "IRON MAN." NOT STARK. AND I DIDN'T MAKE A BAD IRON MAN--EVEN IF I WAS DRINKING ON THE JOB.
YETIS!

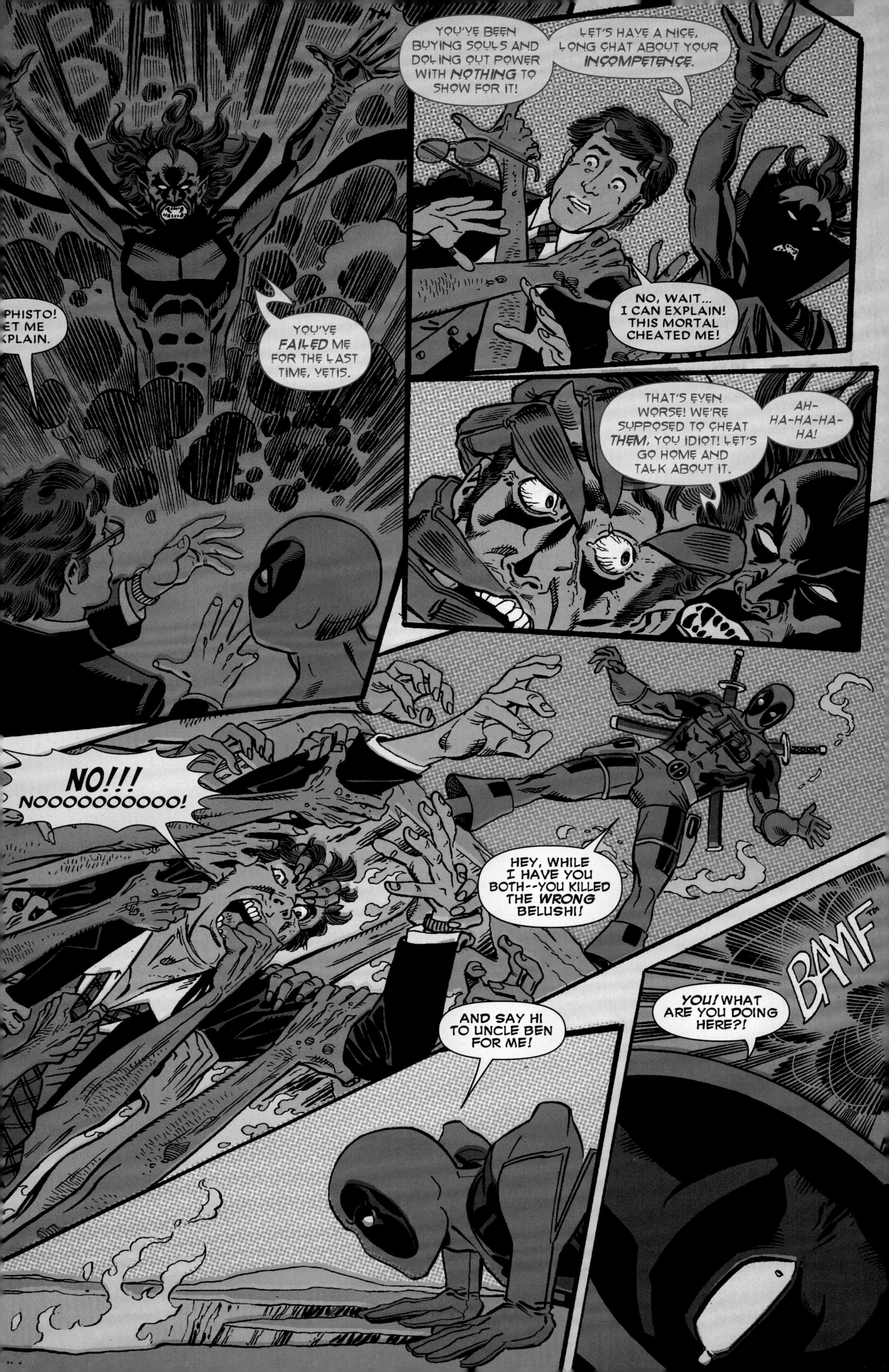
BAMF
YOU'VE BEEN BUYING SOULS AND DOLING OUT POWER WITH NOTHING TO SHOW FOR IT!
LET'S HAVE A NICE, LONG CHAT ABOUT YOUR INCOMPETENCE.
NO, WAIT... I CAN EXPLAIN! THIS MORTAL CHEATED ME!
PHISTO! ET ME XPLAIN.
YOU'VE FAILED ME FOR THE LAST TIME, YETIS.
THAT'S EVEN WORSE! WE'RE SUPPOSED TO CHEAT THEM, YOU IDIOT! LET'S GO HOME AND TALK ABOUT IT.
AH-HA-HA-HA-HA!
NO!!! NOOOOOOOOOO!
HEY, WHILE I HAVE YOU BOTH--YOU KILLED THE WRONG BELUSHI!
AND SAY HI TO UNCLE BEN FOR ME!
BAMF
YOU! WHAT ARE YOU DOING HERE?!

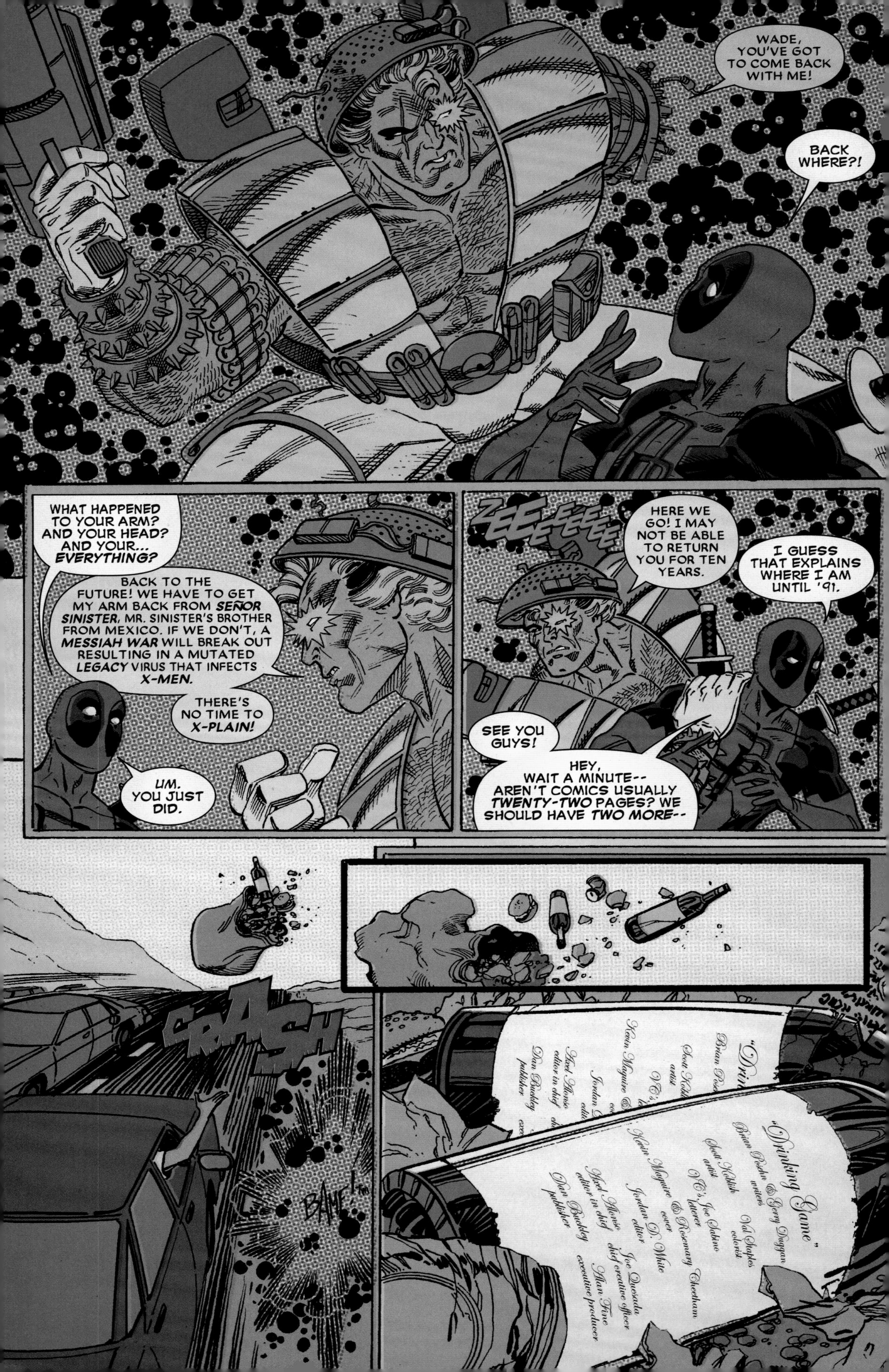

WADE, YOU'VE GOT TO COME BACK WITH ME!
BACK WHERE?!
WHAT HAPPENED TO YOUR ARM? AND YOUR HEAD? AND YOUR... *EVERYTHING?*
BACK TO THE FUTURE! WE HAVE TO GET MY ARM BACK FROM *SEÑOR SINISTER*, MR. SINISTER'S BROTHER FROM MEXICO. IF WE DON'T, A *MESSIAH WAR* WILL BREAK OUT RESULTING IN A MUTATED *LEGACY* VIRUS THAT INFECTS *X-MEN.*
THERE'S NO TIME TO *X-PLAIN!*
UM. YOU JUST DID.
ZEEEEEEEEE
HERE WE GO! I MAY NOT BE ABLE TO RETURN YOU FOR TEN YEARS.
I GUESS THAT EXPLAINS WHERE I AM UNTIL '91.
SEE YOU GUYS!
HEY, WAIT A MINUTE-- AREN'T COMICS USUALLY *TWENTY-TWO* PAGES? WE SHOULD HAVE *TWO MORE--*
CRASH
BAMF!
"Drinking Game"
Brian Posehn & Gerry Duggan writers
Scott Koblish artist
Val Staples colorist
VC's Joe Sabino letterer
Kevin Maguire & Rosemary Cheetham cover
Jordan D. White editor
Axel Alonso editor in chief
Joe Quesada chief creative officer
Dan Buckley publisher
Alan Fine executive producer

Hey readers, glad you joined us for another wacky adventure of the Merc with a Mouth. A lot of great letters this month so let's get right to it, so I can get back to the Marvel bullpen, where we're busy enjoying the '80s, the greatest decade of all time. So like Frankie says, relax... and enjoy our letters column.

---

Dear Deadpool,
I'm turning 7 this week. That's 1 more than 6. My parents say that 7 is too old for comics? How do I convince them that's not true what they said?

Mike Drucker

Mike, your parents might be onto something. A guy running around with katanas and guns is clearly more suited for babies. Maybe we should all quit reading comics. I'm just kidding, your parents are mad stupid. Like Mr. T says, I pity the fools.

Love,
Deadpool

---

Dear Mr. Wilson,
Thank you so much for featuring Iron Man, It's not often a 4th tier Marvel Hero gets to interact with a 3rd tier Marvel hero. Just the other day I was thinking about how Iron Man and that drunkard Tony Stark will sadly never be a viable movie franchise. There are other non-viable movie franchise hero's you should think about working with as well, like maybe you and The Uncanny X-Men could team up or perhaps that justabout Wolverine?! While I know they will never be in movies, I also know that interacting with you is the best I can possibly hope for. When I look at the current state of Super Hero movies I am struck how there is only one franchise that will go well into the 90's and that franchise is currently in the good hands of the Donner company.
Anyway thanks again Deadpool, I have to run, there is a Bob Hope comedy special about to start on NBC, right after Cheers.

Matt Mira

Matt, thanks for the typed letter you sent through the US postal service, which of course is the only way to correspond. As far as super-hero movies, don't hold your breath. In a perfect world there would be a well-made and memorable Daredevil movie and in my opinion, Fantastic Four is good for two flicks that wouldn't be total disappointments. Sadly, we don't live in that world.

Kisses,
Mr. Wilson

---

Dear Deadpool,
I am a really big fan of your comics. Every time I go to the dairy mart, I hope there is a new issue of your comic I can buy, and if there is, I will bring it to school folded up in my pocket to show my friends at recess.
I wanted to write in to ask if I could be your sidekick, but the more I thought about it, the more I worried about getting shot and stabbed and then dying. So instead I was wondering if you needed someone to read about your adventures before they get printed and sent to the dairy mart to make sure they are spelled rite and are good. One time your boot was yellow when it should be red, and I noticed it, so I think I could really help.

Jordan D. White
Naugatuck, CT

Jordan, wow, you noticed my boot was different colors. You're terrific at reading and noticing things. That kind of skill will get you far. That's sarcasm, which my editor just told me doesn't translate well to the written word. Anyway, good luck annoying people.

Angry '80s Deadpool writer

---

Dear Deadpool,
I told the other kids at school that you could beat Spider-Man in a fight and they beat me up. Did you ever get beat up when you were a kid? How did you deal with it? What should I do next time the other kids say Spider-Man is the best? Thanks for being my hero!

Mike Drucker, Age 7

Mike, next time those boys bug you, tell them your mom loves you very, very much and a grown man that writes comic books says you're the coolest kid in the world. They should leave you alone after that. And no, Deadpool didn't get beaten up as a kid, he's @$%&$*% Deadpool.

Sad, delusional '80s Deadpool writer

---

Dead Deadpool--
I am thinking of selling all my shares in Apple computer. I don't think the company is going anywhere?
What do you think?

David Mandel

David,
I agree, Atari forever, brother.

Deadpool

PS. Don't invest in coffee either, no one likes coffee.

---

Dear Deadpool,
I just turned 7 and I want to be you when I grow up! How do I do that?
Is there a swords and jokes training school I can attend? If so, how much is tuition? My parents say I can only go to a state school, so if you know a swords and jokes school in Florida, it would really help me. Also, what are girls like?

Mike Drucker

Mike,
You sure have a lot of time to write us letters. Maybe you should write yourself a life. Zing!!! And girls, what do I know about girls? I write for Marvel and I get my kicks being mean to seven-year-olds.

That same angry '80s Deadpool writer from above

---

Dear Deadpool,
Will we be seeing any fallout from the X-Men team Titans crossover in the pages of dead pool. And if not, why not?

Bendis

Don't worry about it, Bendis, whoever you are. Who writes just their last name? You must think you're a real big shot and that your name means something to me, a mighty Marvel writer. Tell you what, Bendis, instead of butting into our business, why don't you write your own comics, punk?! Just kidding, don't get us fired.

Gerry "Bad Boy" Duggan
(Brian Posehn didn't write this)

---

Dear Deadpool,
I like you and your comical book a lot. I am thirteen and living in a small California winery town in the 1980s. I live with my mom in a tiny apartment. She's kind of a total bitch but one day I'll forgive her. Anyway, I rode my bike twelve miles to get your latest issue because my town doesn't have a comic book store so I had to go to Dada's liquors. He's a foreign guy and he really sticks out in this town. So do I because I'm only thirteen at this time and already a freaking giant. And I'm a nerd in the '80s, which is still a negative thing. Maybe some day hot girls who think being able to quote "Big Bang Theory" (whatever that is) and knowing who Batman is makes them nerdy, will wear T-shirts that say I Heart Nerds. I hear there's a movie called Revenge of the Nerds coming out soon. I hope it's super bloody and makes nerds super popular. Anyway, I love Marvel Comics and want to write for them some day, any advice?

A young Brian Posehn
Sonoma, California

PS. Oh, and the latest issue I mentioned was totally awesome.

Brian, listen up, here's my advice. You should be a comedian first for twenty-five years and show up on people's TVs and the occasional movie. Oh, and most of these movies and TV shows should be not great, but there can be a couple of stand-outs. You should write for TV, too. And marry a pretty lady with low standards and make a beautiful baby that doesn't at all resemble you. Only after you've done all these things should you approach Marvel about a job.

Good luck,
Deadpool.

---

Dear Deadpool writers Mr. Duggan and Mr. Posehn --
Your comic is rad! I love the art and the last issue where Deadpool meets Billy Squier and they team up was the most rocking thing EVER! Keep the comics coming, and make mine Marvel!

Where's the beef--
Patton Oswalt

P.S. Yesterday at school I had another one of my blackouts

---

where I pee my pants and have visions of the future. I saw O.J. Simpson murder his wife in 1994, airplanes hit the World Trade Center in 2001, and a black guy get elected president in 2008! Then there was something about you guys, and some sort of "avoidable death" at the end of 2013, and then I woke up. Luckily, I'm starting Ritalin tomorrow, so no more creepy visions!

There it is, guys--the Days Of Future Past of letters to Marvel comics.

Good luck, to Patton and everyone
Deadpool.

---

Dear Marvel,
Excelsior! Greetings and Salutations from Ms. Meyer's Fifth Grade classroom. I just started reading comics and boy oh boy they are way better than actual books! Ok, here's my question. Any chance Deadpool could team up with a real life hero like Hulk Hogan? Imagine how much fun it would be to see these two side by side fighting crime. Deadpool would be the perfect Robin to Hulk's Batman. Make my dreams come true.

Everybody Wang Chung Tonight!
Paul Scheer (Age 11)
An Undiagnosed Hulkamaniac

P.S. OK to print!
P.P.S. Eat your vitamins and read your comic books.

Paul, thank you for your letter. Your mention of Mr. Hulk Hogan reminds me of a funny story about Andre The Giant--did you know that it was alleged that he needed two hotel rooms on the road? Ask me about it sometime.

Deadpool

---

Dear Deadpool,
This kid in Ms. Bleecker's class said that there might be a Deadpool game out soon. Should I buy it on ColecoVision or Atari? My other question is this. Will it be for one player or two? Also, how come we never see your face?

Gerry Duggan

P.S. In the game can you go up and down or just side to side like Pitfall?
P.S.S. How come the Punisher mini-series on the cover said 4 issues but then there was actually 5? I laughed out loud when I saw that on the newsstand. I wish there was a shorter way to say that I laughed out loud. OW! (I made up that shortcut for OH, WELL--maybe you will help it catch on?

Gerry, as a guy that has traveled through time more times than has happened yet for me to count, I bring you a dire warning from your future: DON'T BUY THE REPLICA STAR TREK COMMUNICATOR WHILE YOU'RE AT THE 1987 NEW YORK COMIC CON. IT BREAKS ON THE WAY HOME, AND THEN YOUR FATHER MAKES YOU JOIN A FOOTBALL TEAM.

Love ya,
Deadpool

# NEXT ISSUE

BACK TO THE PRESENT!

# 8

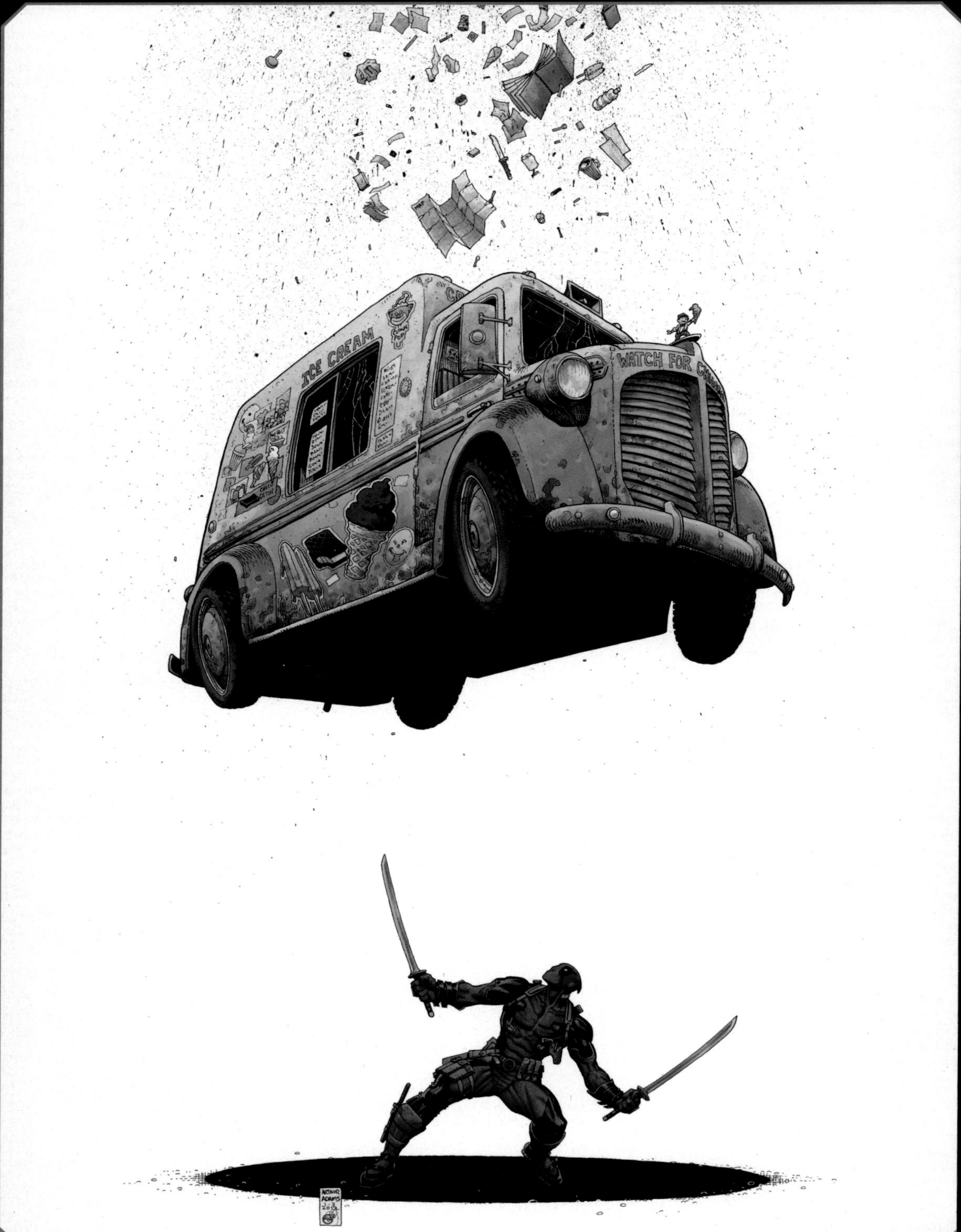
ICE CREAM

# RUNNING WITH THE DEVIL

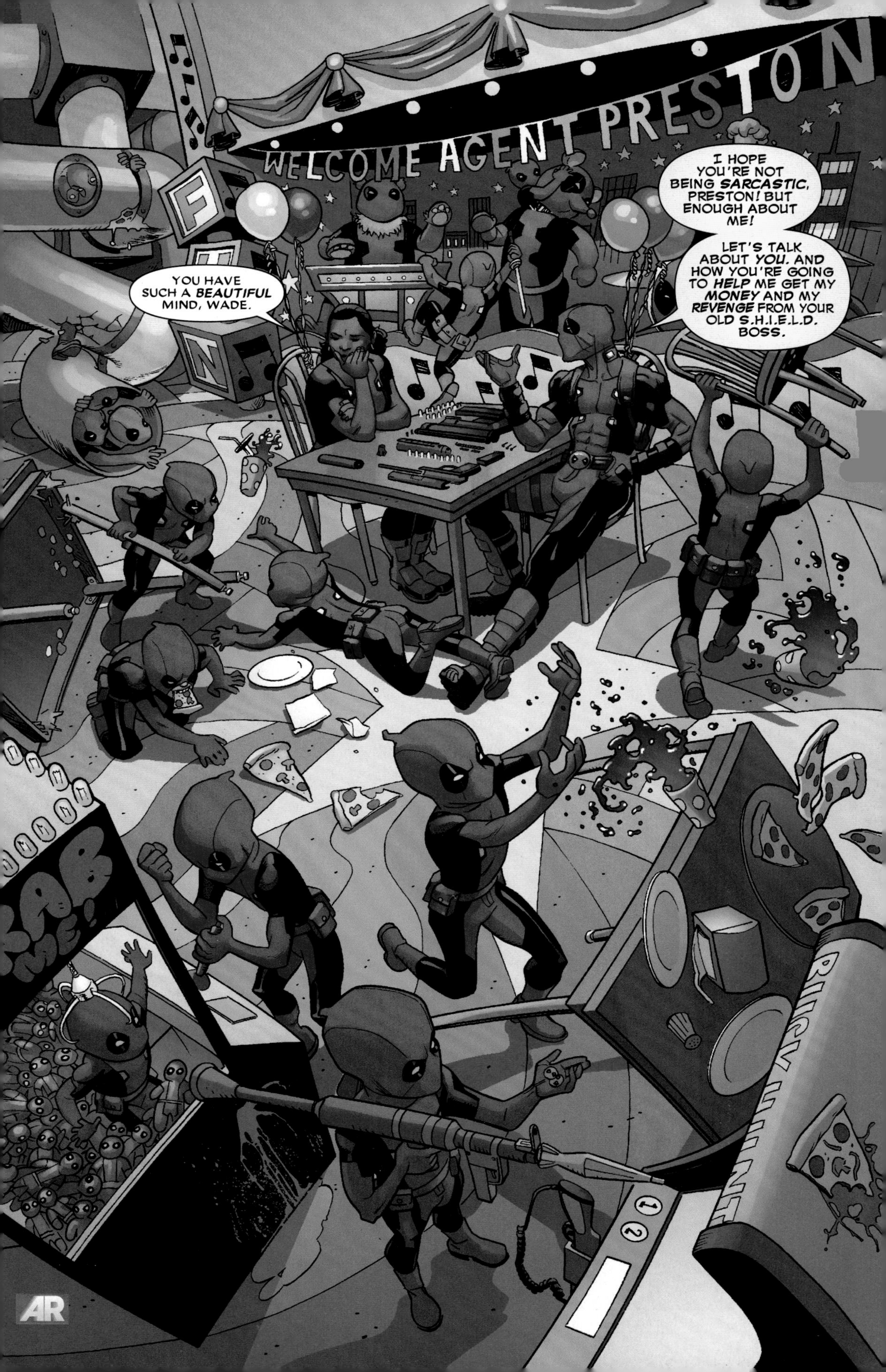
WELCOME AGENT PRESTON
YOU HAVE SUCH A BEAUTIFUL MIND, WADE.
I HOPE YOU'RE NOT BEING SARCASTIC, PRESTON! BUT ENOUGH ABOUT ME!
LET'S TALK ABOUT YOU. AND HOW YOU'RE GOING TO HELP ME GET MY MONEY AND MY REVENGE FROM YOUR OLD S.H.I.E.L.D. BOSS.

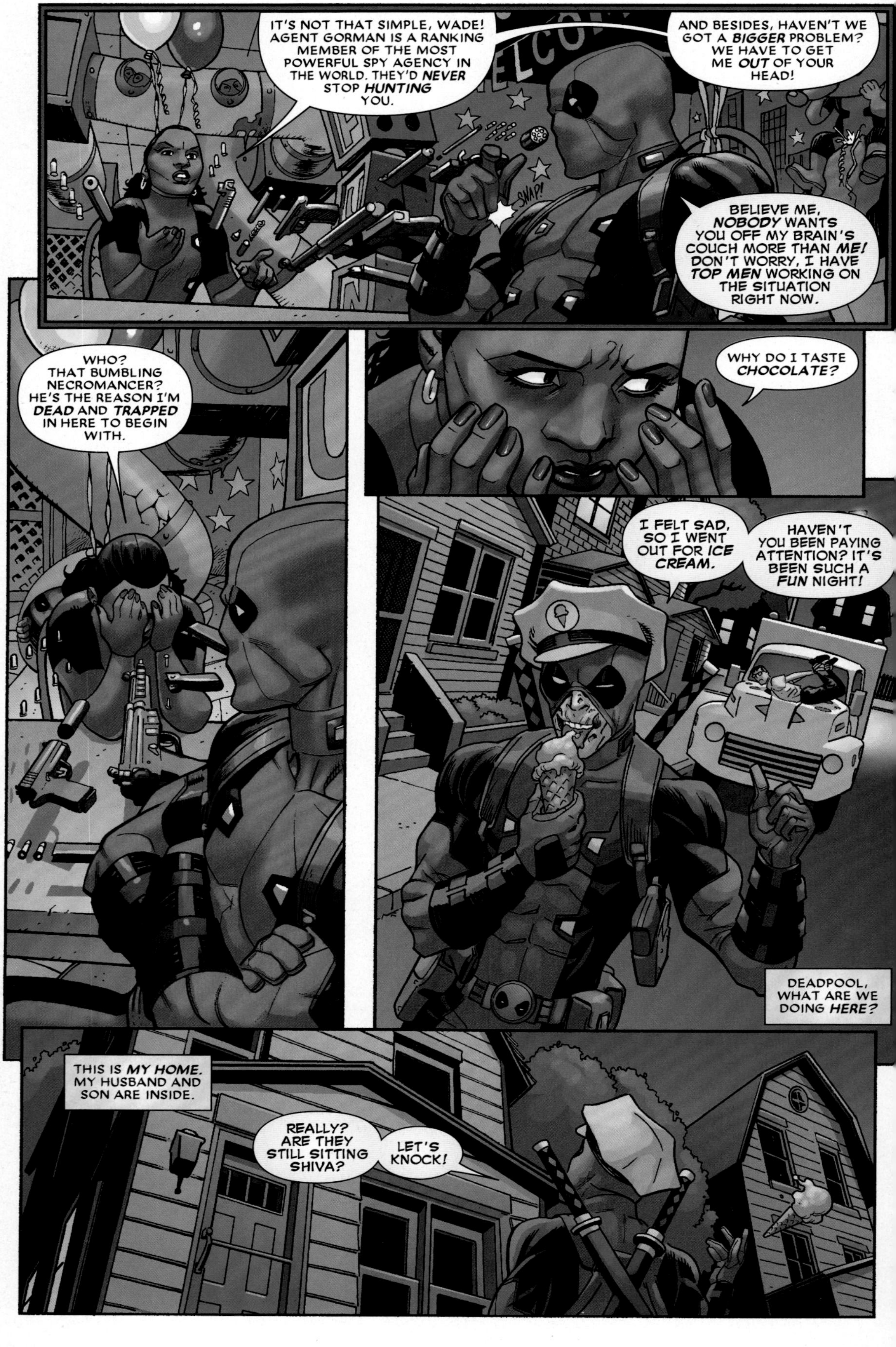

IT'S NOT THAT SIMPLE, WADE! AGENT GORMAN IS A RANKING MEMBER OF THE MOST POWERFUL SPY AGENCY IN THE WORLD. THEY'D NEVER STOP HUNTING YOU.
AND BESIDES, HAVEN'T WE GOT A BIGGER PROBLEM? WE HAVE TO GET ME OUT OF YOUR HEAD!
SNAP!
BELIEVE ME, NOBODY WANTS YOU OFF MY BRAIN'S COUCH MORE THAN ME! DON'T WORRY, I HAVE TOP MEN WORKING ON THE SITUATION RIGHT NOW.
WHO? THAT BUMBLING NECROMANCER? HE'S THE REASON I'M DEAD AND TRAPPED IN HERE TO BEGIN WITH.
WHY DO I TASTE CHOCOLATE?
I FELT SAD, SO I WENT OUT FOR ICE CREAM.
HAVEN'T YOU BEEN PAYING ATTENTION? IT'S BEEN SUCH A FUN NIGHT!
DEADPOOL, WHAT ARE WE DOING HERE?
THIS IS MY HOME. MY HUSBAND AND SON ARE INSIDE.
REALLY? ARE THEY STILL SITTING SHIVA?
LET'S KNOCK!

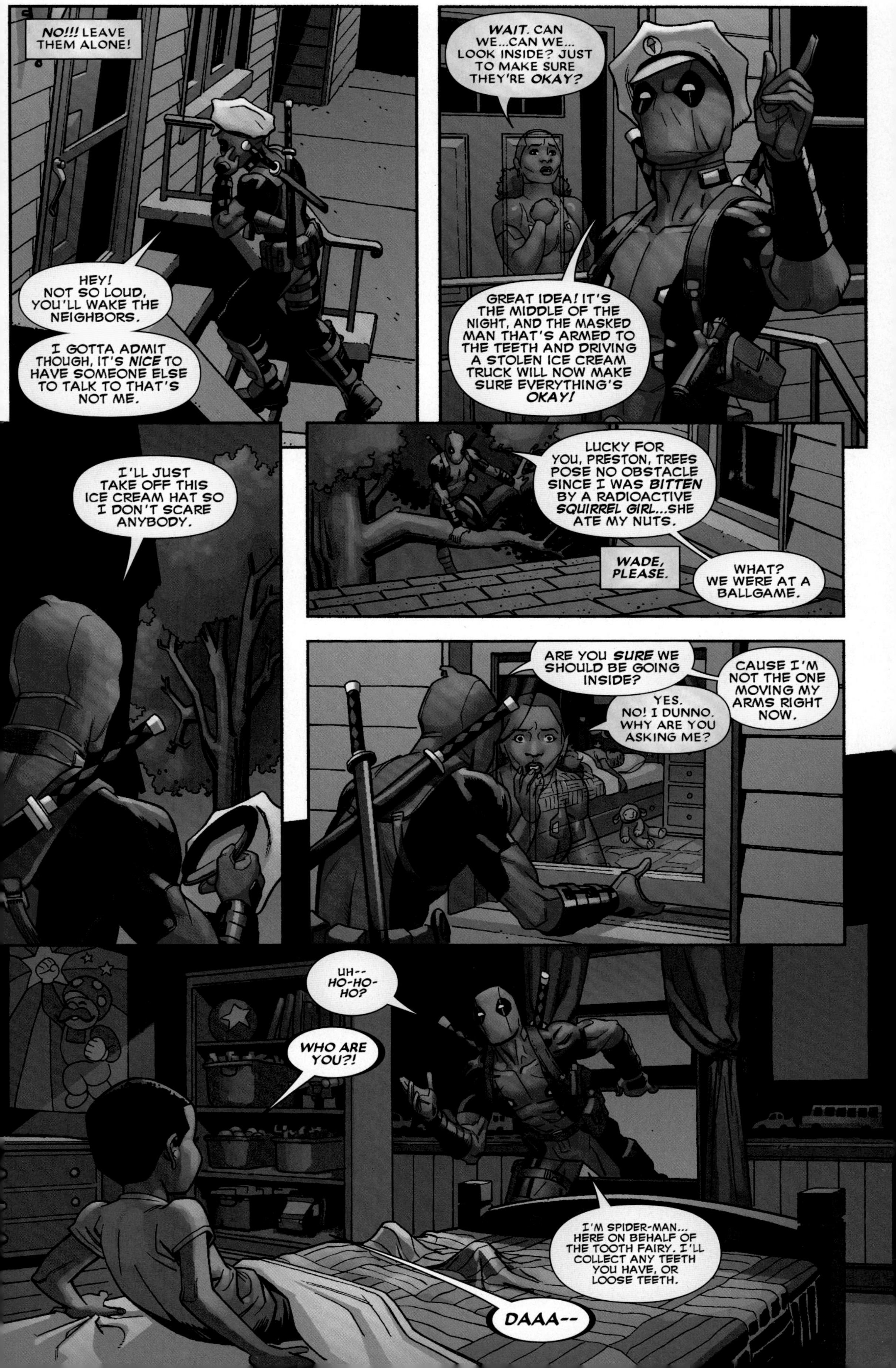
NO!!! LEAVE THEM ALONE!
HEY! NOT SO LOUD, YOU'LL WAKE THE NEIGHBORS.
I GOTTA ADMIT THOUGH, IT'S NICE TO HAVE SOMEONE ELSE TO TALK TO THAT'S NOT ME.
WAIT. CAN WE...CAN WE... LOOK INSIDE? JUST TO MAKE SURE THEY'RE OKAY?
GREAT IDEA! IT'S THE MIDDLE OF THE NIGHT, AND THE MASKED MAN THAT'S ARMED TO THE TEETH AND DRIVING A STOLEN ICE CREAM TRUCK WILL NOW MAKE SURE EVERYTHING'S OKAY!
I'LL JUST TAKE OFF THIS ICE CREAM HAT SO I DON'T SCARE ANYBODY.
LUCKY FOR YOU, PRESTON, TREES POSE NO OBSTACLE SINCE I WAS BITTEN BY A RADIOACTIVE SQUIRREL GIRL...SHE ATE MY NUTS.
WADE, PLEASE.
WHAT? WE WERE AT A BALLGAME.
ARE YOU SURE WE SHOULD BE GOING INSIDE?
CAUSE I'M NOT THE ONE MOVING MY ARMS RIGHT NOW.
YES. NO! I DUNNO. WHY ARE YOU ASKING ME?
UH-- HO-HO-HO?
WHO ARE YOU?!
I'M SPIDER-MAN... HERE ON BEHALF OF THE TOOTH FAIRY. I'LL COLLECT ANY TEETH YOU HAVE, OR LOOSE TEETH.
DAAA--

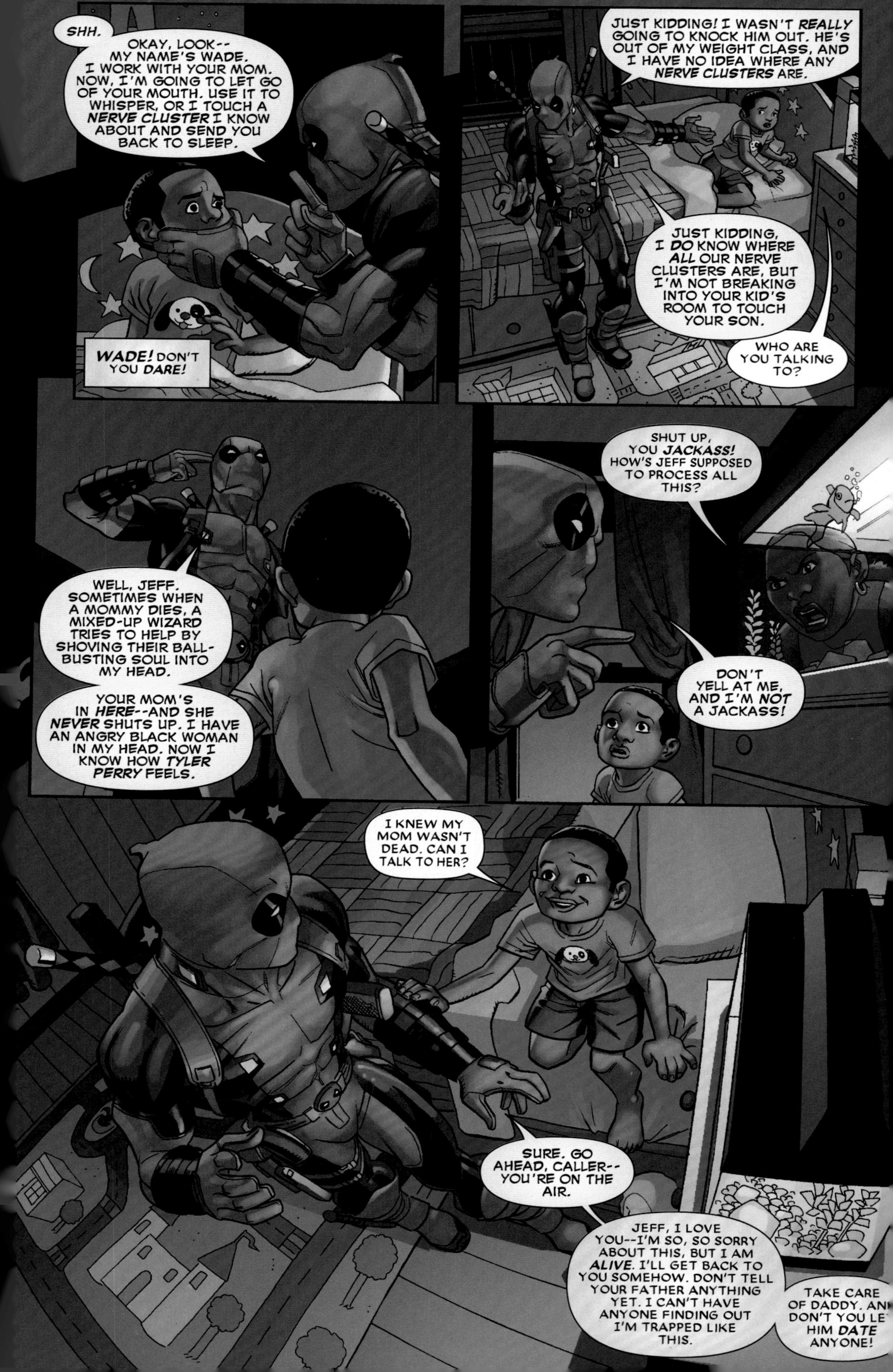
SHH.
OKAY, LOOK-- MY NAME'S WADE. I WORK WITH YOUR MOM. NOW, I'M GOING TO LET GO OF YOUR MOUTH. USE IT TO WHISPER, OR I TOUCH A NERVE CLUSTER I KNOW ABOUT AND SEND YOU BACK TO SLEEP.
WADE! DON'T YOU DARE!
JUST KIDDING! I WASN'T REALLY GOING TO KNOCK HIM OUT. HE'S OUT OF MY WEIGHT CLASS, AND I HAVE NO IDEA WHERE ANY NERVE CLUSTERS ARE.
JUST KIDDING, I DO KNOW WHERE ALL OUR NERVE CLUSTERS ARE, BUT I'M NOT BREAKING INTO YOUR KID'S ROOM TO TOUCH YOUR SON.
WHO ARE YOU TALKING TO?
WELL, JEFF. SOMETIMES WHEN A MOMMY DIES, A MIXED-UP WIZARD TRIES TO HELP BY SHOVING THEIR BALL-BUSTING SOUL INTO MY HEAD.
YOUR MOM'S IN HERE--AND SHE NEVER SHUTS UP. I HAVE AN ANGRY BLACK WOMAN IN MY HEAD. NOW I KNOW HOW TYLER PERRY FEELS.
SHUT UP, YOU JACKASS! HOW'S JEFF SUPPOSED TO PROCESS ALL THIS?
DON'T YELL AT ME, AND I'M NOT A JACKASS!
I KNEW MY MOM WASN'T DEAD. CAN I TALK TO HER?
SURE. GO AHEAD, CALLER-- YOU'RE ON THE AIR.
JEFF, I LOVE YOU--I'M SO, SO SORRY ABOUT THIS, BUT I AM ALIVE. I'LL GET BACK TO YOU SOMEHOW. DON'T TELL YOUR FATHER ANYTHING YET. I CAN'T HAVE ANYONE FINDING OUT I'M TRAPPED LIKE THIS.
TAKE CARE OF DADDY. AN DON'T YOU LE HIM DATE ANYONE!

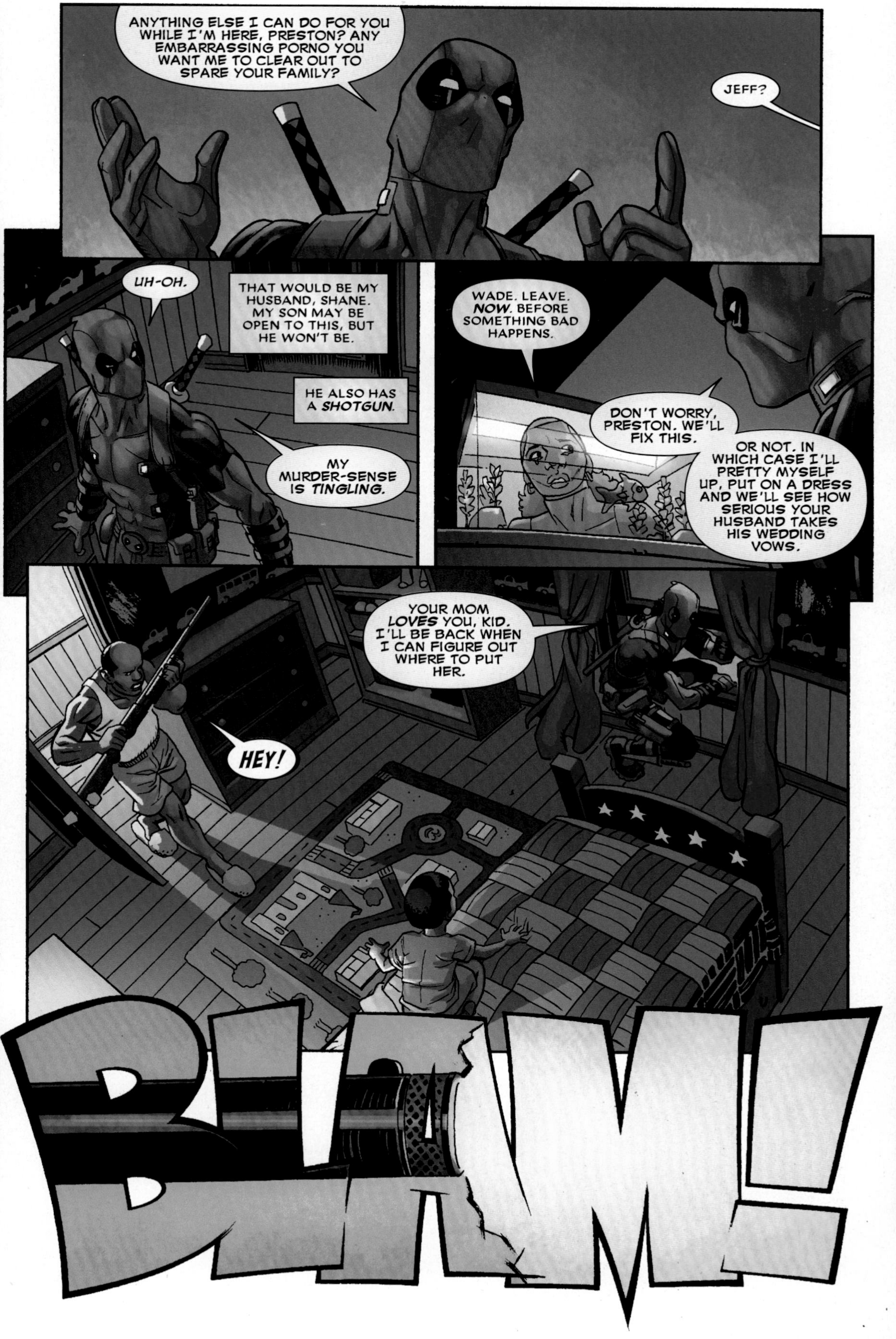

ANYTHING ELSE I CAN DO FOR YOU WHILE I'M HERE, PRESTON? ANY EMBARRASSING PORNO YOU WANT ME TO CLEAR OUT TO SPARE YOUR FAMILY?
JEFF?
UH-OH.
THAT WOULD BE MY HUSBAND, SHANE. MY SON MAY BE OPEN TO THIS, BUT HE WON'T BE.
HE ALSO HAS A *SHOTGUN*.
MY MURDER-SENSE IS *TINGLING*.
WADE. LEAVE. *NOW*. BEFORE SOMETHING BAD HAPPENS.
DON'T WORRY, PRESTON. WE'LL FIX THIS.
OR NOT. IN WHICH CASE I'LL PRETTY MYSELF UP, PUT ON A DRESS AND WE'LL SEE HOW SERIOUS YOUR HUSBAND TAKES HIS WEDDING VOWS.
YOUR MOM *LOVES* YOU, KID. I'LL BE BACK WHEN I CAN FIGURE OUT WHERE TO PUT HER.
HEY!
BLAM!

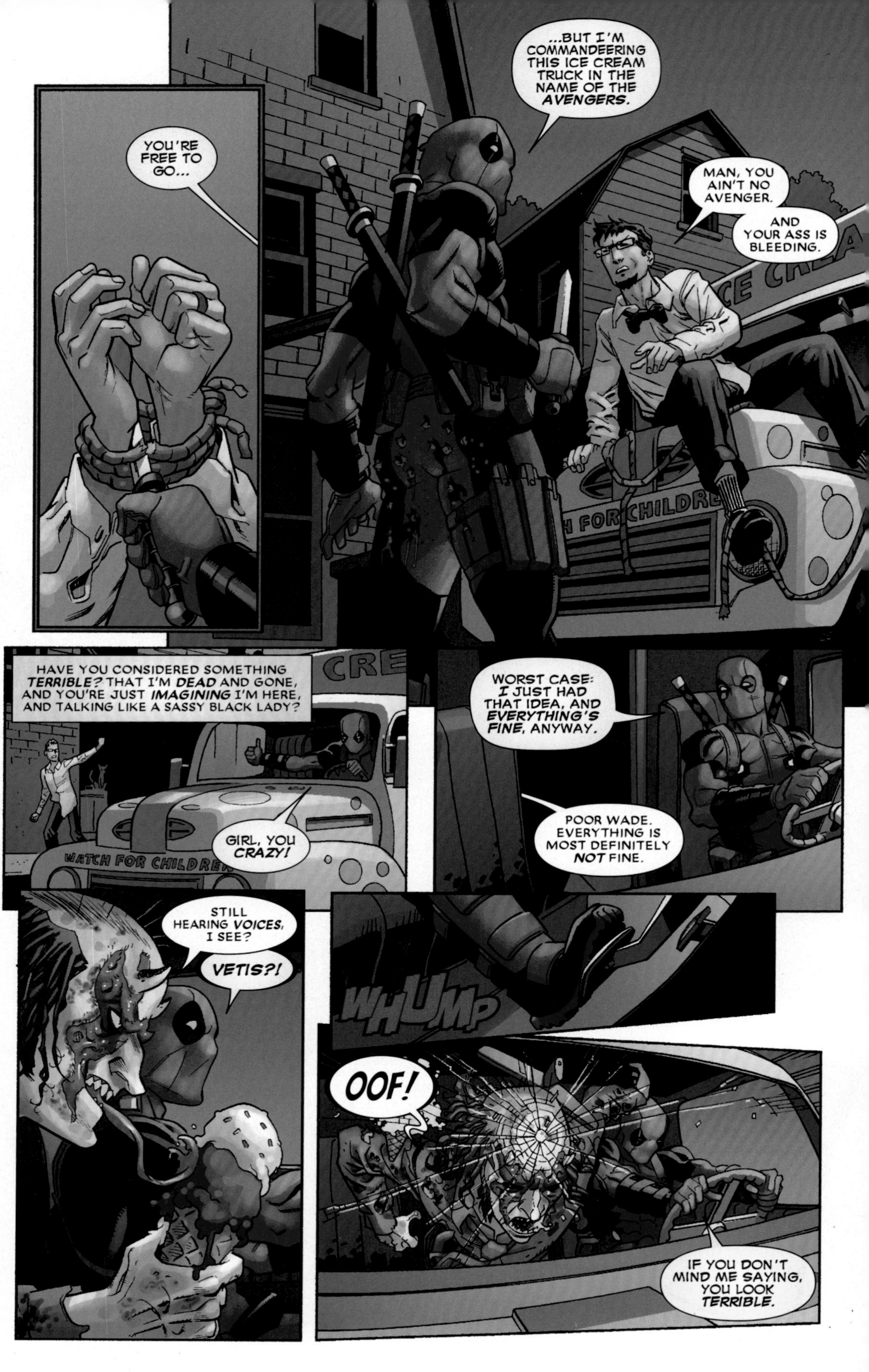

YOU'RE FREE TO GO...
...BUT I'M COMMANDEERING THIS ICE CREAM TRUCK IN THE NAME OF THE *AVENGERS.*
MAN, YOU AIN'T NO AVENGER.
AND YOUR ASS IS BLEEDING.
ICE CREA
H FOR CHILDRE
HAVE YOU CONSIDERED SOMETHING *TERRIBLE?* THAT I'M *DEAD* AND GONE, AND YOU'RE JUST *IMAGINING* I'M HERE, AND TALKING LIKE A SASSY BLACK LADY?
CRE
GIRL, YOU *CRAZY!*
WATCH FOR CHILDREN
WORST CASE: *I* JUST HAD THAT IDEA, AND *EVERYTHING'S FINE,* ANYWAY.
POOR WADE. EVERYTHING IS MOST DEFINITELY *NOT* FINE.
STILL HEARING *VOICES,* I SEE?
*VETIS?!*
WHUMP
OOF!
IF YOU DON'T MIND ME SAYING, YOU LOOK *TERRIBLE.*

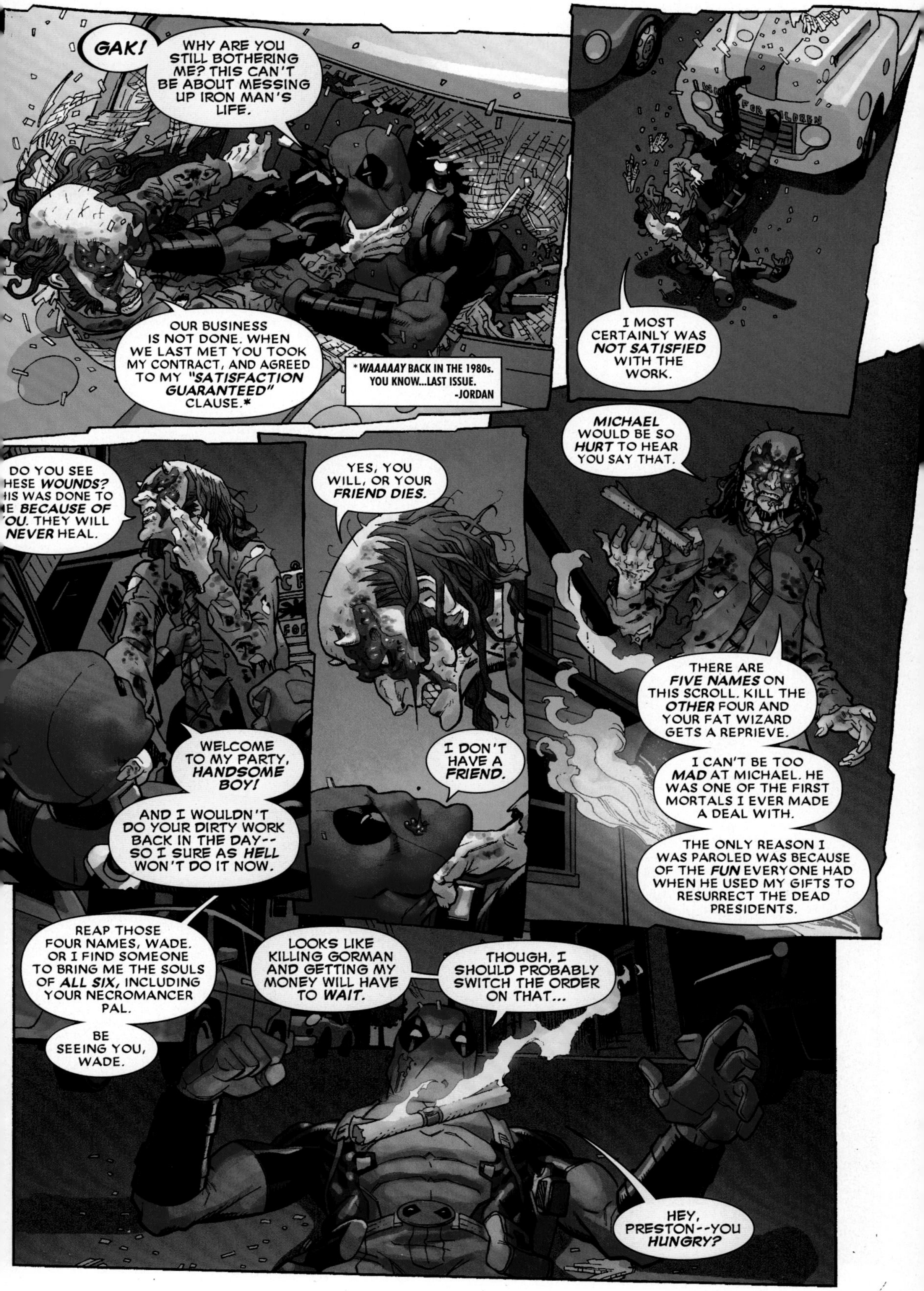
GAK!
WHY ARE YOU STILL BOTHERING ME? THIS CAN'T BE ABOUT MESSING UP IRON MAN'S LIFE.
OUR BUSINESS IS NOT DONE. WHEN WE LAST MET YOU TOOK MY CONTRACT, AND AGREED TO MY "SATISFACTION GUARANTEED" CLAUSE.*
*WAAAAAY BACK IN THE 1980s. YOU KNOW...LAST ISSUE. -JORDAN
I MOST CERTAINLY WAS NOT SATISFIED WITH THE WORK.
DO YOU SEE HESE WOUNDS? HIS WAS DONE TO E BECAUSE OF OU. THEY WILL NEVER HEAL.
WELCOME TO MY PARTY, HANDSOME BOY!
AND I WOULDN'T DO YOUR DIRTY WORK BACK IN THE DAY-- SO I SURE AS HELL WON'T DO IT NOW.
YES, YOU WILL, OR YOUR FRIEND DIES.
I DON'T HAVE A FRIEND.
MICHAEL WOULD BE SO HURT TO HEAR YOU SAY THAT.
THERE ARE FIVE NAMES ON THIS SCROLL. KILL THE OTHER FOUR AND YOUR FAT WIZARD GETS A REPRIEVE.
I CAN'T BE TOO MAD AT MICHAEL. HE WAS ONE OF THE FIRST MORTALS I EVER MADE A DEAL WITH.
THE ONLY REASON I WAS PAROLED WAS BECAUSE OF THE FUN EVERYONE HAD WHEN HE USED MY GIFTS TO RESURRECT THE DEAD PRESIDENTS.
REAP THOSE FOUR NAMES, WADE. OR I FIND SOMEONE TO BRING ME THE SOULS OF ALL SIX, INCLUDING YOUR NECROMANCER PAL.
BE SEEING YOU, WADE.
LOOKS LIKE KILLING GORMAN AND GETTING MY MONEY WILL HAVE TO WAIT.
THOUGH, I SHOULD PROBABLY SWITCH THE ORDER ON THAT...
HEY, PRESTON--YOU HUNGRY?

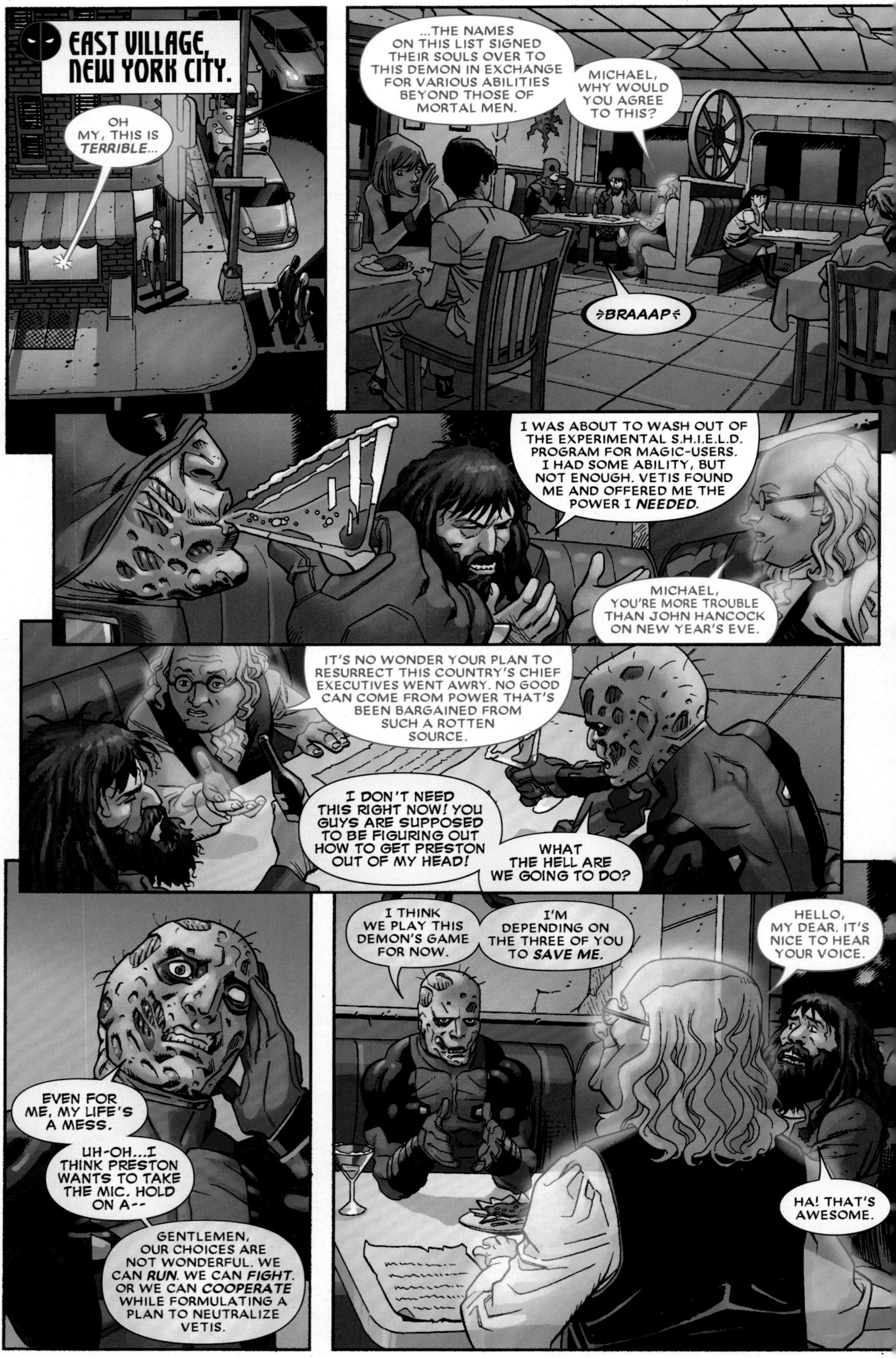
EAST VILLAGE, NEW YORK CITY.
OH MY, THIS IS *TERRIBLE*...
...THE NAMES ON THIS LIST SIGNED THEIR SOULS OVER TO THIS DEMON IN EXCHANGE FOR VARIOUS ABILITIES BEYOND THOSE OF MORTAL MEN.
MICHAEL, WHY WOULD YOU AGREE TO THIS?
BRAAAP
I WAS ABOUT TO WASH OUT OF THE EXPERIMENTAL S.H.I.E.L.D. PROGRAM FOR MAGIC-USERS. I HAD SOME ABILITY, BUT NOT ENOUGH. VETIS FOUND ME AND OFFERED ME THE POWER I *NEEDED.*
MICHAEL, YOU'RE MORE TROUBLE THAN JOHN HANCOCK ON NEW YEAR'S EVE.
IT'S NO WONDER YOUR PLAN TO RESURRECT THIS COUNTRY'S CHIEF EXECUTIVES WENT AWRY. NO GOOD CAN COME FROM POWER THAT'S BEEN BARGAINED FROM SUCH A ROTTEN SOURCE.
I DON'T NEED THIS RIGHT NOW! YOU GUYS ARE SUPPOSED TO BE FIGURING OUT HOW TO GET PRESTON OUT OF MY HEAD!
WHAT THE HELL ARE WE GOING TO DO?
EVEN FOR ME, MY LIFE'S A MESS.
UH-OH...I THINK PRESTON WANTS TO TAKE THE MIC. HOLD ON A--
GENTLEMEN, OUR CHOICES ARE NOT WONDERFUL. WE CAN *RUN*. WE CAN *FIGHT*. OR WE CAN *COOPERATE* WHILE FORMULATING A PLAN TO NEUTRALIZE VETIS.
I THINK WE PLAY THIS DEMON'S GAME FOR NOW.
I'M DEPENDING ON THE THREE OF YOU TO *SAVE ME.*
HELLO, MY DEAR. IT'S NICE TO HEAR YOUR VOICE.
HA! THAT'S AWESOME.

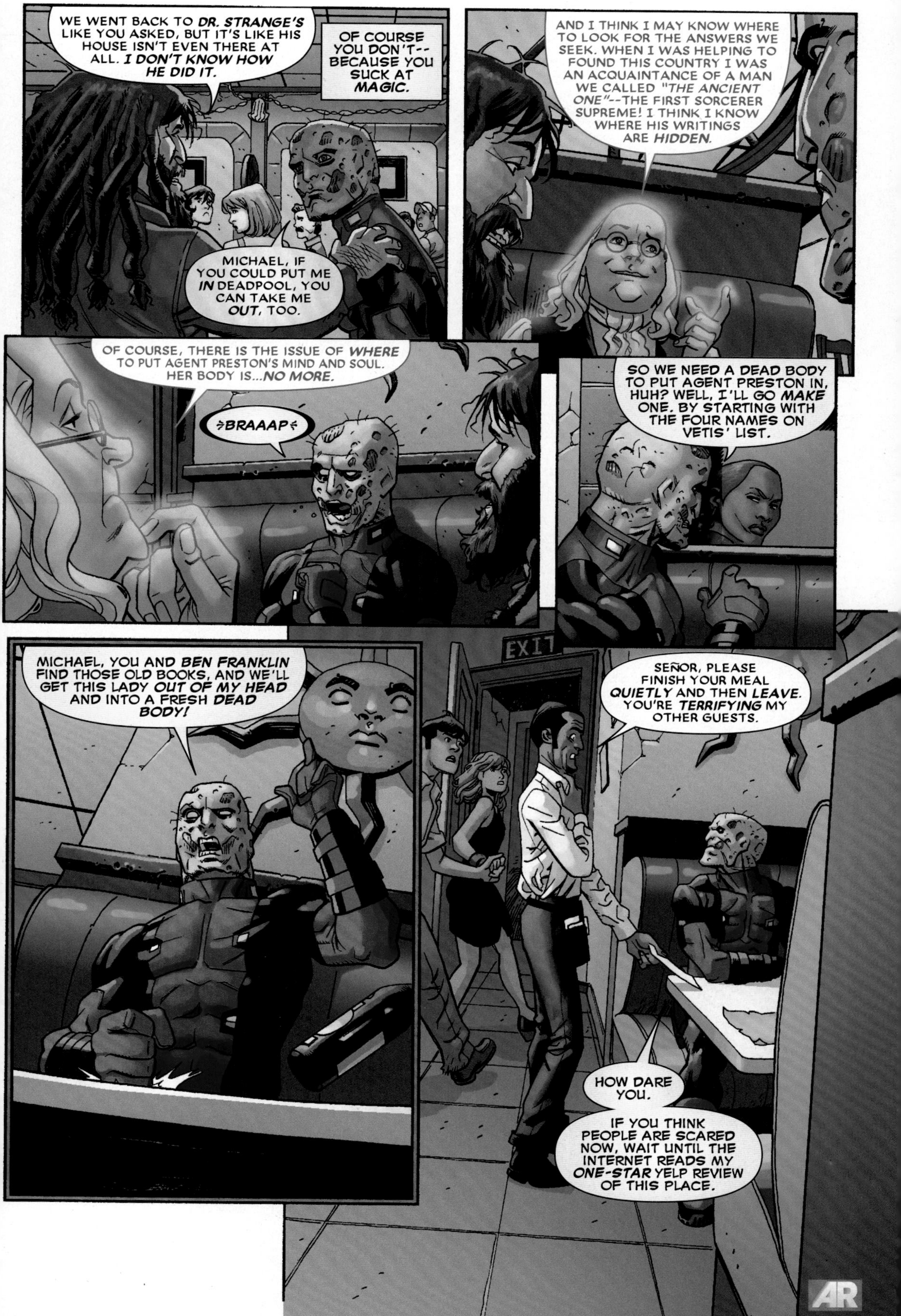
WE WENT BACK TO DR. STRANGE'S LIKE YOU ASKED, BUT IT'S LIKE HIS HOUSE ISN'T EVEN THERE AT ALL. I DON'T KNOW HOW HE DID IT.
OF COURSE YOU DON'T-- BECAUSE YOU SUCK AT MAGIC.
MICHAEL, IF YOU COULD PUT ME IN DEADPOOL, YOU CAN TAKE ME OUT, TOO.
AND I THINK I MAY KNOW WHERE TO LOOK FOR THE ANSWERS WE SEEK. WHEN I WAS HELPING TO FOUND THIS COUNTRY I WAS AN ACQUAINTANCE OF A MAN WE CALLED "THE ANCIENT ONE"--THE FIRST SORCERER SUPREME! I THINK I KNOW WHERE HIS WRITINGS ARE HIDDEN.
OF COURSE, THERE IS THE ISSUE OF WHERE TO PUT AGENT PRESTON'S MIND AND SOUL. HER BODY IS...NO MORE.
BRAAAP
SO WE NEED A DEAD BODY TO PUT AGENT PRESTON IN, HUH? WELL, I'LL GO MAKE ONE. BY STARTING WITH THE FOUR NAMES ON VETIS' LIST.
MICHAEL, YOU AND BEN FRANKLIN FIND THOSE OLD BOOKS, AND WE'LL GET THIS LADY OUT OF MY HEAD AND INTO A FRESH DEAD BODY!
EXIT
SEÑOR, PLEASE FINISH YOUR MEAL QUIETLY AND THEN LEAVE. YOU'RE TERRIFYING MY OTHER GUESTS.
HOW DARE YOU.
IF YOU THINK PEOPLE ARE SCARED NOW, WAIT UNTIL THE INTERNET READS MY ONE-STAR YELP REVIEW OF THIS PLACE.

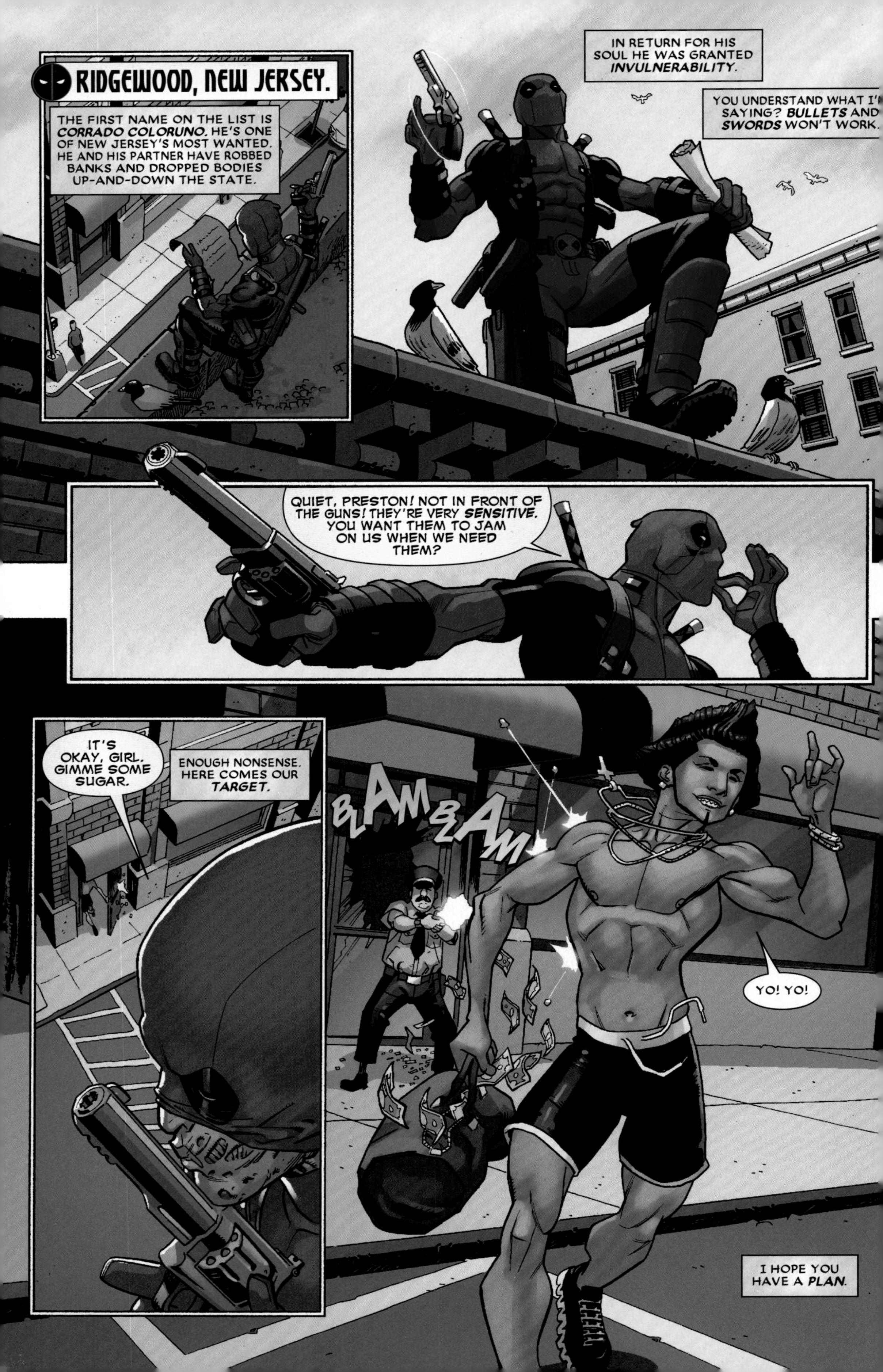
RIDGEWOOD, NEW JERSEY.
THE FIRST NAME ON THE LIST IS CORRADO COLORUNO. HE'S ONE OF NEW JERSEY'S MOST WANTED. HE AND HIS PARTNER HAVE ROBBED BANKS AND DROPPED BODIES UP-AND-DOWN THE STATE.
IN RETURN FOR HIS SOUL HE WAS GRANTED INVULNERABILITY.
YOU UNDERSTAND WHAT I' SAYING? BULLETS AND SWORDS WON'T WORK.
QUIET, PRESTON! NOT IN FRONT OF THE GUNS! THEY'RE VERY SENSITIVE. YOU WANT THEM TO JAM ON US WHEN WE NEED THEM?
IT'S OKAY, GIRL. GIMME SOME SUGAR.
ENOUGH NONSENSE. HERE COMES OUR TARGET.
BLAM BLAM
YO! YO!
I HOPE YOU HAVE A PLAN.

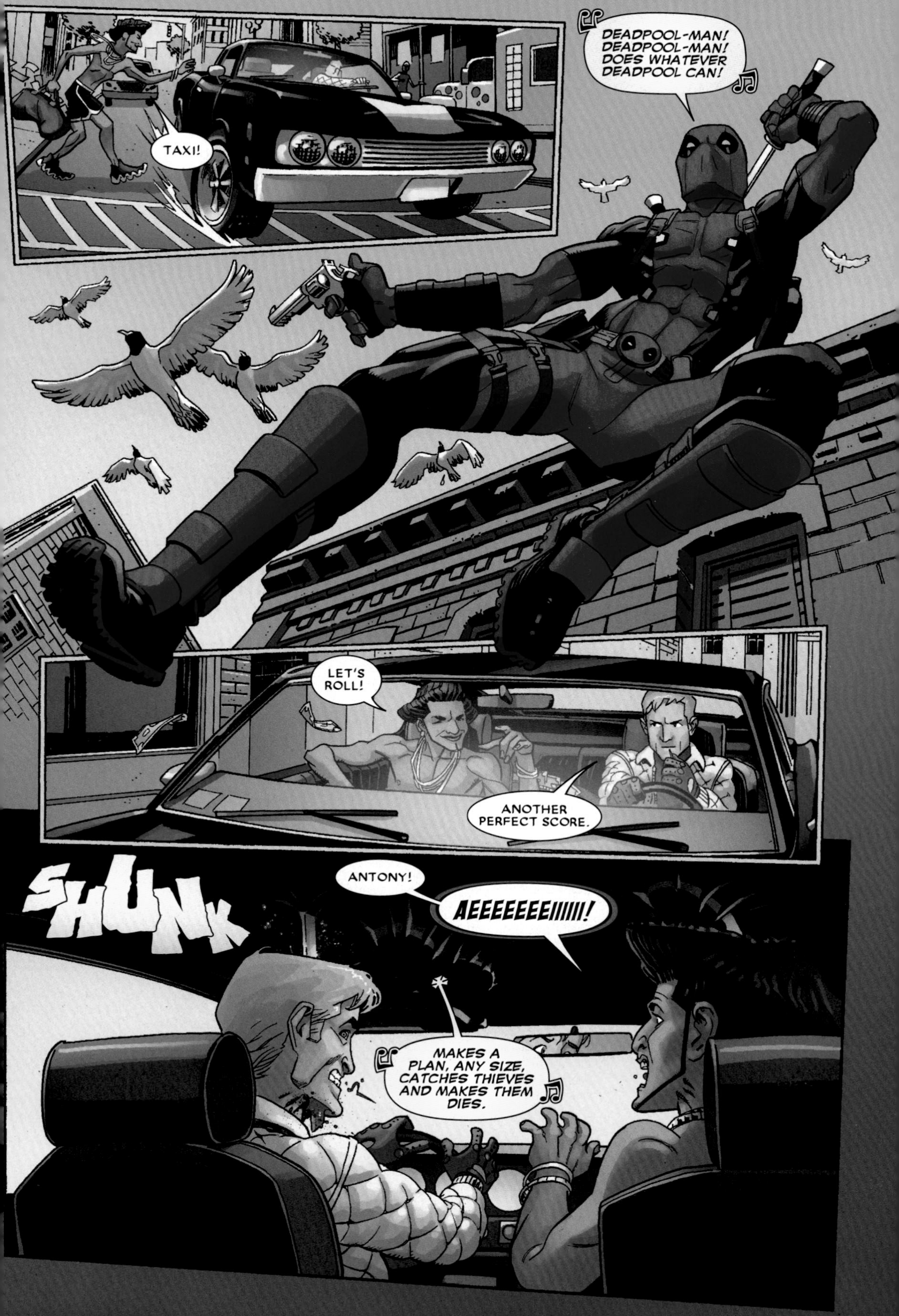
TAXI!
DEADPOOL-MAN! DEADPOOL-MAN! DOES WHATEVER DEADPOOL CAN!
LET'S ROLL!
ANOTHER PERFECT SCORE.
SHUNK
ANTONY!
AEEEEEEEIIIIII!
MAKES A PLAN, ANY SIZE, CATCHES THIEVES AND MAKES THEM DIES.

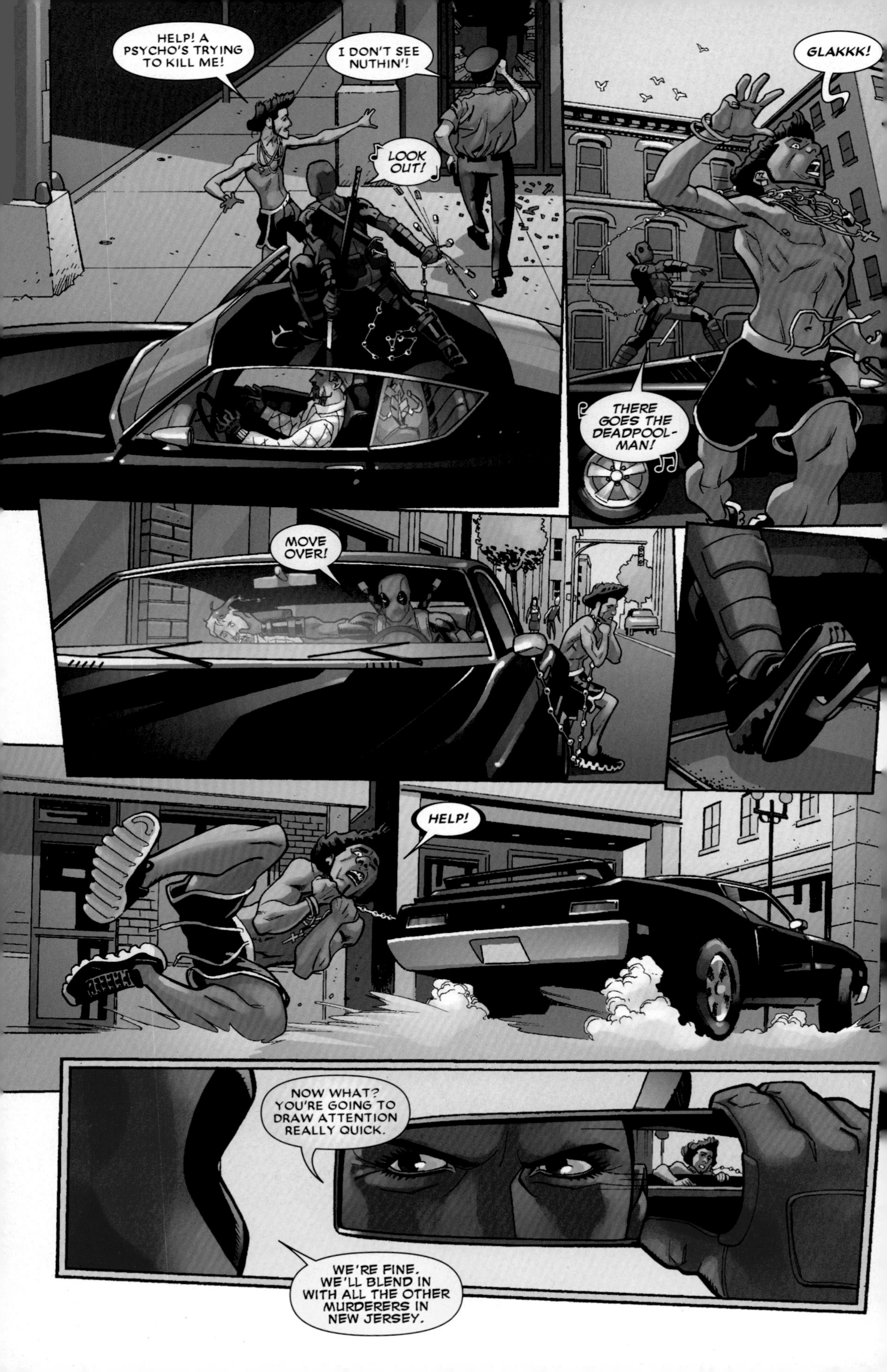
HELP! A PSYCHO'S TRYING TO KILL ME!
I DON'T SEE NUTHIN'!
LOOK OUT!
GLAKKK!
THERE GOES THE DEADPOOL-MAN!
MOVE OVER!
HELP!
NOW WHAT? YOU'RE GOING TO DRAW ATTENTION REALLY QUICK.
WE'RE FINE. WE'LL BLEND IN WITH ALL THE OTHER MURDERERS IN NEW JERSEY.

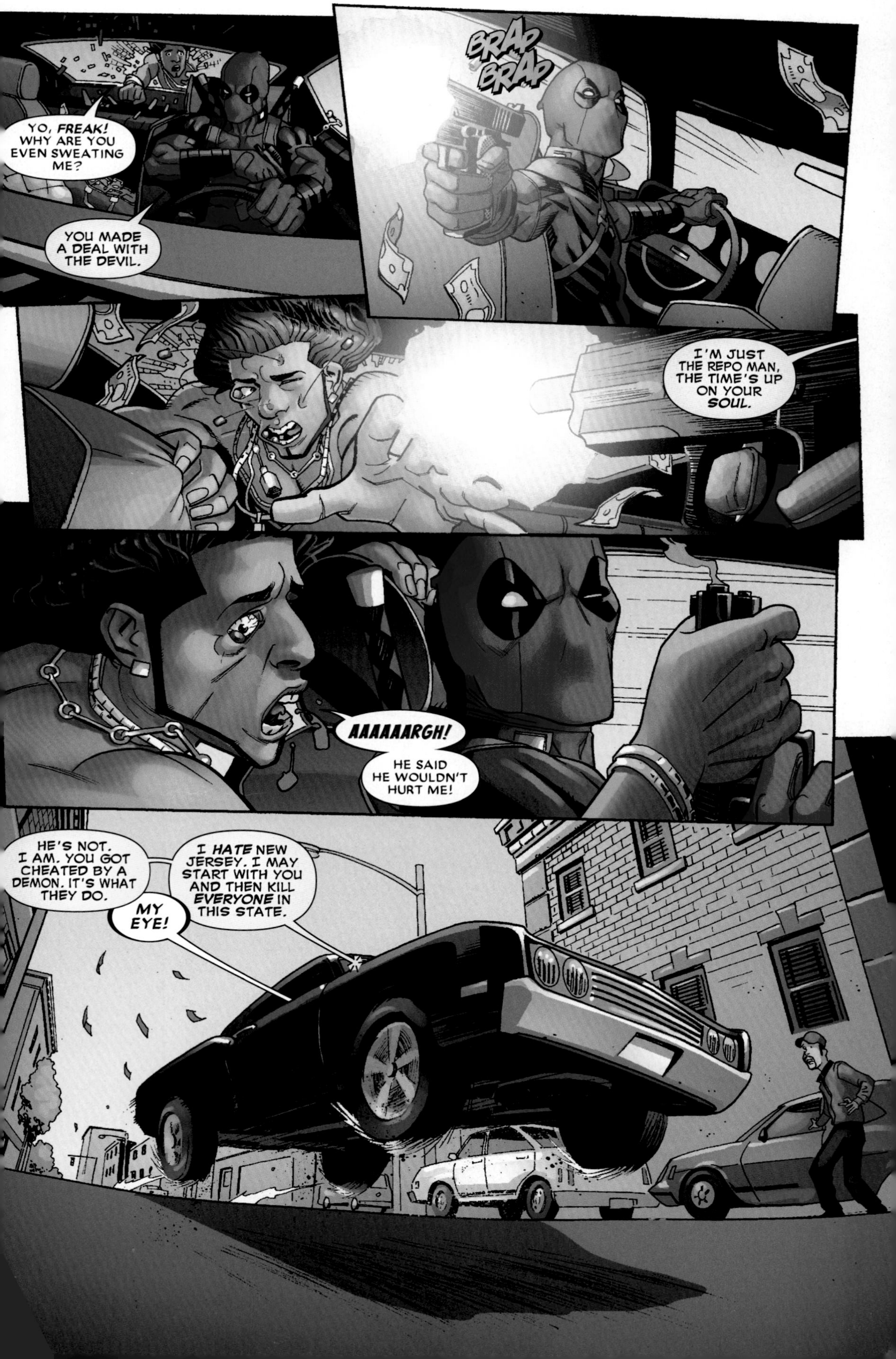
YO, FREAK! WHY ARE YOU EVEN SWEATING ME?
YOU MADE A DEAL WITH THE DEVIL.
BRAP BRAP
I'M JUST THE REPO MAN, THE TIME'S UP ON YOUR SOUL.
AAAAAARGH!
HE SAID HE WOULDN'T HURT ME!
HE'S NOT. I AM. YOU GOT CHEATED BY A DEMON. IT'S WHAT THEY DO.
MY EYE!
I HATE NEW JERSEY. I MAY START WITH YOU AND THEN KILL EVERYONE IN THIS STATE.

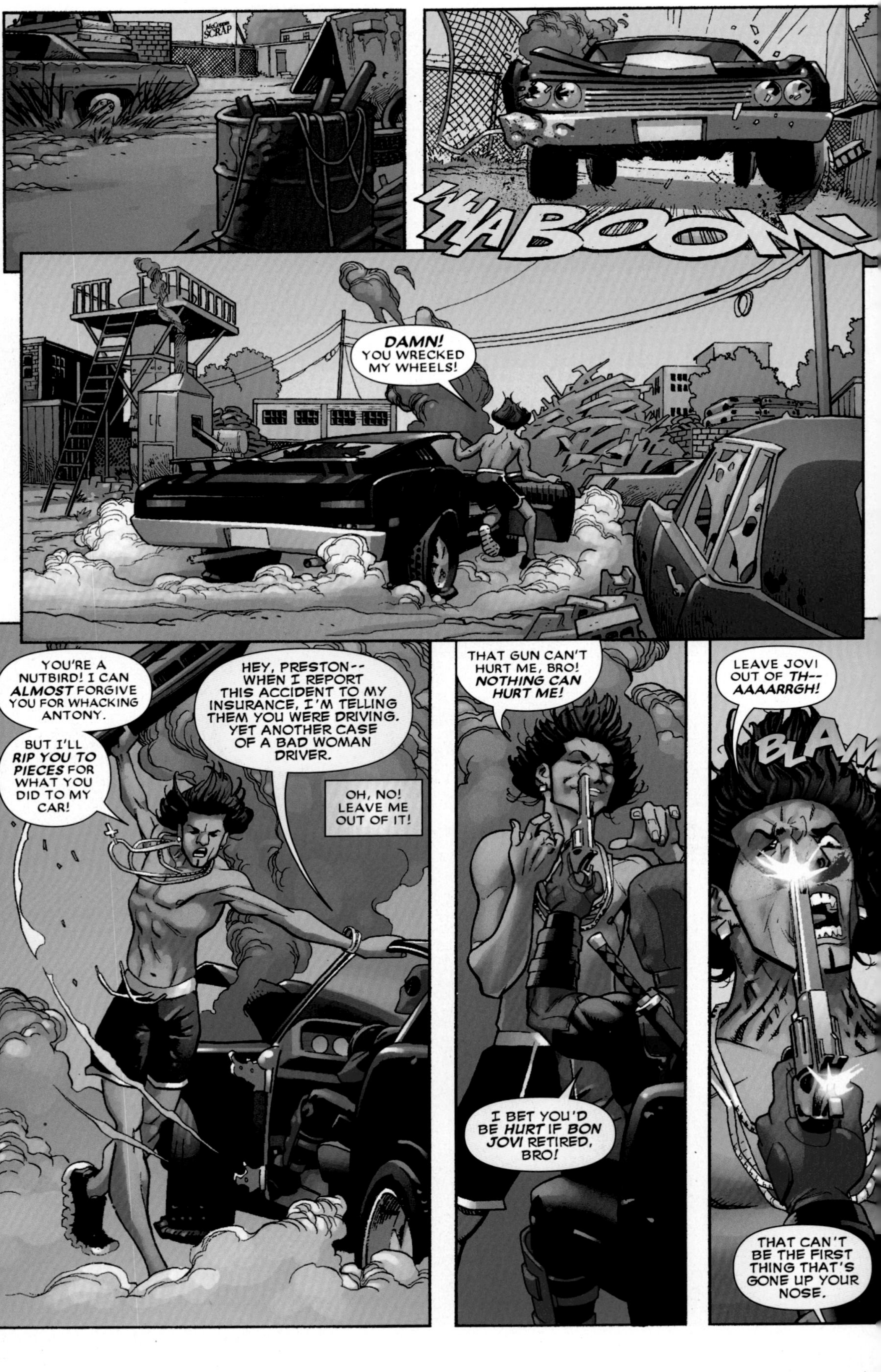

McGUIRE SCRAP
WHABOOM!
DAMN! YOU WRECKED MY WHEELS!
YOU'RE A NUTBIRD! I CAN ALMOST FORGIVE YOU FOR WHACKING ANTONY.
BUT I'LL RIP YOU TO PIECES FOR WHAT YOU DID TO MY CAR!
HEY, PRESTON-- WHEN I REPORT THIS ACCIDENT TO MY INSURANCE, I'M TELLING THEM YOU WERE DRIVING. YET ANOTHER CASE OF A BAD WOMAN DRIVER.
OH, NO! LEAVE ME OUT OF IT!
THAT GUN CAN'T HURT ME, BRO! NOTHING CAN HURT ME!
I BET YOU'D BE HURT IF BON JOVI RETIRED, BRO!
LEAVE JOVI OUT OF TH-- AAAARRGH!
BLAM
THAT CAN'T BE THE FIRST THING THAT'S GONE UP YOUR NOSE.

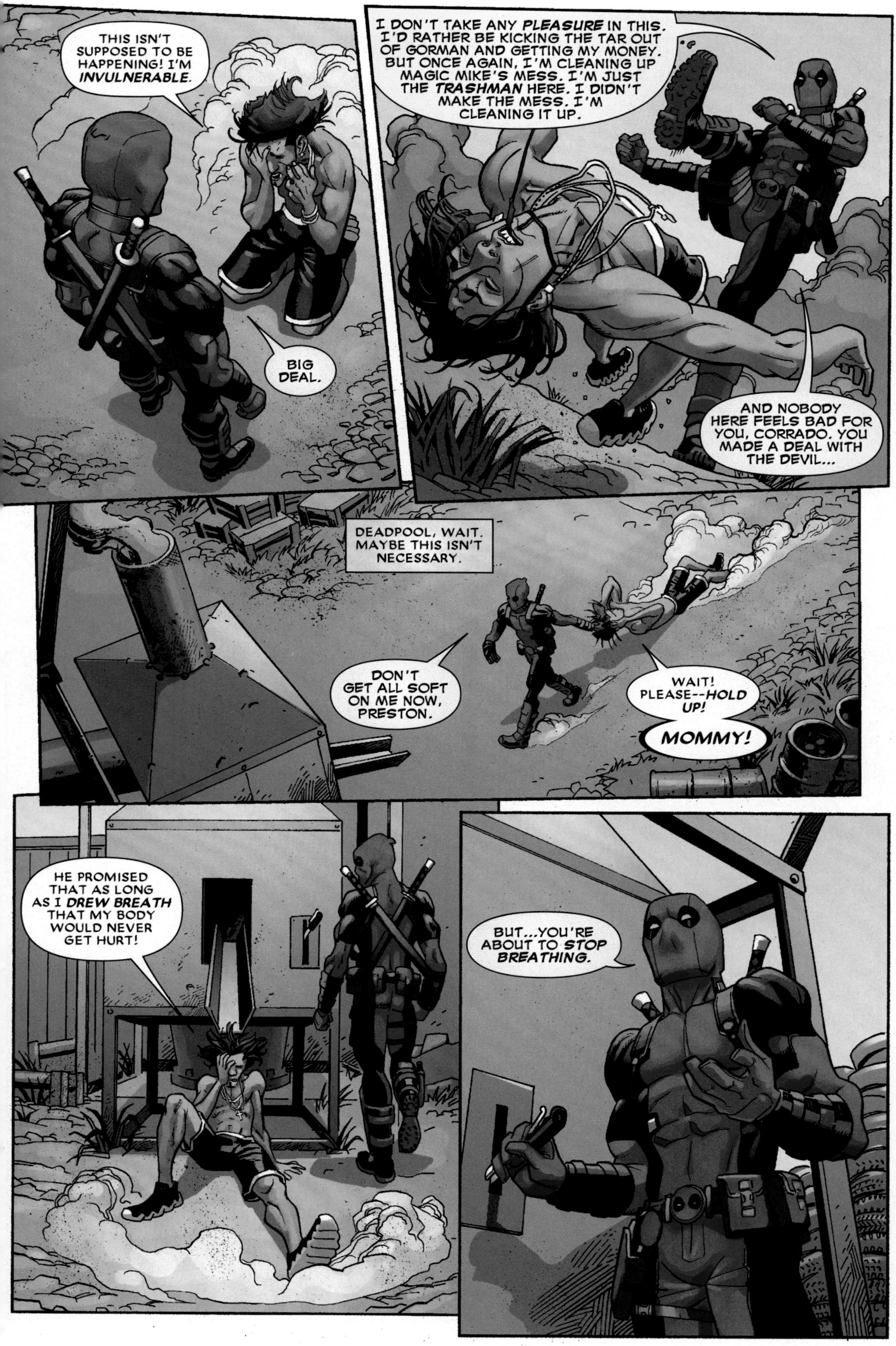
THIS ISN'T SUPPOSED TO BE HAPPENING! I'M INVULNERABLE.
BIG DEAL.
I DON'T TAKE ANY PLEASURE IN THIS. I'D RATHER BE KICKING THE TAR OUT OF GORMAN AND GETTING MY MONEY. BUT ONCE AGAIN, I'M CLEANING UP MAGIC MIKE'S MESS. I'M JUST THE TRASHMAN HERE. I DIDN'T MAKE THE MESS. I'M CLEANING IT UP.
AND NOBODY HERE FEELS BAD FOR YOU, CORRADO. YOU MADE A DEAL WITH THE DEVIL...
DEADPOOL, WAIT. MAYBE THIS ISN'T NECESSARY.
DON'T GET ALL SOFT ON ME NOW, PRESTON.
WAIT! PLEASE--HOLD UP!
MOMMY!
HE PROMISED THAT AS LONG AS I DREW BREATH THAT MY BODY WOULD NEVER GET HURT!
BUT...YOU'RE ABOUT TO STOP BREATHING.

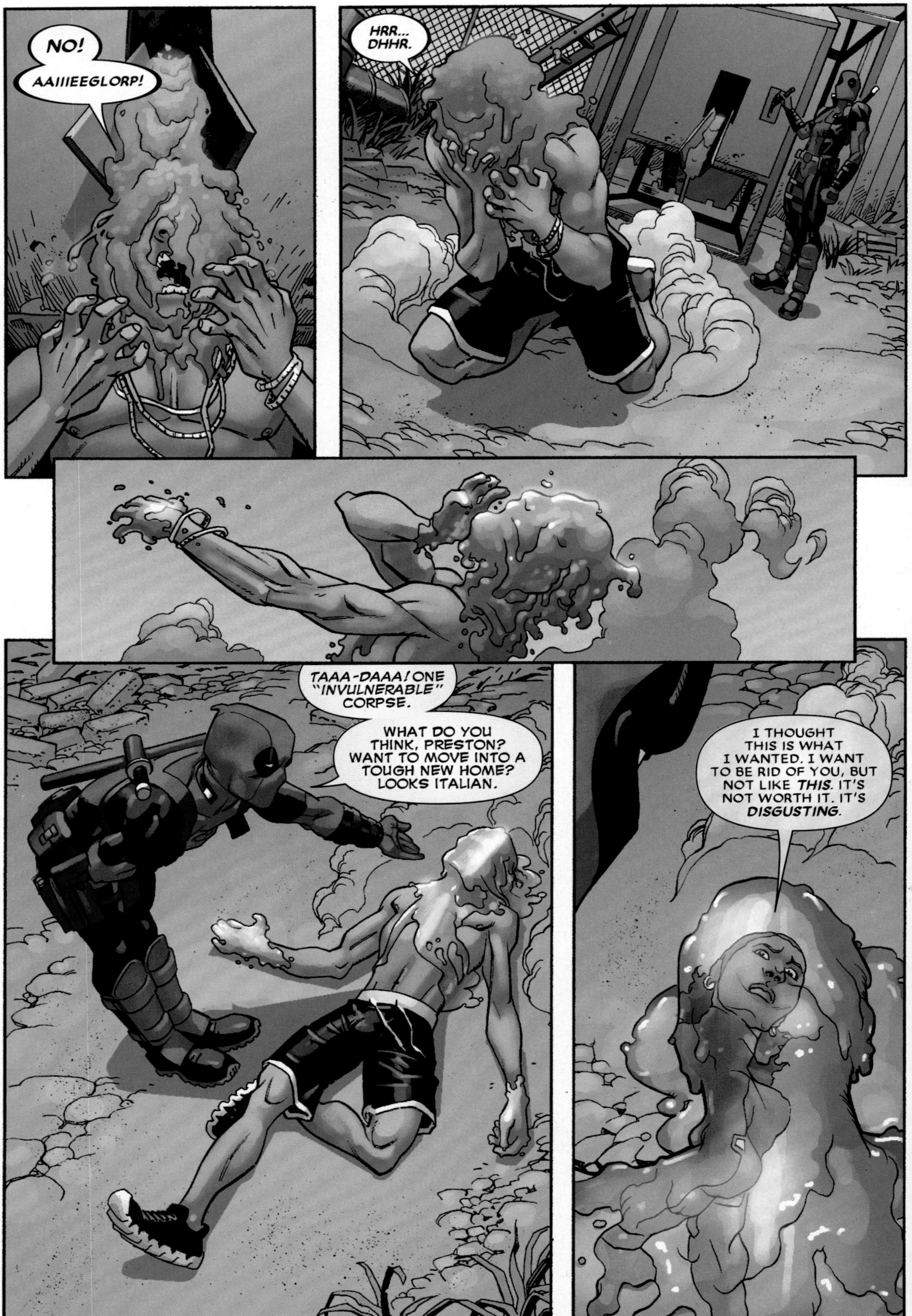
NO!
AAIIIEEGLORP!
HRR... DHHR.
TAAA-DAAA! ONE "INVULNERABLE" CORPSE.
WHAT DO YOU THINK, PRESTON? WANT TO MOVE INTO A TOUGH NEW HOME? LOOKS ITALIAN.
I THOUGHT THIS IS WHAT I WANTED. I WANT TO BE RID OF YOU, BUT NOT LIKE *THIS*. IT'S NOT WORTH IT. IT'S *DISGUSTING*.

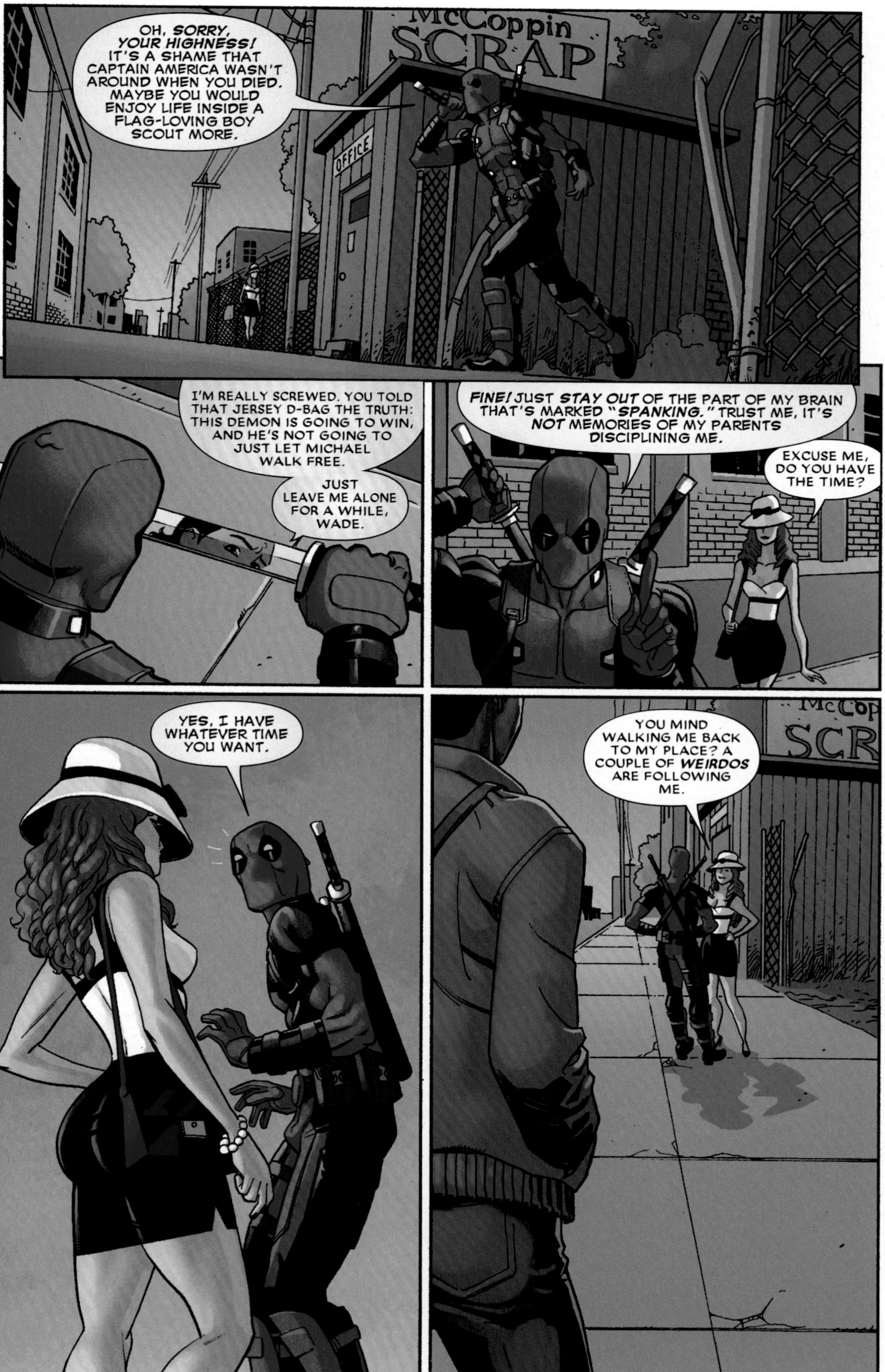
McCoppin SCRAP
OFFICE
OH, SORRY, YOUR HIGHNESS! IT'S A SHAME THAT CAPTAIN AMERICA WASN'T AROUND WHEN YOU DIED. MAYBE YOU WOULD ENJOY LIFE INSIDE A FLAG-LOVING BOY SCOUT MORE.
I'M REALLY SCREWED. YOU TOLD THAT JERSEY D-BAG THE TRUTH: THIS DEMON IS GOING TO WIN, AND HE'S NOT GOING TO JUST LET MICHAEL WALK FREE.
JUST LEAVE ME ALONE FOR A WHILE, WADE.
FINE! JUST STAY OUT OF THE PART OF MY BRAIN THAT'S MARKED "SPANKING." TRUST ME, IT'S NOT MEMORIES OF MY PARENTS DISCIPLINING ME.
EXCUSE ME, DO YOU HAVE THE TIME?
YES, I HAVE WHATEVER TIME YOU WANT.
YOU MIND WALKING ME BACK TO MY PLACE? A COUPLE OF WEIRDOS ARE FOLLOWING ME.

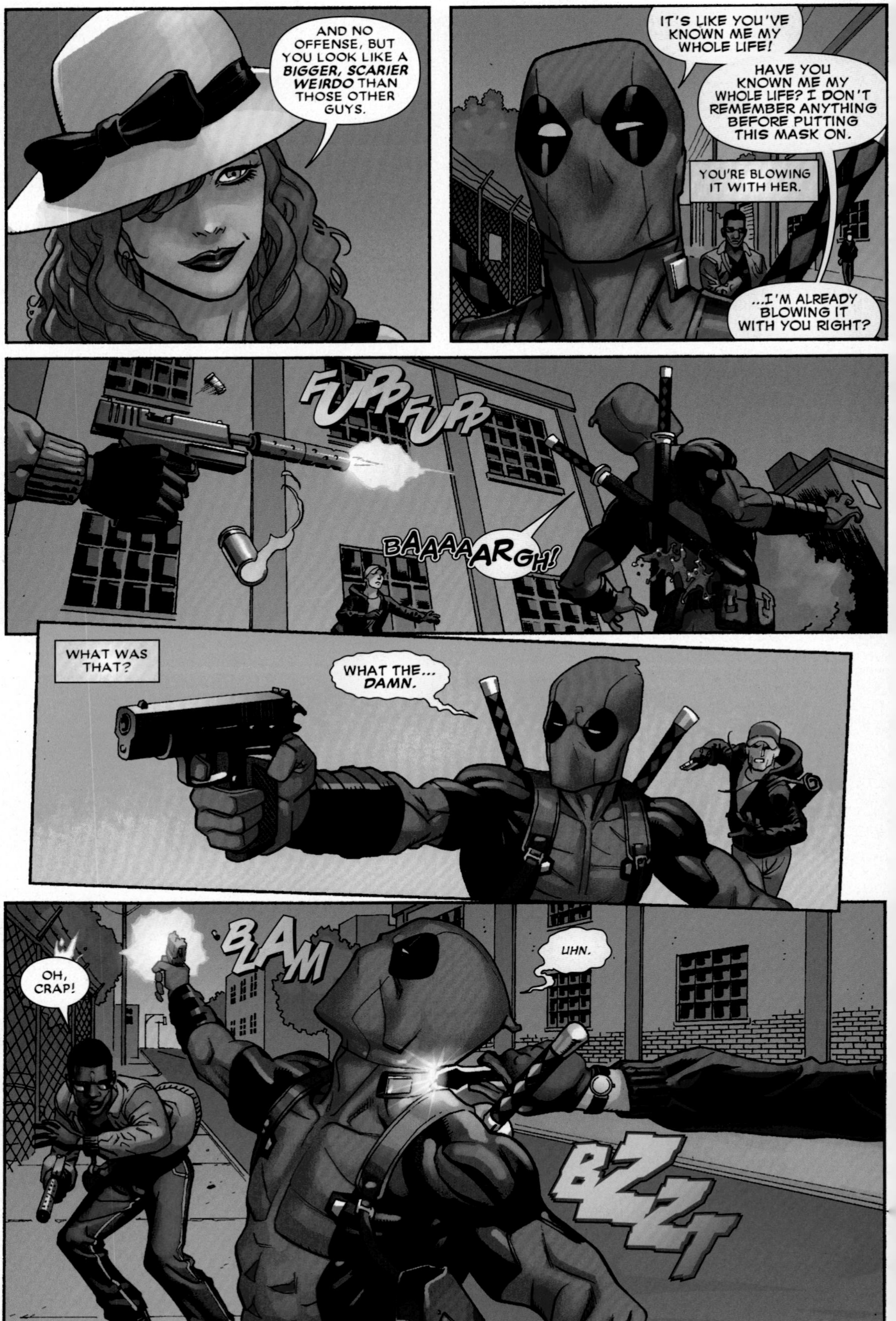
AND NO OFFENSE, BUT YOU LOOK LIKE A BIGGER, SCARIER WEIRDO THAN THOSE OTHER GUYS.
IT'S LIKE YOU'VE KNOWN ME MY WHOLE LIFE!
HAVE YOU KNOWN ME MY WHOLE LIFE? I DON'T REMEMBER ANYTHING BEFORE PUTTING THIS MASK ON.
YOU'RE BLOWING IT WITH HER.
...I'M ALREADY BLOWING IT WITH YOU RIGHT?
FUPP FUPP
BAAAAARGH!
WHAT WAS THAT?
WHAT THE... DAMN.
BLAM
UHN.
OH, CRAP!
BZZZT

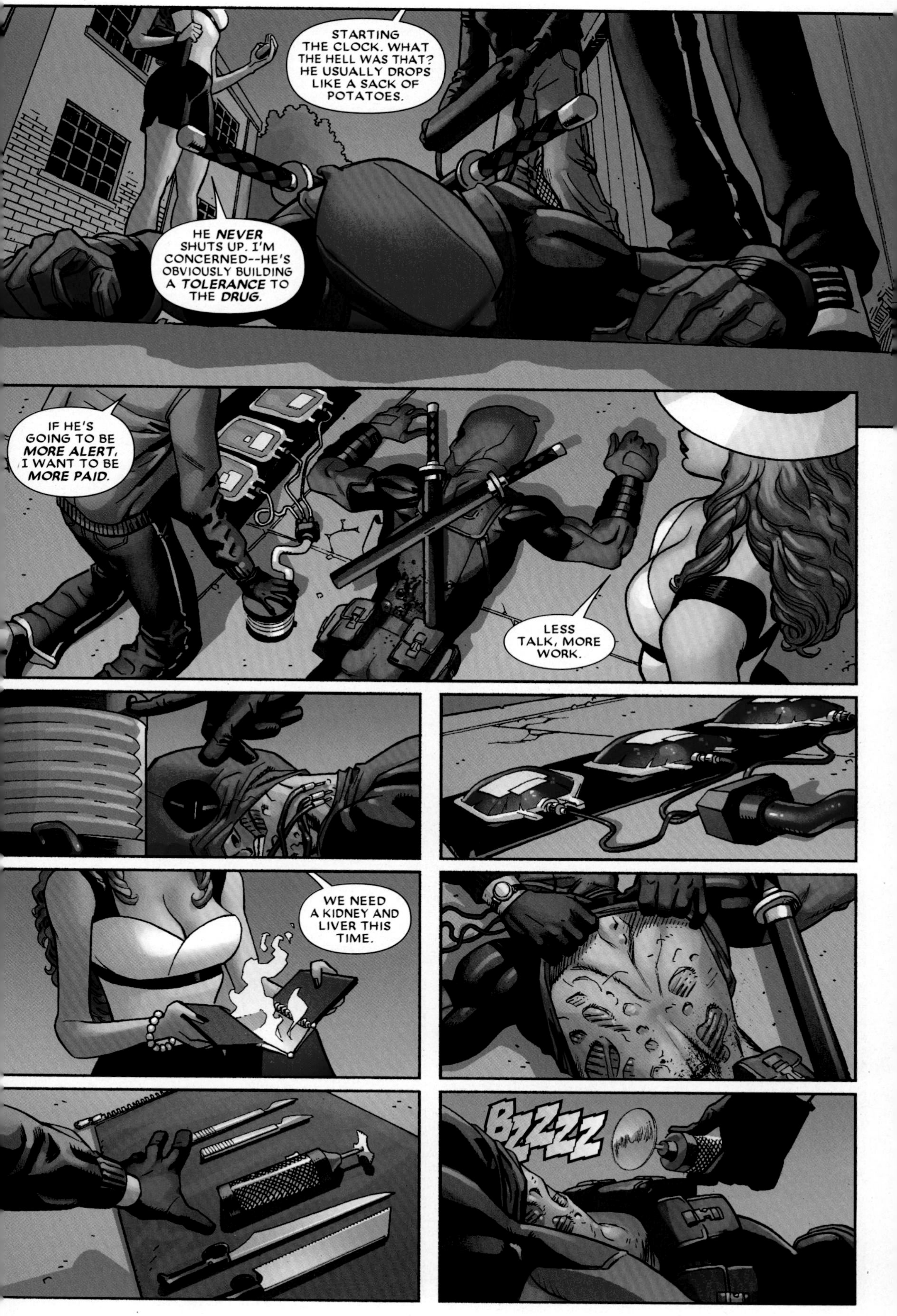
STARTING THE CLOCK. WHAT THE HELL WAS THAT? HE USUALLY DROPS LIKE A SACK OF POTATOES.
HE *NEVER* SHUTS UP. I'M CONCERNED--HE'S OBVIOUSLY BUILDING A *TOLERANCE* TO THE *DRUG*.
IF HE'S GOING TO BE *MORE ALERT*, I WANT TO BE *MORE PAID*.
LESS TALK, MORE WORK.
WE NEED A KIDNEY AND LIVER THIS TIME.
BZZZZ

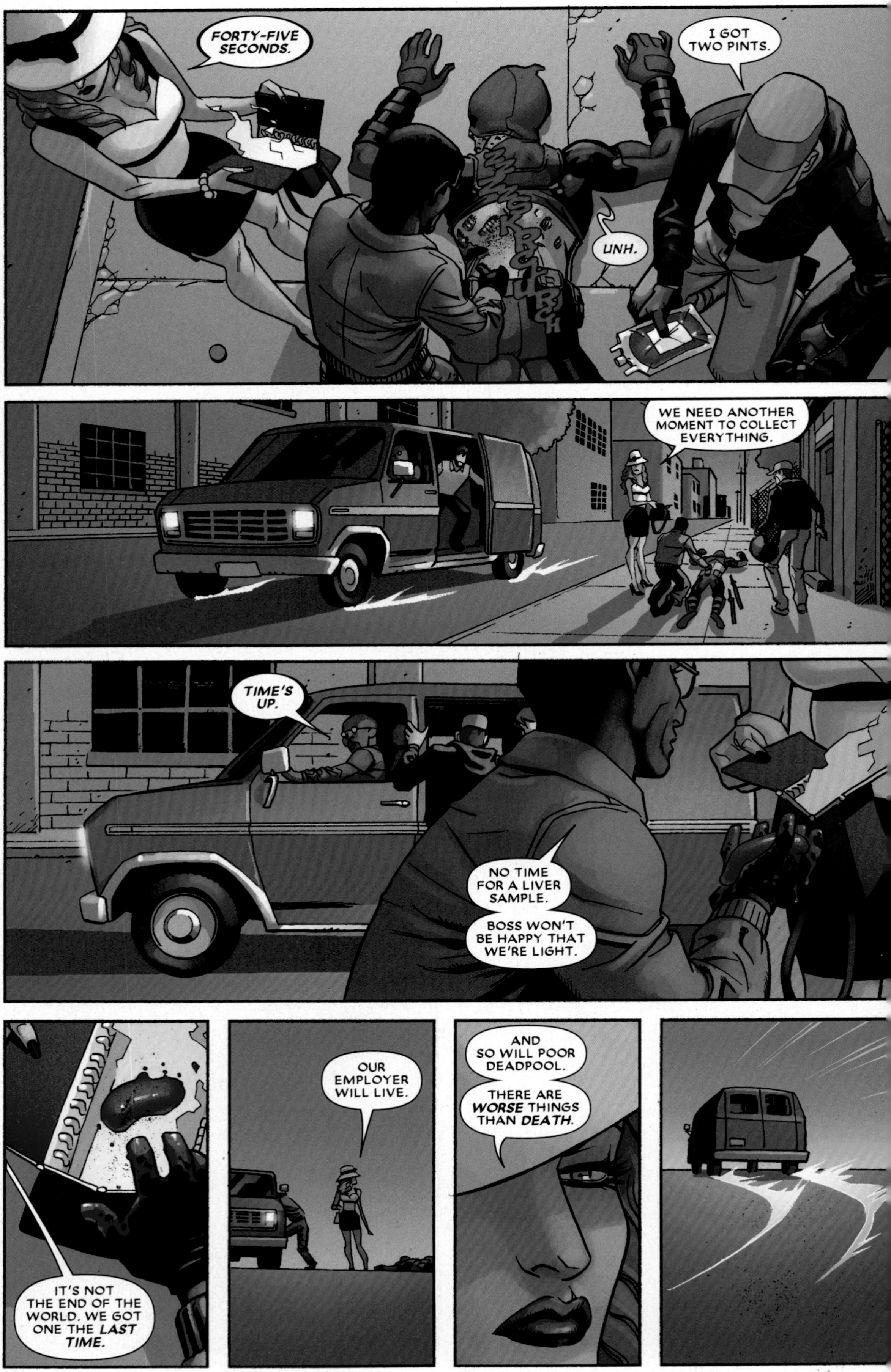
FORTY-FIVE SECONDS.
I GOT TWO PINTS.
UNH.
WE NEED ANOTHER MOMENT TO COLLECT EVERYTHING.
TIME'S UP.
NO TIME FOR A LIVER SAMPLE.
BOSS WON'T BE HAPPY THAT WE'RE LIGHT.
IT'S NOT THE END OF THE WORLD. WE GOT ONE THE LAST TIME.
OUR EMPLOYER WILL LIVE.
AND SO WILL POOR DEADPOOL.
THERE ARE WORSE THINGS THAN DEATH.

# 9

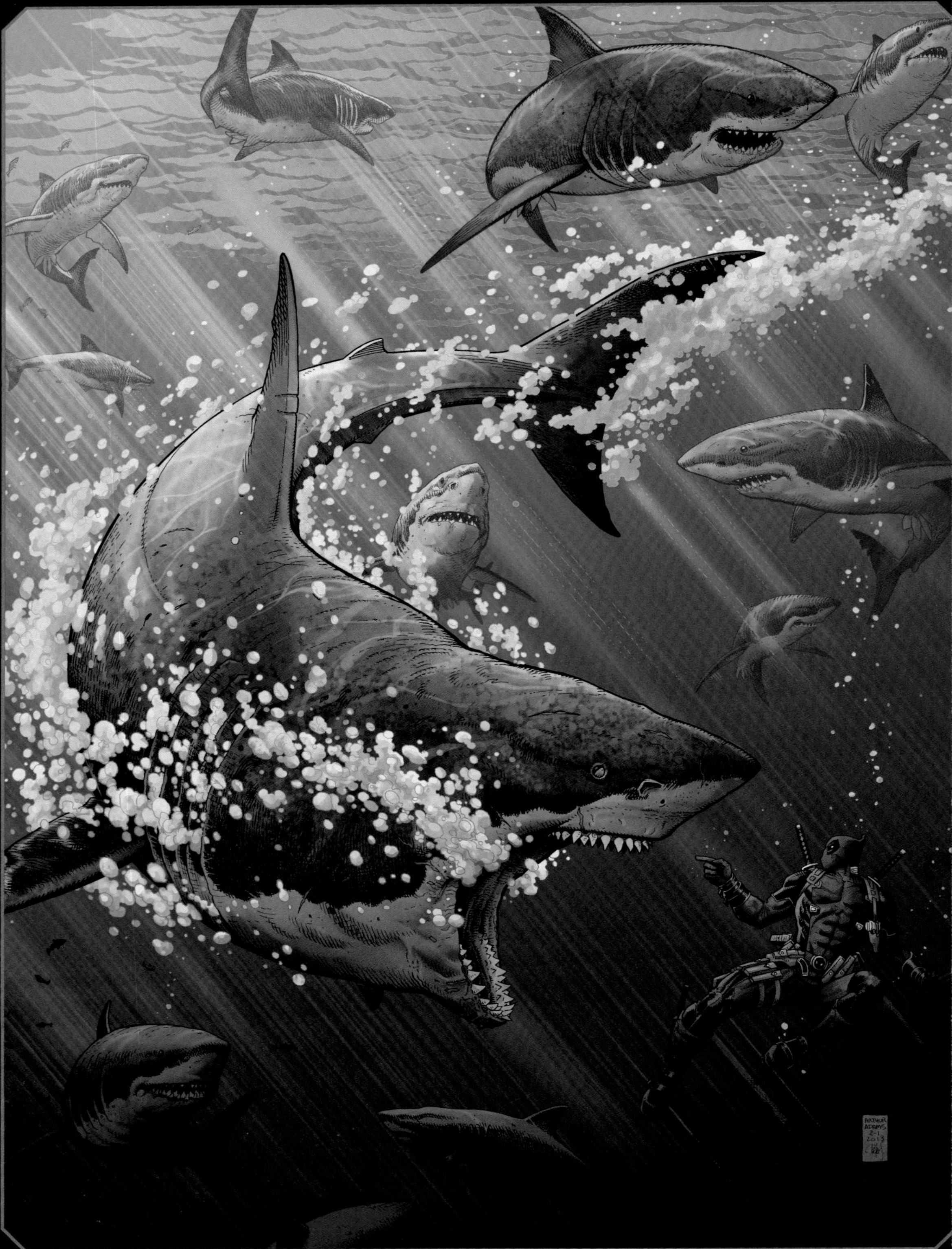

# THE DEVIL & THE DEEP BLUE SEA

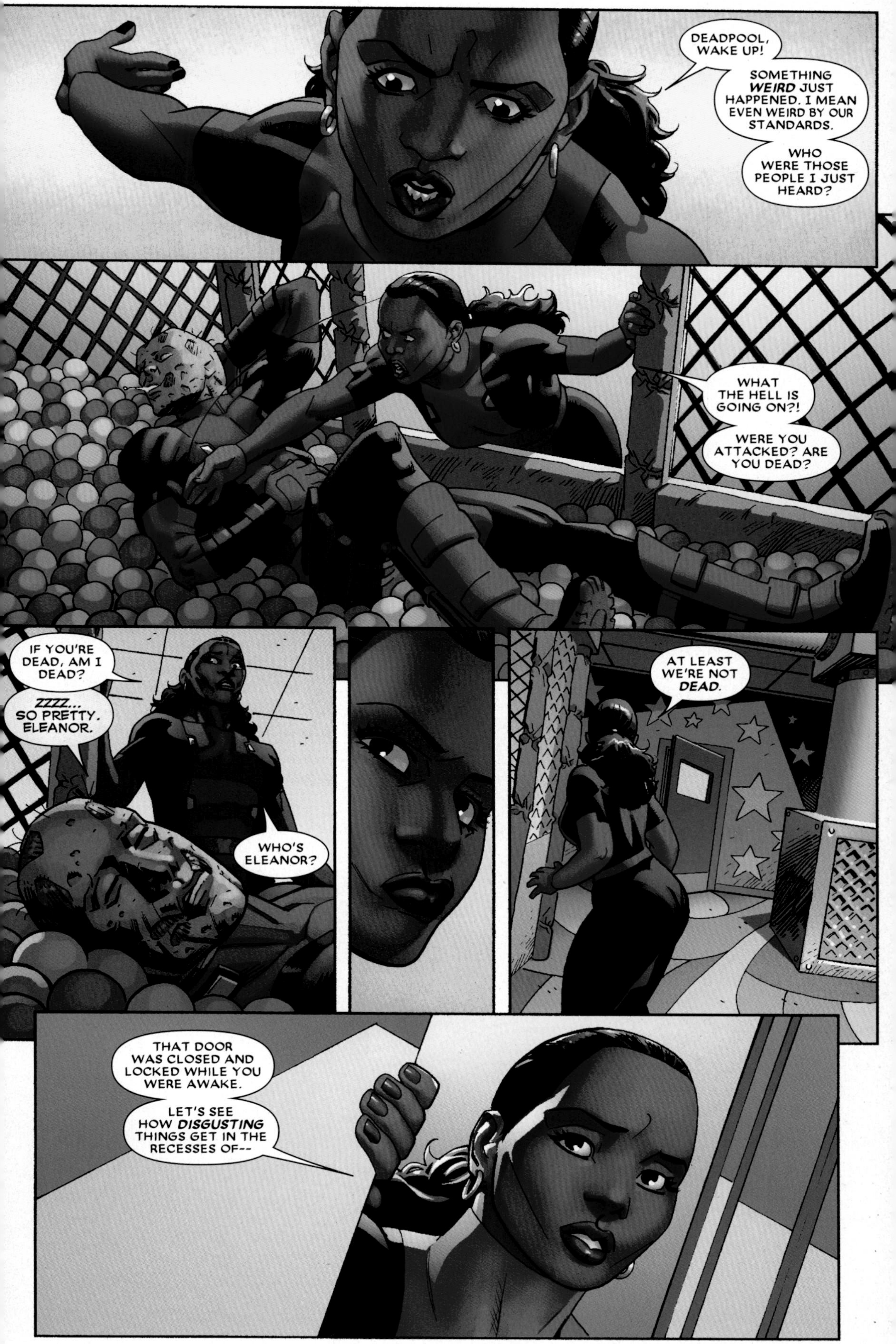

DEADPOOL, WAKE UP!
SOMETHING ***WEIRD*** JUST HAPPENED. I MEAN EVEN WEIRD BY OUR STANDARDS.
WHO WERE THOSE PEOPLE I JUST HEARD?
WHAT THE HELL IS GOING ON?!
WERE YOU ATTACKED? ARE YOU DEAD?
IF YOU'RE DEAD, AM I DEAD?
ZZZZ... SO PRETTY. ELEANOR.
WHO'S ELEANOR?
AT LEAST WE'RE NOT ***DEAD***.
THAT DOOR WAS CLOSED AND LOCKED WHILE YOU WERE AWAKE.
LET'S SEE HOW ***DISGUSTING*** THINGS GET IN THE RECESSES OF--

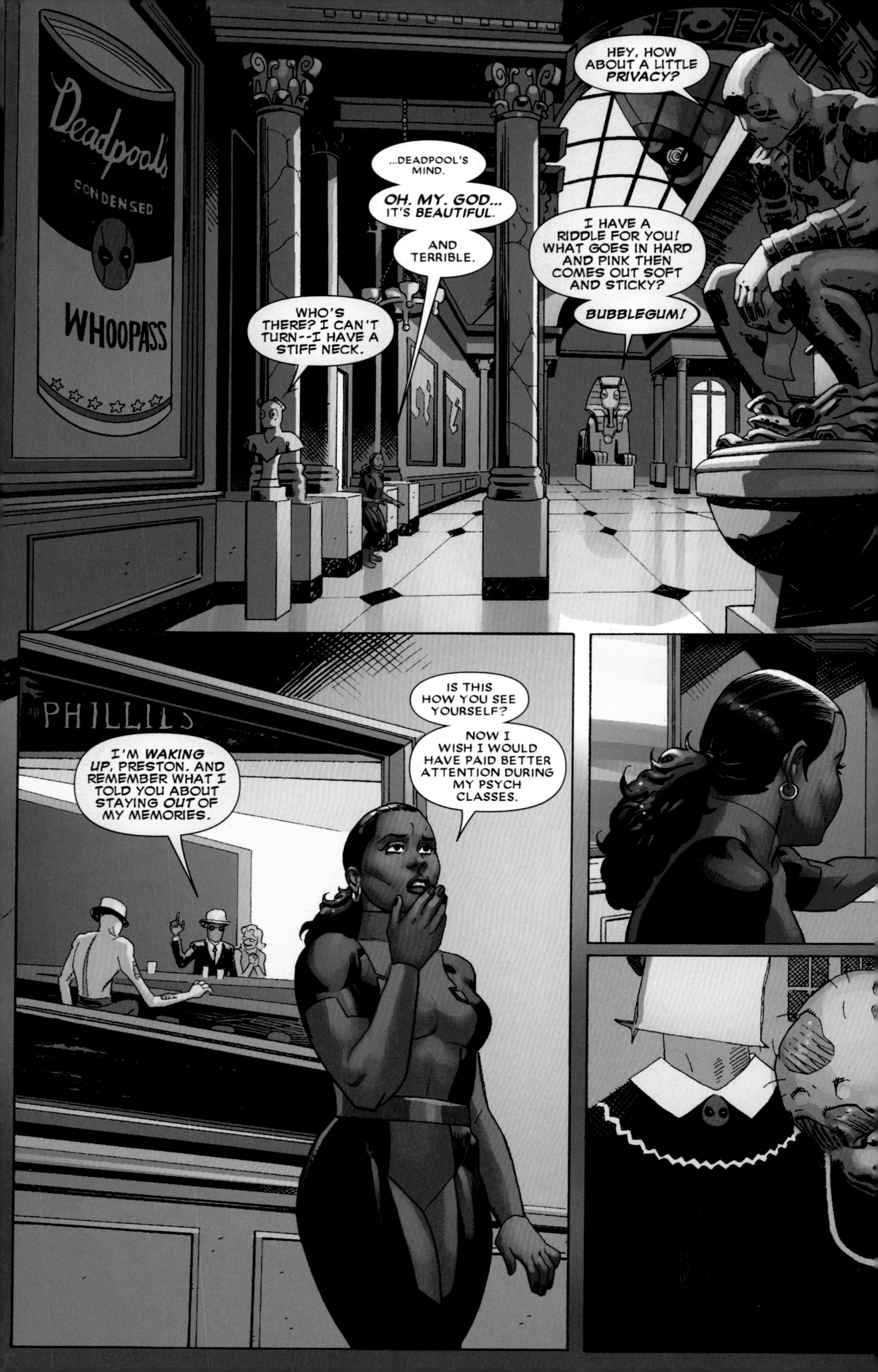
Deadpool's
CONDENSED
WHOOPASS
...DEADPOOL'S MIND.
OH. MY. GOD... IT'S BEAUTIFUL.
AND TERRIBLE.
WHO'S THERE? I CAN'T TURN--I HAVE A STIFF NECK.
HEY, HOW ABOUT A LITTLE PRIVACY?
I HAVE A RIDDLE FOR YOU! WHAT GOES IN HARD AND PINK THEN COMES OUT SOFT AND STICKY?
BUBBLEGUM!
PHILLIES
IS THIS HOW YOU SEE YOURSELF?
NOW I WISH I WOULD HAVE PAID BETTER ATTENTION DURING MY PSYCH CLASSES.
I'M WAKING UP, PRESTON. AND REMEMBER WHAT I TOLD YOU ABOUT STAYING OUT OF MY MEMORIES.

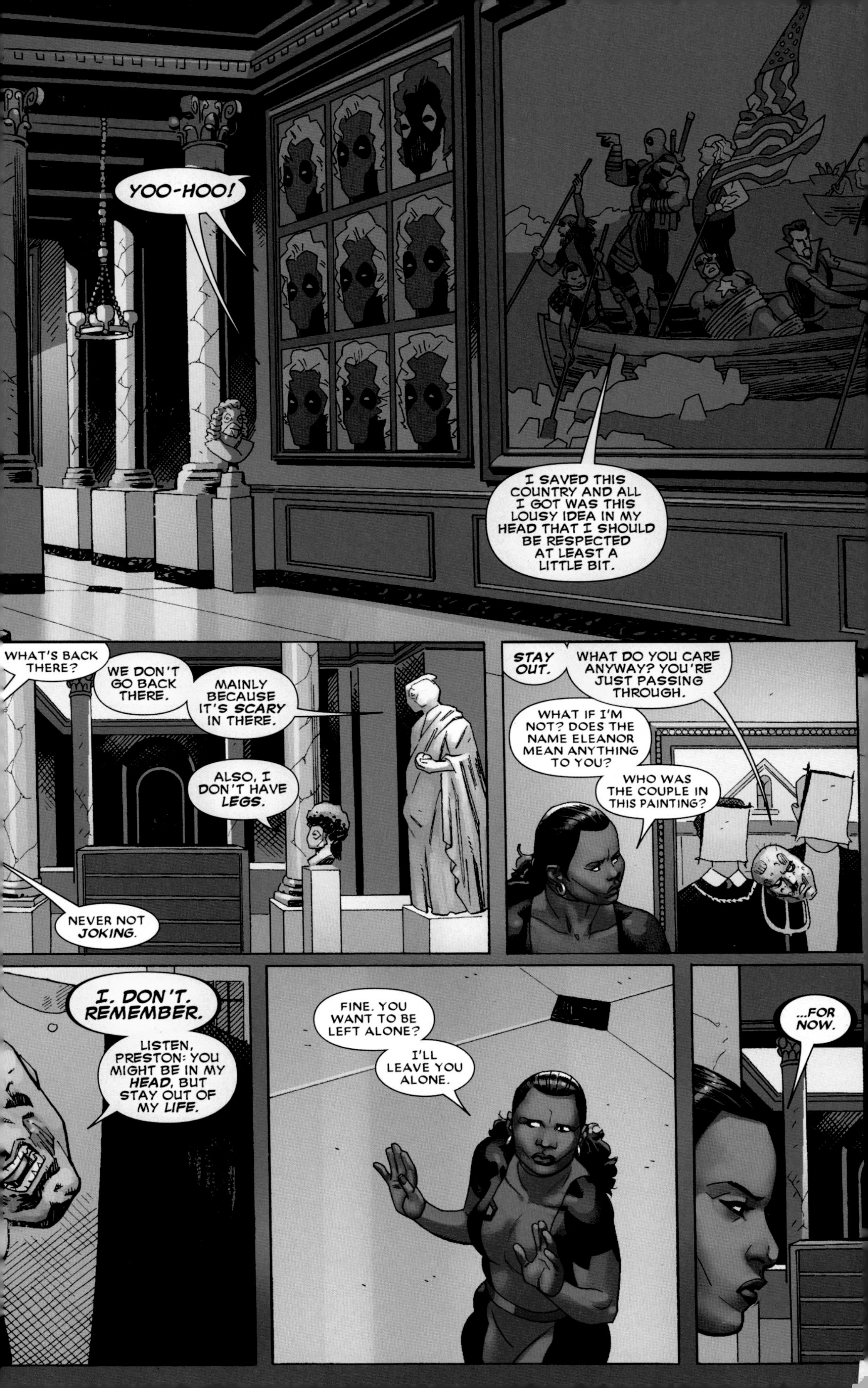
YOO-HOO!
I SAVED THIS COUNTRY AND ALL I GOT WAS THIS LOUSY IDEA IN MY HEAD THAT I SHOULD BE RESPECTED AT LEAST A LITTLE BIT.
WHAT'S BACK THERE?
WE DON'T GO BACK THERE.
MAINLY BECAUSE IT'S SCARY IN THERE.
ALSO, I DON'T HAVE LEGS.
NEVER NOT JOKING.
STAY OUT.
WHAT DO YOU CARE ANYWAY? YOU'RE JUST PASSING THROUGH.
WHAT IF I'M NOT? DOES THE NAME ELEANOR MEAN ANYTHING TO YOU?
WHO WAS THE COUPLE IN THIS PAINTING?
I. DON'T. REMEMBER.
LISTEN, PRESTON: YOU MIGHT BE IN MY HEAD, BUT STAY OUT OF MY LIFE.
FINE. YOU WANT TO BE LEFT ALONE?
I'LL LEAVE YOU ALONE.
...FOR NOW.

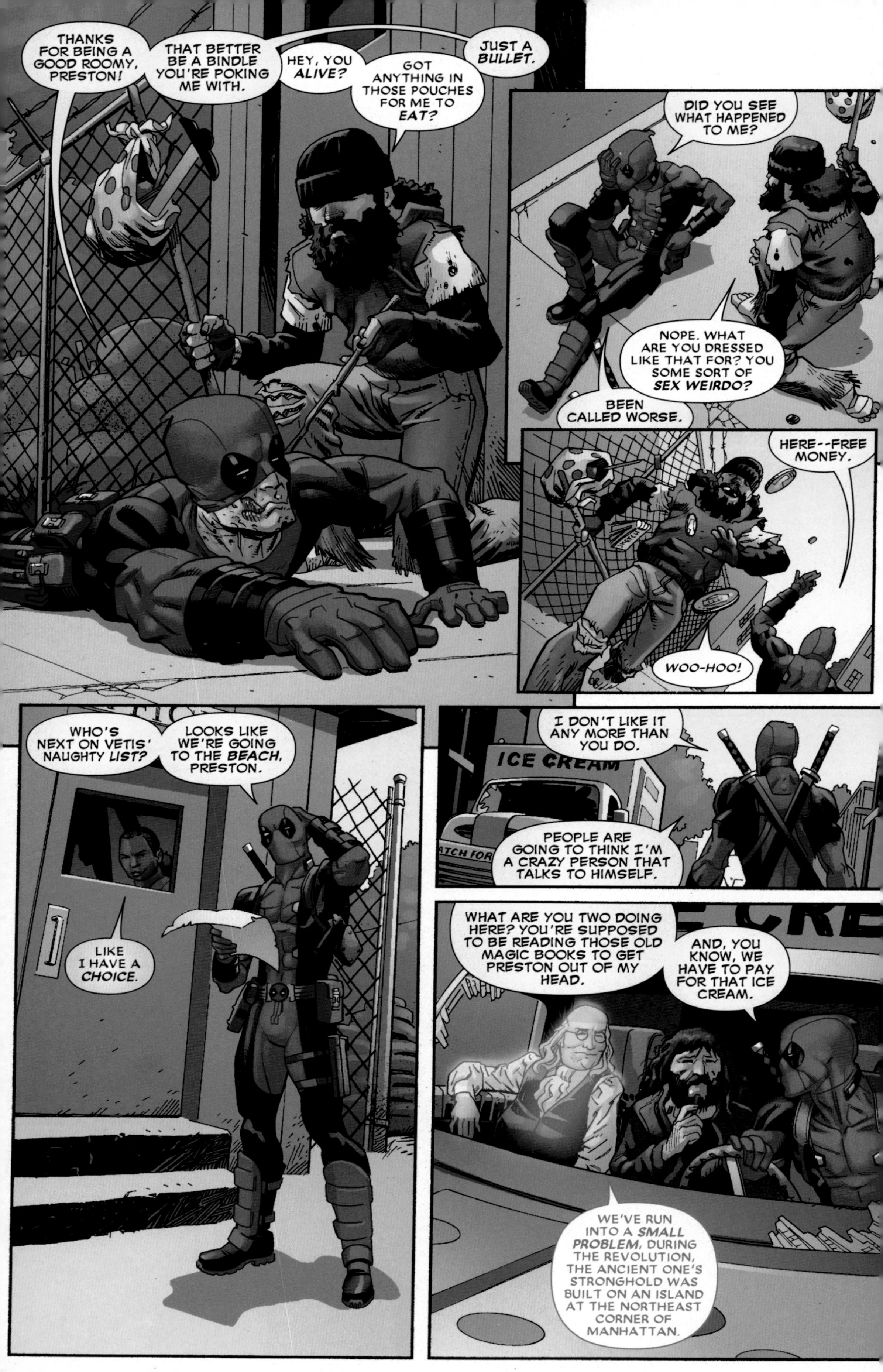
THANKS FOR BEING A GOOD ROOMY, PRESTON!
THAT BETTER BE A BINDLE YOU'RE POKING ME WITH.
HEY, YOU *ALIVE?*
GOT ANYTHING IN THOSE POUCHES FOR ME TO *EAT?*
JUST A *BULLET.*
DID YOU SEE WHAT HAPPENED TO ME?
NOPE. WHAT ARE YOU DRESSED LIKE THAT FOR? YOU SOME SORT OF *SEX WEIRDO?*
BEEN CALLED WORSE.
HERE--FREE MONEY.
WOO-HOO!
WHO'S NEXT ON VETIS' NAUGHTY *LIST?*
LOOKS LIKE WE'RE GOING TO THE *BEACH,* PRESTON.
LIKE I HAVE A *CHOICE.*
ICE CREAM
I DON'T LIKE IT ANY MORE THAN YOU *DO.*
PEOPLE ARE GOING TO THINK I'M A CRAZY PERSON THAT TALKS TO HIMSELF.
WHAT ARE YOU TWO DOING HERE? YOU'RE SUPPOSED TO BE READING THOSE OLD MAGIC BOOKS TO GET PRESTON OUT OF MY HEAD.
AND, YOU KNOW, WE HAVE TO PAY FOR THAT ICE CREAM.
WE'VE RUN INTO A *SMALL PROBLEM,* DURING THE REVOLUTION, THE ANCIENT ONE'S STRONGHOLD WAS BUILT ON AN ISLAND AT THE NORTHEAST CORNER OF MANHATTAN.

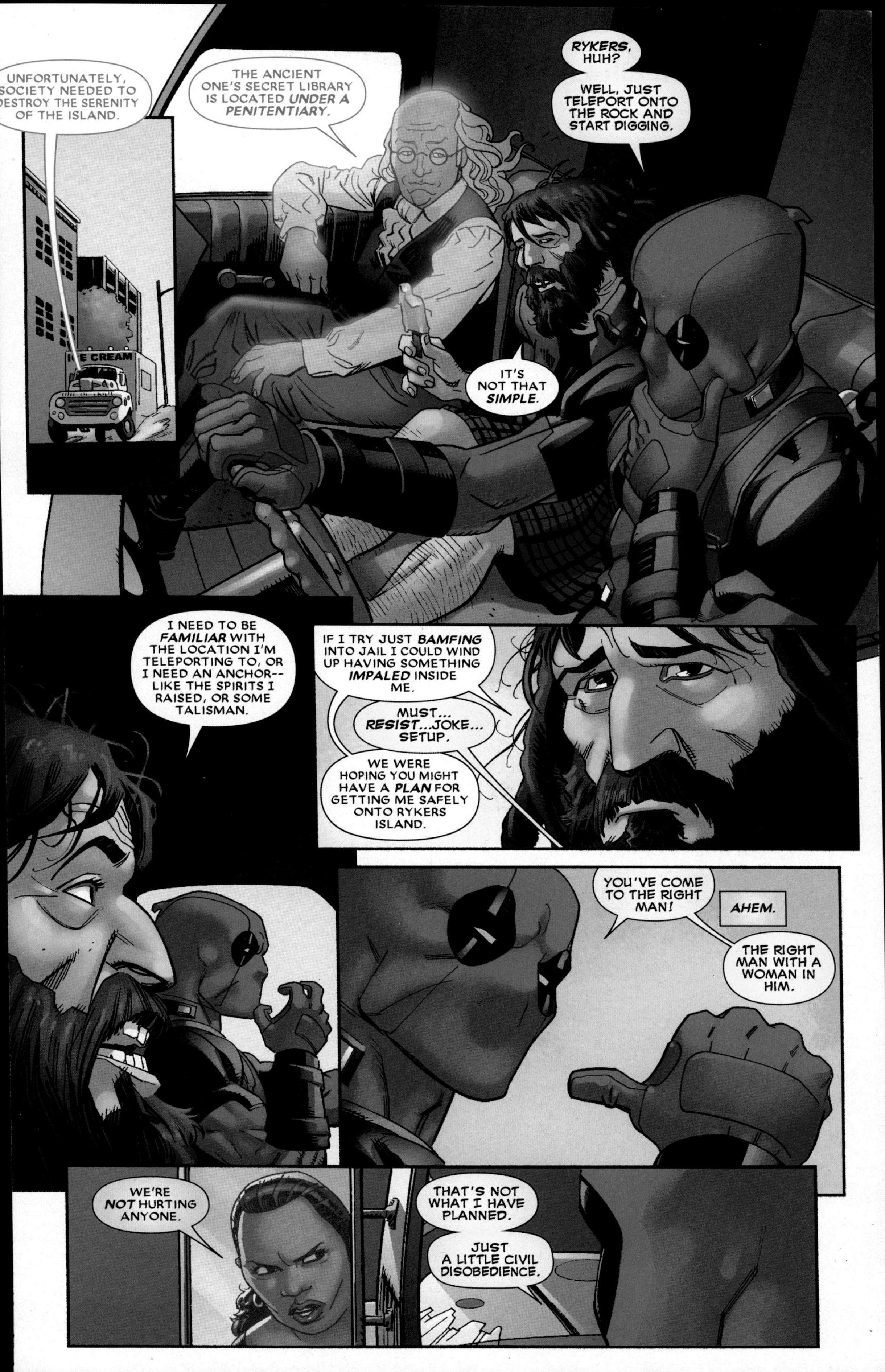
UNFORTUNATELY, SOCIETY NEEDED TO DESTROY THE SERENITY OF THE ISLAND.
THE ANCIENT ONE'S SECRET LIBRARY IS LOCATED UNDER A PENITENTIARY.
ICE CREAM
RYKERS, HUH?
WELL, JUST TELEPORT ONTO THE ROCK AND START DIGGING.
IT'S NOT THAT SIMPLE.
I NEED TO BE FAMILIAR WITH THE LOCATION I'M TELEPORTING TO, OR I NEED AN ANCHOR-- LIKE THE SPIRITS I RAISED, OR SOME TALISMAN.
IF I TRY JUST BAMFING INTO JAIL I COULD WIND UP HAVING SOMETHING IMPALED INSIDE ME.
MUST... RESIST...JOKE... SETUP.
WE WERE HOPING YOU MIGHT HAVE A PLAN FOR GETTING ME SAFELY ONTO RYKERS ISLAND.
YOU'VE COME TO THE RIGHT MAN!
AHEM.
THE RIGHT MAN WITH A WOMAN IN HIM.
WE'RE NOT HURTING ANYONE.
THAT'S NOT WHAT I HAVE PLANNED.
JUST A LITTLE CIVIL DISOBEDIENCE.

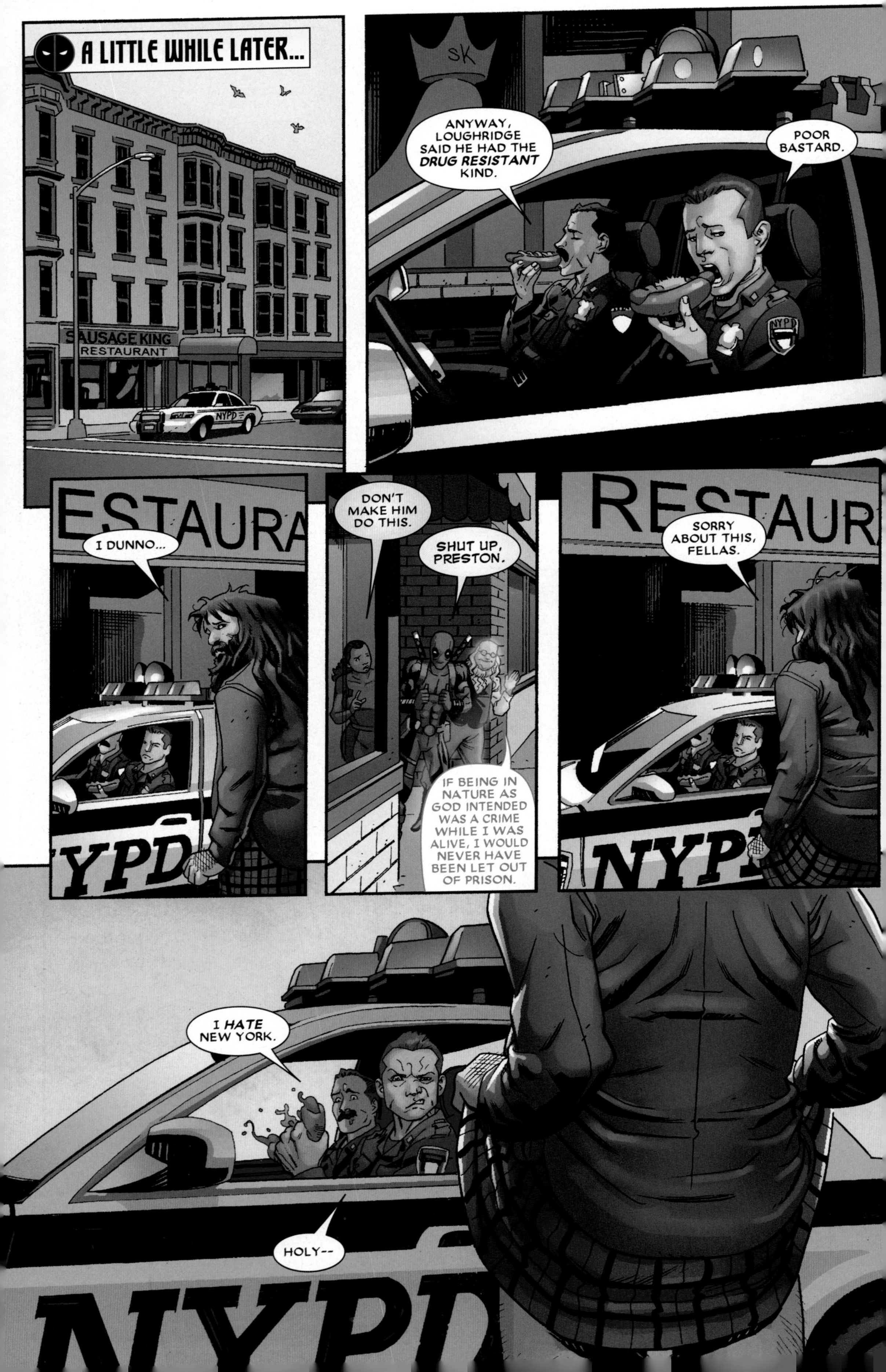
A LITTLE WHILE LATER...
SAUSAGE KING
RESTAURANT
NYPD
SK
ANYWAY, LOUGHRIDGE SAID HE HAD THE *DRUG RESISTANT* KIND.
POOR BASTARD.
NYPD
ESTAURA
I DUNNO...
NYPD
DON'T MAKE HIM DO THIS.
SHUT UP, PRESTON.
IF BEING IN NATURE AS GOD INTENDED WAS A CRIME WHILE I WAS ALIVE, I WOULD NEVER HAVE BEEN LET OUT OF PRISON.
RESTAURA
SORRY ABOUT THIS, FELLAS.
NYPI
I *HATE* NEW YORK.
HOLY--
NYPD

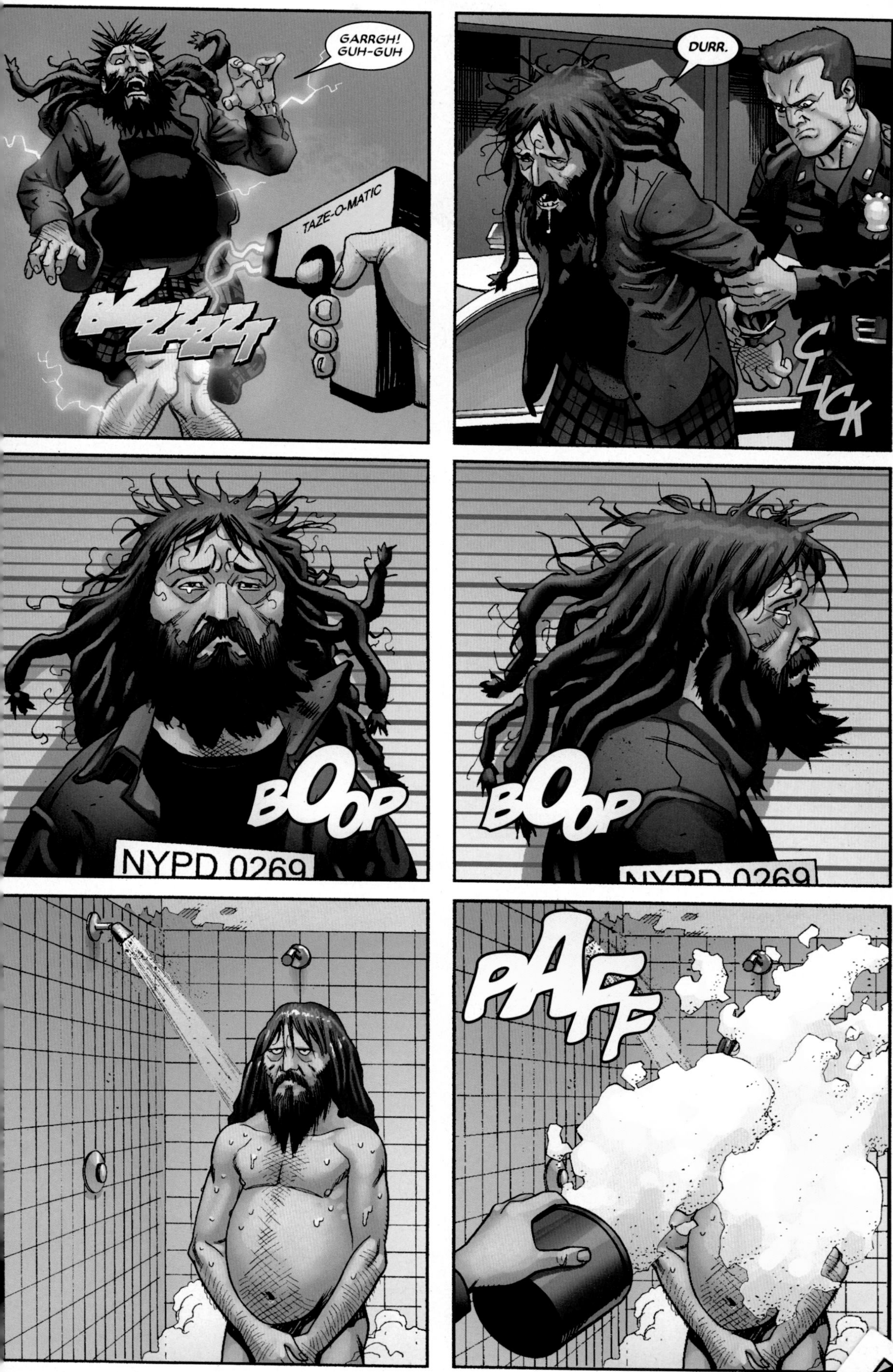

GARRGH! GUH-GUH
TAZE-O-MATIC
BZZZZZT
DURR.
CLICK
BOOP
NYPD 0269
BOOP
NYPD 0269
PAFF

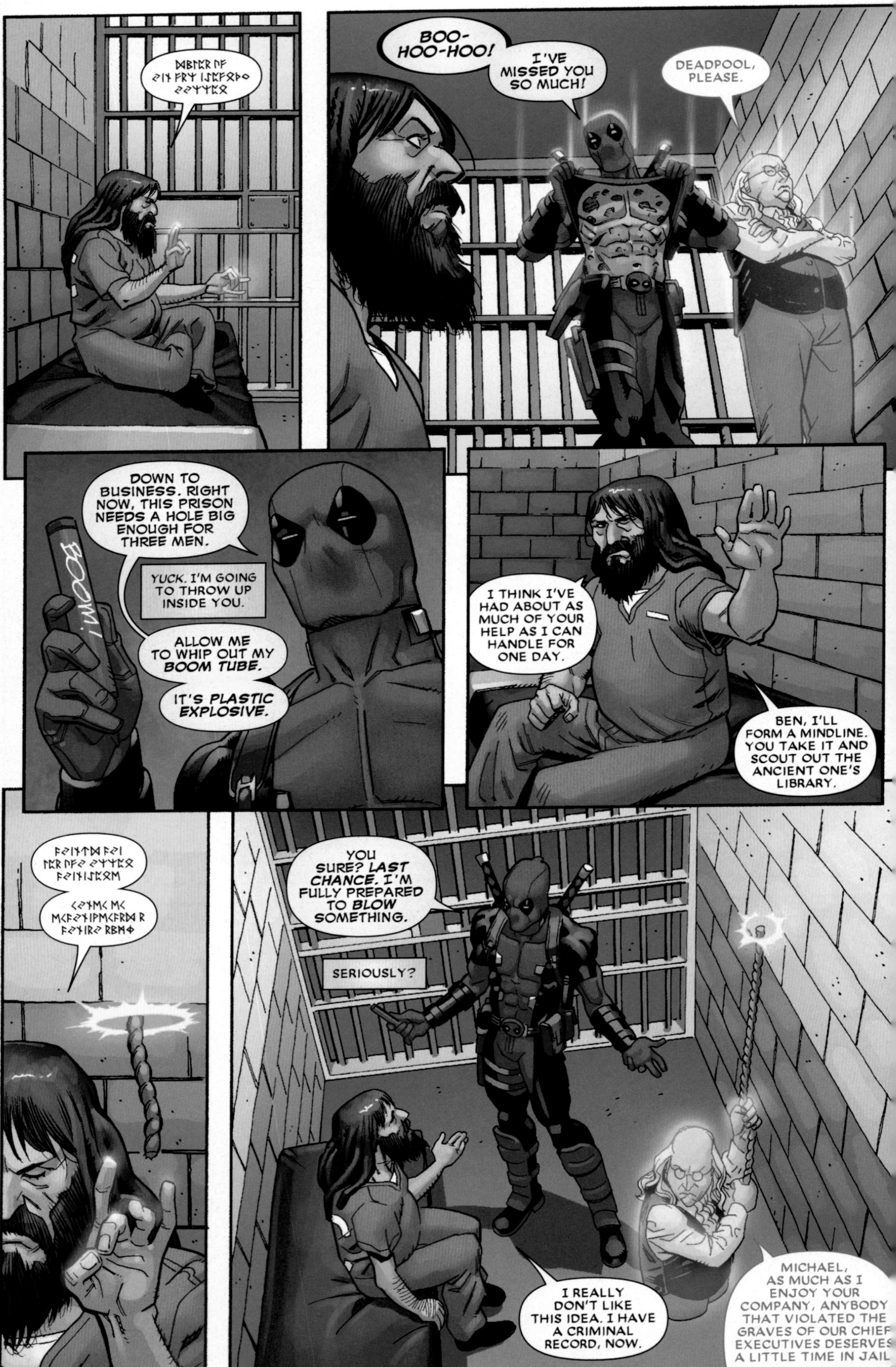
BOO-HOO-HOO!
I'VE MISSED YOU SO MUCH!
DEADPOOL, PLEASE.
DOWN TO BUSINESS. RIGHT NOW, THIS PRISON NEEDS A HOLE BIG ENOUGH FOR THREE MEN.
BOOM!
YUCK. I'M GOING TO THROW UP INSIDE YOU.
ALLOW ME TO WHIP OUT MY BOOM TUBE.
IT'S PLASTIC EXPLOSIVE.
I THINK I'VE HAD ABOUT AS MUCH OF YOUR HELP AS I CAN HANDLE FOR ONE DAY.
BEN, I'LL FORM A MINDLINE. YOU TAKE IT AND SCOUT OUT THE ANCIENT ONE'S LIBRARY.
YOU SURE? LAST CHANCE. I'M FULLY PREPARED TO BLOW SOMETHING.
SERIOUSLY?
I REALLY DON'T LIKE THIS IDEA. I HAVE A CRIMINAL RECORD, NOW.
MICHAEL, AS MUCH AS I ENJOY YOUR COMPANY, ANYBODY THAT VIOLATED THE GRAVES OF OUR CHIEF EXECUTIVES DESERVES A LITTLE TIME IN JAIL.

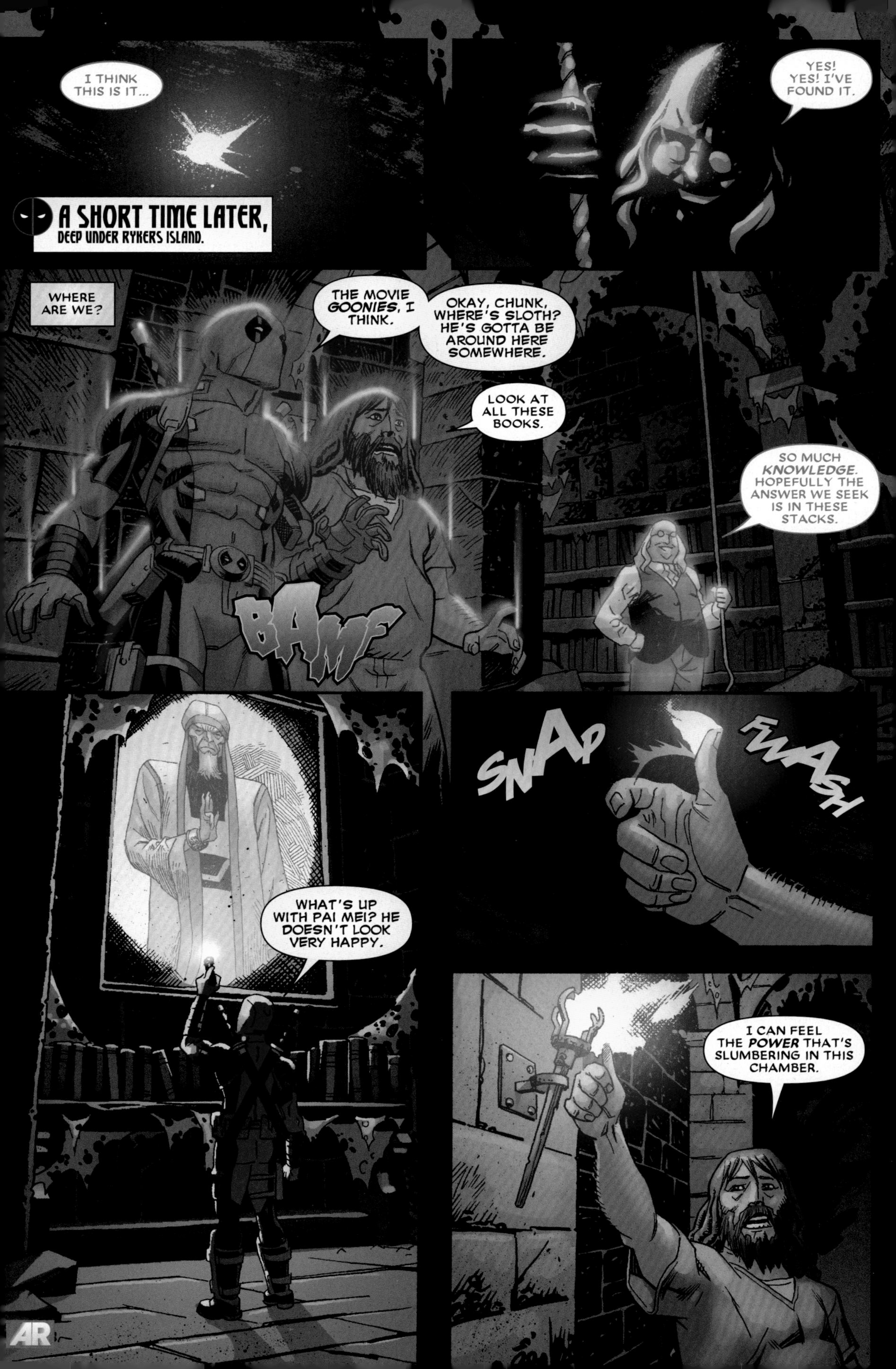
I THINK THIS IS IT...
A SHORT TIME LATER, DEEP UNDER RYKERS ISLAND.
YES! YES! I'VE FOUND IT.
WHERE ARE WE?
THE MOVIE GOONIES, I THINK.
OKAY, CHUNK, WHERE'S SLOTH? HE'S GOTTA BE AROUND HERE SOMEWHERE.
LOOK AT ALL THESE BOOKS.
SO MUCH KNOWLEDGE. HOPEFULLY THE ANSWER WE SEEK IS IN THESE STACKS.
BAMF
WHAT'S UP WITH PAI MEI? HE DOESN'T LOOK VERY HAPPY.
SNAP
FWASH
I CAN FEEL THE POWER THAT'S SLUMBERING IN THIS CHAMBER.
AR

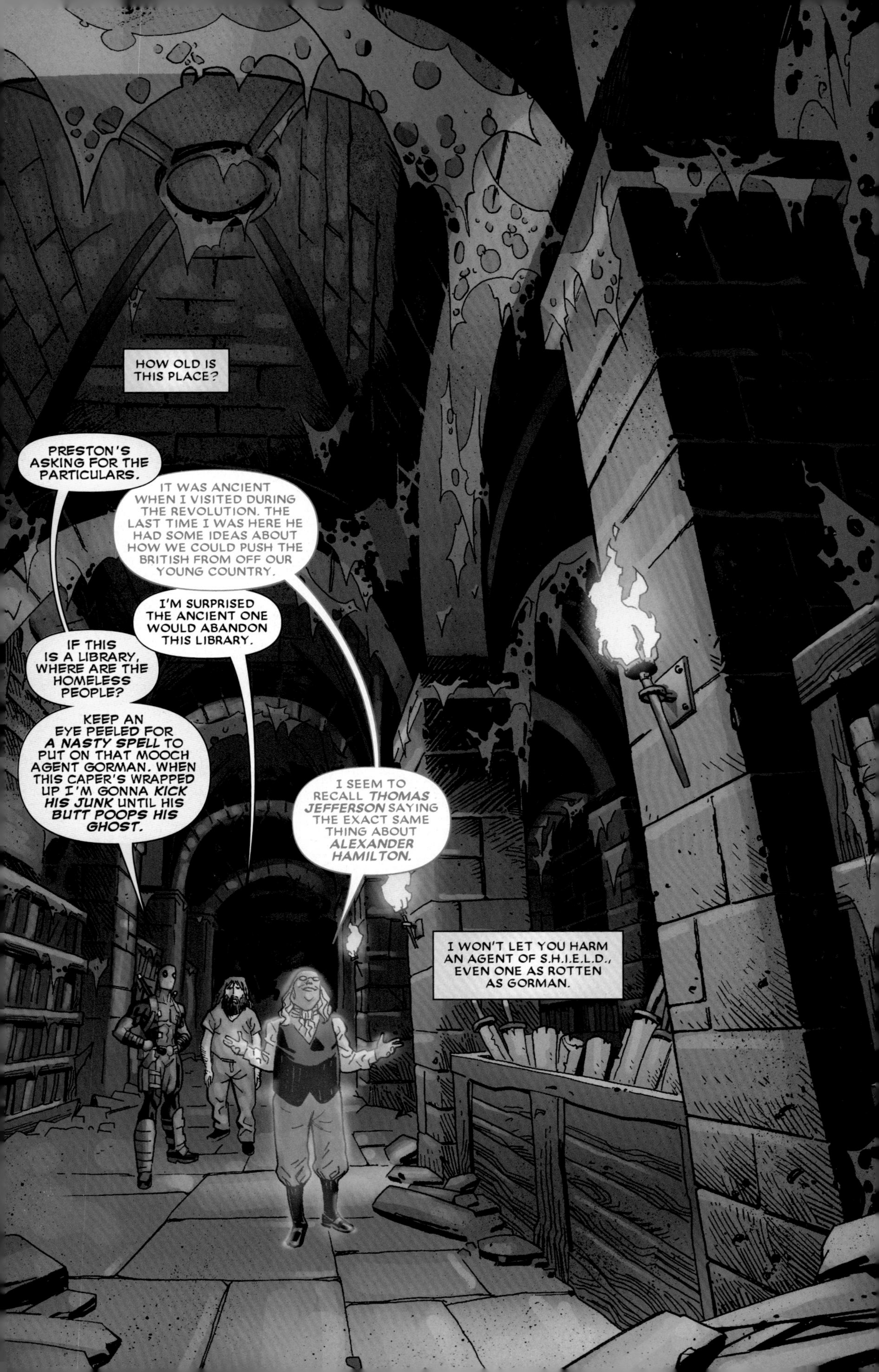

HOW OLD IS THIS PLACE?
PRESTON'S ASKING FOR THE PARTICULARS.
IT WAS ANCIENT WHEN I VISITED DURING THE REVOLUTION. THE LAST TIME I WAS HERE HE HAD SOME IDEAS ABOUT HOW WE COULD PUSH THE BRITISH FROM OFF OUR YOUNG COUNTRY.
I'M SURPRISED THE ANCIENT ONE WOULD ABANDON THIS LIBRARY.
IF THIS IS A LIBRARY, WHERE ARE THE HOMELESS PEOPLE?
KEEP AN EYE PEELED FOR A NASTY SPELL TO PUT ON THAT MOOCH AGENT GORMAN. WHEN THIS CAPER'S WRAPPED UP I'M GONNA KICK HIS JUNK UNTIL HIS BUTT POOPS HIS GHOST.
I SEEM TO RECALL THOMAS JEFFERSON SAYING THE EXACT SAME THING ABOUT ALEXANDER HAMILTON.
I WON'T LET YOU HARM AN AGENT OF S.H.I.E.L.D., EVEN ONE AS ROTTEN AS GORMAN.

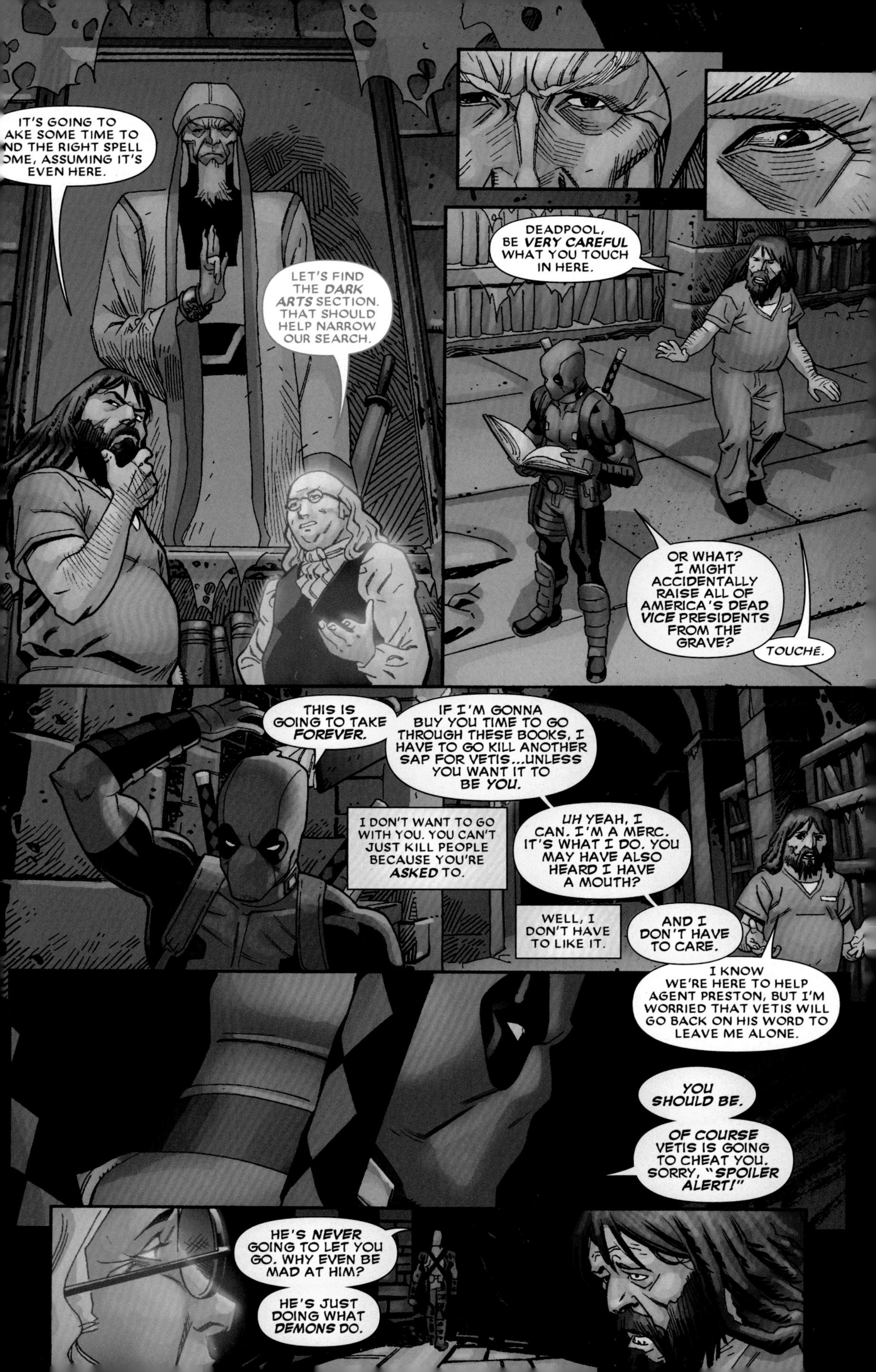
IT'S GOING TO AKE SOME TIME TO ND THE RIGHT SPELL OME, ASSUMING IT'S EVEN HERE.
LET'S FIND THE DARK ARTS SECTION. THAT SHOULD HELP NARROW OUR SEARCH.
DEADPOOL, BE VERY CAREFUL WHAT YOU TOUCH IN HERE.
OR WHAT? I MIGHT ACCIDENTALLY RAISE ALL OF AMERICA'S DEAD VICE PRESIDENTS FROM THE GRAVE?
TOUCHÉ.
THIS IS GOING TO TAKE FOREVER.
IF I'M GONNA BUY YOU TIME TO GO THROUGH THESE BOOKS, I HAVE TO GO KILL ANOTHER SAP FOR VETIS...UNLESS YOU WANT IT TO BE YOU.
I DON'T WANT TO GO WITH YOU. YOU CAN'T JUST KILL PEOPLE BECAUSE YOU'RE ASKED TO.
UH YEAH, I CAN. I'M A MERC. IT'S WHAT I DO. YOU MAY HAVE ALSO HEARD I HAVE A MOUTH?
WELL, I DON'T HAVE TO LIKE IT.
AND I DON'T HAVE TO CARE.
I KNOW WE'RE HERE TO HELP AGENT PRESTON, BUT I'M WORRIED THAT VETIS WILL GO BACK ON HIS WORD TO LEAVE ME ALONE.
YOU SHOULD BE.
OF COURSE VETIS IS GOING TO CHEAT YOU. SORRY, "SPOILER ALERT!"
HE'S NEVER GOING TO LET YOU GO. WHY EVEN BE MAD AT HIM?
HE'S JUST DOING WHAT DEMONS DO.

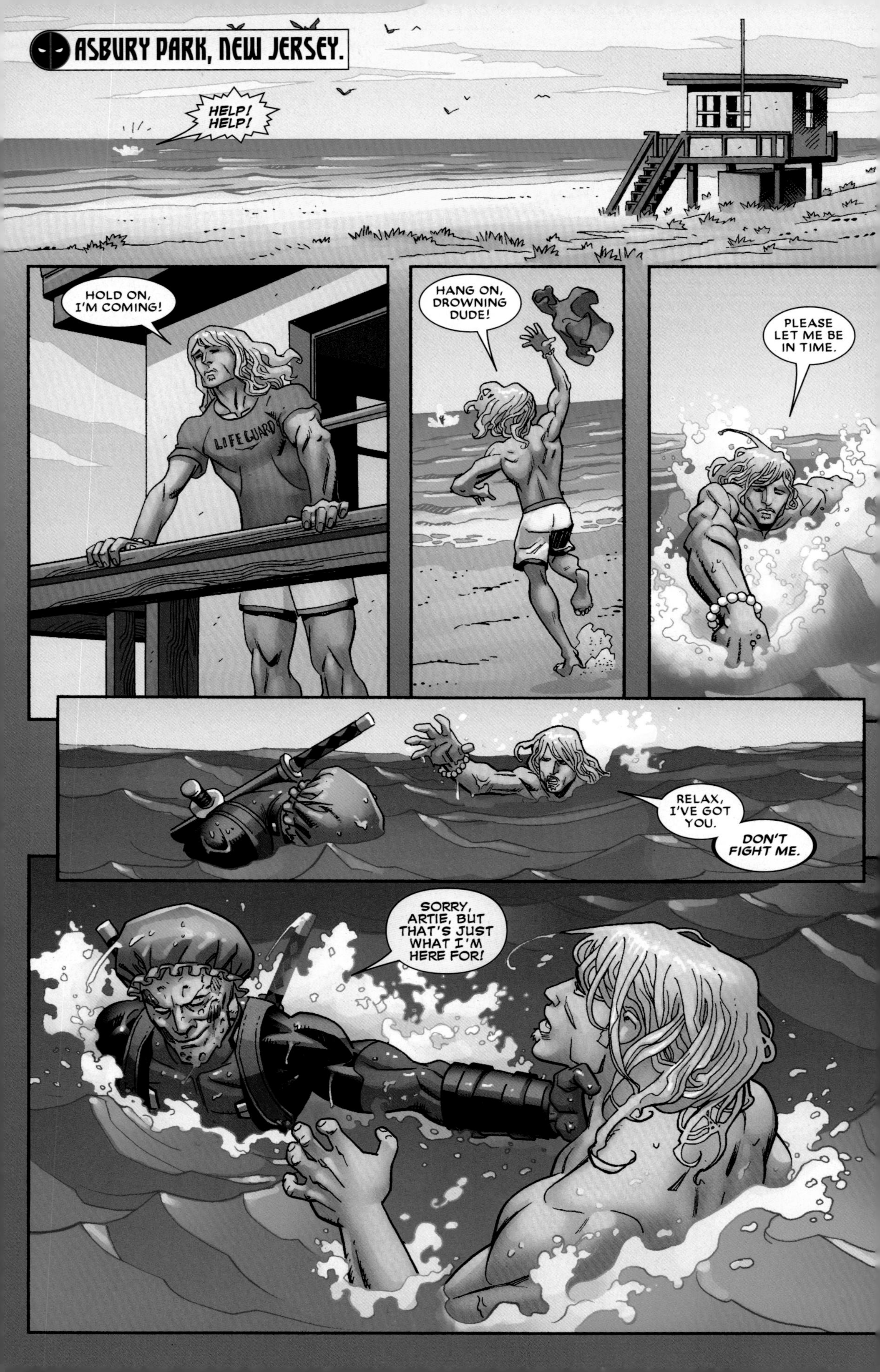

ASBURY PARK, NEW JERSEY.
HELP! HELP!
HOLD ON, I'M COMING!
LIFEGUARD
HANG ON, DROWNING DUDE!
PLEASE LET ME BE IN TIME.
RELAX, I'VE GOT YOU.
DON'T FIGHT ME.
SORRY, ARTIE, BUT THAT'S JUST WHAT I'M HERE FOR!

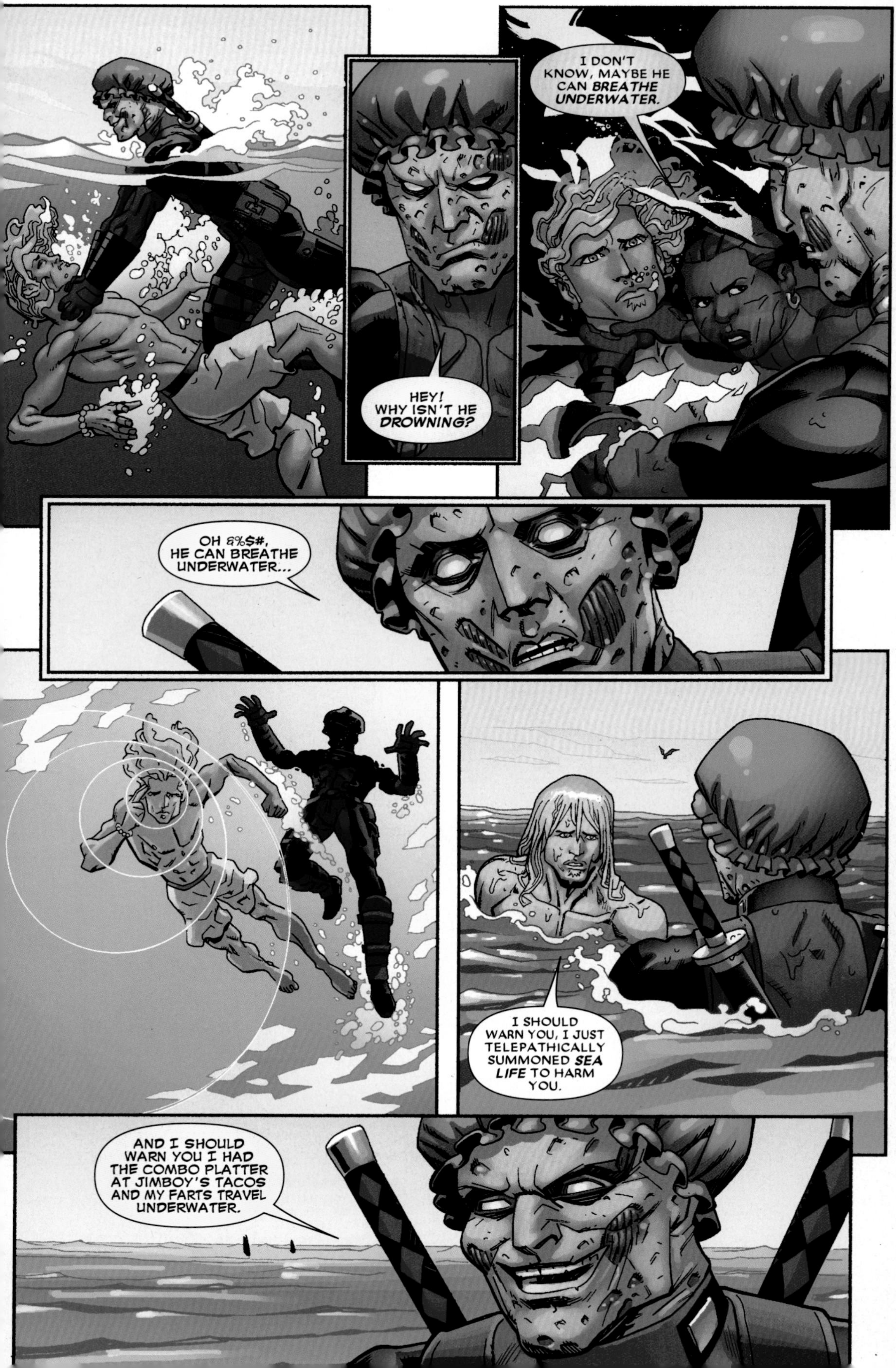
HEY! WHY ISN'T HE DROWNING?
I DON'T KNOW, MAYBE HE CAN BREATHE UNDERWATER.
OH &%$#, HE CAN BREATHE UNDERWATER...
I SHOULD WARN YOU, I JUST TELEPATHICALLY SUMMONED SEA LIFE TO HARM YOU.
AND I SHOULD WARN YOU I HAD THE COMBO PLATTER AT JIMBOY'S TACOS AND MY FARTS TRAVEL UNDERWATER.

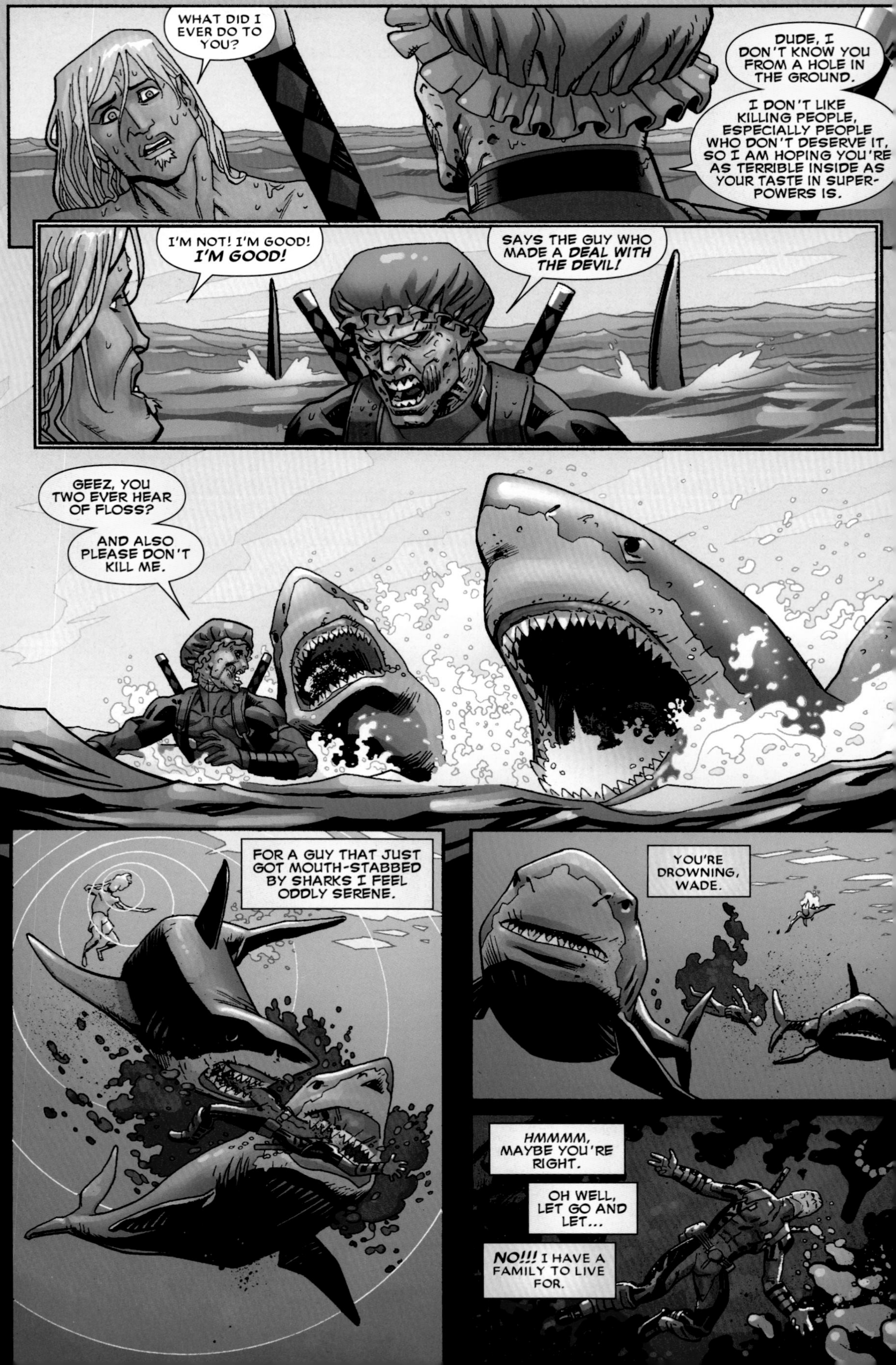
WHAT DID I EVER DO TO YOU?
DUDE, I DON'T KNOW YOU FROM A HOLE IN THE GROUND.
I DON'T LIKE KILLING PEOPLE, ESPECIALLY PEOPLE WHO DON'T DESERVE IT, SO I AM HOPING YOU'RE AS TERRIBLE INSIDE AS YOUR TASTE IN SUPER-POWERS IS.
I'M NOT! I'M GOOD! I'M GOOD!
SAYS THE GUY WHO MADE A DEAL WITH THE DEVIL!
GEEZ, YOU TWO EVER HEAR OF FLOSS?
AND ALSO PLEASE DON'T KILL ME.
FOR A GUY THAT JUST GOT MOUTH-STABBED BY SHARKS I FEEL ODDLY SERENE.
YOU'RE DROWNING, WADE.
HMMMM, MAYBE YOU'RE RIGHT.
OH WELL, LET GO AND LET...
NO!!! I HAVE A FAMILY TO LIVE FOR.

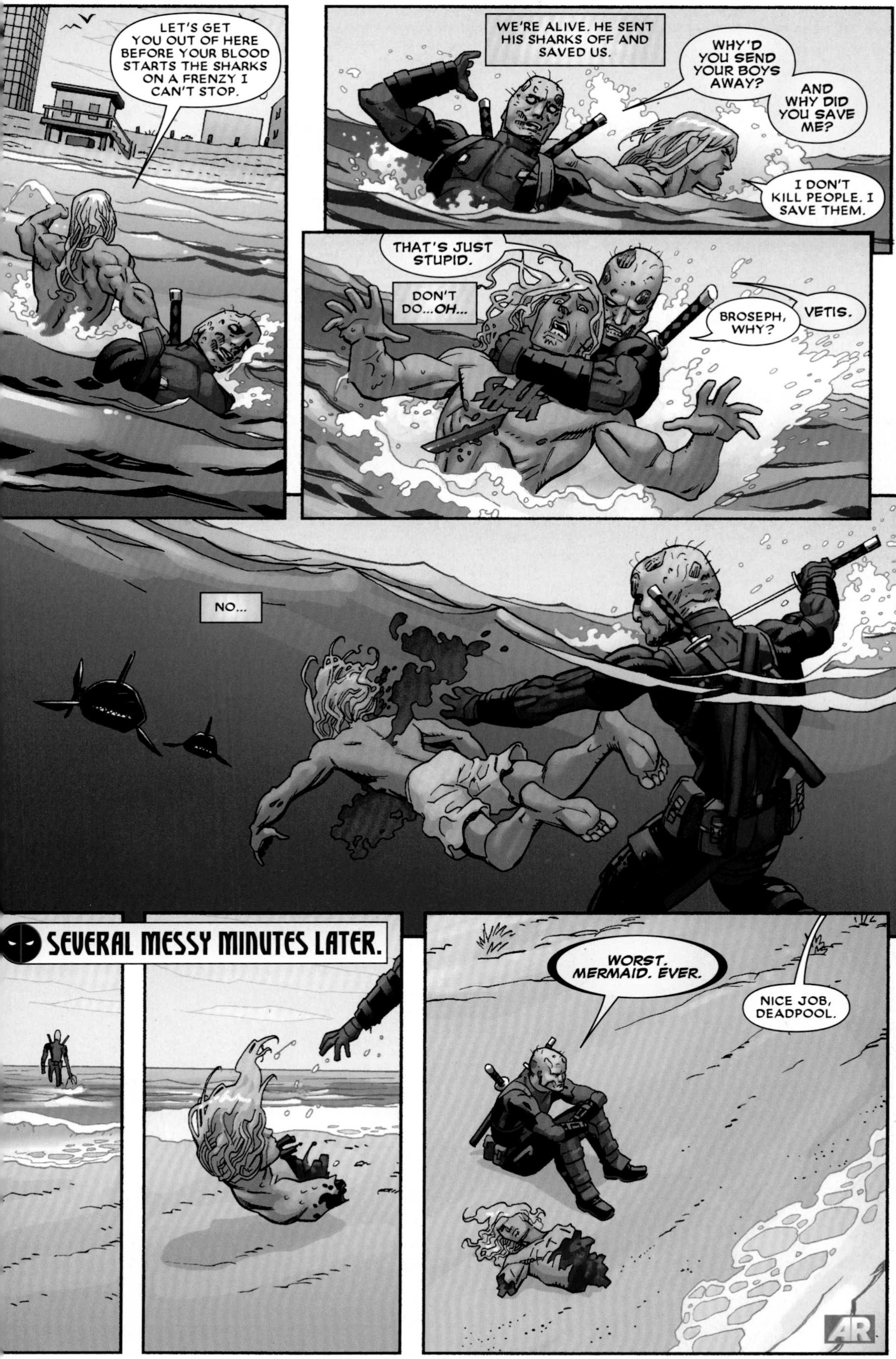

LET'S GET YOU OUT OF HERE BEFORE YOUR BLOOD STARTS THE SHARKS ON A FRENZY I CAN'T STOP.
WE'RE ALIVE. HE SENT HIS SHARKS OFF AND SAVED US.
WHY'D YOU SEND YOUR BOYS AWAY?
AND WHY DID YOU SAVE ME?
I DON'T KILL PEOPLE. I SAVE THEM.
THAT'S JUST STUPID.
DON'T DO...OH...
BROSEPH, WHY?
VETIS.
SHLUK
NO...
SEVERAL MESSY MINUTES LATER.
WORST. MERMAID. EVER.
NICE JOB, DEADPOOL.
AR

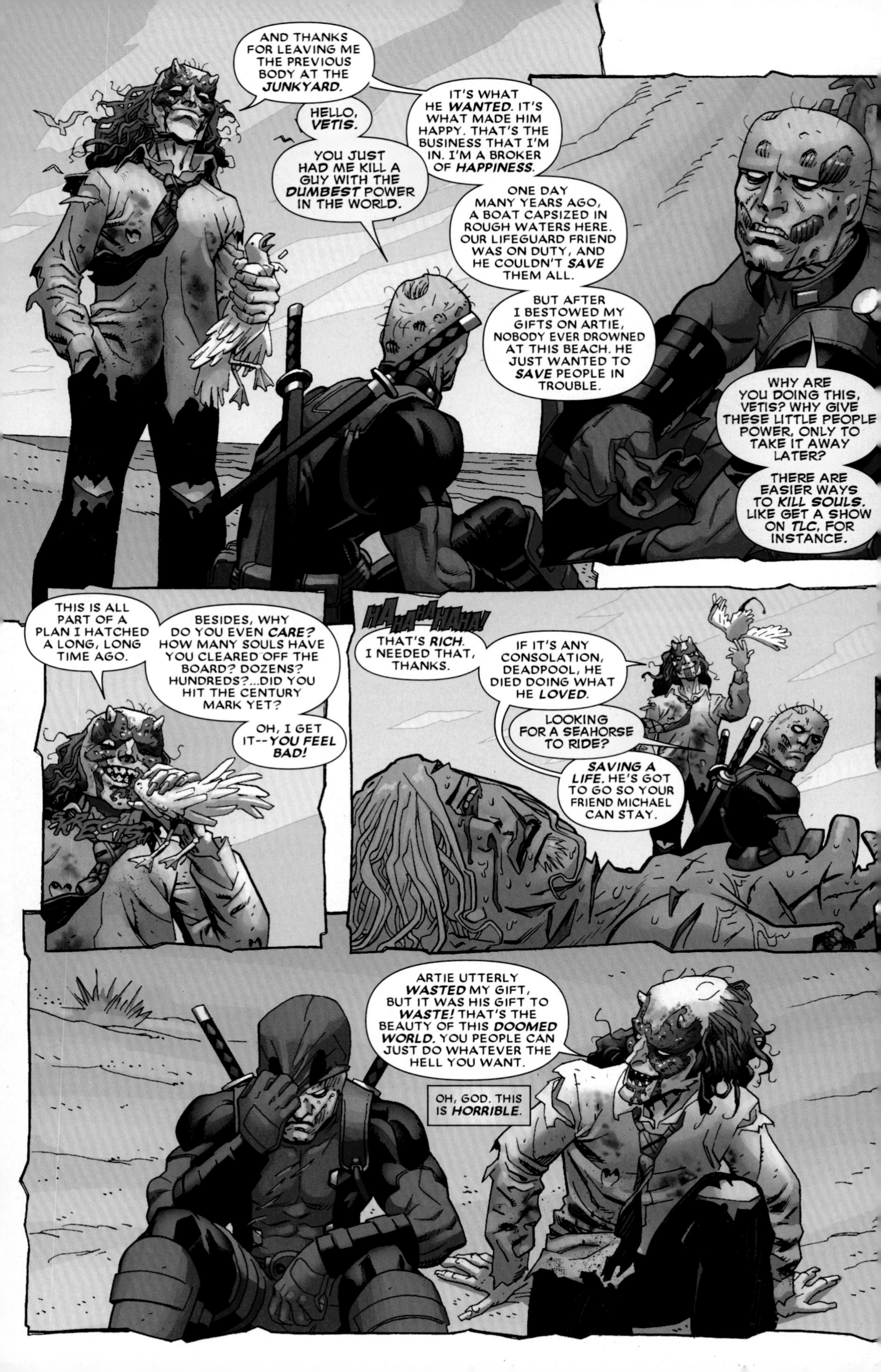

AND THANKS FOR LEAVING ME THE PREVIOUS BODY AT THE JUNKYARD.
HELLO, VETIS.
YOU JUST HAD ME KILL A GUY WITH THE DUMBEST POWER IN THE WORLD.
IT'S WHAT HE WANTED. IT'S WHAT MADE HIM HAPPY. THAT'S THE BUSINESS THAT I'M IN. I'M A BROKER OF HAPPINESS.
ONE DAY MANY YEARS AGO, A BOAT CAPSIZED IN ROUGH WATERS HERE. OUR LIFEGUARD FRIEND WAS ON DUTY, AND HE COULDN'T SAVE THEM ALL.
BUT AFTER I BESTOWED MY GIFTS ON ARTIE, NOBODY EVER DROWNED AT THIS BEACH. HE JUST WANTED TO SAVE PEOPLE IN TROUBLE.
WHY ARE YOU DOING THIS, VETIS? WHY GIVE THESE LITTLE PEOPLE POWER, ONLY TO TAKE IT AWAY LATER?
THERE ARE EASIER WAYS TO KILL SOULS. LIKE GET A SHOW ON TLC, FOR INSTANCE.
THIS IS ALL PART OF A PLAN I HATCHED A LONG, LONG TIME AGO.
BESIDES, WHY DO YOU EVEN CARE? HOW MANY SOULS HAVE YOU CLEARED OFF THE BOARD? DOZENS? HUNDREDS?...DID YOU HIT THE CENTURY MARK YET?
OH, I GET IT--YOU FEEL BAD!
HAHAHAHAHA!
THAT'S RICH. I NEEDED THAT, THANKS.
IF IT'S ANY CONSOLATION, DEADPOOL, HE DIED DOING WHAT HE LOVED.
LOOKING FOR A SEAHORSE TO RIDE?
SAVING A LIFE. HE'S GOT TO GO SO YOUR FRIEND MICHAEL CAN STAY.
ARTIE UTTERLY WASTED MY GIFT, BUT IT WAS HIS GIFT TO WASTE! THAT'S THE BEAUTY OF THIS DOOMED WORLD. YOU PEOPLE CAN JUST DO WHATEVER THE HELL YOU WANT.
OH, GOD. THIS IS HORRIBLE.

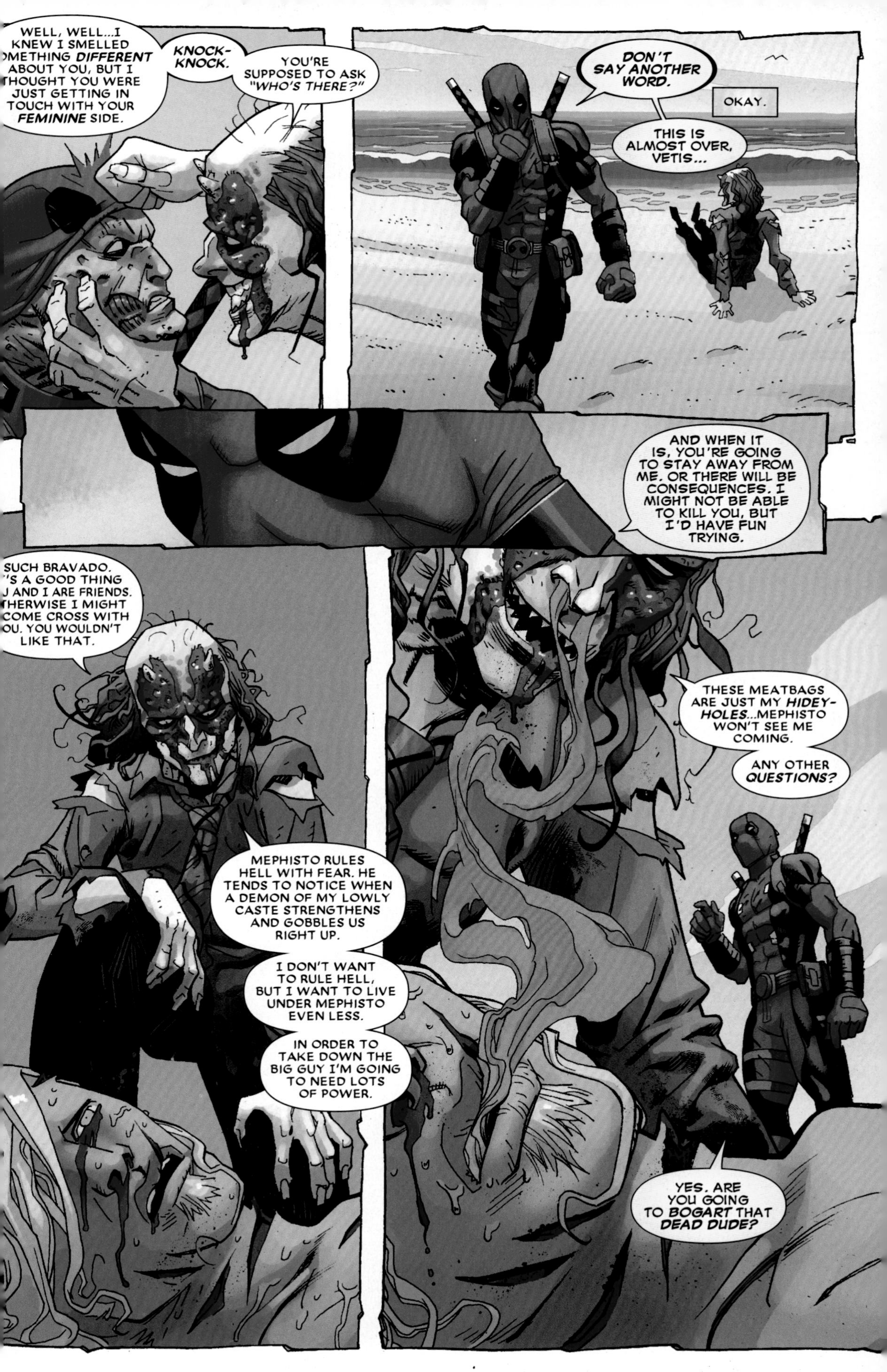
WELL, WELL...I KNEW I SMELLED OMETHING DIFFERENT ABOUT YOU, BUT I THOUGHT YOU WERE JUST GETTING IN TOUCH WITH YOUR FEMININE SIDE.
KNOCK-KNOCK.
YOU'RE SUPPOSED TO ASK "WHO'S THERE?"
DON'T SAY ANOTHER WORD.
OKAY.
THIS IS ALMOST OVER, VETIS...
AND WHEN IT IS, YOU'RE GOING TO STAY AWAY FROM ME. OR THERE WILL BE CONSEQUENCES. I MIGHT NOT BE ABLE TO KILL YOU, BUT I'D HAVE FUN TRYING.
SUCH BRAVADO. 'S A GOOD THING U AND I ARE FRIENDS. THERWISE I MIGHT COME CROSS WITH OU. YOU WOULDN'T LIKE THAT.
MEPHISTO RULES HELL WITH FEAR. HE TENDS TO NOTICE WHEN A DEMON OF MY LOWLY CASTE STRENGTHENS AND GOBBLES US RIGHT UP.
I DON'T WANT TO RULE HELL, BUT I WANT TO LIVE UNDER MEPHISTO EVEN LESS.
IN ORDER TO TAKE DOWN THE BIG GUY I'M GOING TO NEED LOTS OF POWER.
THESE MEATBAGS ARE JUST MY HIDEY-HOLES...MEPHISTO WON'T SEE ME COMING.
ANY OTHER QUESTIONS?
YES. ARE YOU GOING TO BOGART THAT DEAD DUDE?

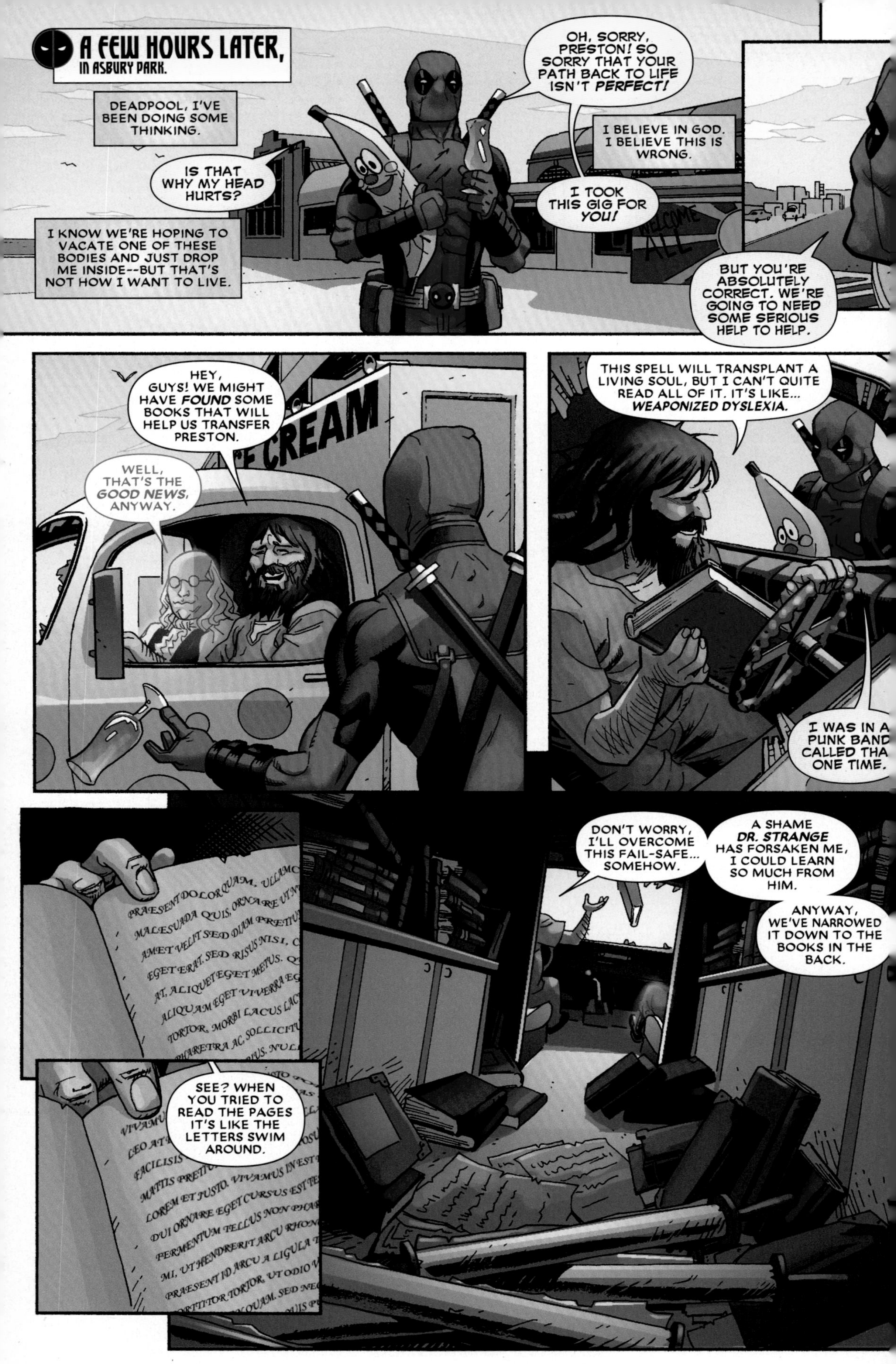

A FEW HOURS LATER, IN ASBURY PARK.
DEADPOOL, I'VE BEEN DOING SOME THINKING.
IS THAT WHY MY HEAD HURTS?
I KNOW WE'RE HOPING TO VACATE ONE OF THESE BODIES AND JUST DROP ME INSIDE--BUT THAT'S NOT HOW I WANT TO LIVE.
OH, SORRY, PRESTON! SO SORRY THAT YOUR PATH BACK TO LIFE ISN'T PERFECT!
I BELIEVE IN GOD. I BELIEVE THIS IS WRONG.
I TOOK THIS GIG FOR YOU!
BUT YOU'RE ABSOLUTELY CORRECT. WE'RE GOING TO NEED SOME SERIOUS HELP TO HELP.
HEY, GUYS! WE MIGHT HAVE FOUND SOME BOOKS THAT WILL HELP US TRANSFER PRESTON.
WELL, THAT'S THE GOOD NEWS, ANYWAY.
THIS SPELL WILL TRANSPLANT A LIVING SOUL, BUT I CAN'T QUITE READ ALL OF IT. IT'S LIKE... WEAPONIZED DYSLEXIA.
I WAS IN A PUNK BAND CALLED THA ONE TIME.
SEE? WHEN YOU TRIED TO READ THE PAGES IT'S LIKE THE LETTERS SWIM AROUND.
DON'T WORRY, I'LL OVERCOME THIS FAIL-SAFE... SOMEHOW.
A SHAME DR. STRANGE HAS FORSAKEN ME, I COULD LEARN SO MUCH FROM HIM.
ANYWAY, WE'VE NARROWED IT DOWN TO THE BOOKS IN THE BACK.

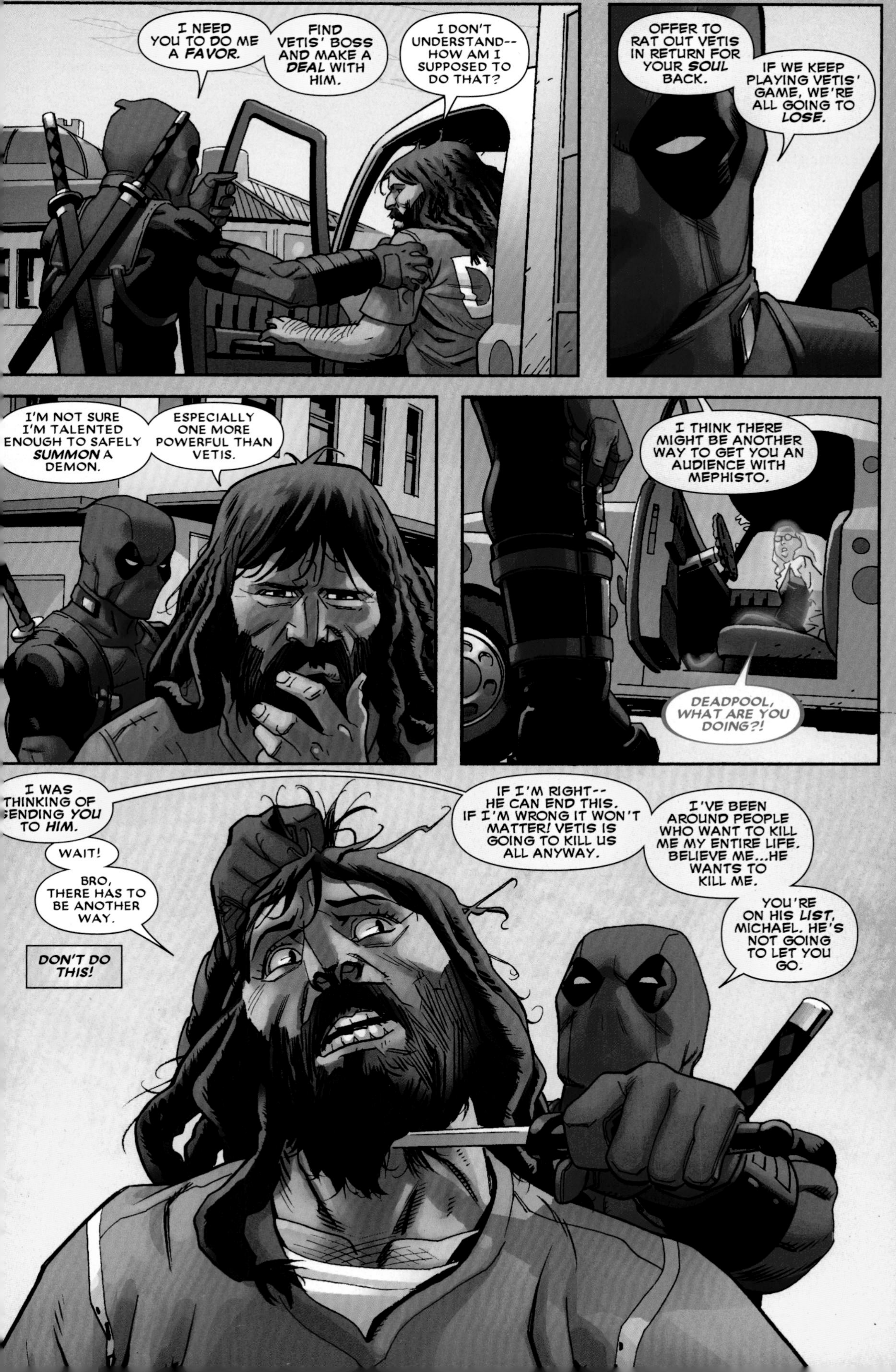
I NEED YOU TO DO ME A FAVOR.
FIND VETIS' BOSS AND MAKE A DEAL WITH HIM.
I DON'T UNDERSTAND--HOW AM I SUPPOSED TO DO THAT?
OFFER TO RAT OUT VETIS IN RETURN FOR YOUR SOUL BACK.
IF WE KEEP PLAYING VETIS' GAME, WE'RE ALL GOING TO LOSE.
I'M NOT SURE I'M TALENTED ENOUGH TO SAFELY SUMMON A DEMON.
ESPECIALLY ONE MORE POWERFUL THAN VETIS.
I THINK THERE MIGHT BE ANOTHER WAY TO GET YOU AN AUDIENCE WITH MEPHISTO.
DEADPOOL, WHAT ARE YOU DOING?!
I WAS THINKING OF SENDING YOU TO HIM.
WAIT!
BRO, THERE HAS TO BE ANOTHER WAY.
DON'T DO THIS!
IF I'M RIGHT--HE CAN END THIS. IF I'M WRONG IT WON'T MATTER! VETIS IS GOING TO KILL US ALL ANYWAY.
I'VE BEEN AROUND PEOPLE WHO WANT TO KILL ME MY ENTIRE LIFE. BELIEVE ME...HE WANTS TO KILL ME.
YOU'RE ON HIS LIST, MICHAEL. HE'S NOT GOING TO LET YOU GO.

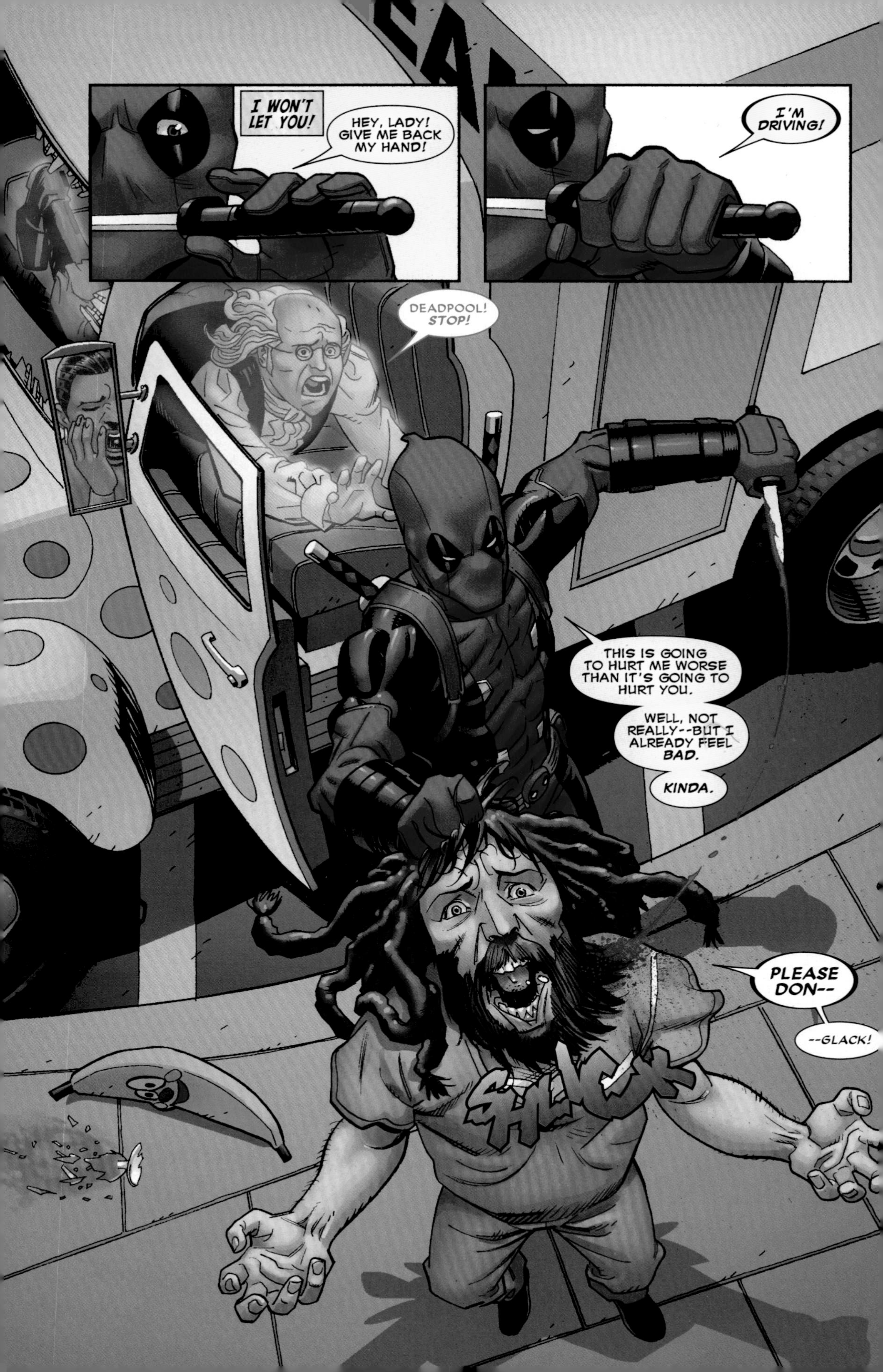
I WON'T LET YOU!
HEY, LADY! GIVE ME BACK MY HAND!
I'M DRIVING!
DEADPOOL! STOP!
THIS IS GOING TO HURT ME WORSE THAN IT'S GOING TO HURT YOU.
WELL, NOT REALLY--BUT I ALREADY FEEL BAD.
KINDA.
PLEASE DON--
--GLACK!
SHLUCK

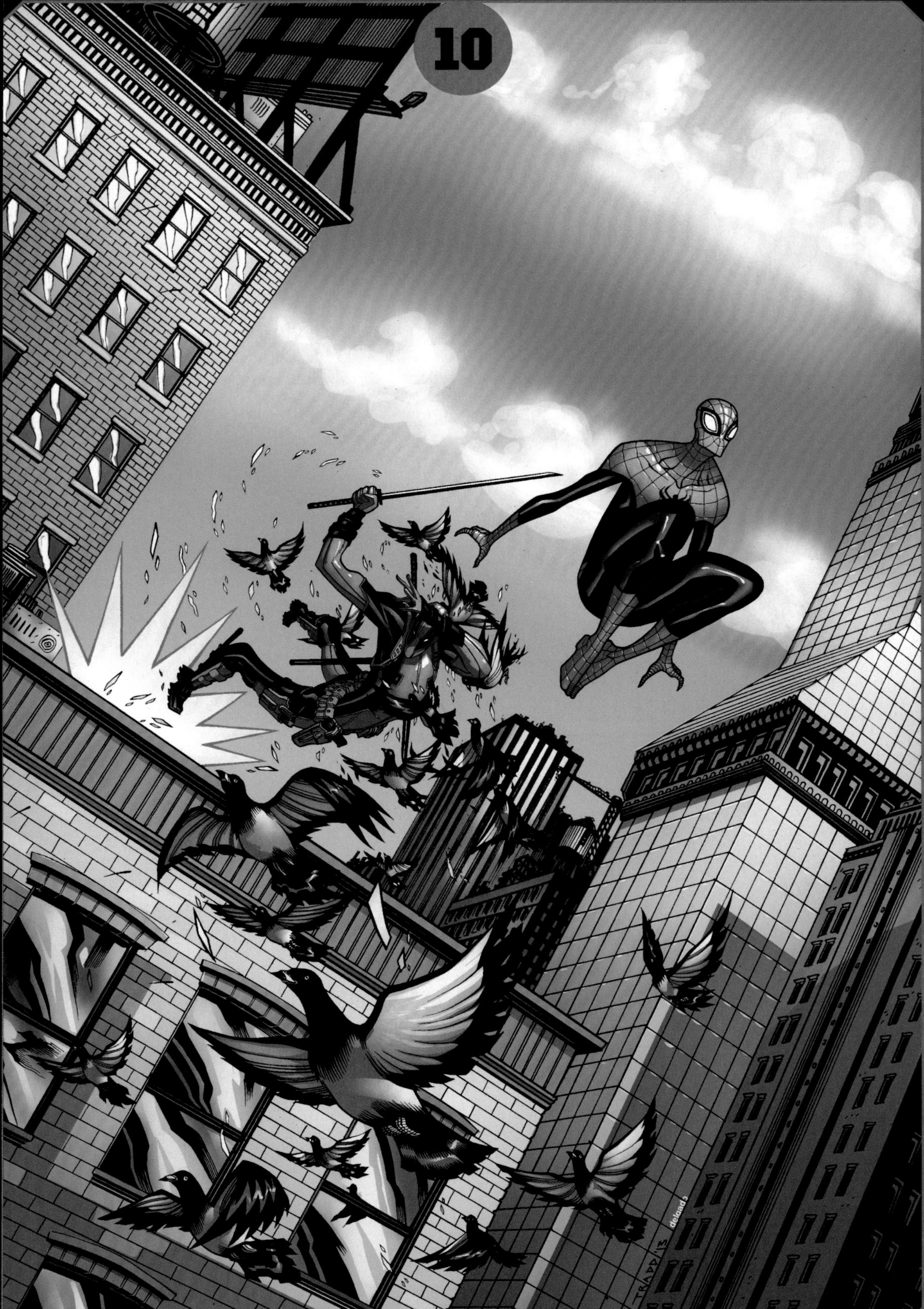
10
TRADD '13

EIGHT LEGS TO KICK YOU

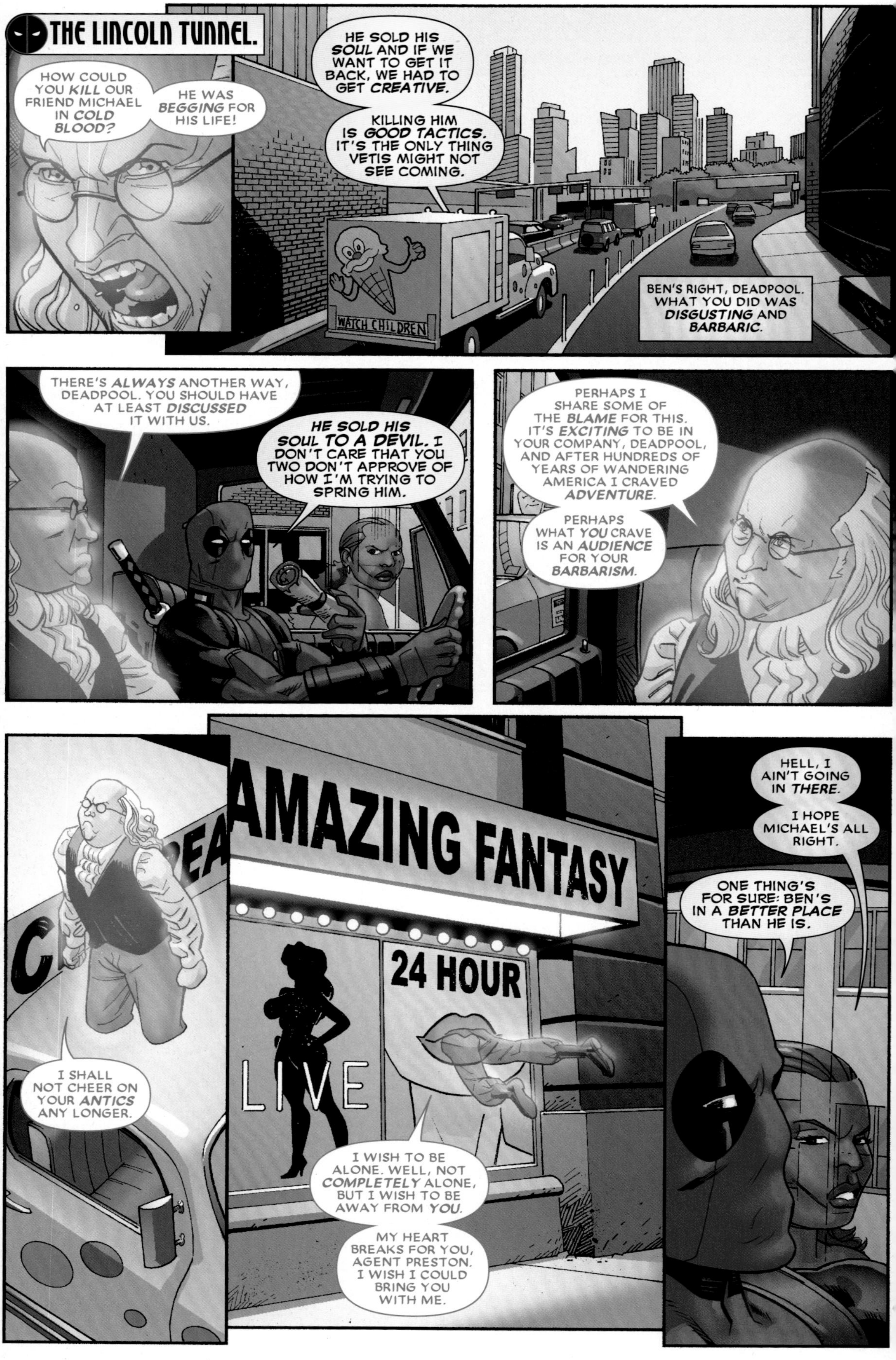
THE LINCOLN TUNNEL.
HOW COULD YOU KILL OUR FRIEND MICHAEL IN COLD BLOOD?
HE WAS BEGGING FOR HIS LIFE!
HE SOLD HIS SOUL AND IF WE WANT TO GET IT BACK, WE HAD TO GET CREATIVE.
KILLING HIM IS GOOD TACTICS. IT'S THE ONLY THING VETIS MIGHT NOT SEE COMING.
WATCH CHILDREN
BEN'S RIGHT, DEADPOOL. WHAT YOU DID WAS DISGUSTING AND BARBARIC.
THERE'S ALWAYS ANOTHER WAY, DEADPOOL. YOU SHOULD HAVE AT LEAST DISCUSSED IT WITH US.
HE SOLD HIS SOUL TO A DEVIL. I DON'T CARE THAT YOU TWO DON'T APPROVE OF HOW I'M TRYING TO SPRING HIM.
PERHAPS I SHARE SOME OF THE BLAME FOR THIS. IT'S EXCITING TO BE IN YOUR COMPANY, DEADPOOL, AND AFTER HUNDREDS OF YEARS OF WANDERING AMERICA I CRAVED ADVENTURE.
PERHAPS WHAT YOU CRAVE IS AN AUDIENCE FOR YOUR BARBARISM.
I SHALL NOT CHEER ON YOUR ANTICS ANY LONGER.
AMAZING FANTASY
24 HOUR
LIVE
I WISH TO BE ALONE. WELL, NOT COMPLETELY ALONE, BUT I WISH TO BE AWAY FROM YOU.
MY HEART BREAKS FOR YOU, AGENT PRESTON. I WISH I COULD BRING YOU WITH ME.
HELL, I AIN'T GOING IN THERE.
I HOPE MICHAEL'S ALL RIGHT.
ONE THING'S FOR SURE: BEN'S IN A BETTER PLACE THAN HE IS.

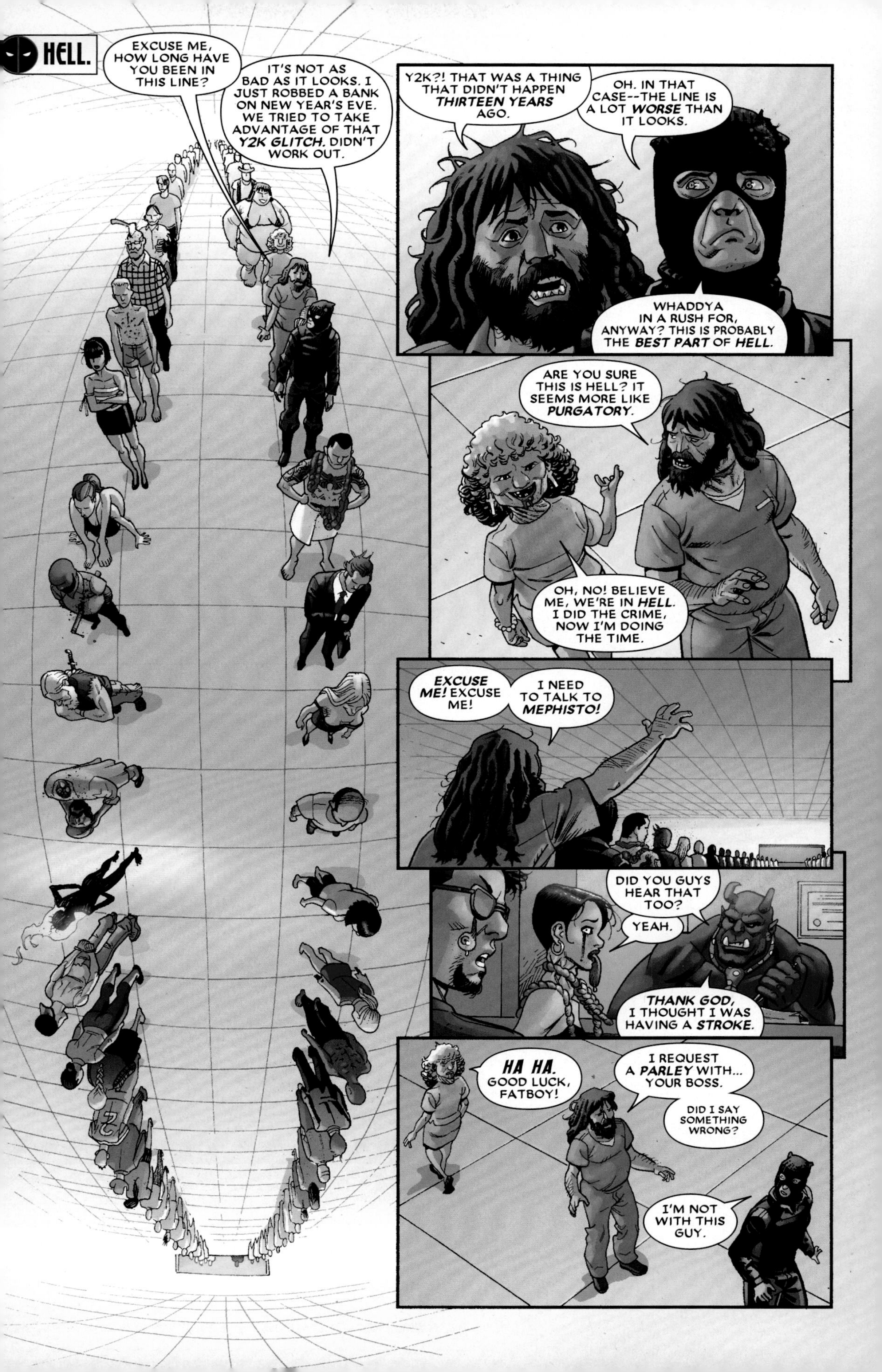
HELL.
EXCUSE ME, HOW LONG HAVE YOU BEEN IN THIS LINE?
IT'S NOT AS BAD AS IT LOOKS. I JUST ROBBED A BANK ON NEW YEAR'S EVE. WE TRIED TO TAKE ADVANTAGE OF THAT Y2K GLITCH. DIDN'T WORK OUT.
Y2K?! THAT WAS A THING THAT DIDN'T HAPPEN THIRTEEN YEARS AGO.
OH. IN THAT CASE--THE LINE IS A LOT WORSE THAN IT LOOKS.
WHADDYA IN A RUSH FOR, ANYWAY? THIS IS PROBABLY THE BEST PART OF HELL.
ARE YOU SURE THIS IS HELL? IT SEEMS MORE LIKE PURGATORY.
OH, NO! BELIEVE ME, WE'RE IN HELL. I DID THE CRIME, NOW I'M DOING THE TIME.
EXCUSE ME! EXCUSE ME!
I NEED TO TALK TO MEPHISTO!
DID YOU GUYS HEAR THAT TOO?
YEAH.
THANK GOD, I THOUGHT I WAS HAVING A STROKE.
HA HA. GOOD LUCK, FATBOY!
I REQUEST A PARLEY WITH... YOUR BOSS.
DID I SAY SOMETHING WRONG?
I'M NOT WITH THIS GUY.

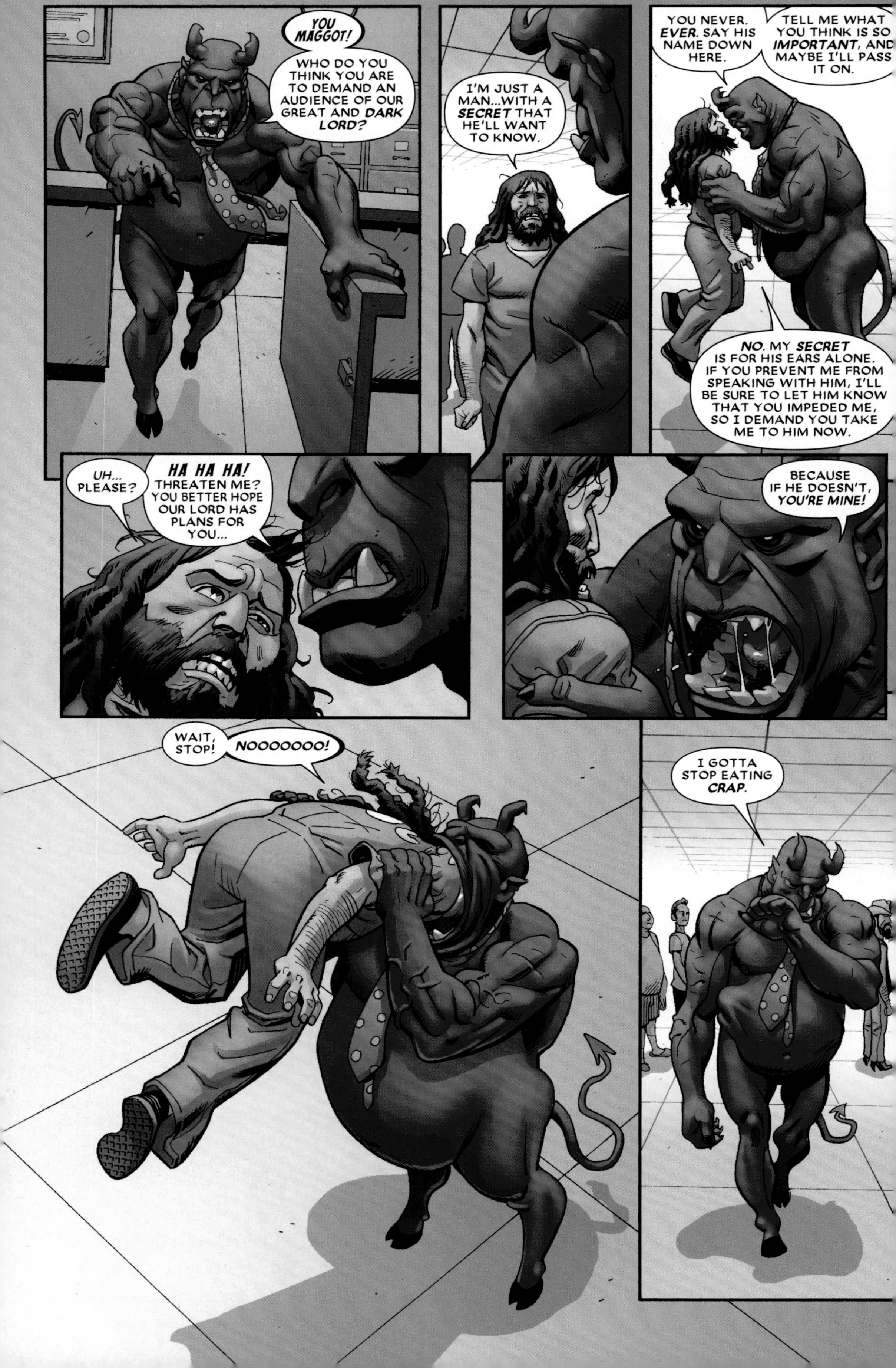
YOU MAGGOT!
WHO DO YOU THINK YOU ARE TO DEMAND AN AUDIENCE OF OUR GREAT AND DARK LORD?
I'M JUST A MAN...WITH A SECRET THAT HE'LL WANT TO KNOW.
YOU NEVER. EVER. SAY HIS NAME DOWN HERE.
TELL ME WHAT YOU THINK IS SO IMPORTANT, AND MAYBE I'LL PASS IT ON.
NO. MY SECRET IS FOR HIS EARS ALONE. IF YOU PREVENT ME FROM SPEAKING WITH HIM, I'LL BE SURE TO LET HIM KNOW THAT YOU IMPEDED ME, SO I DEMAND YOU TAKE ME TO HIM NOW.
HA HA HA! THREATEN ME? YOU BETTER HOPE OUR LORD HAS PLANS FOR YOU...
UH... PLEASE?
BECAUSE IF HE DOESN'T, YOU'RE MINE!
WAIT, STOP!
NOOOOOOO!
I GOTTA STOP EATING CRAP.

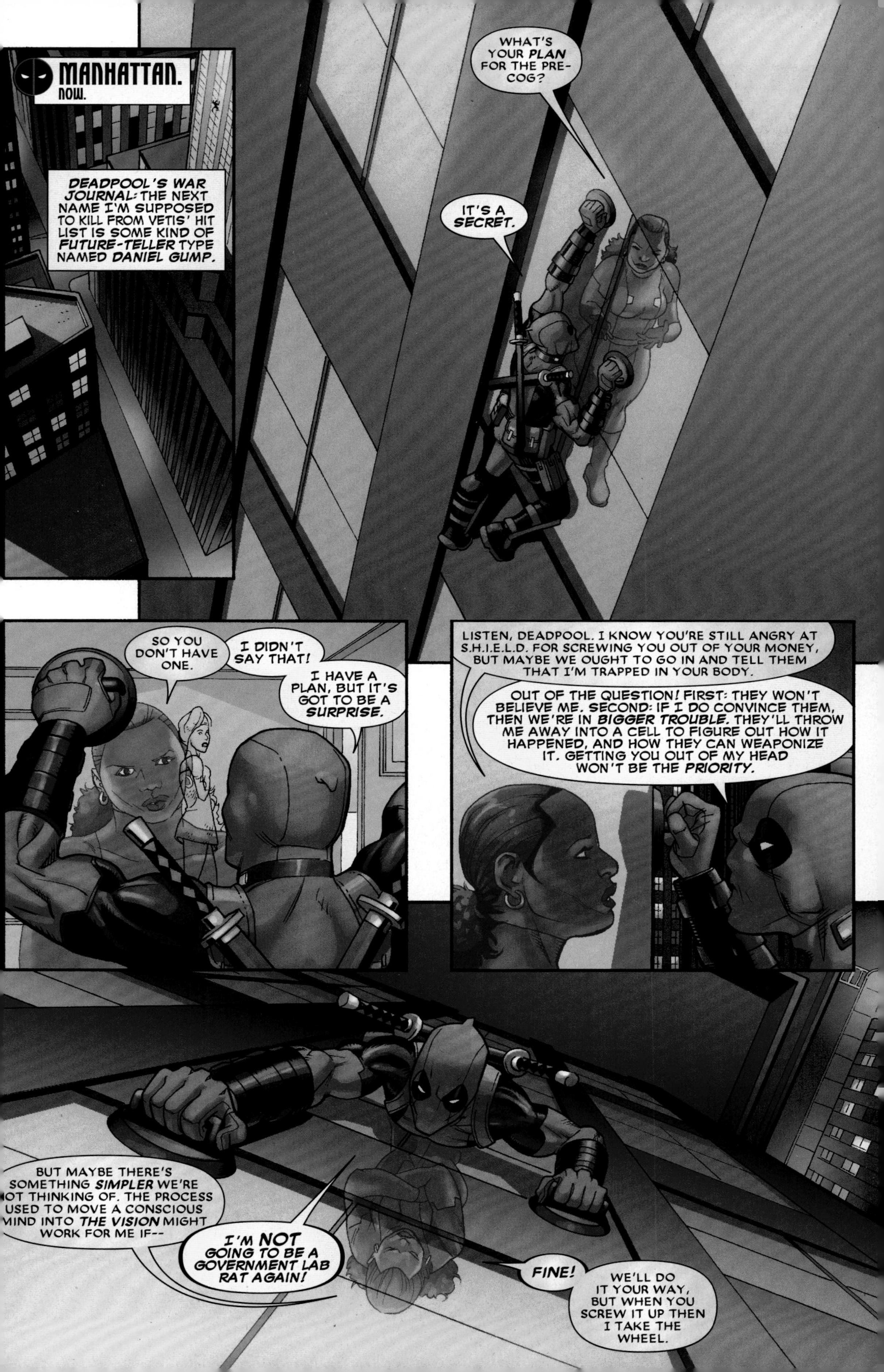

MANHATTAN. now.
DEADPOOL'S WAR JOURNAL: THE NEXT NAME I'M SUPPOSED TO KILL FROM VETIS' HIT LIST IS SOME KIND OF FUTURE-TELLER TYPE NAMED DANIEL GUMP.
WHAT'S YOUR PLAN FOR THE PRE-COG?
IT'S A SECRET.
SO YOU DON'T HAVE ONE.
I DIDN'T SAY THAT!
I HAVE A PLAN, BUT IT'S GOT TO BE A SURPRISE.
LISTEN, DEADPOOL. I KNOW YOU'RE STILL ANGRY AT S.H.I.E.L.D. FOR SCREWING YOU OUT OF YOUR MONEY, BUT MAYBE WE OUGHT TO GO IN AND TELL THEM THAT I'M TRAPPED IN YOUR BODY.
OUT OF THE QUESTION! FIRST: THEY WON'T BELIEVE ME. SECOND: IF I DO CONVINCE THEM, THEN WE'RE IN BIGGER TROUBLE. THEY'LL THROW ME AWAY INTO A CELL TO FIGURE OUT HOW IT HAPPENED, AND HOW THEY CAN WEAPONIZE IT. GETTING YOU OUT OF MY HEAD WON'T BE THE PRIORITY.
BUT MAYBE THERE'S SOMETHING SIMPLER WE'RE OT THINKING OF. THE PROCESS USED TO MOVE A CONSCIOUS MIND INTO THE VISION MIGHT WORK FOR ME IF--
I'M NOT GOING TO BE A GOVERNMENT LAB RAT AGAIN!
FINE!
WE'LL DO IT YOUR WAY, BUT WHEN YOU SCREW IT UP THEN I TAKE THE WHEEL.

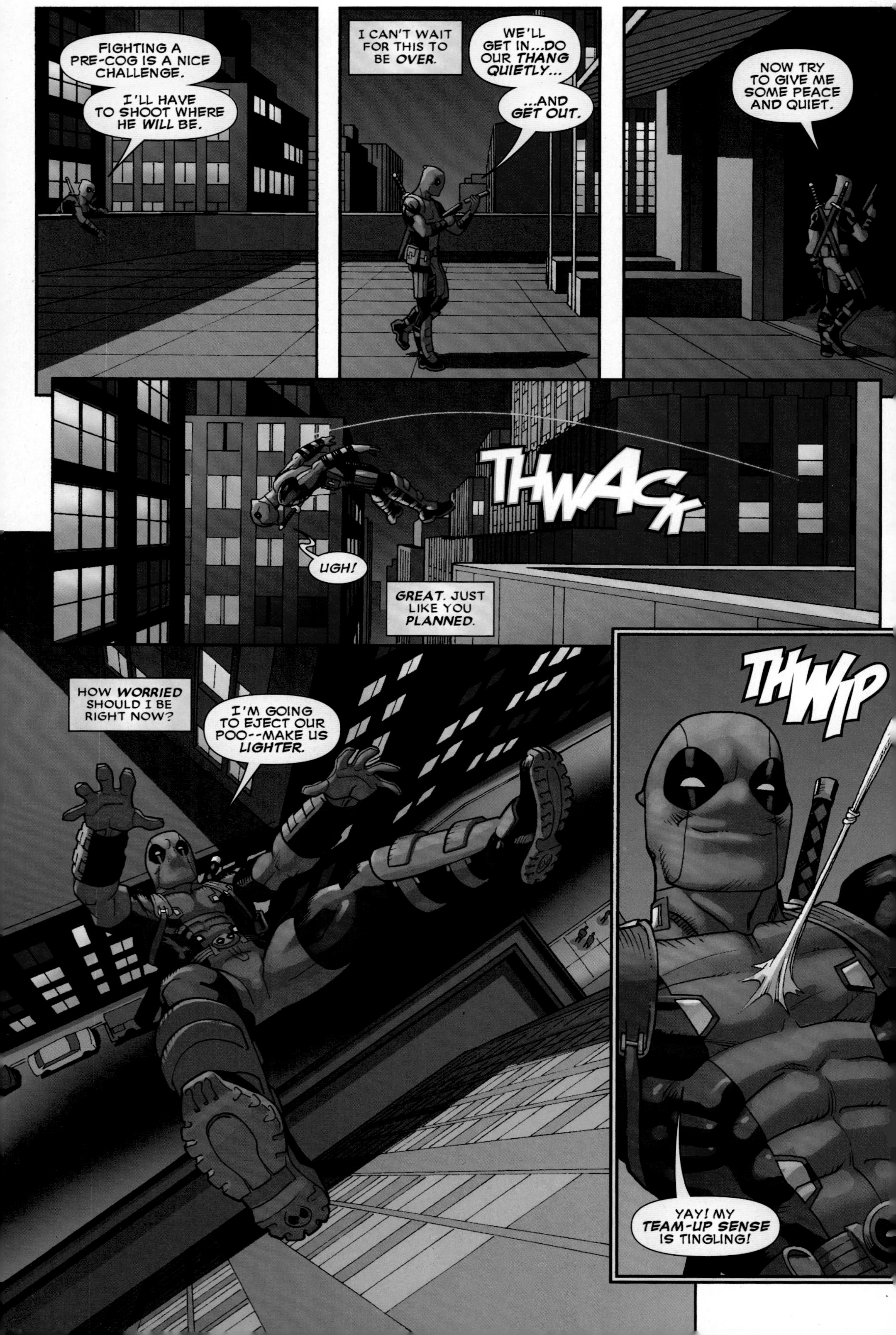
FIGHTING A PRE-COG IS A NICE CHALLENGE.
I'LL HAVE TO SHOOT WHERE HE WILL BE.
I CAN'T WAIT FOR THIS TO BE OVER.
WE'LL GET IN...DO OUR THANG QUIETLY...
...AND GET OUT.
NOW TRY TO GIVE ME SOME PEACE AND QUIET.
THWACK
UGH!
GREAT. JUST LIKE YOU PLANNED.
HOW WORRIED SHOULD I BE RIGHT NOW?
I'M GOING TO EJECT OUR POO--MAKE US LIGHTER.
THWIP
YAY! MY TEAM-UP SENSE IS TINGLING!

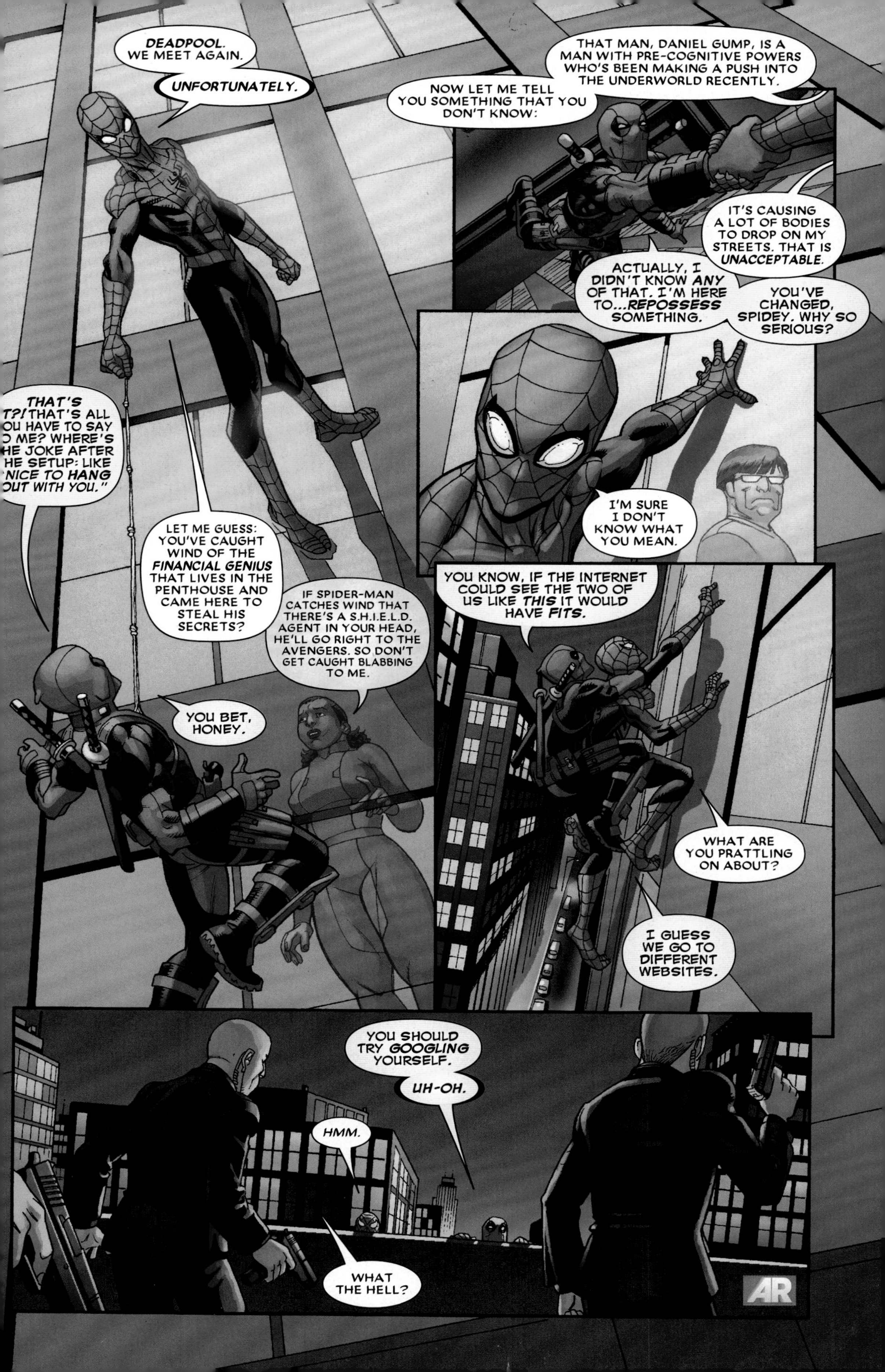
DEADPOOL. WE MEET AGAIN.
UNFORTUNATELY.
NOW LET ME TELL YOU SOMETHING THAT YOU DON'T KNOW:
THAT MAN, DANIEL GUMP, IS A MAN WITH PRE-COGNITIVE POWERS WHO'S BEEN MAKING A PUSH INTO THE UNDERWORLD RECENTLY.
IT'S CAUSING A LOT OF BODIES TO DROP ON MY STREETS. THAT IS UNACCEPTABLE.
ACTUALLY, I DIDN'T KNOW ANY OF THAT. I'M HERE TO...REPOSSESS SOMETHING.
YOU'VE CHANGED, SPIDEY. WHY SO SERIOUS?
I'M SURE I DON'T KNOW WHAT YOU MEAN.
THAT'S IT?! THAT'S ALL YOU HAVE TO SAY TO ME? WHERE'S THE JOKE AFTER THE SETUP: LIKE "NICE TO HANG OUT WITH YOU."
LET ME GUESS: YOU'VE CAUGHT WIND OF THE FINANCIAL GENIUS THAT LIVES IN THE PENTHOUSE AND CAME HERE TO STEAL HIS SECRETS?
IF SPIDER-MAN CATCHES WIND THAT THERE'S A S.H.I.E.L.D. AGENT IN YOUR HEAD, HE'LL GO RIGHT TO THE AVENGERS. SO DON'T GET CAUGHT BLABBING TO ME.
YOU BET, HONEY.
YOU KNOW, IF THE INTERNET COULD SEE THE TWO OF US LIKE THIS IT WOULD HAVE FITS.
WHAT ARE YOU PRATTLING ON ABOUT?
I GUESS WE GO TO DIFFERENT WEBSITES.
YOU SHOULD TRY GOOGLING YOURSELF.
UH-OH.
HMM.
WHAT THE HELL?
AR

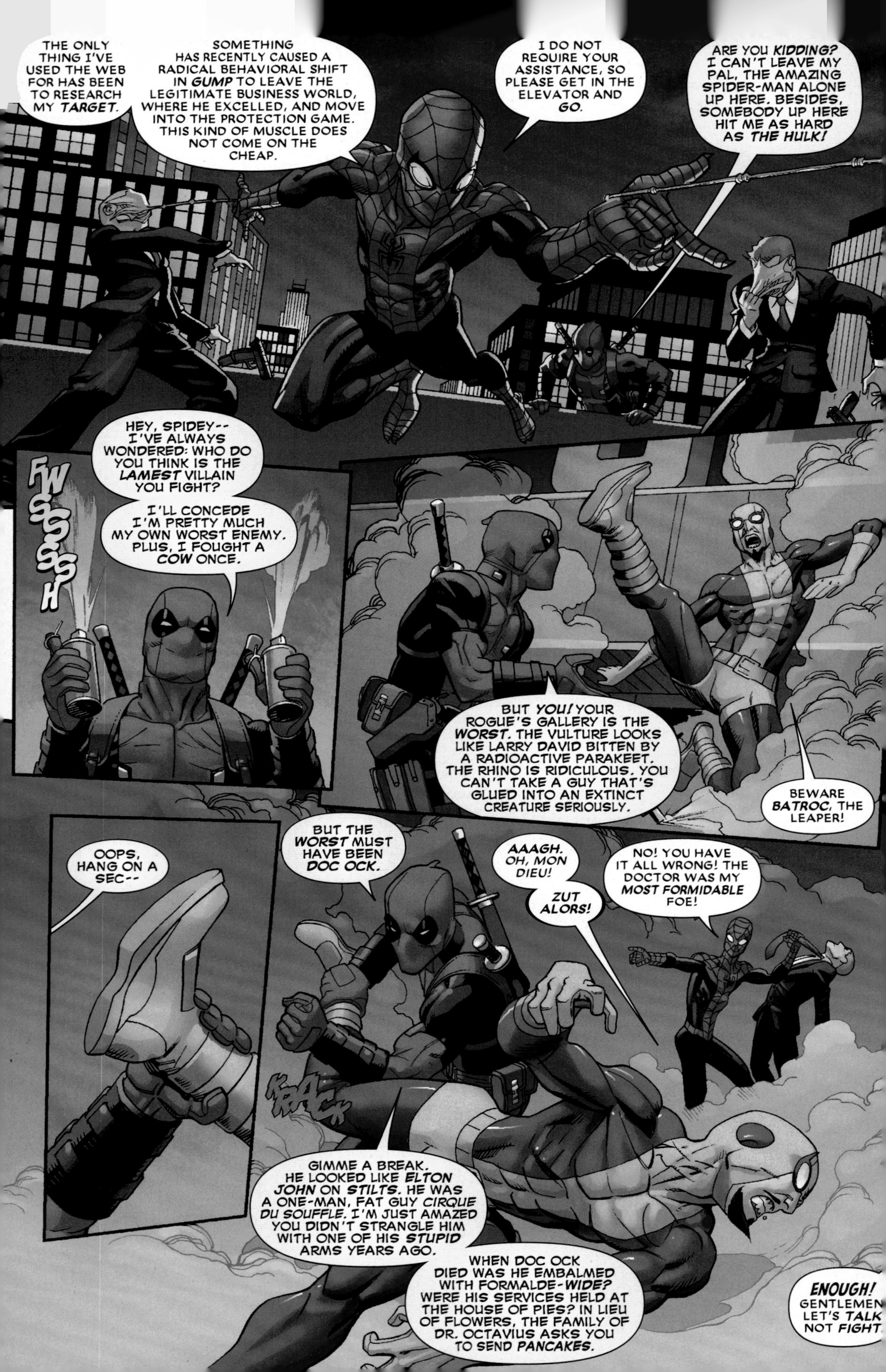
THE ONLY THING I'VE USED THE WEB FOR HAS BEEN TO RESEARCH MY TARGET.
SOMETHING HAS RECENTLY CAUSED A RADICAL BEHAVIORAL SHIFT IN GUMP TO LEAVE THE LEGITIMATE BUSINESS WORLD, WHERE HE EXCELLED, AND MOVE INTO THE PROTECTION GAME. THIS KIND OF MUSCLE DOES NOT COME ON THE CHEAP.
I DO NOT REQUIRE YOUR ASSISTANCE, SO PLEASE GET IN THE ELEVATOR AND GO.
ARE YOU KIDDING? I CAN'T LEAVE MY PAL, THE AMAZING SPIDER-MAN ALONE UP HERE. BESIDES, SOMEBODY UP HERE HIT ME AS HARD AS THE HULK!
FWSSSSH
HEY, SPIDEY-- I'VE ALWAYS WONDERED: WHO DO YOU THINK IS THE LAMEST VILLAIN YOU FIGHT?
I'LL CONCEDE I'M PRETTY MUCH MY OWN WORST ENEMY. PLUS, I FOUGHT A COW ONCE.
BUT YOU! YOUR ROGUE'S GALLERY IS THE WORST. THE VULTURE LOOKS LIKE LARRY DAVID BITTEN BY A RADIOACTIVE PARAKEET. THE RHINO IS RIDICULOUS. YOU CAN'T TAKE A GUY THAT'S GLUED INTO AN EXTINCT CREATURE SERIOUSLY.
BEWARE BATROC, THE LEAPER!
OOPS, HANG ON A SEC--
BUT THE WORST MUST HAVE BEEN DOC OCK.
AAAGH. OH, MON DIEU!
ZUT ALORS!
NO! YOU HAVE IT ALL WRONG! THE DOCTOR WAS MY MOST FORMIDABLE FOE!
KRACK
GIMME A BREAK. HE LOOKED LIKE ELTON JOHN ON STILTS. HE WAS A ONE-MAN, FAT GUY CIRQUE DU SOUFFLE. I'M JUST AMAZED YOU DIDN'T STRANGLE HIM WITH ONE OF HIS STUPID ARMS YEARS AGO.
WHEN DOC OCK DIED WAS HE EMBALMED WITH FORMALDE-WIDE? WERE HIS SERVICES HELD AT THE HOUSE OF PIES? IN LIEU OF FLOWERS, THE FAMILY OF DR. OCTAVIUS ASKS YOU TO SEND PANCAKES.
ENOUGH! GENTLEMEN LET'S TALK NOT FIGHT.

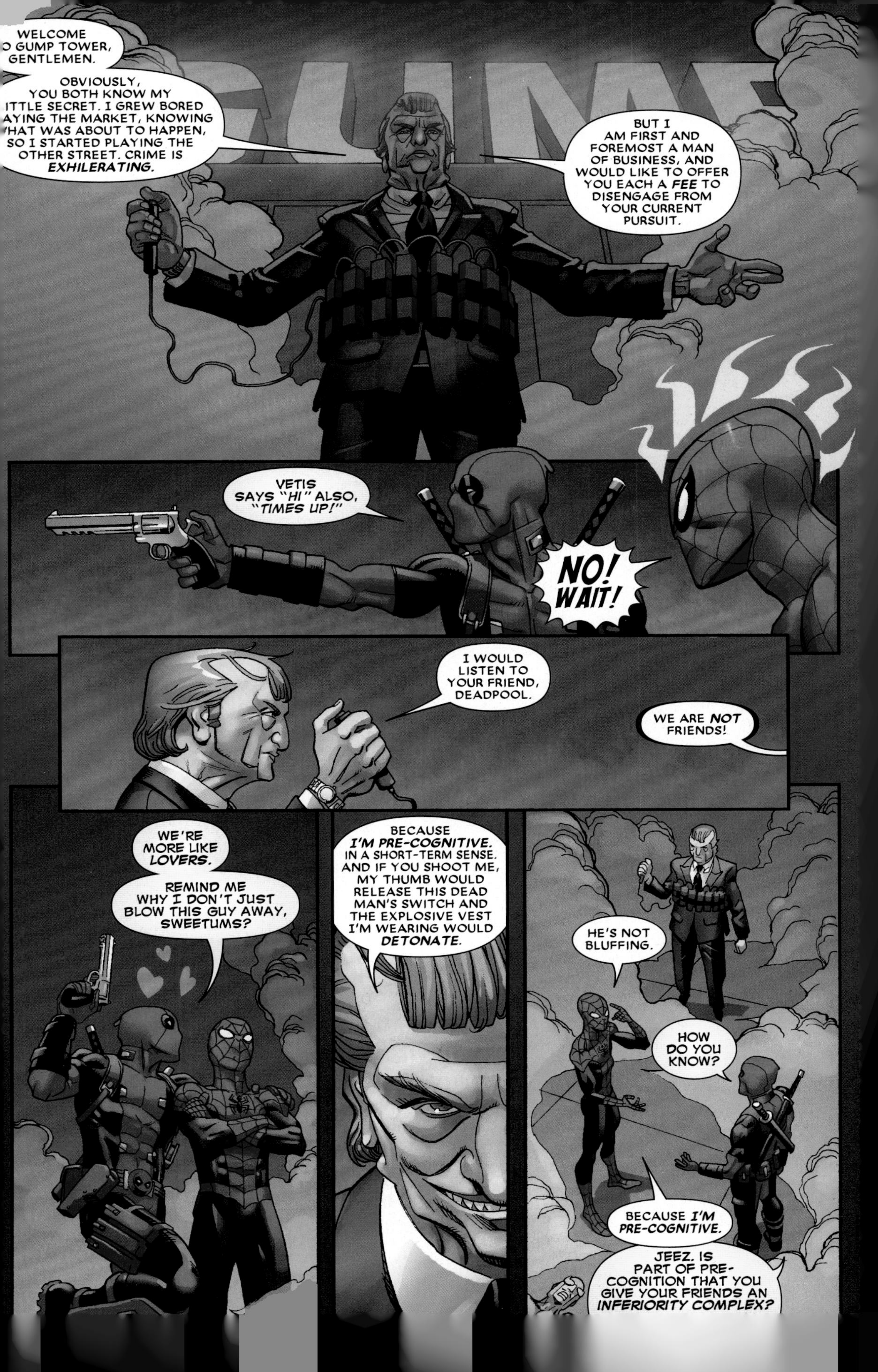
WELCOME O GUMP TOWER, GENTLEMEN.
OBVIOUSLY, YOU BOTH KNOW MY ITTLE SECRET. I GREW BORED AYING THE MARKET, KNOWING VHAT WAS ABOUT TO HAPPEN, SO I STARTED PLAYING THE OTHER STREET. CRIME IS *EXHILERATING.*
BUT I AM FIRST AND FOREMOST A MAN OF BUSINESS, AND WOULD LIKE TO OFFER YOU EACH A *FEE* TO DISENGAGE FROM YOUR CURRENT PURSUIT.
VETIS SAYS "*HI*" ALSO, "*TIMES UP!*"
NO! WAIT!
I WOULD LISTEN TO YOUR FRIEND, DEADPOOL.
WE ARE *NOT* FRIENDS!
WE'RE MORE LIKE *LOVERS.*
REMIND ME WHY I DON'T JUST BLOW THIS GUY AWAY, SWEETUMS?
BECAUSE *I'M PRE-COGNITIVE.* IN A SHORT-TERM SENSE. AND IF YOU SHOOT ME, MY THUMB WOULD RELEASE THIS DEAD MAN'S SWITCH AND THE EXPLOSIVE VEST I'M WEARING WOULD *DETONATE.*
HE'S NOT BLUFFING.
HOW DO YOU KNOW?
BECAUSE *I'M PRE-COGNITIVE.*
JEEZ. IS PART OF PRE-COGNITION THAT YOU GIVE YOUR FRIENDS AN *INFERIORITY COMPLEX?*

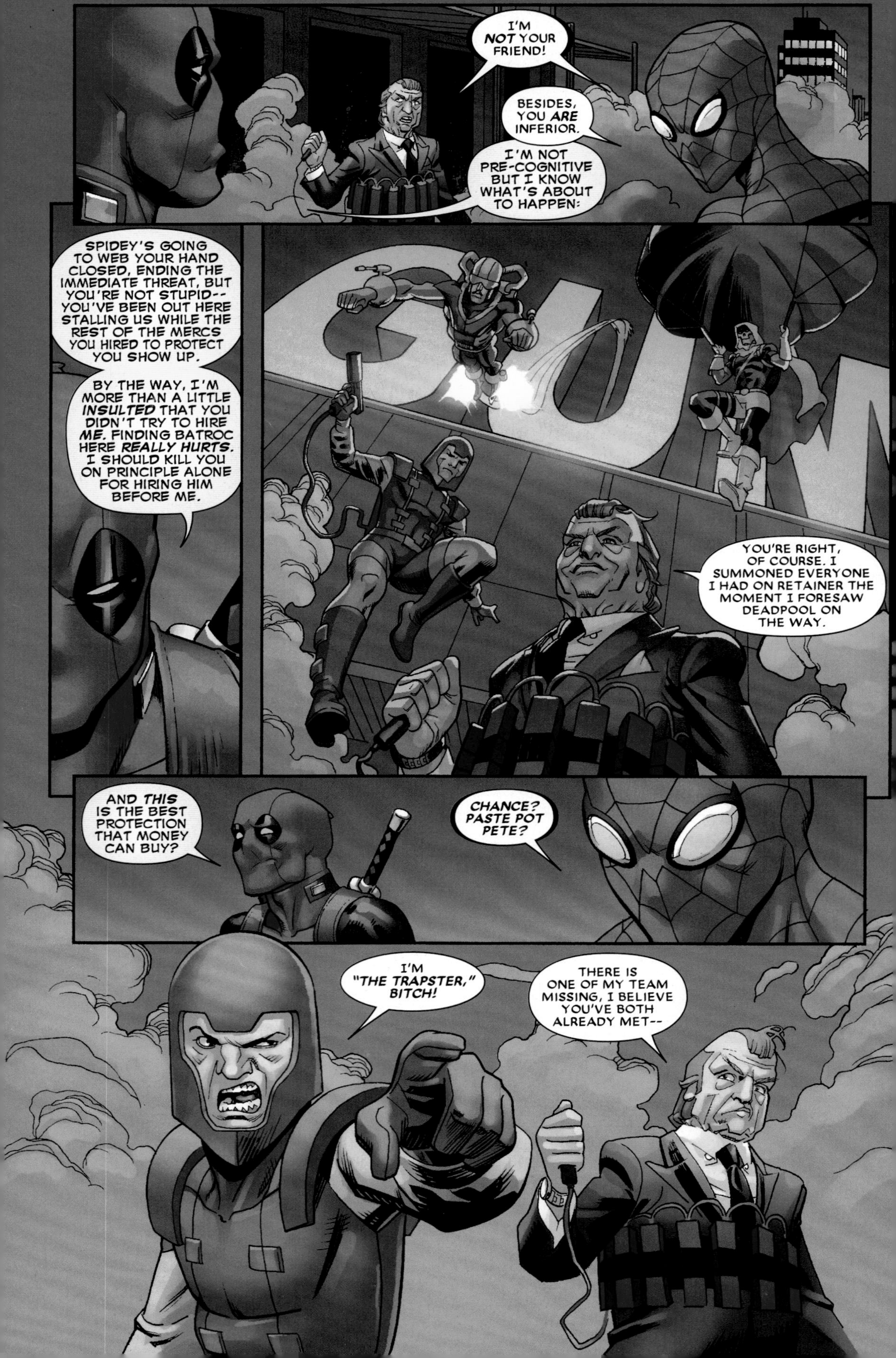
I'M *NOT* YOUR FRIEND!
BESIDES, YOU *ARE* INFERIOR.
I'M NOT PRE-COGNITIVE BUT I KNOW WHAT'S ABOUT TO HAPPEN:
SPIDEY'S GOING TO WEB YOUR HAND CLOSED, ENDING THE IMMEDIATE THREAT, BUT YOU'RE NOT STUPID-- YOU'VE BEEN OUT HERE STALLING US WHILE THE REST OF THE MERCS YOU HIRED TO PROTECT YOU SHOW UP.
BY THE WAY, I'M MORE THAN A LITTLE *INSULTED* THAT YOU DIDN'T TRY TO HIRE *ME*. FINDING BATROC HERE *REALLY HURTS*. I SHOULD KILL YOU ON PRINCIPLE ALONE FOR HIRING HIM BEFORE ME.
YOU'RE RIGHT, OF COURSE. I SUMMONED EVERYONE I HAD ON RETAINER THE MOMENT I FORESAW DEADPOOL ON THE WAY.
AND *THIS* IS THE BEST PROTECTION THAT MONEY CAN BUY?
*CHANCE? PASTE POT PETE?*
I'M *"THE TRAPSTER," BITCH!*
THERE IS ONE OF MY TEAM MISSING, I BELIEVE YOU'VE BOTH ALREADY MET--

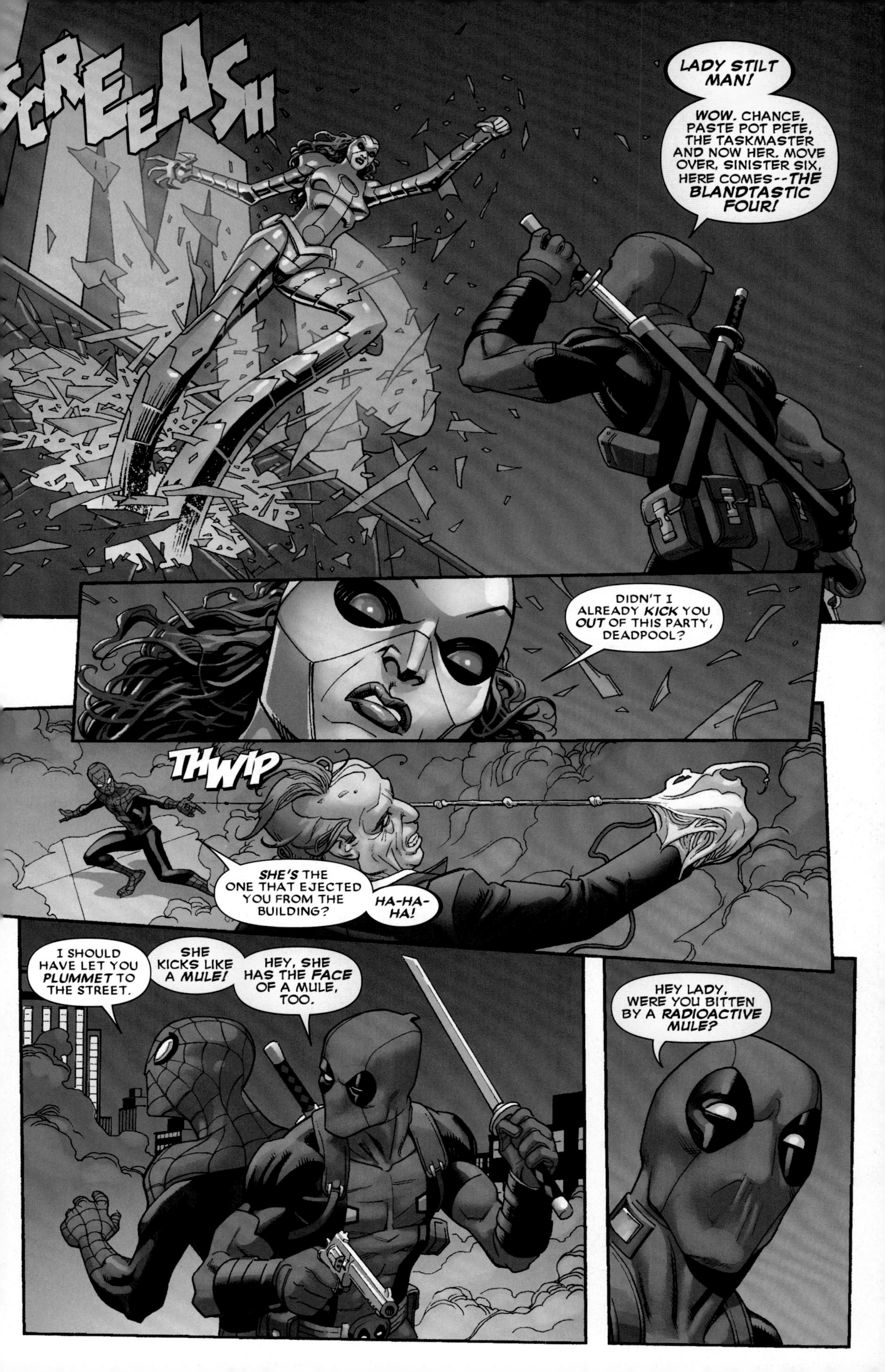
SCREEEASH
LADY STILT MAN!
WOW. CHANCE, PASTE POT PETE, THE TASKMASTER AND NOW HER. MOVE OVER, SINISTER SIX, HERE COMES--THE BLANDTASTIC FOUR!
DIDN'T I ALREADY KICK YOU OUT OF THIS PARTY, DEADPOOL?
THWIP
SHE'S THE ONE THAT EJECTED YOU FROM THE BUILDING?
HA-HA-HA!
I SHOULD HAVE LET YOU PLUMMET TO THE STREET.
SHE KICKS LIKE A MULE!
HEY, SHE HAS THE FACE OF A MULE, TOO.
HEY LADY, WERE YOU BITTEN BY A RADIOACTIVE MULE?

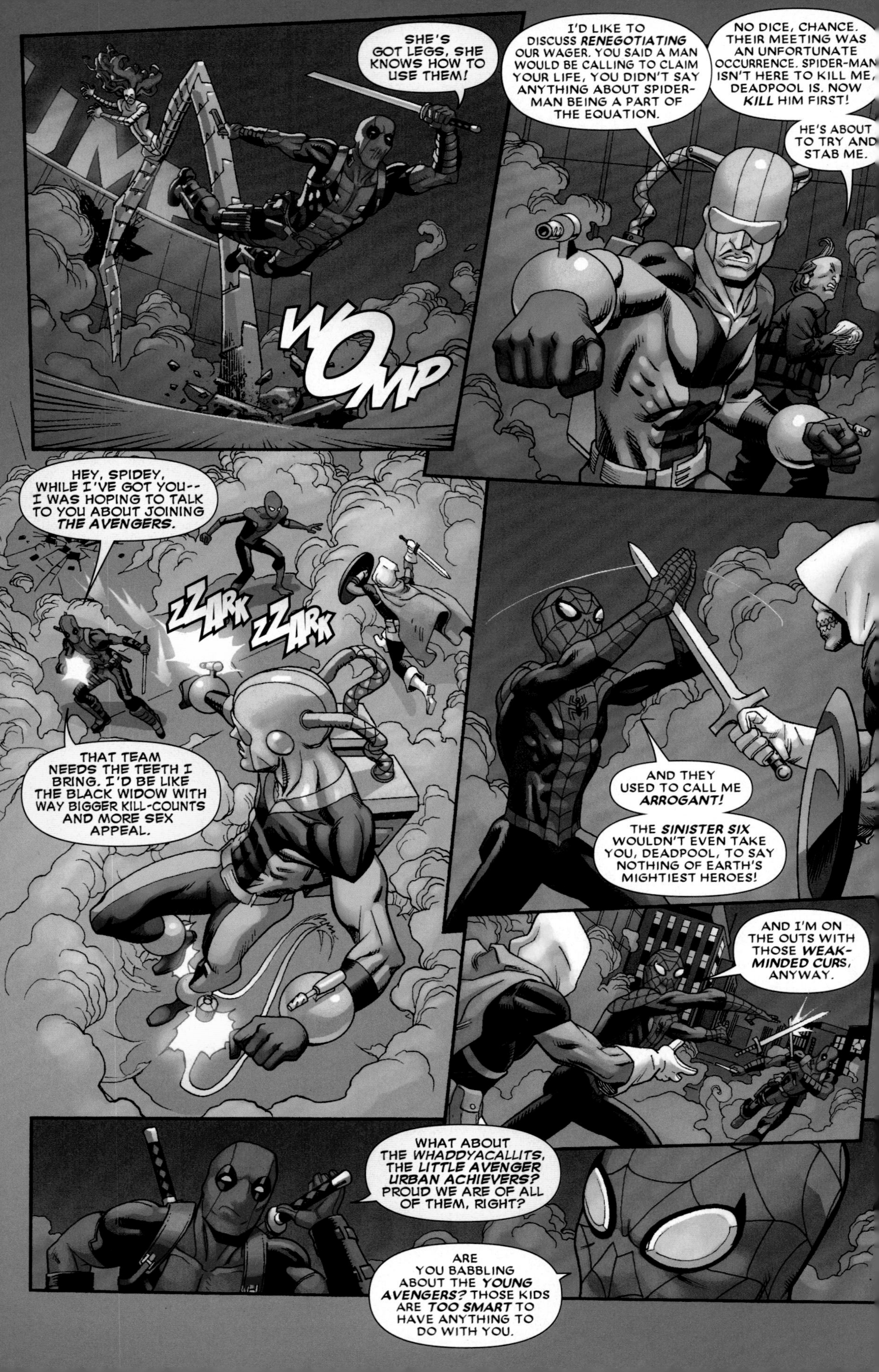
SHE'S GOT LEGS, SHE KNOWS HOW TO USE THEM!
WOMP
I'D LIKE TO DISCUSS RENEGOTIATING OUR WAGER. YOU SAID A MAN WOULD BE CALLING TO CLAIM YOUR LIFE, YOU DIDN'T SAY ANYTHING ABOUT SPIDER-MAN BEING A PART OF THE EQUATION.
NO DICE, CHANCE. THEIR MEETING WAS AN UNFORTUNATE OCCURRENCE. SPIDER-MAN ISN'T HERE TO KILL ME, DEADPOOL IS. NOW KILL HIM FIRST!
HE'S ABOUT TO TRY AND STAB ME.
HEY, SPIDEY, WHILE I'VE GOT YOU-- I WAS HOPING TO TALK TO YOU ABOUT JOINING THE AVENGERS.
ZZARK ZZARK
THAT TEAM NEEDS THE TEETH I BRING. I'D BE LIKE THE BLACK WIDOW WITH WAY BIGGER KILL-COUNTS AND MORE SEX APPEAL.
AND THEY USED TO CALL ME ARROGANT!
THE SINISTER SIX WOULDN'T EVEN TAKE YOU, DEADPOOL, TO SAY NOTHING OF EARTH'S MIGHTIEST HEROES!
AND I'M ON THE OUTS WITH THOSE WEAK-MINDED CURS, ANYWAY.
WHAT ABOUT THE WHADDYACALLITS, THE LITTLE AVENGER URBAN ACHIEVERS? PROUD WE ARE OF ALL OF THEM, RIGHT?
ARE YOU BABBLING ABOUT THE YOUNG AVENGERS? THOSE KIDS ARE TOO SMART TO HAVE ANYTHING TO DO WITH YOU.

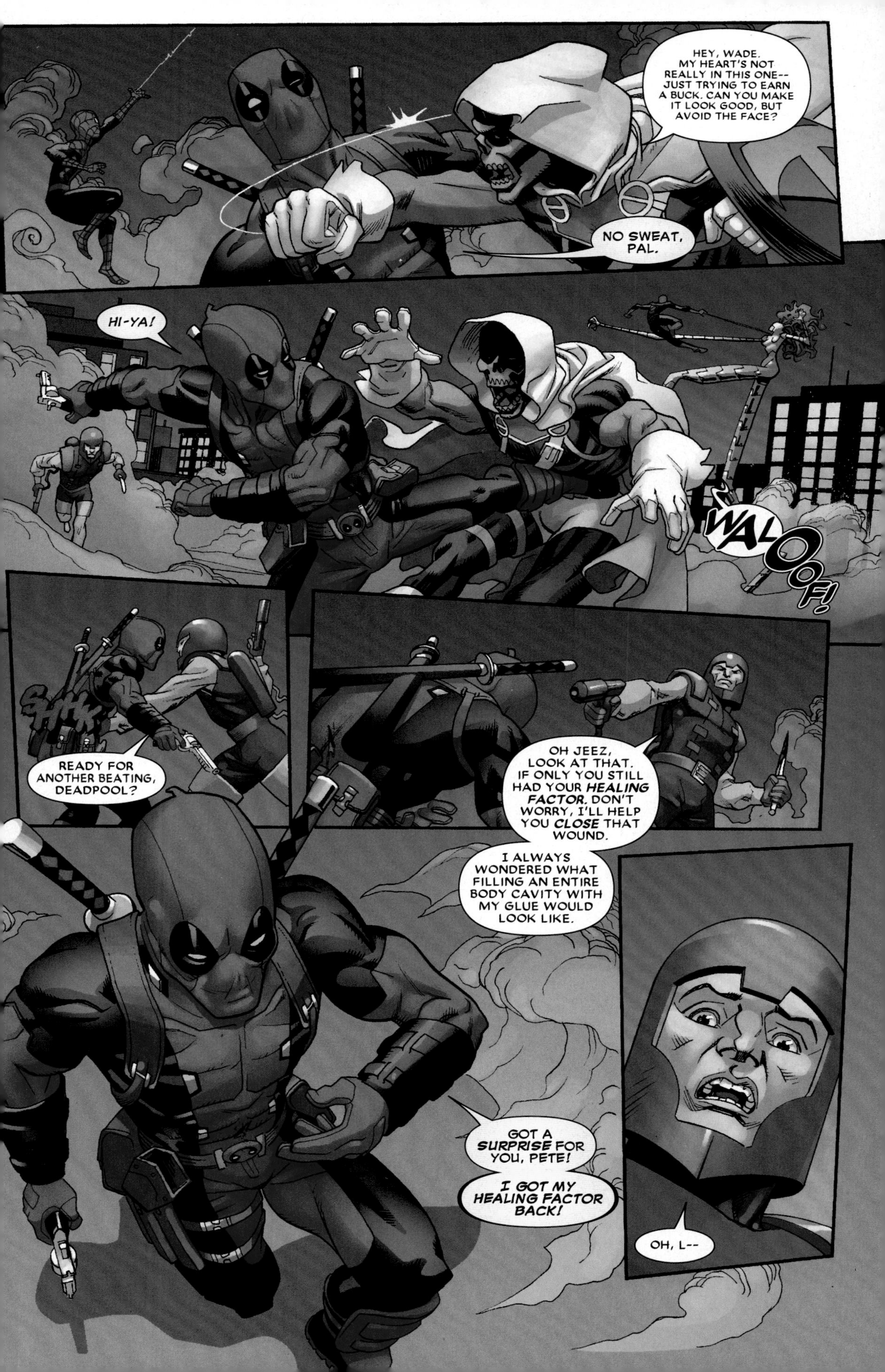
HEY, WADE. MY HEART'S NOT REALLY IN THIS ONE-- JUST TRYING TO EARN A BUCK. CAN YOU MAKE IT LOOK GOOD, BUT AVOID THE FACE?
NO SWEAT, PAL.
HI-YA!
WALOOF!
READY FOR ANOTHER BEATING, DEADPOOL?
OH JEEZ, LOOK AT THAT. IF ONLY YOU STILL HAD YOUR HEALING FACTOR. DON'T WORRY, I'LL HELP YOU CLOSE THAT WOUND.
I ALWAYS WONDERED WHAT FILLING AN ENTIRE BODY CAVITY WITH MY GLUE WOULD LOOK LIKE.
GOT A SURPRISE FOR YOU, PETE!
I GOT MY HEALING FACTOR BACK!
OH, L--

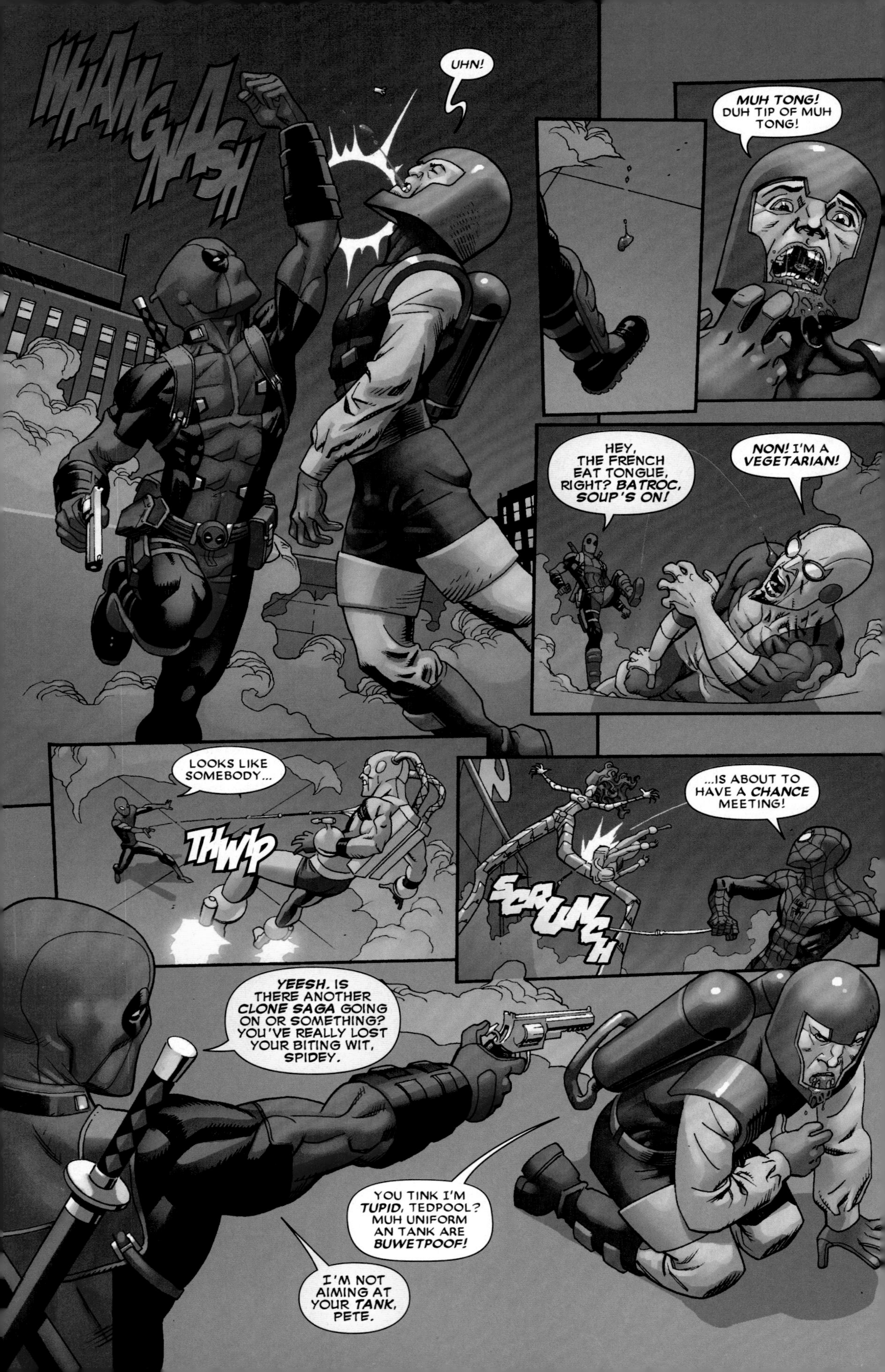
WHANGWASH
UHN!
MUH TONG! DUH TIP OF MUH TONG!
HEY, THE FRENCH EAT TONGUE, RIGHT? BATROC, SOUP'S ON!
NON! I'M A VEGETARIAN!
LOOKS LIKE SOMEBODY...
THWIP
...IS ABOUT TO HAVE A CHANCE MEETING!
SCRUNCH
YEESH. IS THERE ANOTHER CLONE SAGA GOING ON OR SOMETHING? YOU'VE REALLY LOST YOUR BITING WIT, SPIDEY.
YOU TINK I'M TUPID, TEDPOOL? MUH UNIFORM AN TANK ARE BUWETPOOF!
I'M NOT AIMING AT YOUR TANK, PETE.

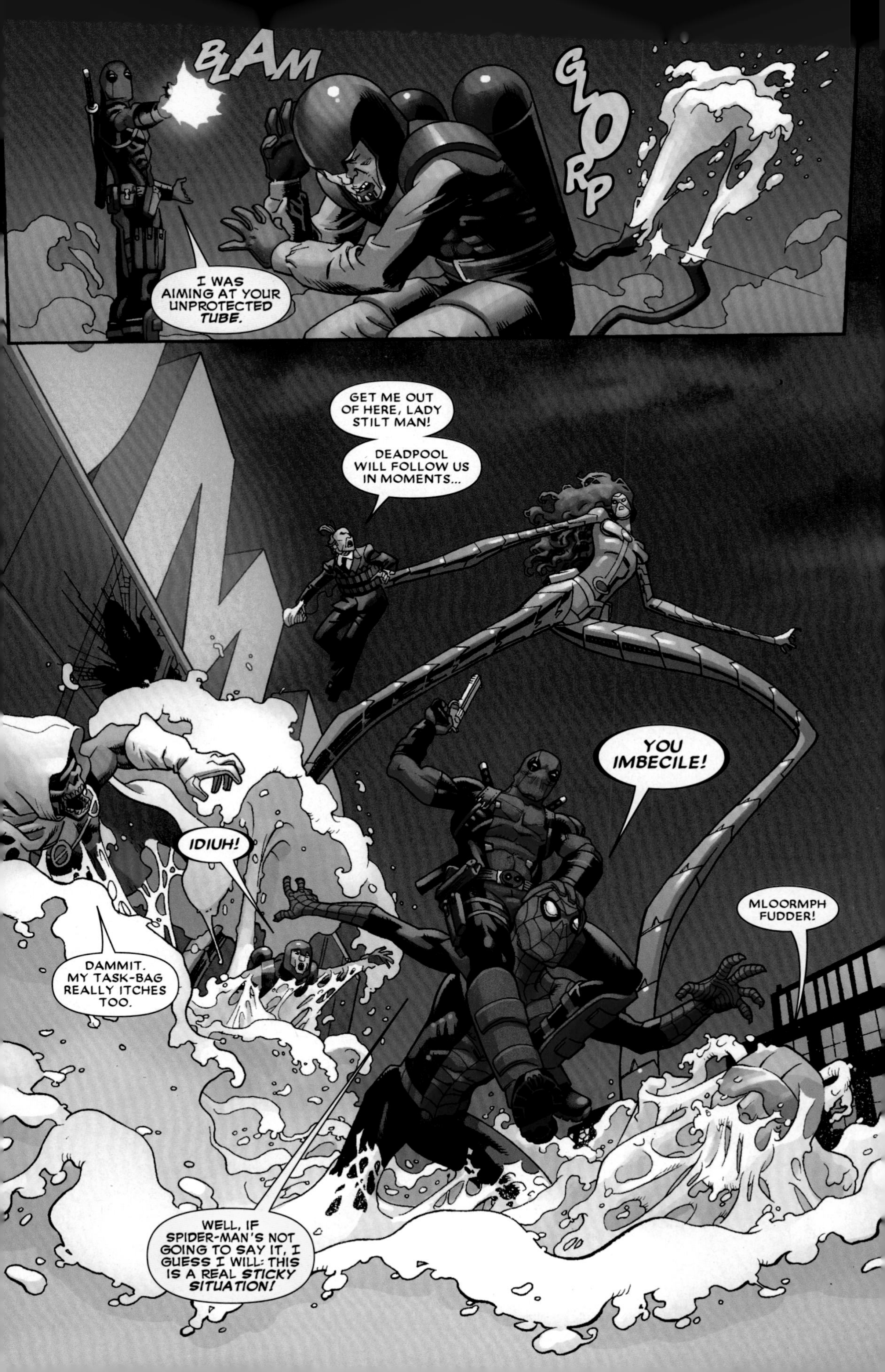
BLAM
GLORP
I WAS AIMING AT YOUR UNPROTECTED TUBE.
GET ME OUT OF HERE, LADY STILT MAN!
DEADPOOL WILL FOLLOW US IN MOMENTS...
YOU IMBECILE!
IDIUH!
DAMMIT. MY TASK-BAG REALLY ITCHES TOO.
MLOORMPH FUDDER!
WELL, IF SPIDER-MAN'S NOT GOING TO SAY IT, I GUESS I WILL: THIS IS A REAL STICKY SITUATION!

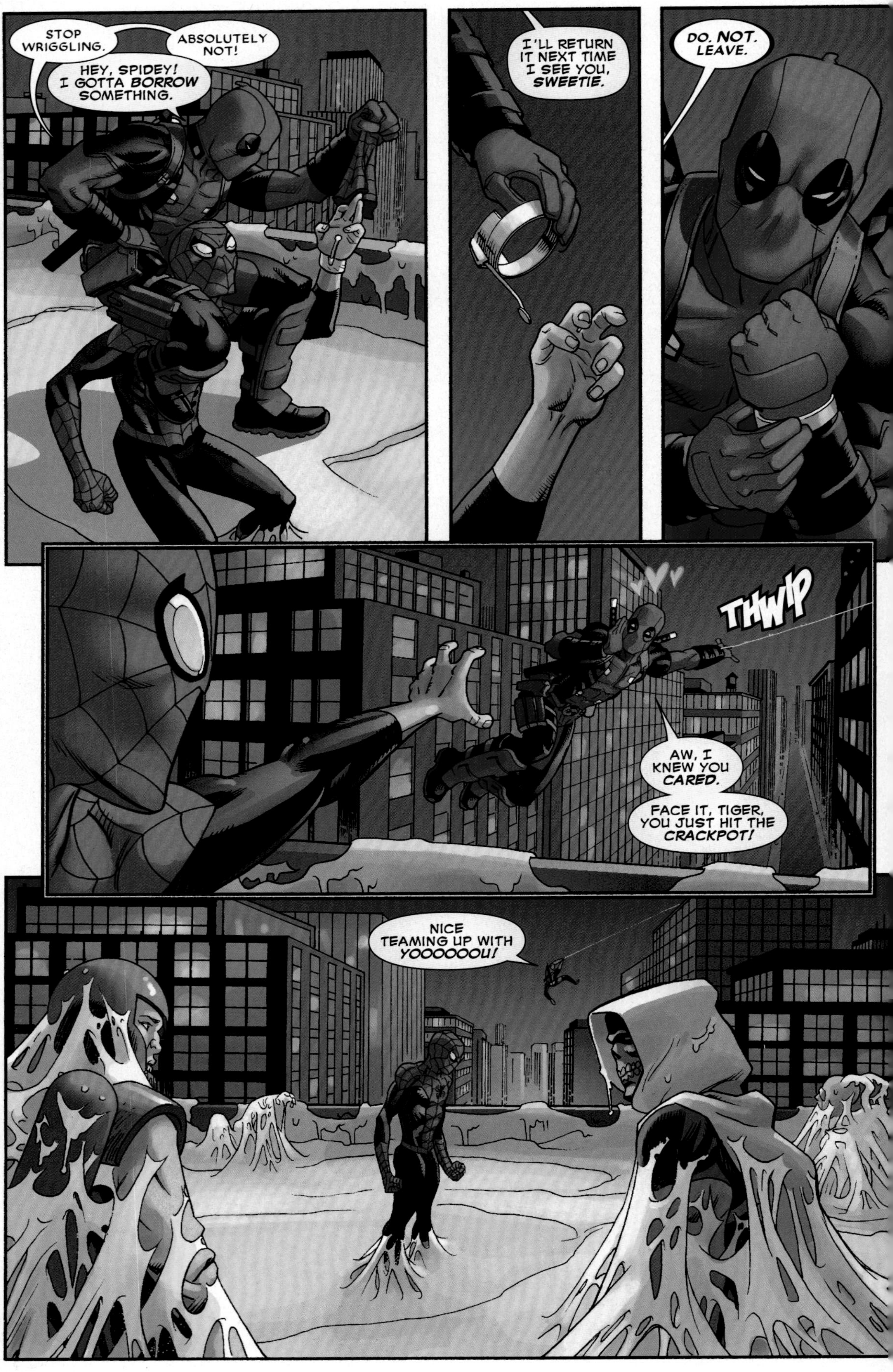
STOP WRIGGLING.
ABSOLUTELY NOT!
HEY, SPIDEY! I GOTTA BORROW SOMETHING.
I'LL RETURN IT NEXT TIME I SEE YOU, SWEETIE.
DO. NOT. LEAVE.
THWIP
AW, I KNEW YOU CARED.
FACE IT, TIGER, YOU JUST HIT THE CRACKPOT!
NICE TEAMING UP WITH YOOOOOOU!

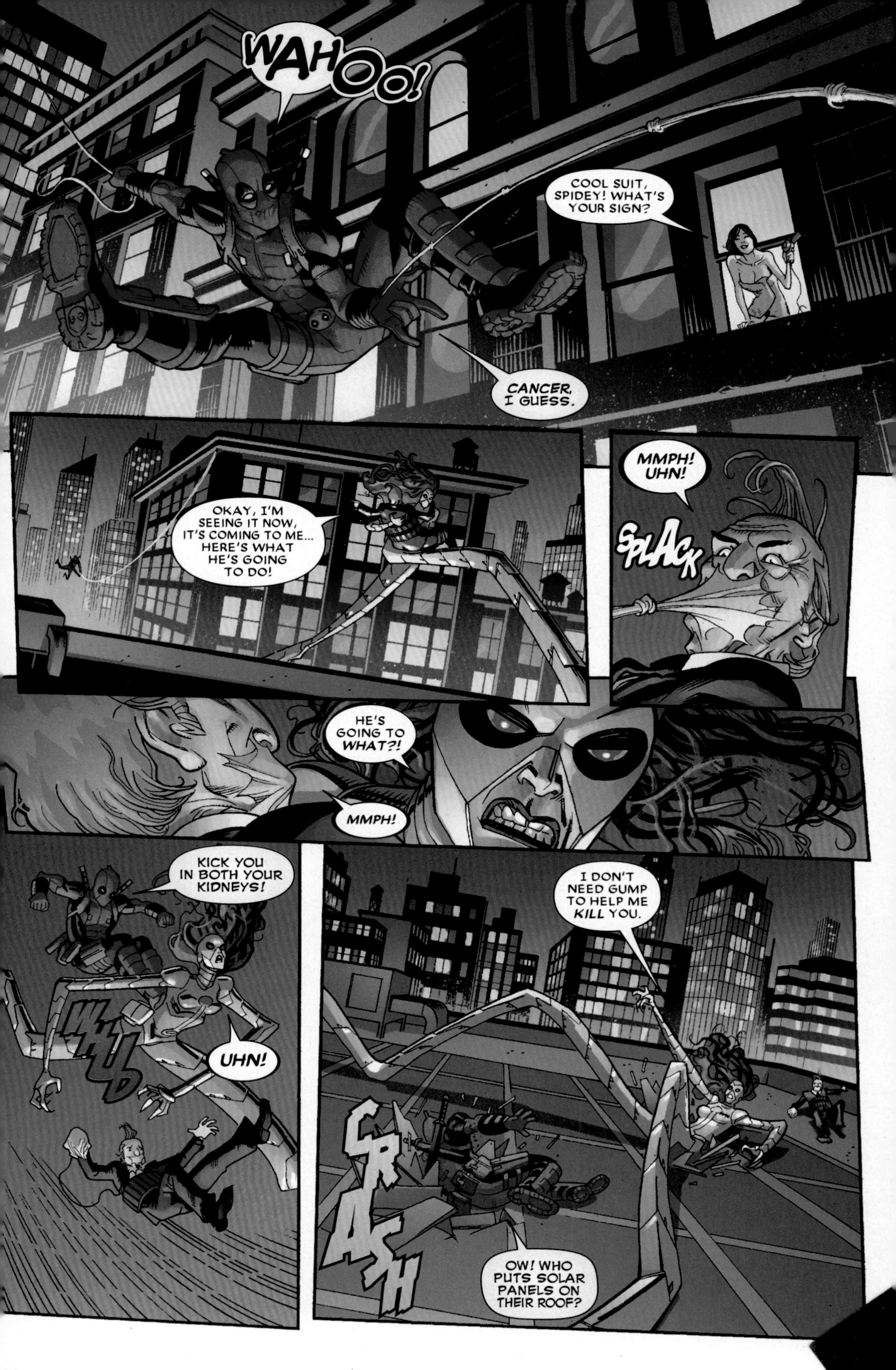

WAHOOO!
COOL SUIT, SPIDEY! WHAT'S YOUR SIGN?
CANCER, I GUESS.
OKAY, I'M SEEING IT NOW, IT'S COMING TO ME... HERE'S WHAT HE'S GOING TO DO!
MMPH! UHN!
SPLACK
HE'S GOING TO WHAT?!
MMPH!
KICK YOU IN BOTH YOUR KIDNEYS!
WHUD
UHN!
I DON'T NEED GUMP TO HELP ME KILL YOU.
CRASH
OW! WHO PUTS SOLAR PANELS ON THEIR ROOF?

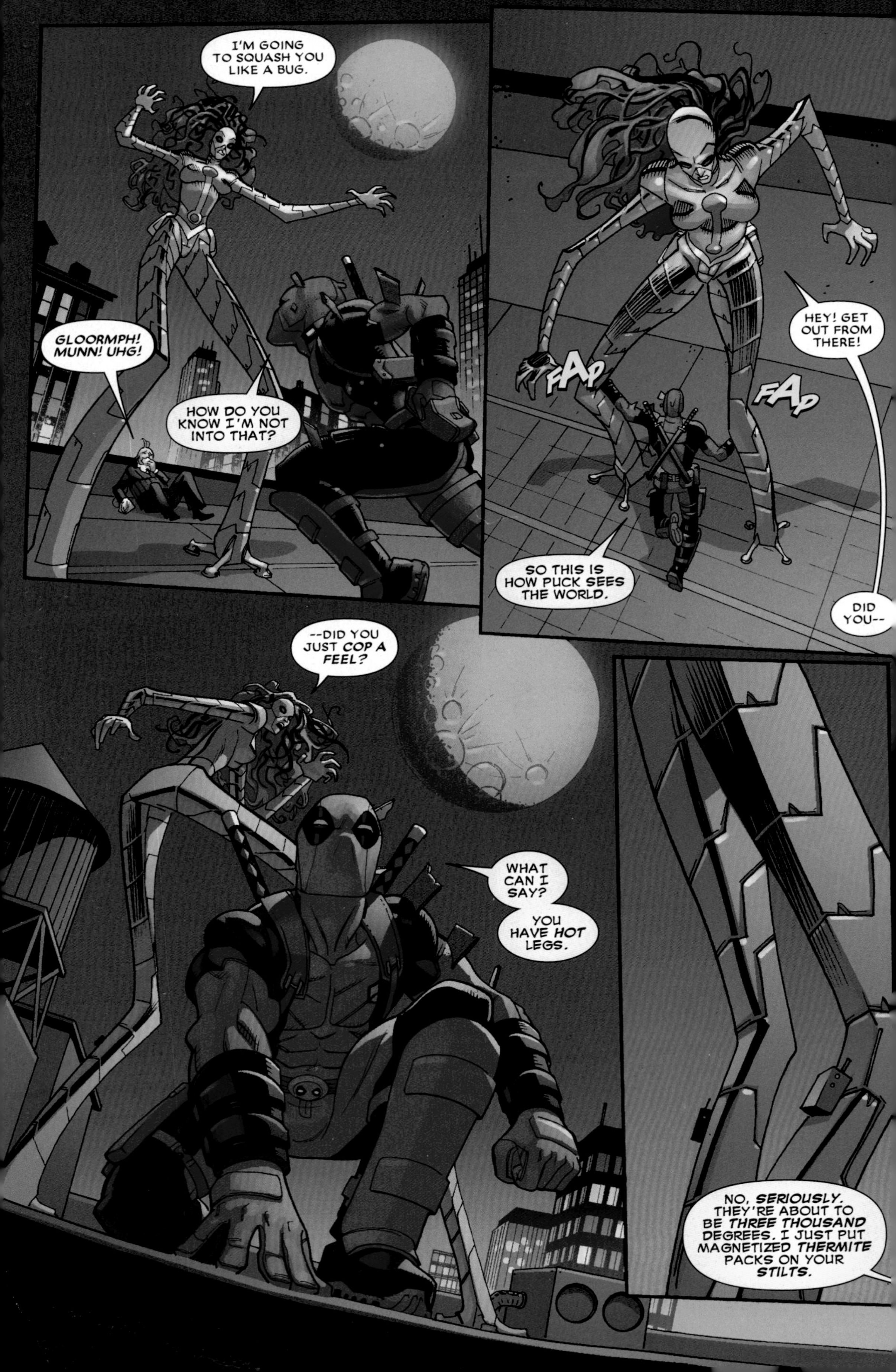
I'M GOING TO SQUASH YOU LIKE A BUG.
GLOORMPH! MUNN! UHG!
HOW DO YOU KNOW I'M NOT INTO THAT?
FAP
FAP
SO THIS IS HOW PUCK SEES THE WORLD.
HEY! GET OUT FROM THERE!
DID YOU--
--DID YOU JUST COP A FEEL?
WHAT CAN I SAY?
YOU HAVE HOT LEGS.
NO, SERIOUSLY. THEY'RE ABOUT TO BE THREE THOUSAND DEGREES. I JUST PUT MAGNETIZED THERMITE PACKS ON YOUR STILTS.

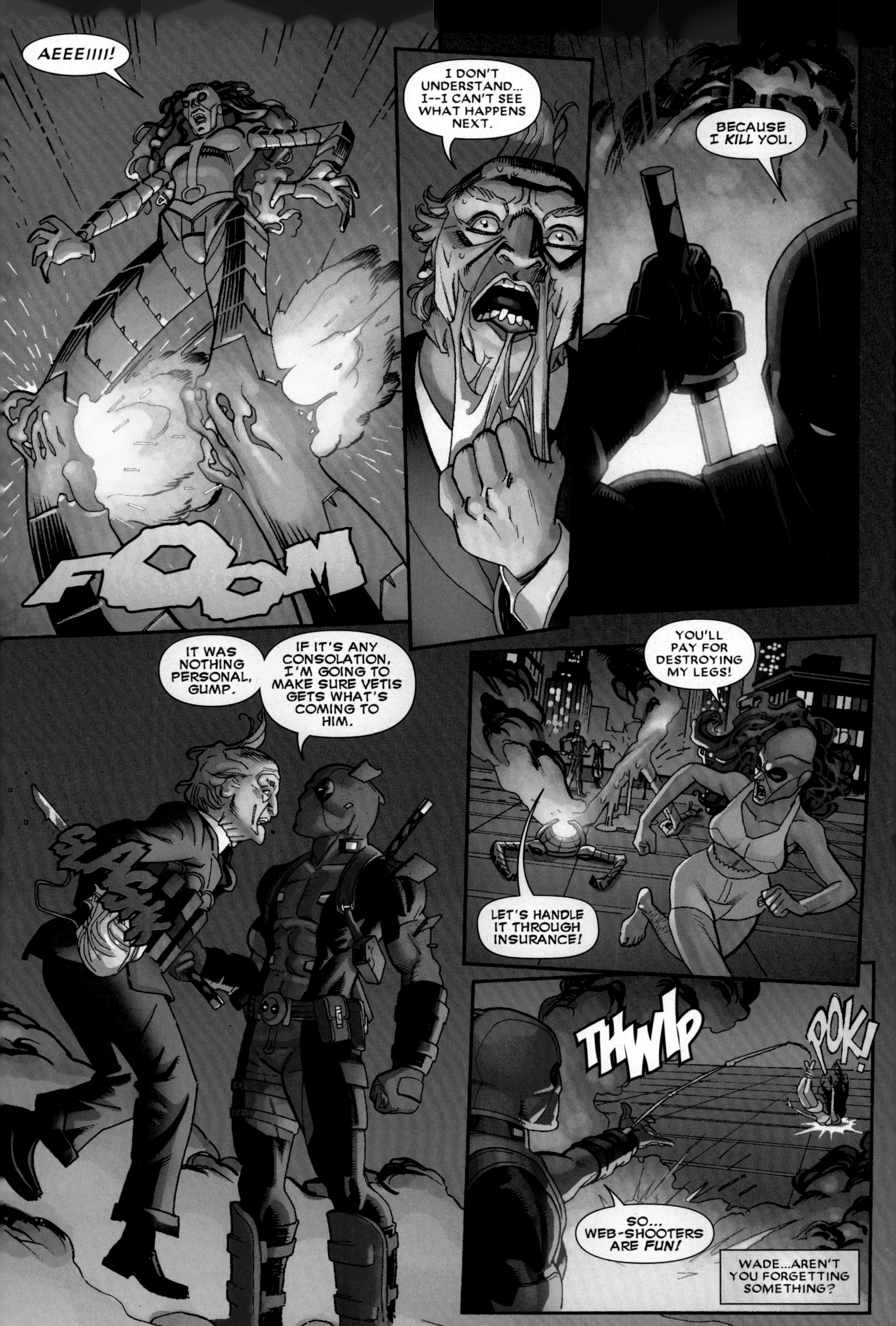
AEEEIIII!
FOOM
I DON'T UNDERSTAND... I--I CAN'T SEE WHAT HAPPENS NEXT.
BECAUSE I KILL YOU.
IT WAS NOTHING PERSONAL, GUMP.
IF IT'S ANY CONSOLATION, I'M GOING TO MAKE SURE VETIS GETS WHAT'S COMING TO HIM.
YOU'LL PAY FOR DESTROYING MY LEGS!
LET'S HANDLE IT THROUGH INSURANCE!
THWIP
POK!
SO... WEB-SHOOTERS ARE FUN!
WADE...AREN'T YOU FORGETTING SOMETHING?

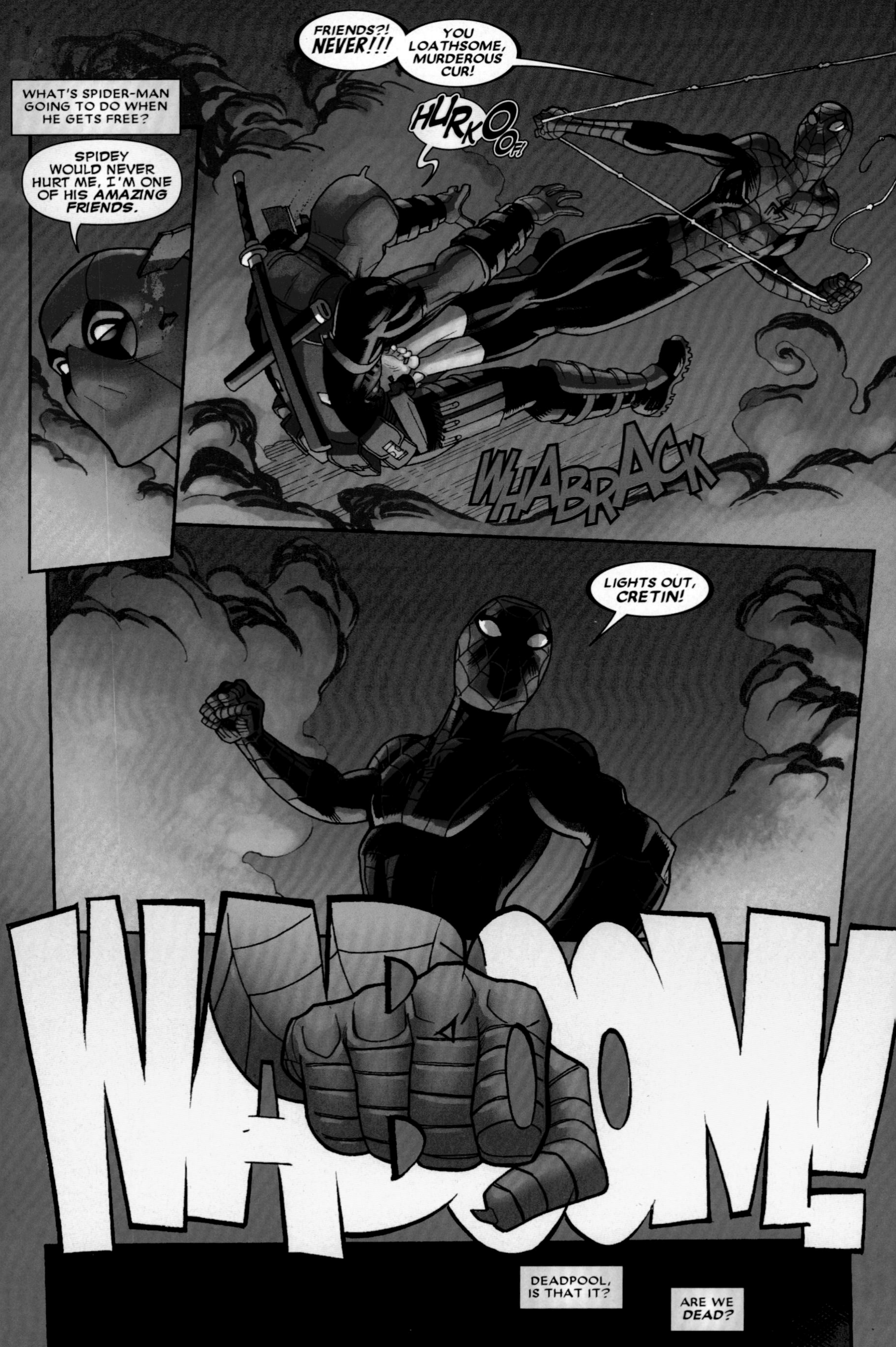
WHAT'S SPIDER-MAN GOING TO DO WHEN HE GETS FREE?
SPIDEY WOULD NEVER HURT ME, I'M ONE OF HIS *AMAZING FRIENDS.*
FRIENDS?! *NEVER!!!*
YOU LOATHSOME, MURDEROUS CUR!
HURK
OOOF!
WHABRACK
LIGHTS OUT, *CRETIN!*
WADOOM!
DEADPOOL, IS THAT IT?
ARE WE *DEAD?*

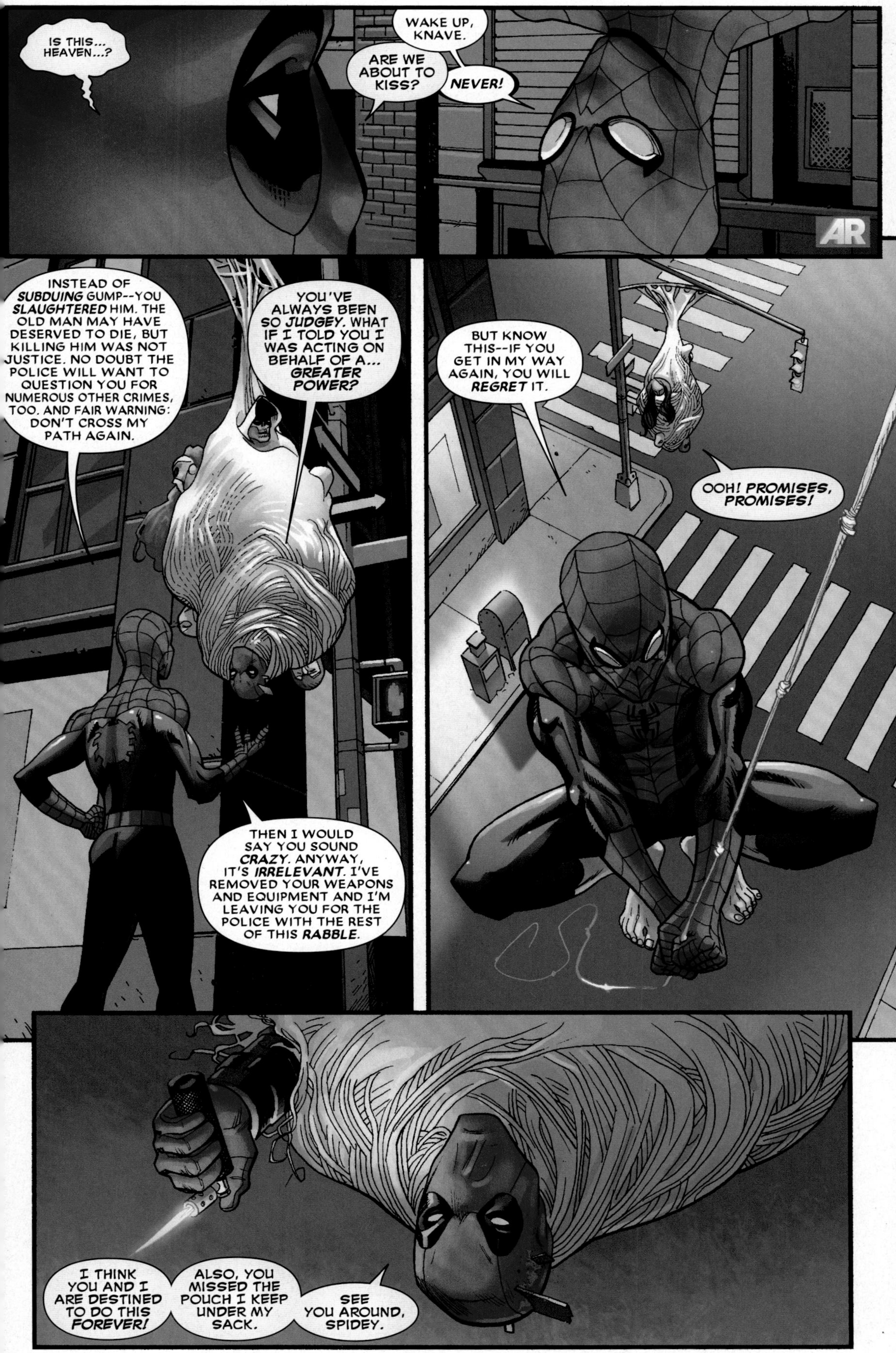
IS THIS... HEAVEN...?
WAKE UP, KNAVE.
ARE WE ABOUT TO KISS?
NEVER!
AR
INSTEAD OF SUBDUING GUMP--YOU SLAUGHTERED HIM. THE OLD MAN MAY HAVE DESERVED TO DIE, BUT KILLING HIM WAS NOT JUSTICE. NO DOUBT THE POLICE WILL WANT TO QUESTION YOU FOR NUMEROUS OTHER CRIMES, TOO. AND FAIR WARNING: DON'T CROSS MY PATH AGAIN.
YOU'VE ALWAYS BEEN SO JUDGEY. WHAT IF I TOLD YOU I WAS ACTING ON BEHALF OF A... GREATER POWER?
THEN I WOULD SAY YOU SOUND CRAZY. ANYWAY, IT'S IRRELEVANT. I'VE REMOVED YOUR WEAPONS AND EQUIPMENT AND I'M LEAVING YOU FOR THE POLICE WITH THE REST OF THIS RABBLE.
BUT KNOW THIS--IF YOU GET IN MY WAY AGAIN, YOU WILL REGRET IT.
OOH! PROMISES, PROMISES!
I THINK YOU AND I ARE DESTINED TO DO THIS FOREVER!
ALSO, YOU MISSED THE POUCH I KEEP UNDER MY SACK.
SEE YOU AROUND, SPIDEY.

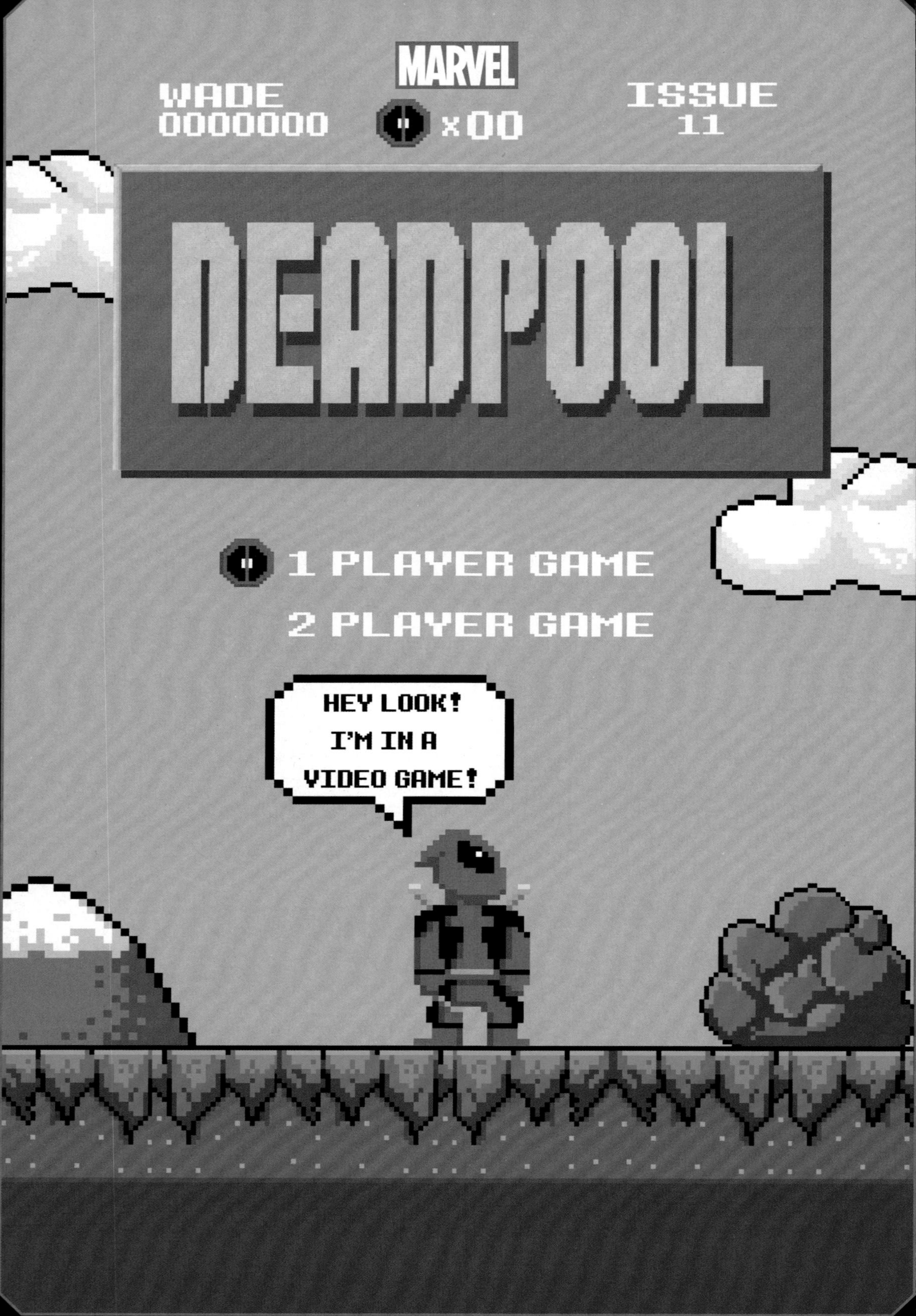
MARVEL
WADE
0000000
x00
ISSUE
11
DEADPOOL
1 PLAYER GAME
2 PLAYER GAME
HEY LOOK! I'M IN A VIDEO GAME!

#11 8-BIT VARIANT
BY MATTHEW WAITE

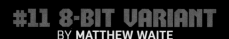

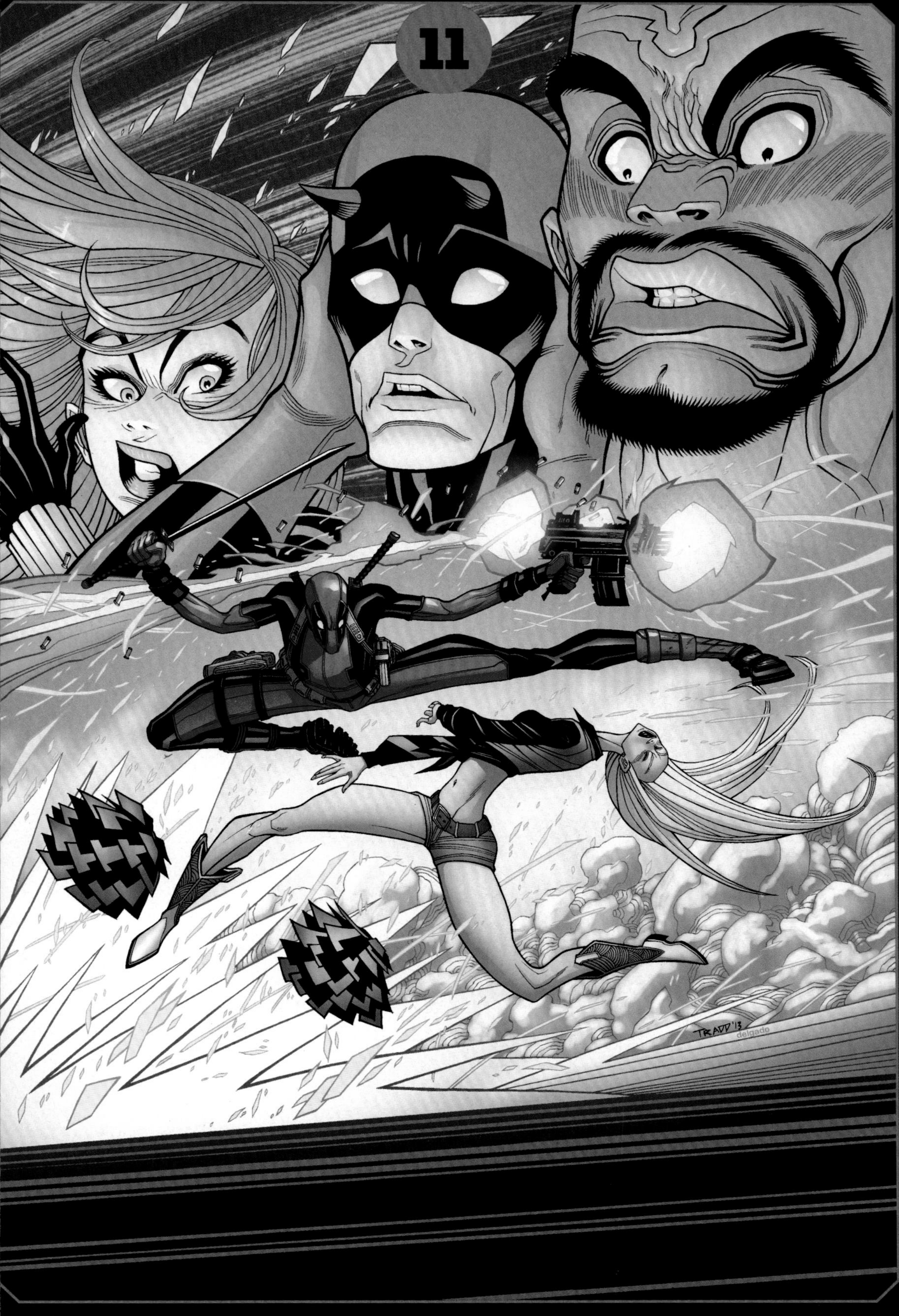
11
TRADD'13
delgado

# DARE TO BE DEVILED

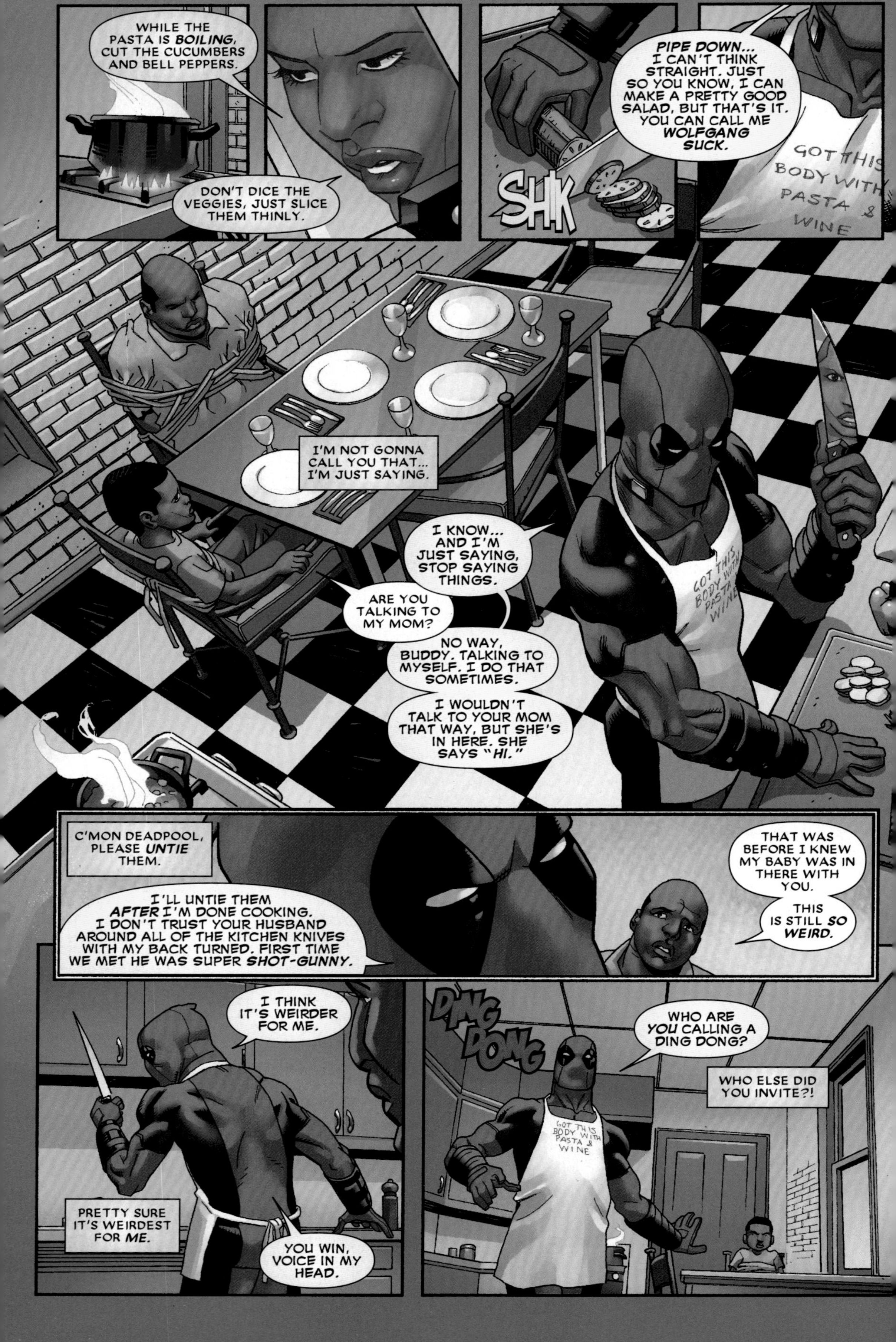
WHILE THE PASTA IS BOILING, CUT THE CUCUMBERS AND BELL PEPPERS.
DON'T DICE THE VEGGIES, JUST SLICE THEM THINLY.
SHIK
PIPE DOWN... I CAN'T THINK STRAIGHT. JUST SO YOU KNOW, I CAN MAKE A PRETTY GOOD SALAD, BUT THAT'S IT. YOU CAN CALL ME WOLFGANG SUCK.
GOT THIS BODY WITH PASTA & WINE
I'M NOT GONNA CALL YOU THAT... I'M JUST SAYING.
I KNOW... AND I'M JUST SAYING, STOP SAYING THINGS.
ARE YOU TALKING TO MY MOM?
NO WAY, BUDDY. TALKING TO MYSELF. I DO THAT SOMETIMES.
I WOULDN'T TALK TO YOUR MOM THAT WAY, BUT SHE'S IN HERE. SHE SAYS "HI."
C'MON DEADPOOL, PLEASE UNTIE THEM.
I'LL UNTIE THEM AFTER I'M DONE COOKING. I DON'T TRUST YOUR HUSBAND AROUND ALL OF THE KITCHEN KNIVES WITH MY BACK TURNED. FIRST TIME WE MET HE WAS SUPER SHOT-GUNNY.
THAT WAS BEFORE I KNEW MY BABY WAS IN THERE WITH YOU.
THIS IS STILL SO WEIRD.
I THINK IT'S WEIRDER FOR ME.
PRETTY SURE IT'S WEIRDEST FOR ME.
YOU WIN, VOICE IN MY HEAD.
DING DONG
WHO ARE YOU CALLING A DING DONG?
WHO ELSE DID YOU INVITE?!
GOT THIS BODY WITH PASTA & WINE

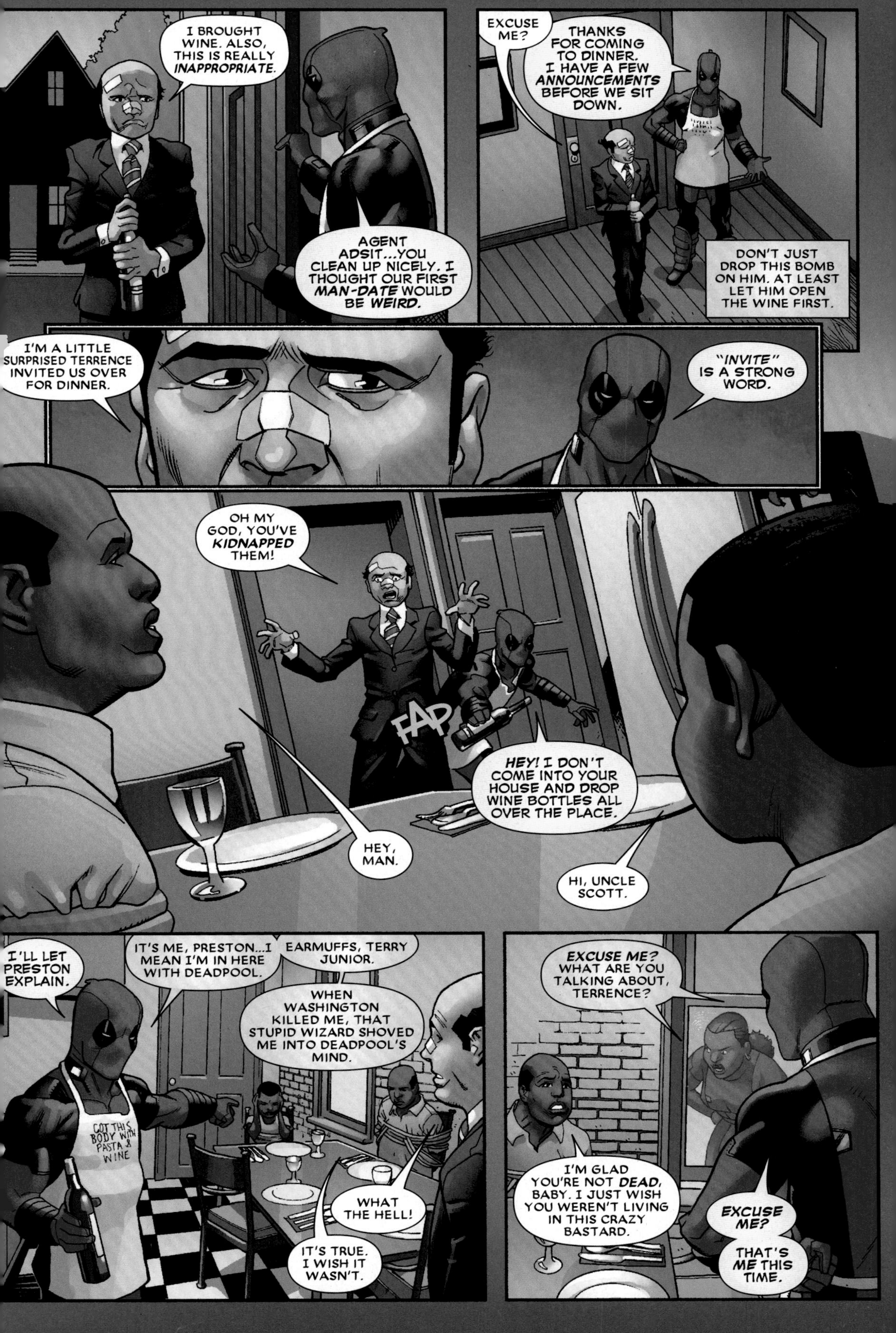
I BROUGHT WINE. ALSO, THIS IS REALLY INAPPROPRIATE.
AGENT ADSIT...YOU CLEAN UP NICELY. I THOUGHT OUR FIRST MAN-DATE WOULD BE WEIRD.
EXCUSE ME?
THANKS FOR COMING TO DINNER. I HAVE A FEW ANNOUNCEMENTS BEFORE WE SIT DOWN.
DON'T JUST DROP THIS BOMB ON HIM. AT LEAST LET HIM OPEN THE WINE FIRST.
I'M A LITTLE SURPRISED TERRENCE INVITED US OVER FOR DINNER.
"INVITE" IS A STRONG WORD.
OH MY GOD, YOU'VE KIDNAPPED THEM!
FAP
HEY! I DON'T COME INTO YOUR HOUSE AND DROP WINE BOTTLES ALL OVER THE PLACE.
HEY, MAN.
HI, UNCLE SCOTT.
I'LL LET PRESTON EXPLAIN.
IT'S ME, PRESTON...I MEAN I'M IN HERE WITH DEADPOOL.
EARMUFFS, TERRY JUNIOR.
WHEN WASHINGTON KILLED ME, THAT STUPID WIZARD SHOVED ME INTO DEADPOOL'S MIND.
GOT THIS BODY WITH PASTA & WINE
WHAT THE HELL!
IT'S TRUE. I WISH IT WASN'T.
EXCUSE ME? WHAT ARE YOU TALKING ABOUT, TERRENCE?
I'M GLAD YOU'RE NOT DEAD, BABY. I JUST WISH YOU WEREN'T LIVING IN THIS CRAZY BASTARD.
EXCUSE ME?
THAT'S ME THIS TIME.

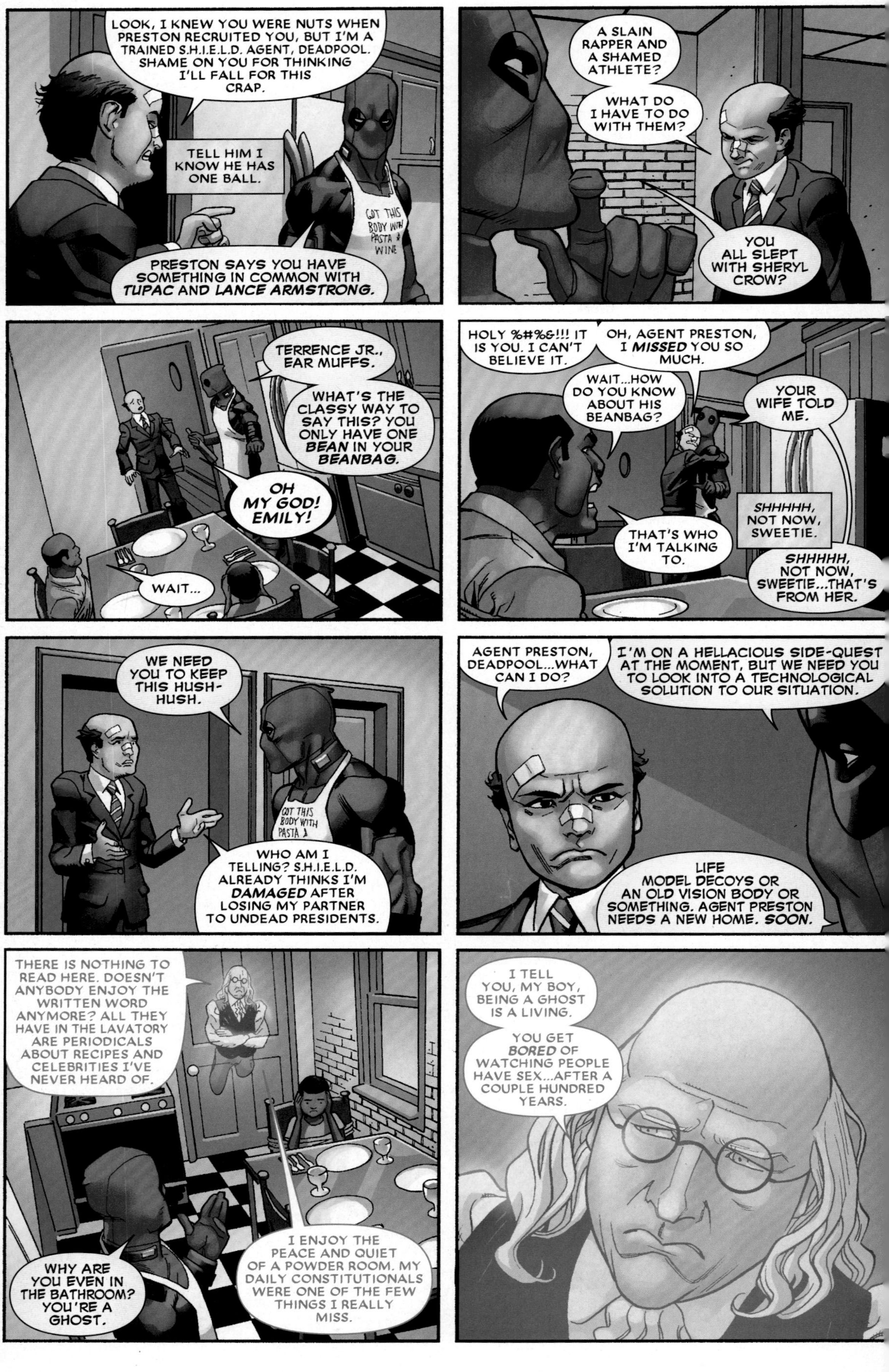
LOOK, I KNEW YOU WERE NUTS WHEN PRESTON RECRUITED YOU, BUT I'M A TRAINED S.H.I.E.L.D. AGENT, DEADPOOL. SHAME ON YOU FOR THINKING I'LL FALL FOR THIS CRAP.
TELL HIM I KNOW HE HAS ONE BALL.
GOT THIS BODY WITH PASTA & WINE
PRESTON SAYS YOU HAVE SOMETHING IN COMMON WITH TUPAC AND LANCE ARMSTRONG.
A SLAIN RAPPER AND A SHAMED ATHLETE?
WHAT DO I HAVE TO DO WITH THEM?
YOU ALL SLEPT WITH SHERYL CROW?
TERRENCE JR., EAR MUFFS.
WHAT'S THE CLASSY WAY TO SAY THIS? YOU ONLY HAVE ONE BEAN IN YOUR BEANBAG.
OH MY GOD! EMILY!
WAIT...
HOLY %#%&!!! IT IS YOU. I CAN'T BELIEVE IT.
OH, AGENT PRESTON, I MISSED YOU SO MUCH.
WAIT...HOW DO YOU KNOW ABOUT HIS BEANBAG?
YOUR WIFE TOLD ME.
THAT'S WHO I'M TALKING TO.
SHHHHH, NOT NOW, SWEETIE.
SHHHHH, NOT NOW, SWEETIE...THAT'S FROM HER.
WE NEED YOU TO KEEP THIS HUSH-HUSH.
GOT THIS BODY WITH PASTA &
WHO AM I TELLING? S.H.I.E.L.D. ALREADY THINKS I'M DAMAGED AFTER LOSING MY PARTNER TO UNDEAD PRESIDENTS.
AGENT PRESTON, DEADPOOL...WHAT CAN I DO?
I'M ON A HELLACIOUS SIDE-QUEST AT THE MOMENT, BUT WE NEED YOU TO LOOK INTO A TECHNOLOGICAL SOLUTION TO OUR SITUATION.
LIFE MODEL DECOYS OR AN OLD VISION BODY OR SOMETHING. AGENT PRESTON NEEDS A NEW HOME. SOON.
THERE IS NOTHING TO READ HERE. DOESN'T ANYBODY ENJOY THE WRITTEN WORD ANYMORE? ALL THEY HAVE IN THE LAVATORY ARE PERIODICALS ABOUT RECIPES AND CELEBRITIES I'VE NEVER HEARD OF.
WHY ARE YOU EVEN IN THE BATHROOM? YOU'RE A GHOST.
I ENJOY THE PEACE AND QUIET OF A POWDER ROOM. MY DAILY CONSTITUTIONALS WERE ONE OF THE FEW THINGS I REALLY MISS.
I TELL YOU, MY BOY, BEING A GHOST IS A LIVING.
YOU GET BORED OF WATCHING PEOPLE HAVE SEX...AFTER A COUPLE HUNDRED YEARS.

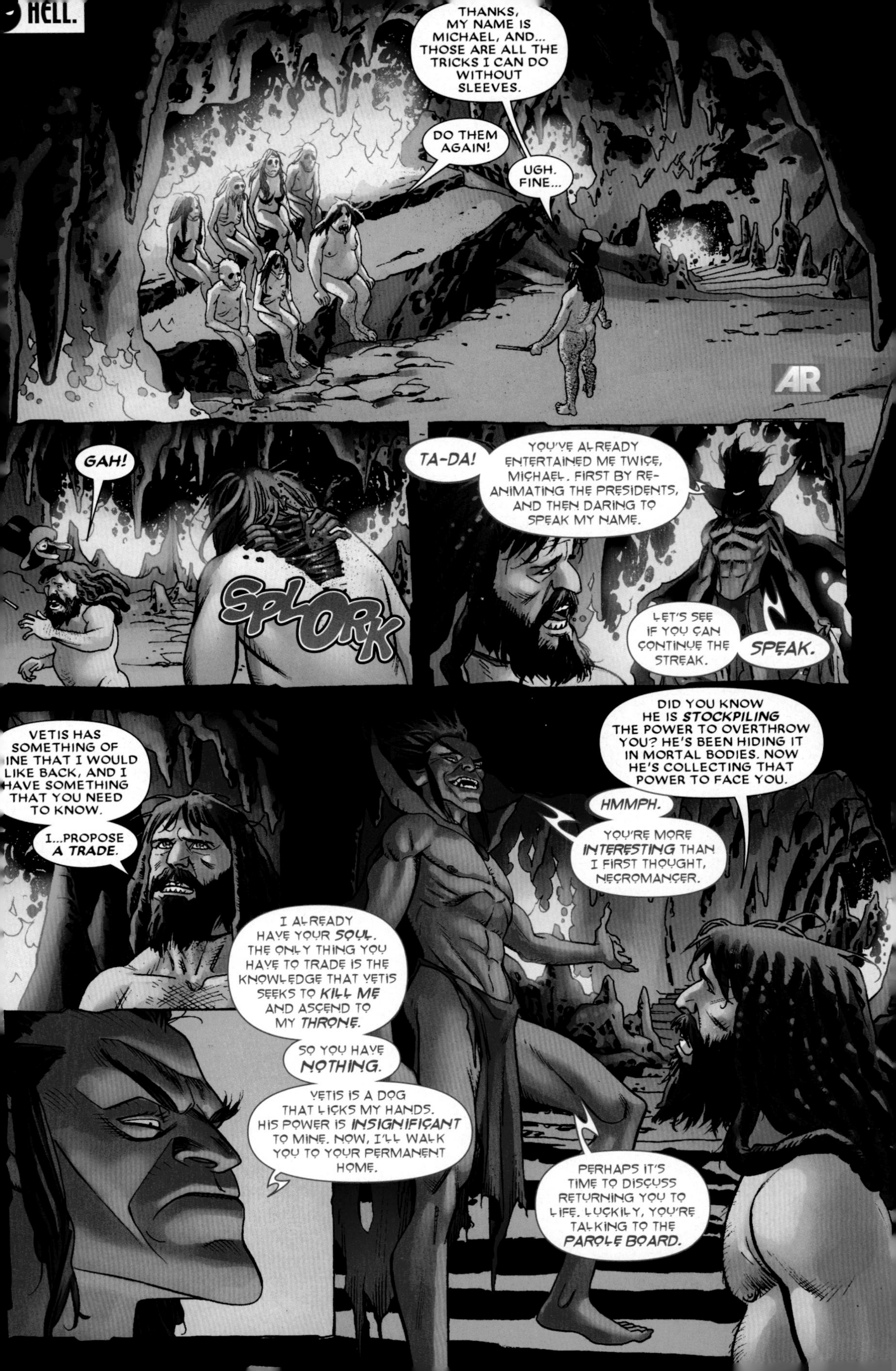
THANKS, MY NAME IS MICHAEL, AND... THOSE ARE ALL THE TRICKS I CAN DO WITHOUT SLEEVES.
DO THEM AGAIN!
UGH. FINE...
AR
GAH!
SPLORK
TA-DA!
YOU'VE ALREADY ENTERTAINED ME TWICE, MICHAEL. FIRST BY RE-ANIMATING THE PRESIDENTS, AND THEN DARING TO SPEAK MY NAME.
LET'S SEE IF YOU CAN CONTINUE THE STREAK.
SPEAK.
VETIS HAS SOMETHING OF INE THAT I WOULD LIKE BACK, AND I HAVE SOMETHING THAT YOU NEED TO KNOW.
I...PROPOSE A TRADE.
DID YOU KNOW HE IS STOCKPILING THE POWER TO OVERTHROW YOU? HE'S BEEN HIDING IT IN MORTAL BODIES. NOW HE'S COLLECTING THAT POWER TO FACE YOU.
HMMPH.
YOU'RE MORE INTERESTING THAN I FIRST THOUGHT, NECROMANCER.
I ALREADY HAVE YOUR SOUL. THE ONLY THING YOU HAVE TO TRADE IS THE KNOWLEDGE THAT VETIS SEEKS TO KILL ME AND ASCEND TO MY THRONE.
SO YOU HAVE NOTHING.
VETIS IS A DOG THAT LICKS MY HANDS. HIS POWER IS INSIGNIFICANT TO MINE. NOW, I'LL WALK YOU TO YOUR PERMANENT HOME.
PERHAPS IT'S TIME TO DISCUSS RETURNING YOU TO LIFE. LUCKILY, YOU'RE TALKING TO THE PAROLE BOARD.

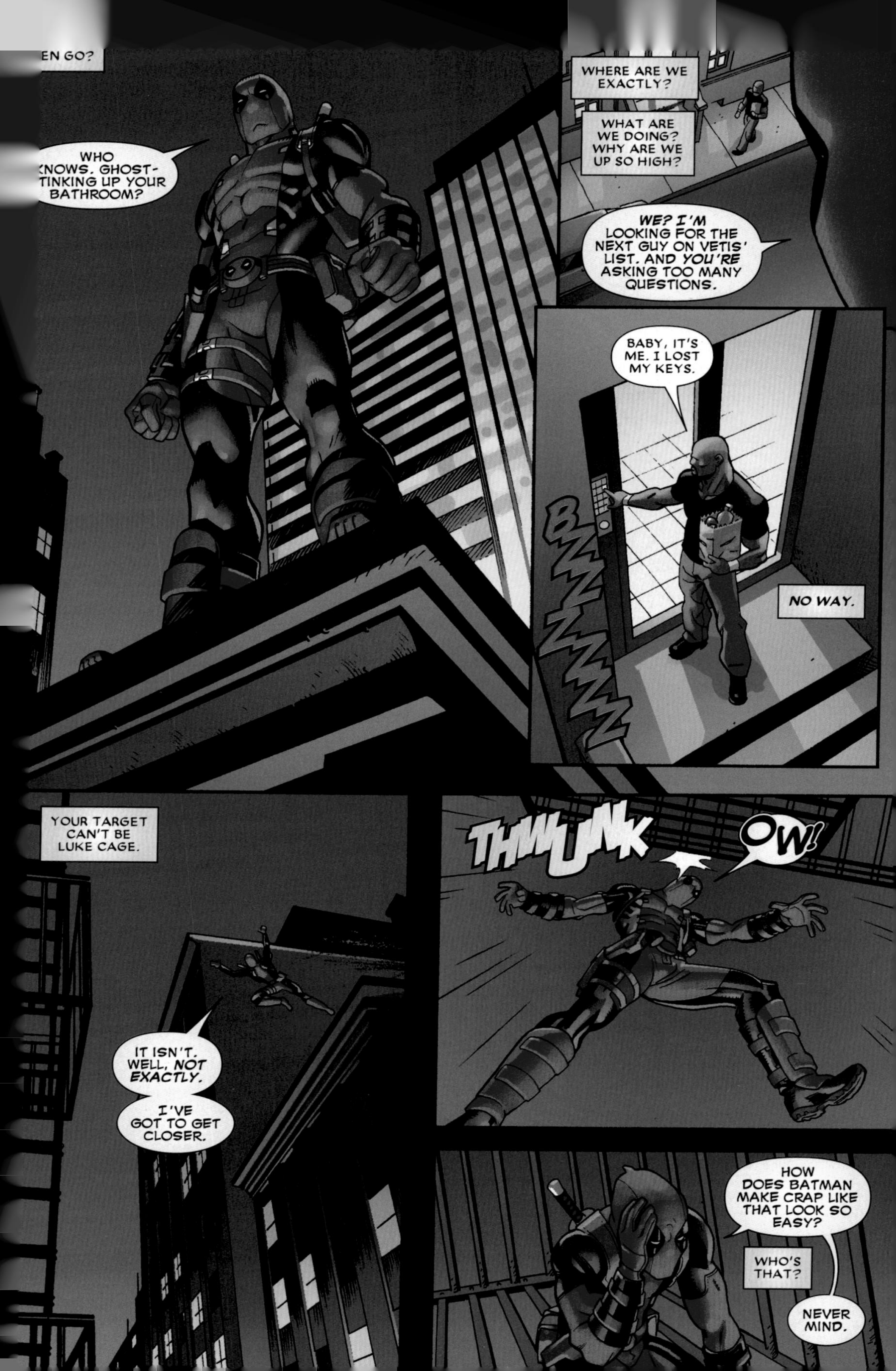

EN GO?
WHO KNOWS. GHOST-TINKING UP YOUR BATHROOM?
WHERE ARE WE EXACTLY?
WHAT ARE WE DOING? WHY ARE WE UP SO HIGH?
WE? I'M LOOKING FOR THE NEXT GUY ON VETIS' LIST. AND YOU'RE ASKING TOO MANY QUESTIONS.
BABY, IT'S ME. I LOST MY KEYS.
BZZZZZZZ
NO WAY.
YOUR TARGET CAN'T BE LUKE CAGE.
IT ISN'T. WELL, NOT EXACTLY.
I'VE GOT TO GET CLOSER.
THWUNK
OW!
HOW DOES BATMAN MAKE CRAP LIKE THAT LOOK SO EASY?
WHO'S THAT?
NEVER MIND.

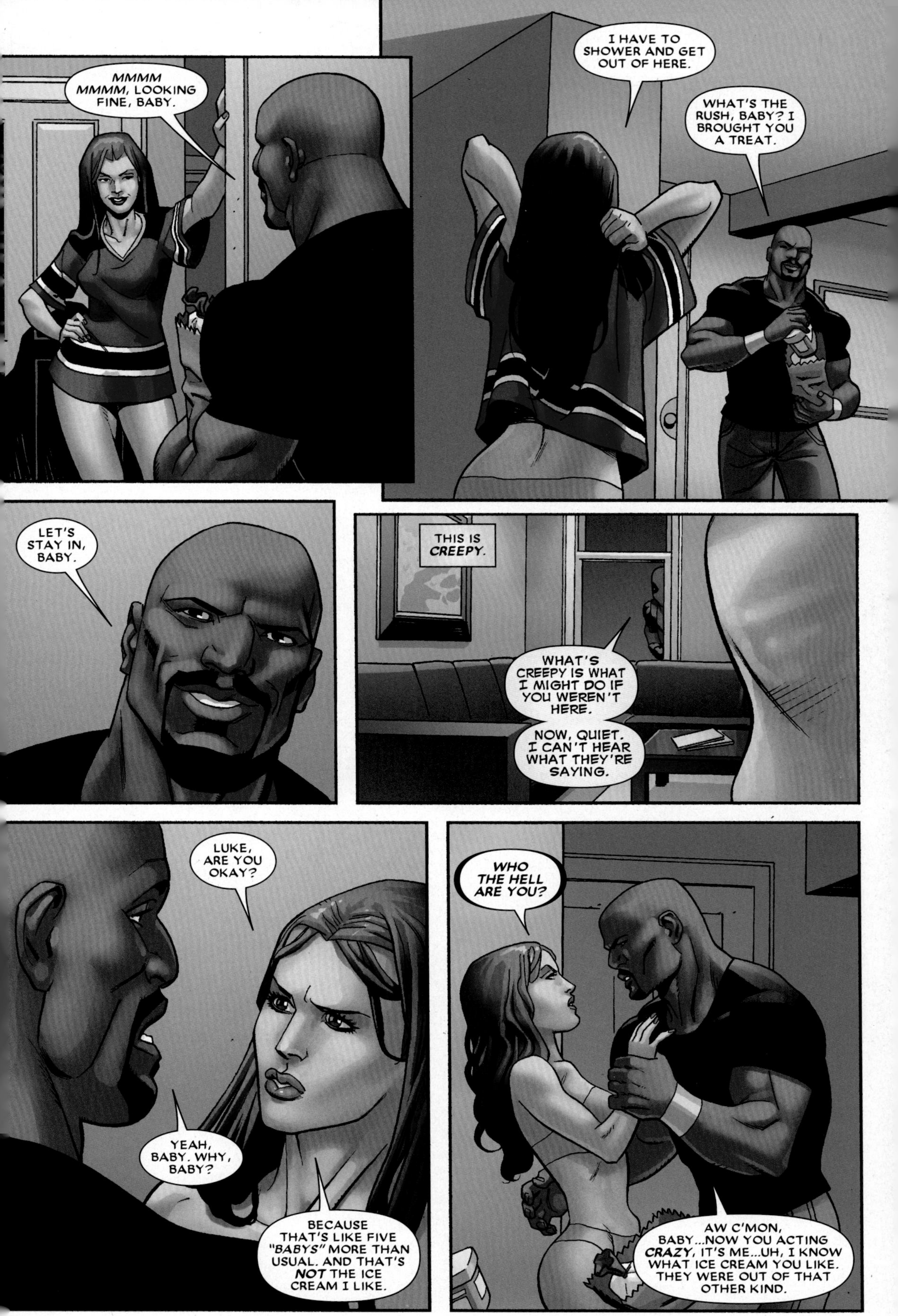
MMMM MMMM, LOOKING FINE, BABY.
I HAVE TO SHOWER AND GET OUT OF HERE.
WHAT'S THE RUSH, BABY? I BROUGHT YOU A TREAT.
LET'S STAY IN, BABY.
THIS IS CREEPY.
WHAT'S CREEPY IS WHAT I MIGHT DO IF YOU WEREN'T HERE.
NOW, QUIET. I CAN'T HEAR WHAT THEY'RE SAYING.
LUKE, ARE YOU OKAY?
YEAH, BABY. WHY, BABY?
BECAUSE THAT'S LIKE FIVE "BABYS" MORE THAN USUAL. AND THAT'S NOT THE ICE CREAM I LIKE.
WHO THE HELL ARE YOU?
AW C'MON, BABY...NOW YOU ACTING CRAZY, IT'S ME...UH, I KNOW WHAT ICE CREAM YOU LIKE. THEY WERE OUT OF THAT OTHER KIND.

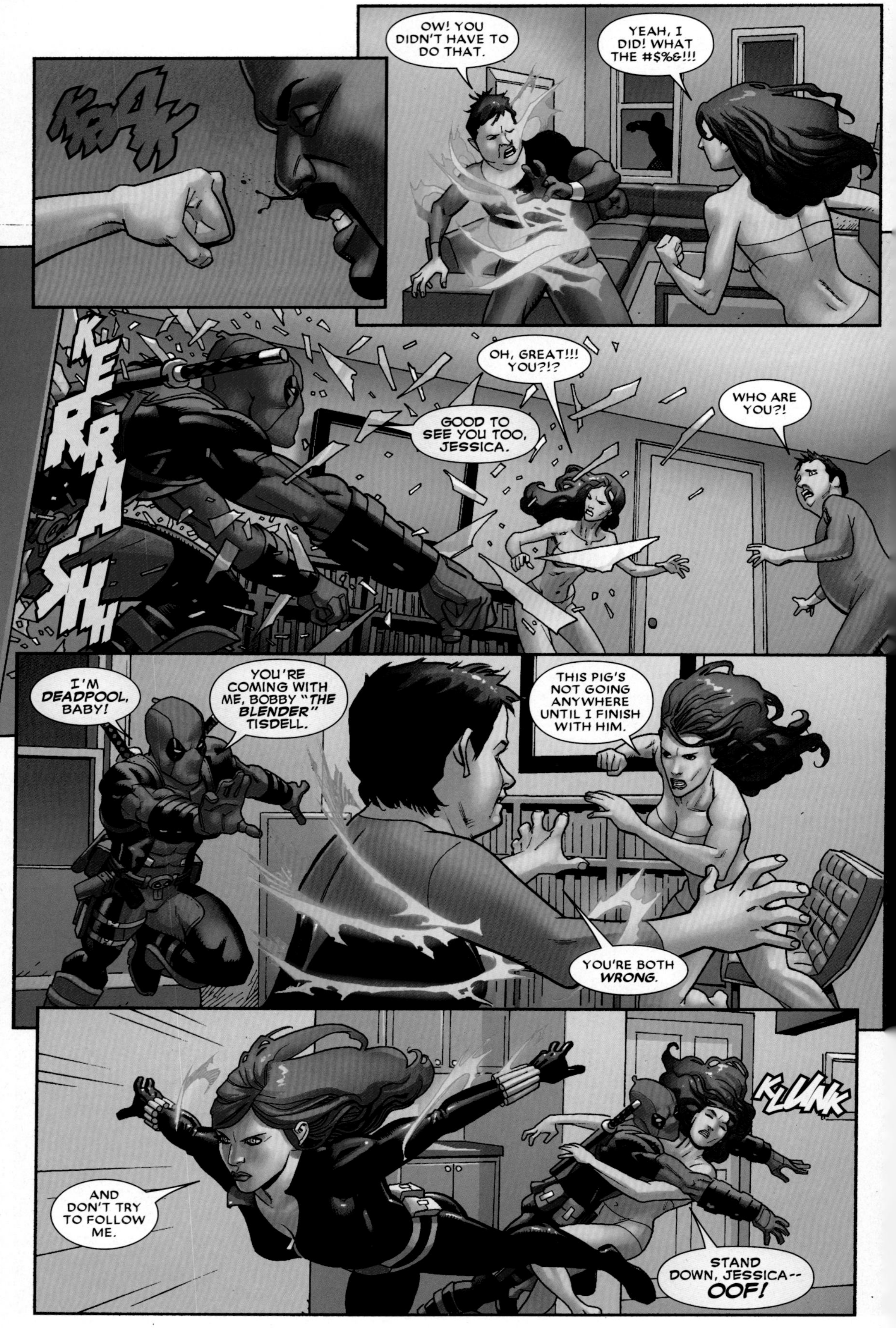
KRAK
OW! YOU DIDN'T HAVE TO DO THAT.
YEAH, I DID! WHAT THE #$%&!!!
KERRASHH
OH, GREAT!!! YOU?!?
GOOD TO SEE YOU TOO, JESSICA.
WHO ARE YOU?!
I'M DEADPOOL, BABY!
YOU'RE COMING WITH ME, BOBBY "THE BLENDER" TISDELL.
THIS PIG'S NOT GOING ANYWHERE UNTIL I FINISH WITH HIM.
YOU'RE BOTH WRONG.
KLUNK
AND DON'T TRY TO FOLLOW ME.
STAND DOWN, JESSICA-- OOF!

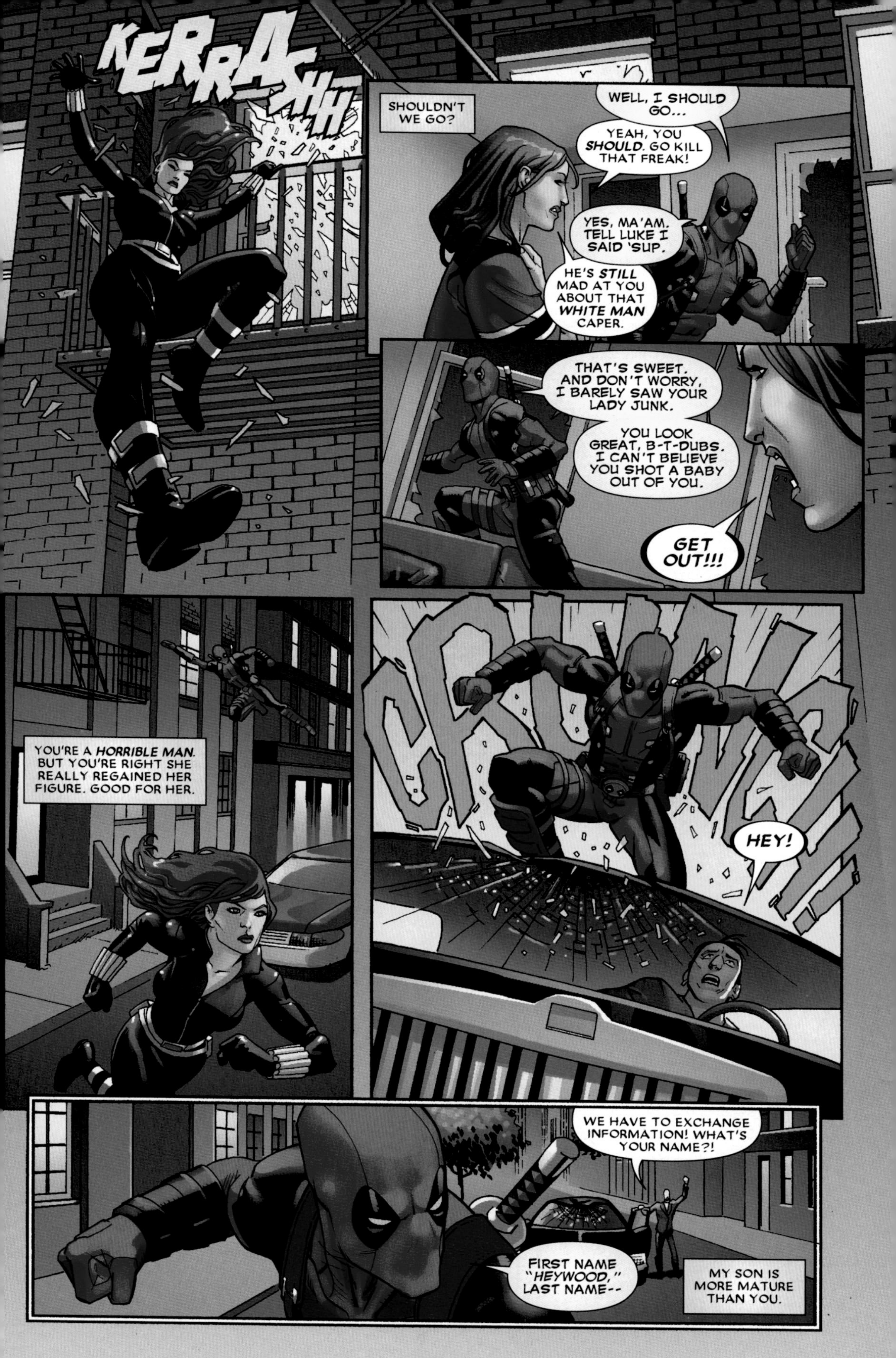
KERRASHH
SHOULDN'T WE GO?
WELL, I SHOULD GO...
YEAH, YOU SHOULD. GO KILL THAT FREAK!
YES, MA'AM. TELL LUKE I SAID 'SUP.
HE'S STILL MAD AT YOU ABOUT THAT WHITE MAN CAPER.
THAT'S SWEET. AND DON'T WORRY, I BARELY SAW YOUR LADY JUNK.
YOU LOOK GREAT, B-T-DUBS. I CAN'T BELIEVE YOU SHOT A BABY OUT OF YOU.
GET OUT!!!
YOU'RE A HORRIBLE MAN. BUT YOU'RE RIGHT SHE REALLY REGAINED HER FIGURE. GOOD FOR HER.
HEY!
WE HAVE TO EXCHANGE INFORMATION! WHAT'S YOUR NAME?!
FIRST NAME "HEYWOOD," LAST NAME--
MY SON IS MORE MATURE THAN YOU.

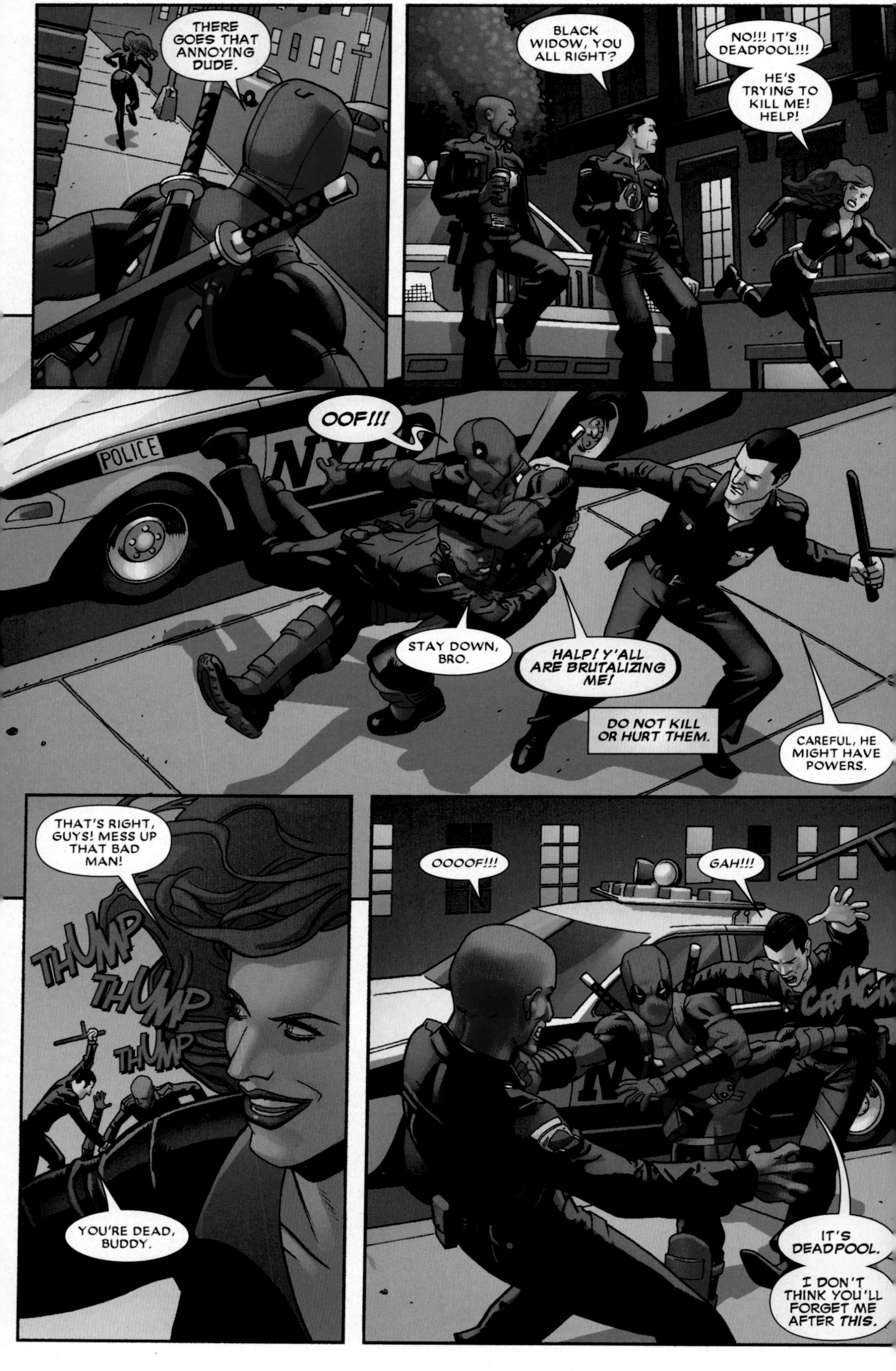
THERE GOES THAT ANNOYING DUDE.
BLACK WIDOW, YOU ALL RIGHT?
NO!!! IT'S DEADPOOL!!!
HE'S TRYING TO KILL ME! HELP!
POLICE
OOF!!!
STAY DOWN, BRO.
HALP! Y'ALL ARE BRUTALIZING ME!
DO NOT KILL OR HURT THEM.
CAREFUL, HE MIGHT HAVE POWERS.
THAT'S RIGHT, GUYS! MESS UP THAT BAD MAN!
THUMP
THUMP
THUMP
YOU'RE DEAD, BUDDY.
OOOOF!!!
GAH!!!
CRACK
IT'S DEADPOOL.
I DON'T THINK YOU'LL FORGET ME AFTER THIS.

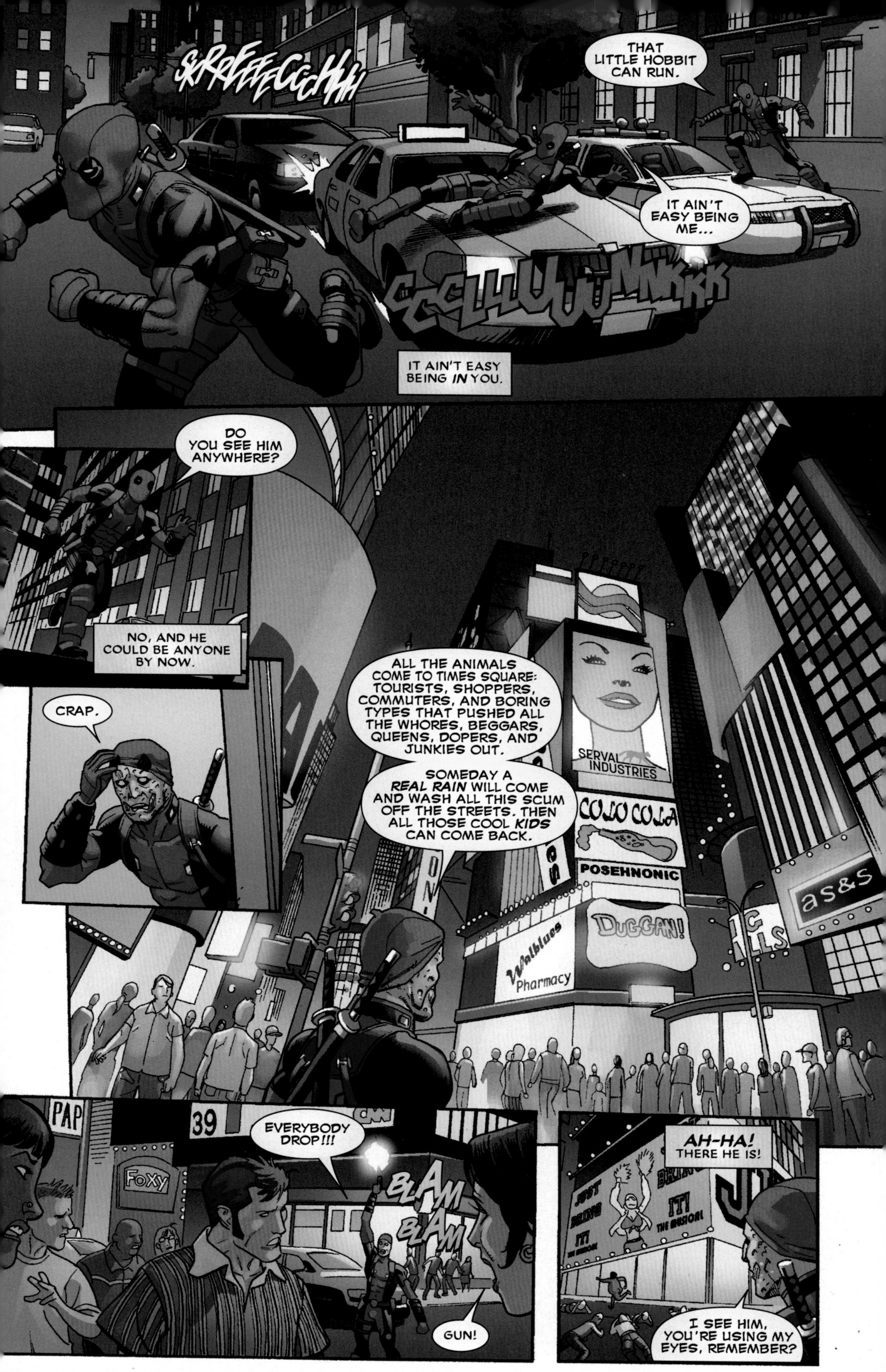
SKRREEEECCCHHH
THAT LITTLE HOBBIT CAN RUN.
IT AIN'T EASY BEING ME...
CCCLLUUUUNNKKK
IT AIN'T EASY BEING *IN* YOU.
DO YOU SEE HIM ANYWHERE?
NO, AND HE COULD BE ANYONE BY NOW.
CRAP.
ALL THE ANIMALS COME TO TIMES SQUARE: TOURISTS, SHOPPERS, COMMUTERS, AND BORING TYPES THAT PUSHED ALL THE WHORES, BEGGARS, QUEENS, DOPERS, AND JUNKIES OUT.
SOMEDAY A *REAL RAIN* WILL COME AND WASH ALL THIS SCUM OFF THE STREETS. THEN ALL THOSE COOL *KIDS* CAN COME BACK.
SERVAL INDUSTRIES
COLO COLA
POSEHNONIC
DUGGAN!
Walblues Pharmacy
as&s
PAP
39
Foxy
EVERYBODY DROP!!!
BLAM
BLAM
GUN!
*AH-HA!* THERE HE IS!
I SEE HIM, YOU'RE USING MY EYES, REMEMBER?

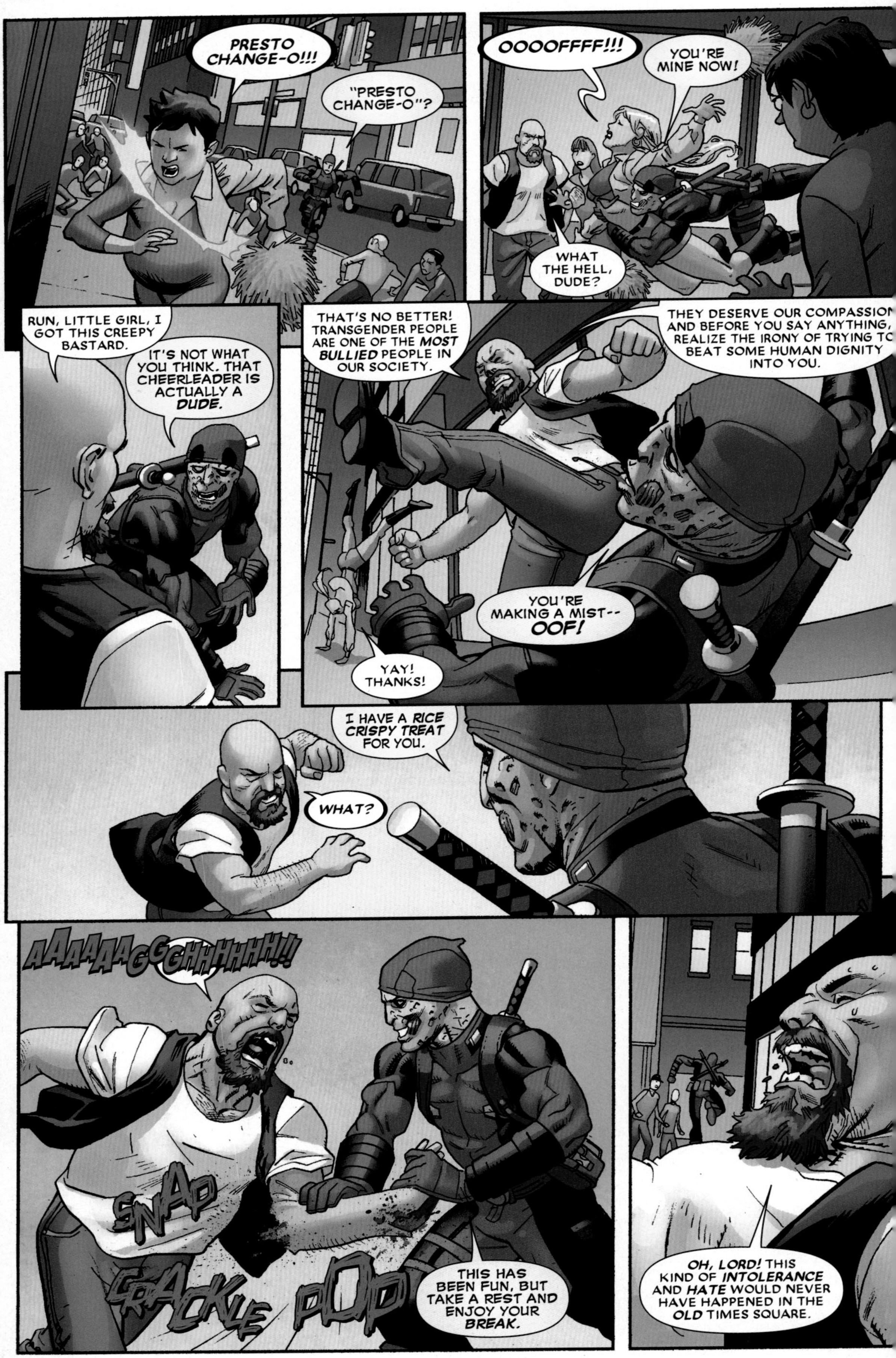
PRESTO CHANGE-O!!!
"PRESTO CHANGE-O"?
OOOOFFFF!!!
YOU'RE MINE NOW!
WHAT THE HELL, DUDE?
RUN, LITTLE GIRL, I GOT THIS CREEPY BASTARD.
IT'S NOT WHAT YOU THINK. THAT CHEERLEADER IS ACTUALLY A DUDE.
THAT'S NO BETTER! TRANSGENDER PEOPLE ARE ONE OF THE MOST BULLIED PEOPLE IN OUR SOCIETY.
THEY DESERVE OUR COMPASSION AND BEFORE YOU SAY ANYTHING, REALIZE THE IRONY OF TRYING TO BEAT SOME HUMAN DIGNITY INTO YOU.
YOU'RE MAKING A MIST--OOF!
YAY! THANKS!
I HAVE A RICE CRISPY TREAT FOR YOU.
WHAT?
AAAAAAGGGHHHHHH!!!
SNAP
CRACKLE
POP
THIS HAS BEEN FUN, BUT TAKE A REST AND ENJOY YOUR BREAK.
OH, LORD! THIS KIND OF INTOLERANCE AND HATE WOULD NEVER HAVE HAPPENED IN THE OLD TIMES SQUARE.

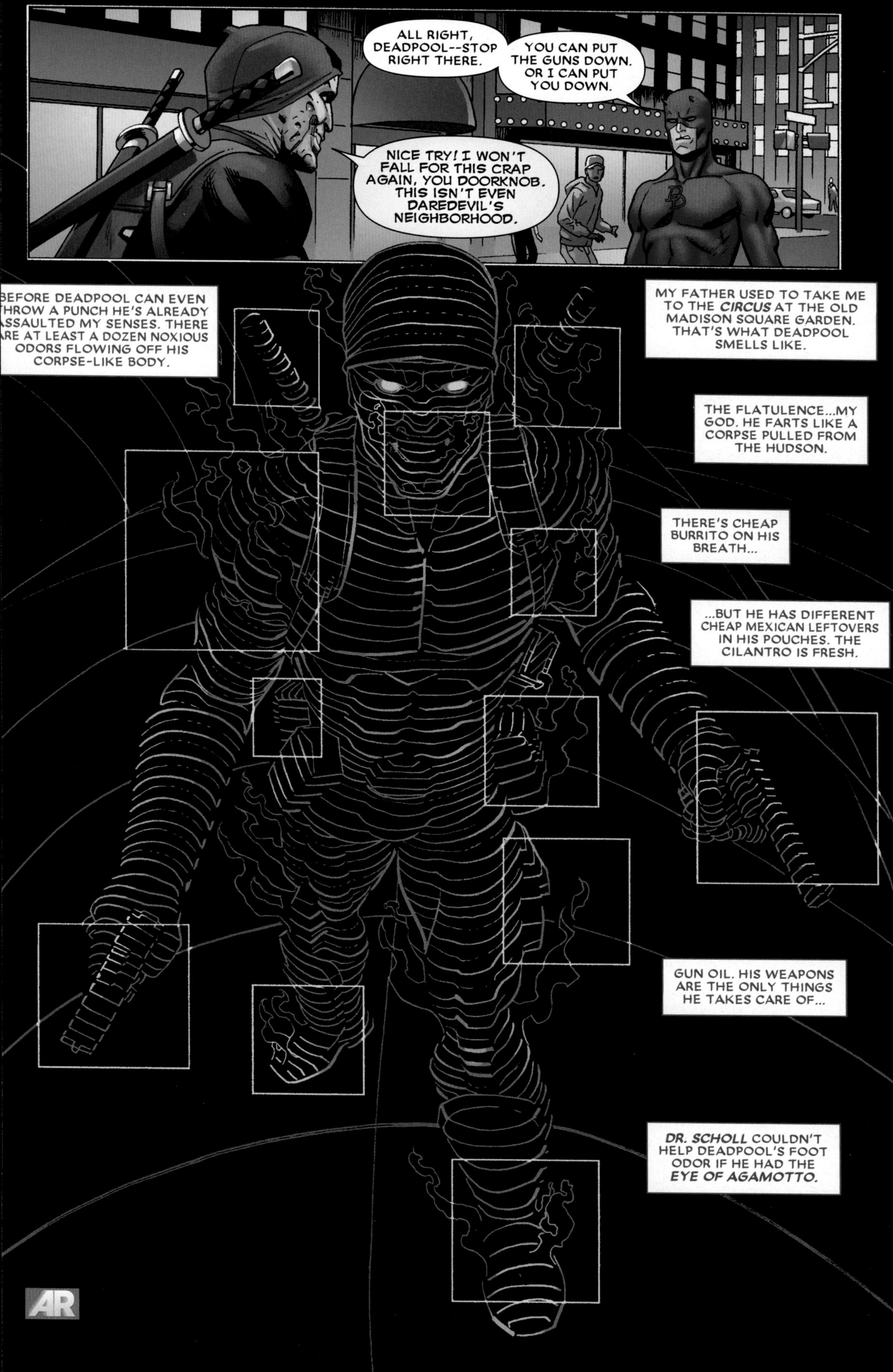
ALL RIGHT, DEADPOOL--STOP RIGHT THERE.
YOU CAN PUT THE GUNS DOWN. OR I CAN PUT YOU DOWN.
NICE TRY! I WON'T FALL FOR THIS CRAP AGAIN, YOU DOORKNOB. THIS ISN'T EVEN DAREDEVIL'S NEIGHBORHOOD.
BEFORE DEADPOOL CAN EVEN THROW A PUNCH HE'S ALREADY ASSAULTED MY SENSES. THERE ARE AT LEAST A DOZEN NOXIOUS ODORS FLOWING OFF HIS CORPSE-LIKE BODY.
MY FATHER USED TO TAKE ME TO THE *CIRCUS* AT THE OLD MADISON SQUARE GARDEN. THAT'S WHAT DEADPOOL SMELLS LIKE.
THE FLATULENCE...MY GOD. HE FARTS LIKE A CORPSE PULLED FROM THE HUDSON.
THERE'S CHEAP BURRITO ON HIS BREATH...
...BUT HE HAS DIFFERENT CHEAP MEXICAN LEFTOVERS IN HIS POUCHES. THE CILANTRO IS FRESH.
GUN OIL. HIS WEAPONS ARE THE ONLY THINGS HE TAKES CARE OF...
*DR. SCHOLL* COULDN'T HELP DEADPOOL'S FOOT ODOR IF HE HAD THE *EYE OF AGAMOTTO.*

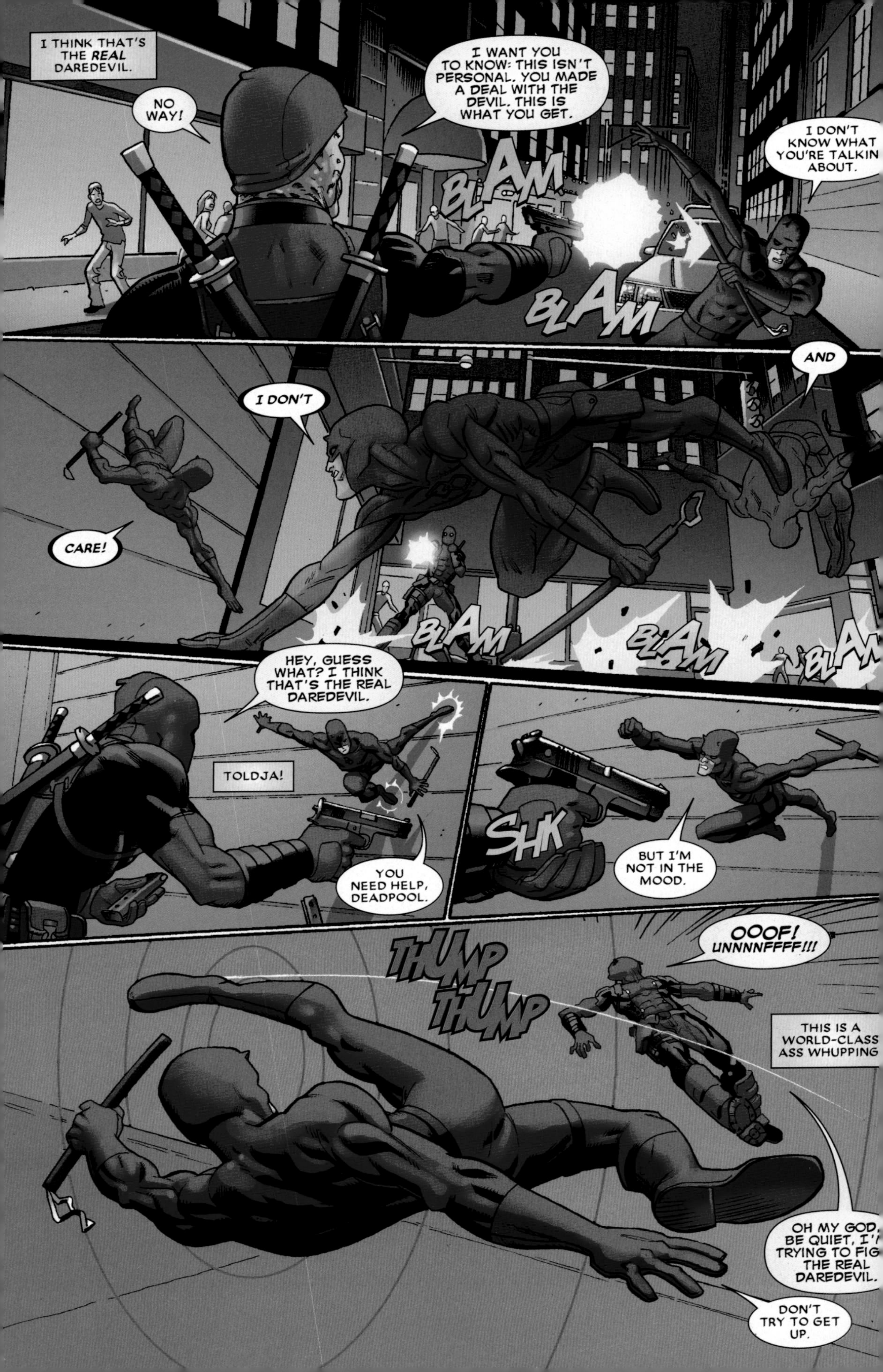
I THINK THAT'S THE REAL DAREDEVIL.
NO WAY!
I WANT YOU TO KNOW: THIS ISN'T PERSONAL. YOU MADE A DEAL WITH THE DEVIL. THIS IS WHAT YOU GET.
BLAM
I DON'T KNOW WHAT YOU'RE TALKIN ABOUT.
BLAM
I DON'T
AND
CARE!
BLAM
BLAM
BLAM
HEY, GUESS WHAT? I THINK THAT'S THE REAL DAREDEVIL.
TOLDJA!
YOU NEED HELP, DEADPOOL.
SHK
BUT I'M NOT IN THE MOOD.
THUMP THUMP
OOOF! UNNNNFFFF!!!
THIS IS A WORLD-CLASS ASS WHUPPING
OH MY GOD, BE QUIET, I' TRYING TO FIG THE REAL DAREDEVIL.
DON'T TRY TO GET UP.

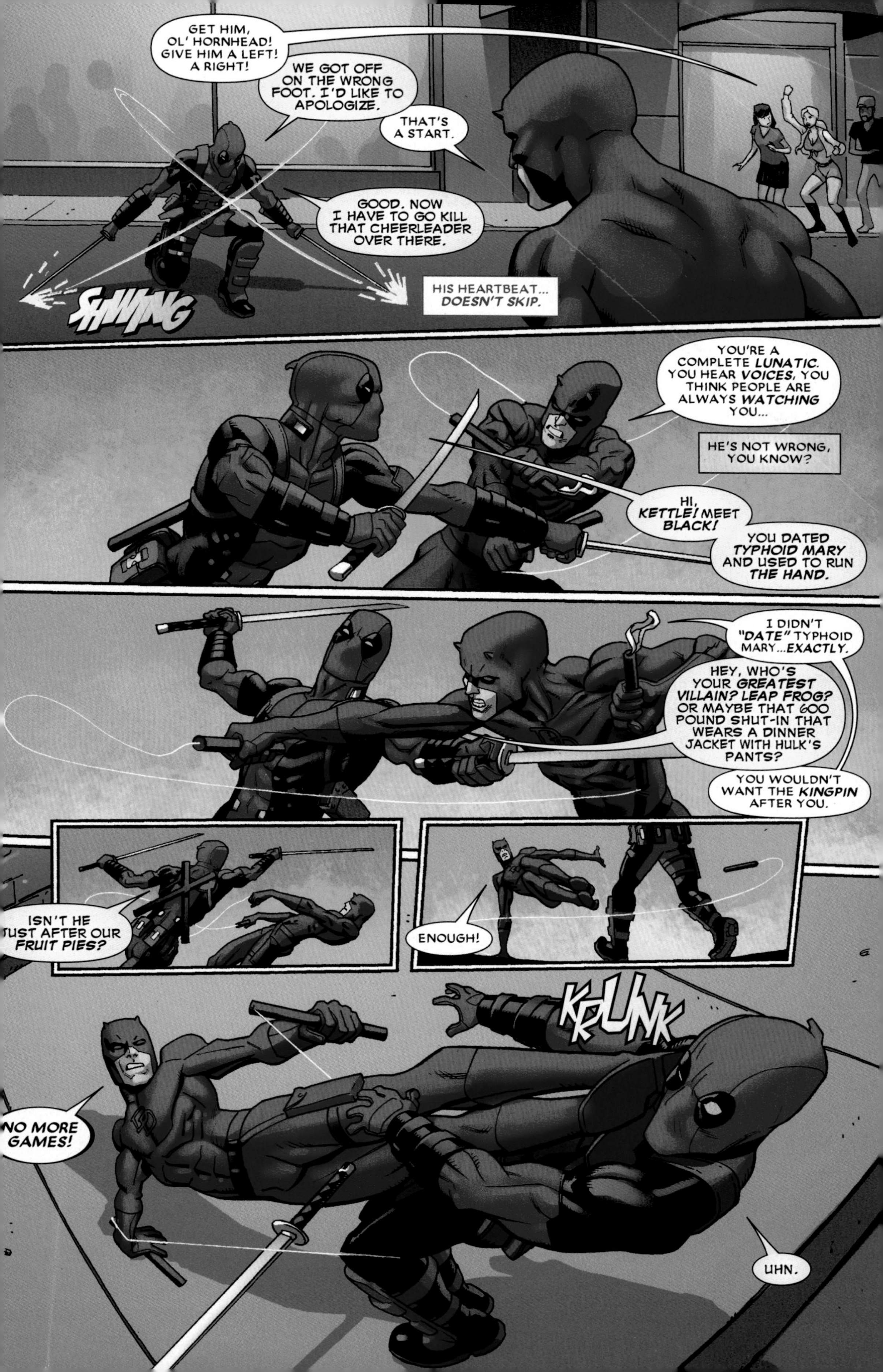
GET HIM, OL' HORNHEAD! GIVE HIM A LEFT! A RIGHT!
WE GOT OFF ON THE WRONG FOOT. I'D LIKE TO APOLOGIZE.
THAT'S A START.
GOOD. NOW I HAVE TO GO KILL THAT CHEERLEADER OVER THERE.
SHWING
HIS HEARTBEAT... DOESN'T SKIP.
YOU'RE A COMPLETE LUNATIC. YOU HEAR VOICES, YOU THINK PEOPLE ARE ALWAYS WATCHING YOU...
HE'S NOT WRONG, YOU KNOW?
HI, KETTLE! MEET BLACK!
YOU DATED TYPHOID MARY AND USED TO RUN THE HAND.
I DIDN'T "DATE" TYPHOID MARY...EXACTLY.
HEY, WHO'S YOUR GREATEST VILLAIN? LEAP FROG? OR MAYBE THAT 600 POUND SHUT-IN THAT WEARS A DINNER JACKET WITH HULK'S PANTS?
YOU WOULDN'T WANT THE KINGPIN AFTER YOU.
ISN'T HE JUST AFTER OUR FRUIT PIES?
ENOUGH!
KRUNK
NO MORE GAMES!
UHN.

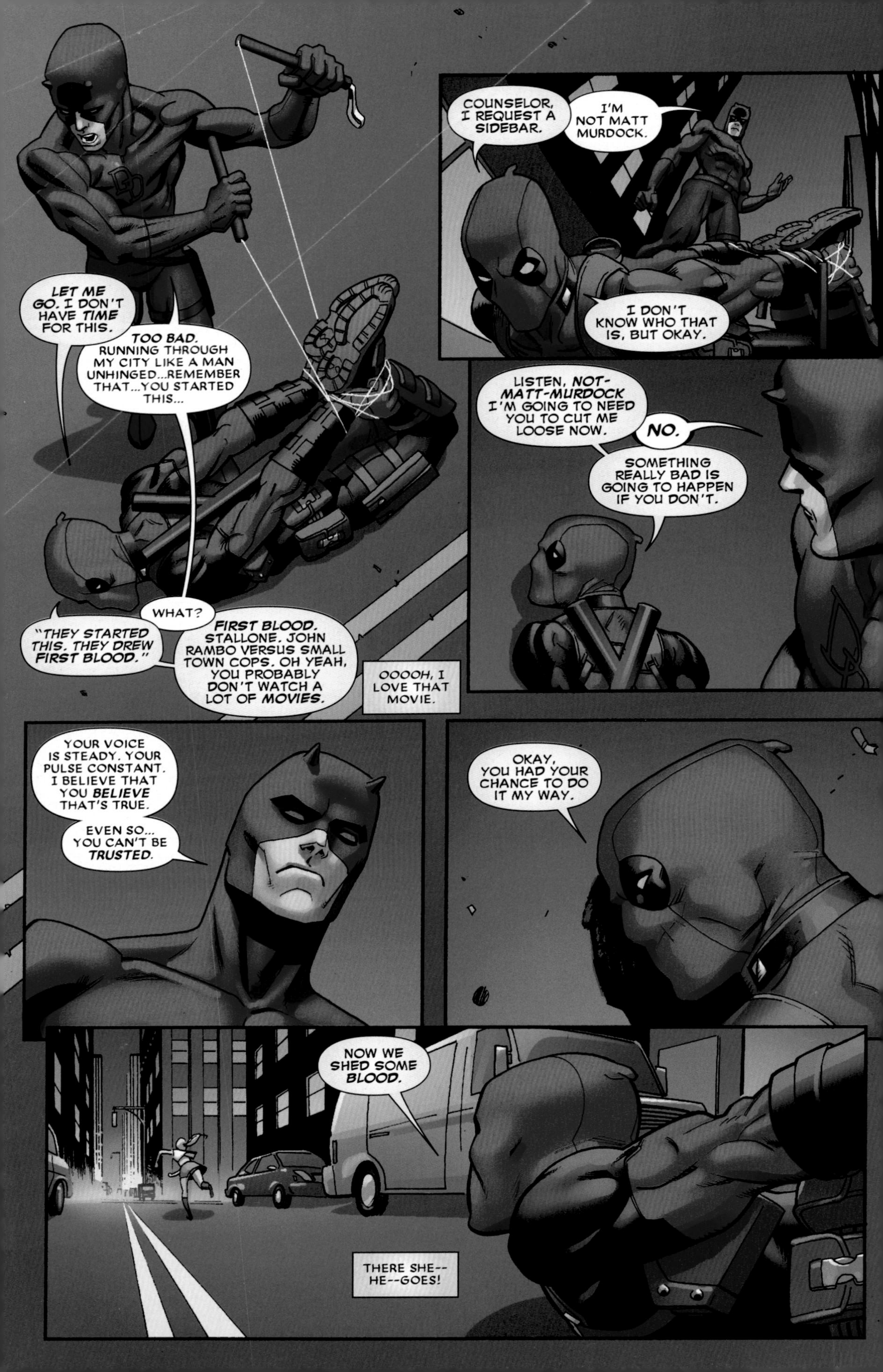
LET ME GO. I DON'T HAVE TIME FOR THIS.
TOO BAD. RUNNING THROUGH MY CITY LIKE A MAN UNHINGED...REMEMBER THAT...YOU STARTED THIS...
"THEY STARTED THIS. THEY DREW FIRST BLOOD."
WHAT?
FIRST BLOOD. STALLONE. JOHN RAMBO VERSUS SMALL TOWN COPS. OH YEAH, YOU PROBABLY DON'T WATCH A LOT OF MOVIES.
OOOOH, I LOVE THAT MOVIE.
COUNSELOR, I REQUEST A SIDEBAR.
I'M NOT MATT MURDOCK.
I DON'T KNOW WHO THAT IS, BUT OKAY.
LISTEN, NOT-MATT-MURDOCK I'M GOING TO NEED YOU TO CUT ME LOOSE NOW.
NO.
SOMETHING REALLY BAD IS GOING TO HAPPEN IF YOU DON'T.
YOUR VOICE IS STEADY. YOUR PULSE CONSTANT. I BELIEVE THAT YOU BELIEVE THAT'S TRUE.
EVEN SO... YOU CAN'T BE TRUSTED.
OKAY, YOU HAD YOUR CHANCE TO DO IT MY WAY.
NOW WE SHED SOME BLOOD.
THERE SHE--HE--GOES!

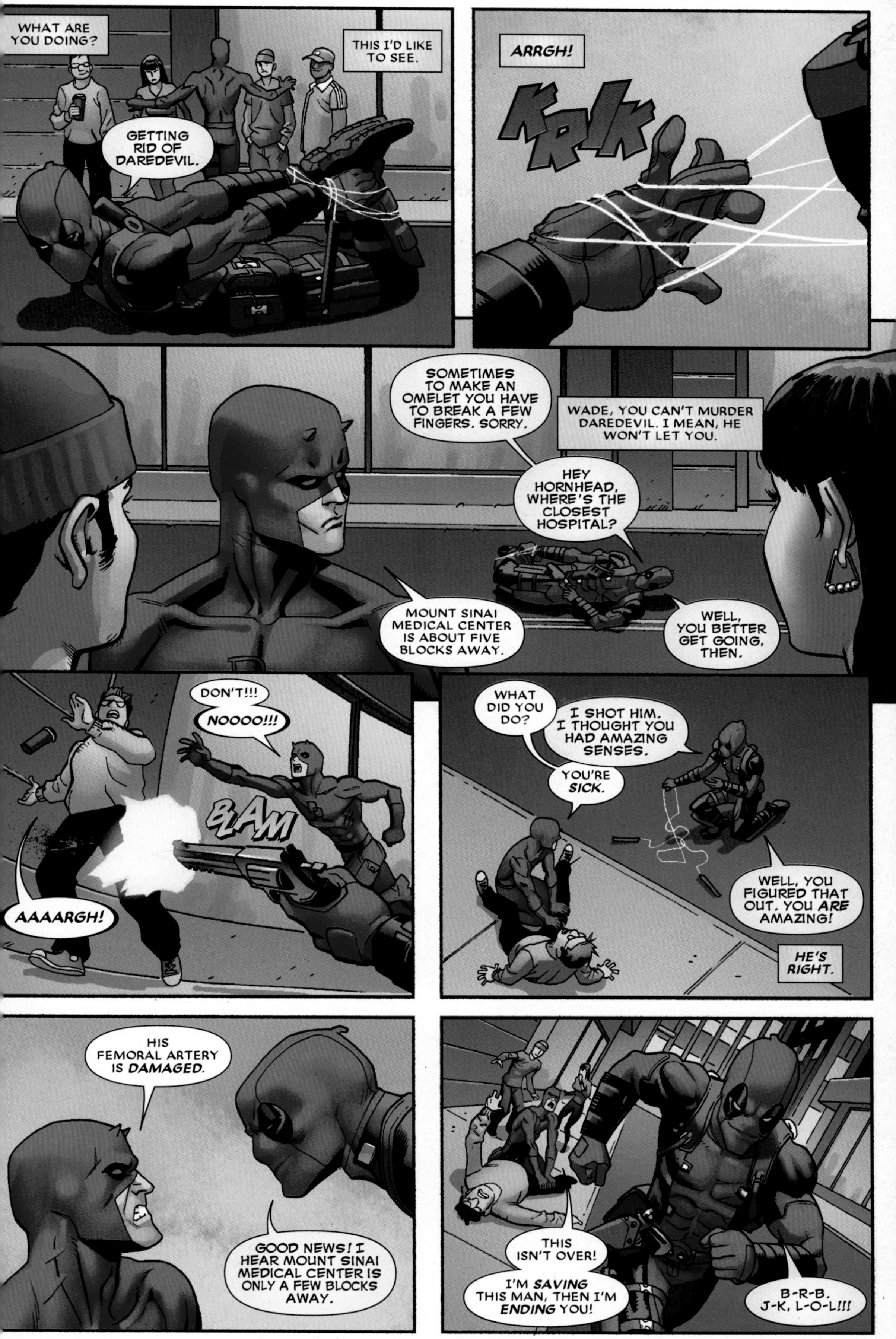

WHAT ARE YOU DOING?
GETTING RID OF DAREDEVIL.
THIS I'D LIKE TO SEE.
ARRGH!
KRIK
SOMETIMES TO MAKE AN OMELET YOU HAVE TO BREAK A FEW FINGERS. SORRY.
WADE, YOU CAN'T MURDER DAREDEVIL. I MEAN, HE WON'T LET YOU.
HEY HORNHEAD, WHERE'S THE CLOSEST HOSPITAL?
MOUNT SINAI MEDICAL CENTER IS ABOUT FIVE BLOCKS AWAY.
WELL, YOU BETTER GET GOING, THEN.
DON'T!!!
NOOOO!!!
BLAM
AAAARGH!
WHAT DID YOU DO?
I SHOT HIM. I THOUGHT YOU HAD AMAZING SENSES.
YOU'RE SICK.
WELL, YOU FIGURED THAT OUT. YOU ARE AMAZING!
HE'S RIGHT.
HIS FEMORAL ARTERY IS DAMAGED.
GOOD NEWS! I HEAR MOUNT SINAI MEDICAL CENTER IS ONLY A FEW BLOCKS AWAY.
THIS ISN'T OVER!
I'M SAVING THIS MAN, THEN I'M ENDING YOU!
B-R-B. J-K, L-O-L!!!

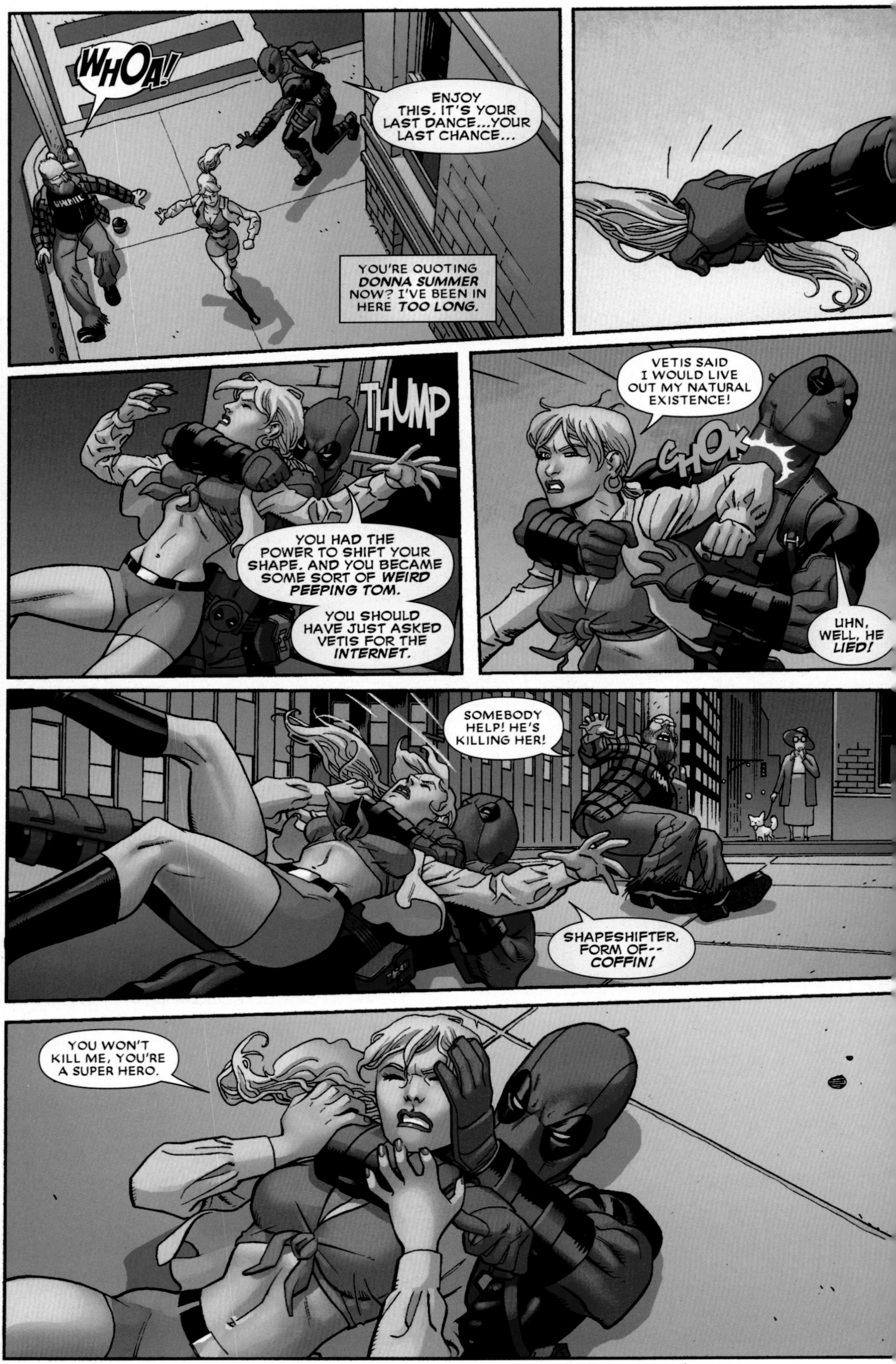
WHOA!
ENJOY THIS. IT'S YOUR LAST DANCE...YOUR LAST CHANCE...
YOU'RE QUOTING DONNA SUMMER NOW? I'VE BEEN IN HERE TOO LONG.
THUMP
YOU HAD THE POWER TO SHIFT YOUR SHAPE. AND YOU BECAME SOME SORT OF WEIRD PEEPING TOM.
YOU SHOULD HAVE JUST ASKED VETIS FOR THE INTERNET.
VETIS SAID I WOULD LIVE OUT MY NATURAL EXISTENCE!
CHOK
UHN, WELL, HE LIED!
SOMEBODY HELP! HE'S KILLING HER!
SHAPESHIFTER, FORM OF-- COFFIN!
YOU WON'T KILL ME, YOU'RE A SUPER HERO.

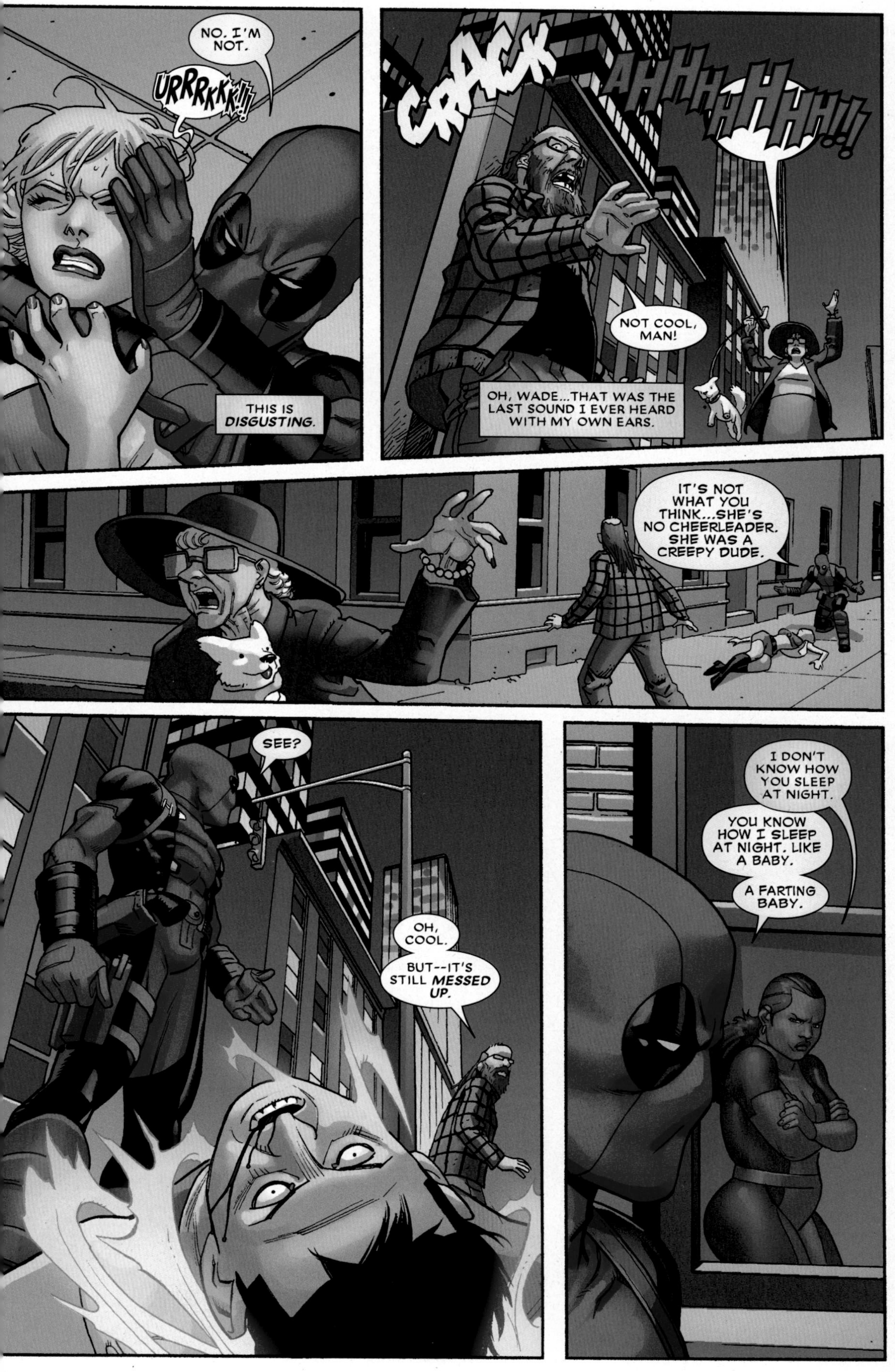

NO. I'M NOT.
URRRKKK!!!
THIS IS DISGUSTING.
CRACK
AHHHHHHHHH!!!
NOT COOL, MAN!
OH, WADE...THAT WAS THE LAST SOUND I EVER HEARD WITH MY OWN EARS.
IT'S NOT WHAT YOU THINK...SHE'S NO CHEERLEADER. SHE WAS A CREEPY DUDE.
SEE?
OH, COOL.
BUT--IT'S STILL MESSED UP.
I DON'T KNOW HOW YOU SLEEP AT NIGHT.
YOU KNOW HOW I SLEEP AT NIGHT. LIKE A BABY.
A FARTING BABY.

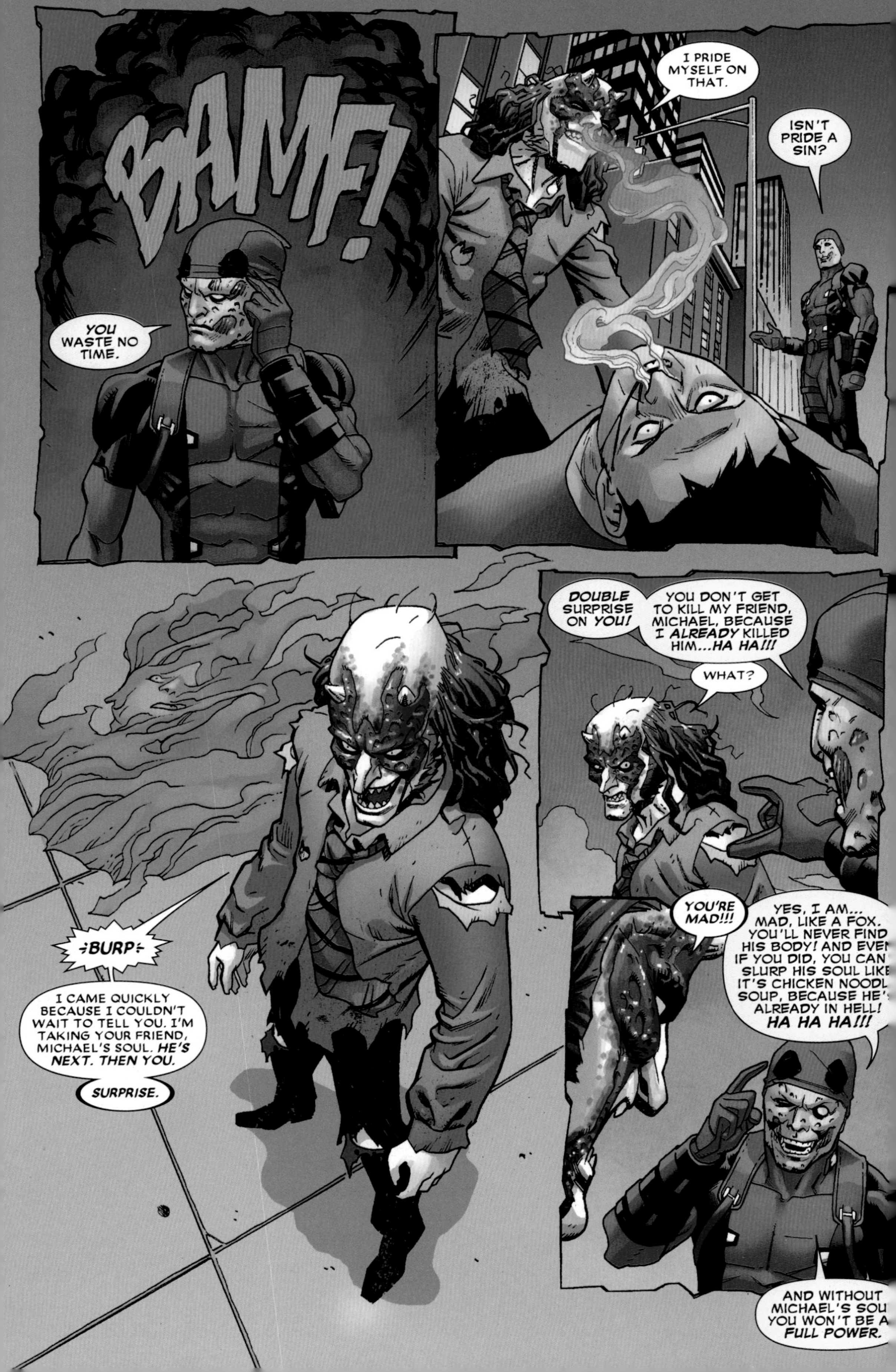
BAMF!
YOU WASTE NO TIME.
I PRIDE MYSELF ON THAT.
ISN'T PRIDE A SIN?
BURP
I CAME QUICKLY BECAUSE I COULDN'T WAIT TO TELL YOU. I'M TAKING YOUR FRIEND, MICHAEL'S SOUL. HE'S NEXT. THEN YOU.
SURPRISE.
DOUBLE SURPRISE ON YOU!
YOU DON'T GET TO KILL MY FRIEND, MICHAEL, BECAUSE I ALREADY KILLED HIM...HA HA!!!
WHAT?
YOU'RE MAD!!!
YES, I AM... MAD, LIKE A FOX. YOU'LL NEVER FIND HIS BODY! AND EVEN IF YOU DID, YOU CAN SLURP HIS SOUL LIKE IT'S CHICKEN NOODL SOUP, BECAUSE HE' ALREADY IN HELL! HA HA HA!!!
AND WITHOUT MICHAEL'S SOU YOU WON'T BE A FULL POWER.

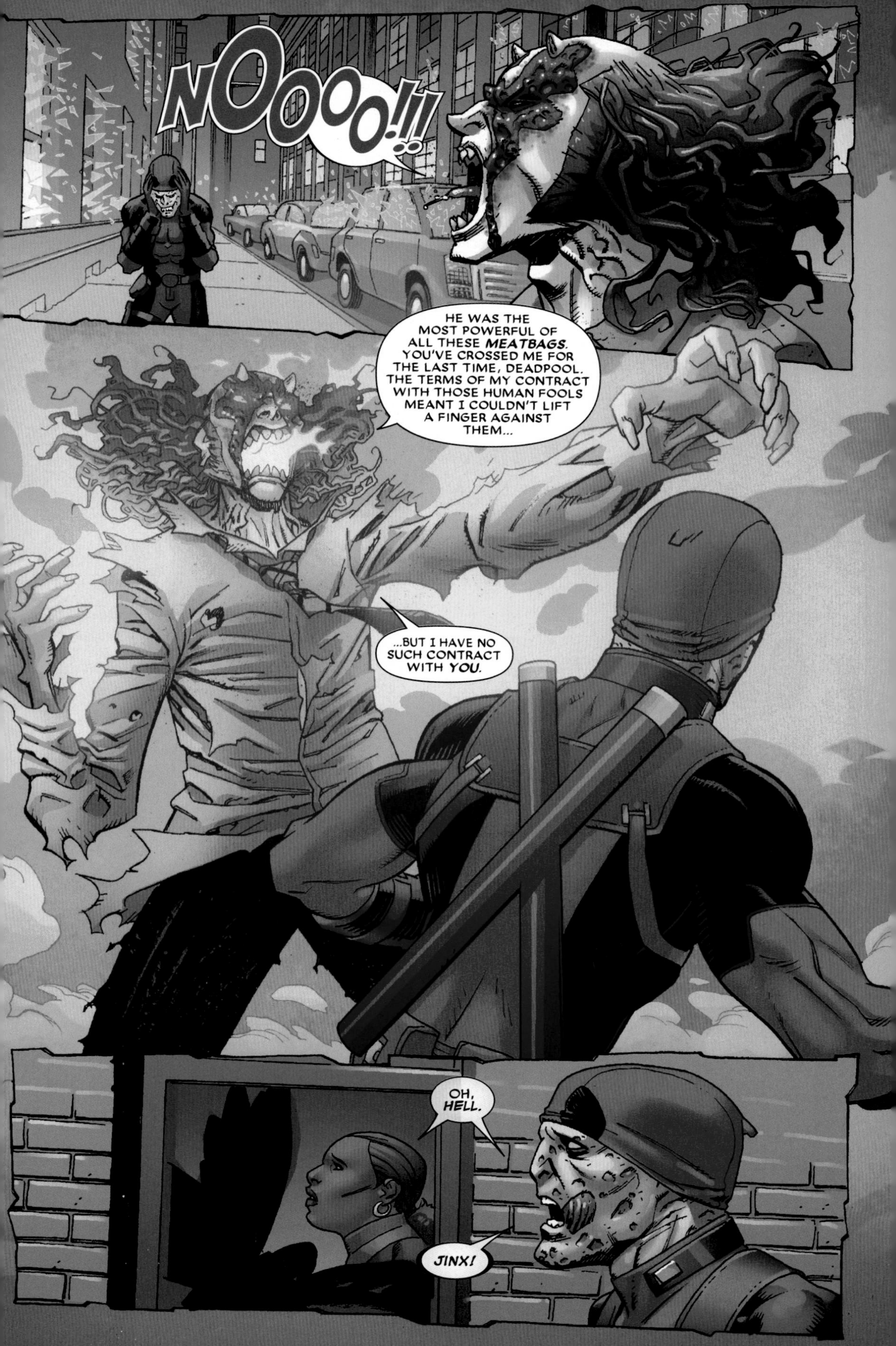
NOOOO!!!
HE WAS THE MOST POWERFUL OF ALL THESE MEATBAGS. YOU'VE CROSSED ME FOR THE LAST TIME, DEADPOOL. THE TERMS OF MY CONTRACT WITH THOSE HUMAN FOOLS MEANT I COULDN'T LIFT A FINGER AGAINST THEM...
...BUT I HAVE NO SUCH CONTRACT WITH YOU.
OH, HELL.
JINX!

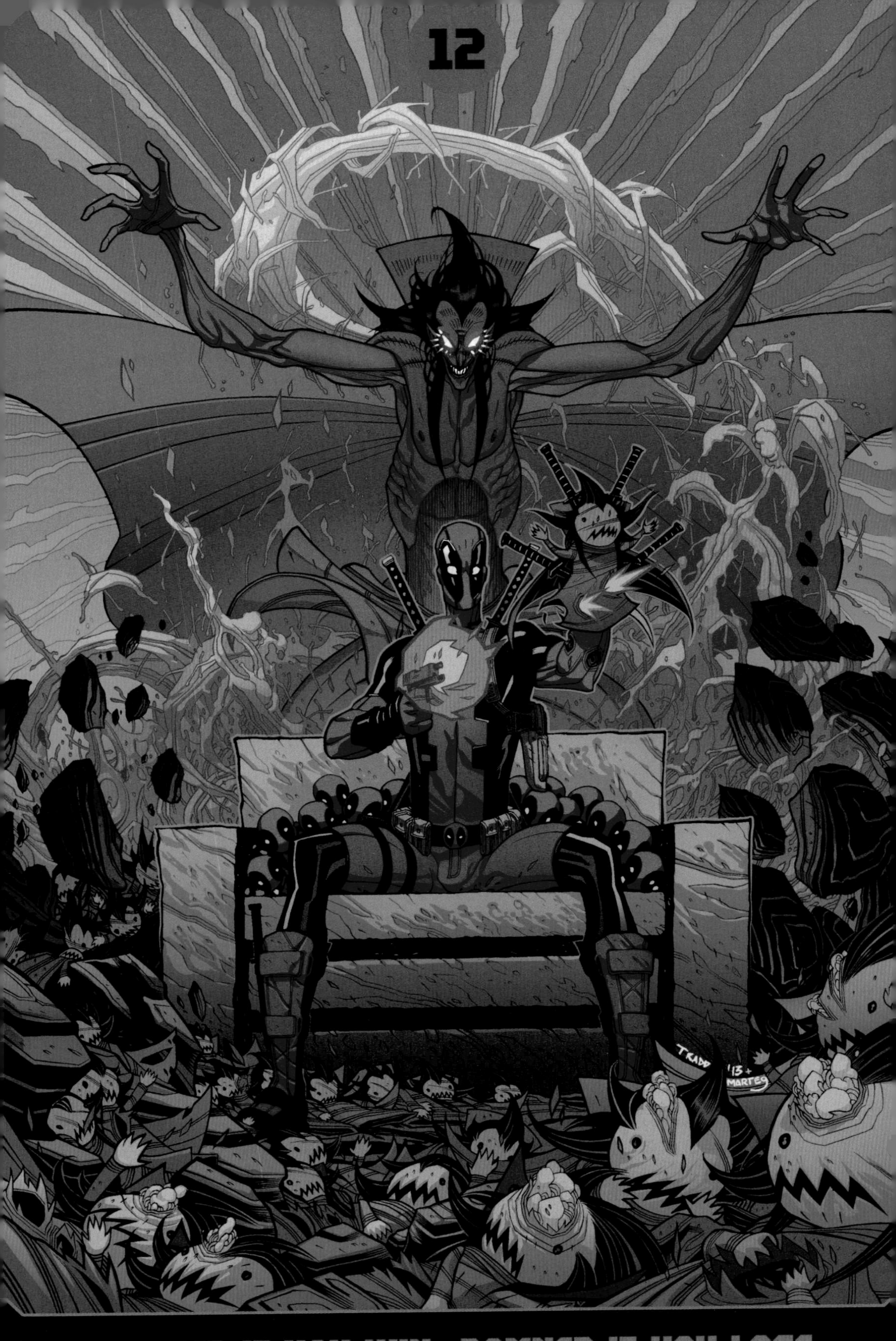
12

DAMNED IF YOU WIN, DAMNED IF YOU LOSE

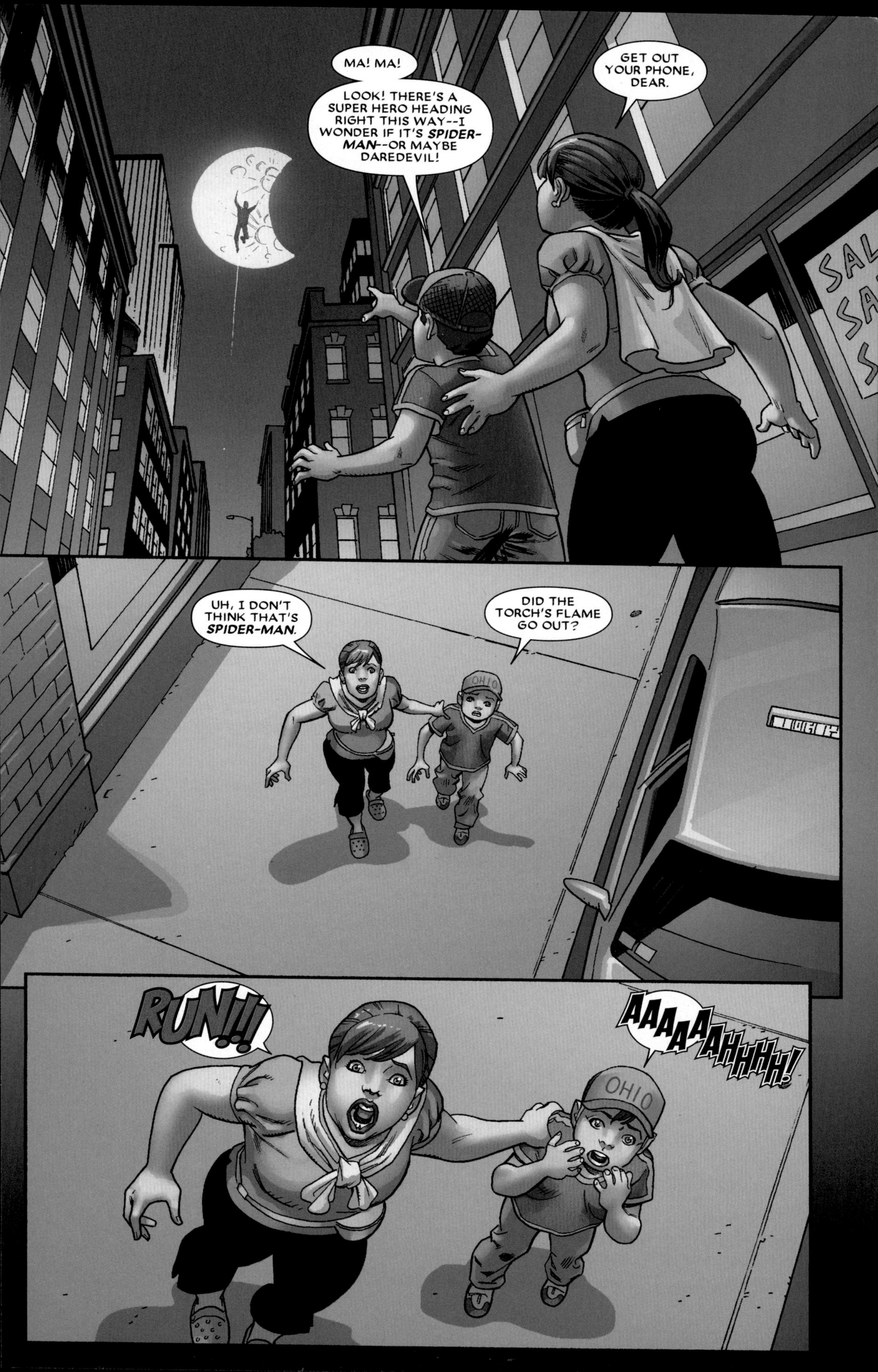
MA! MA!
LOOK! THERE'S A SUPER HERO HEADING RIGHT THIS WAY--I WONDER IF IT'S SPIDER-MAN--OR MAYBE DAREDEVIL!
GET OUT YOUR PHONE, DEAR.
SAL
SA
S
UH, I DON'T THINK THAT'S SPIDER-MAN.
DID THE TORCH'S FLAME GO OUT?
OHIO
RUN!!!
AAAAAAHHHH!
OHIO

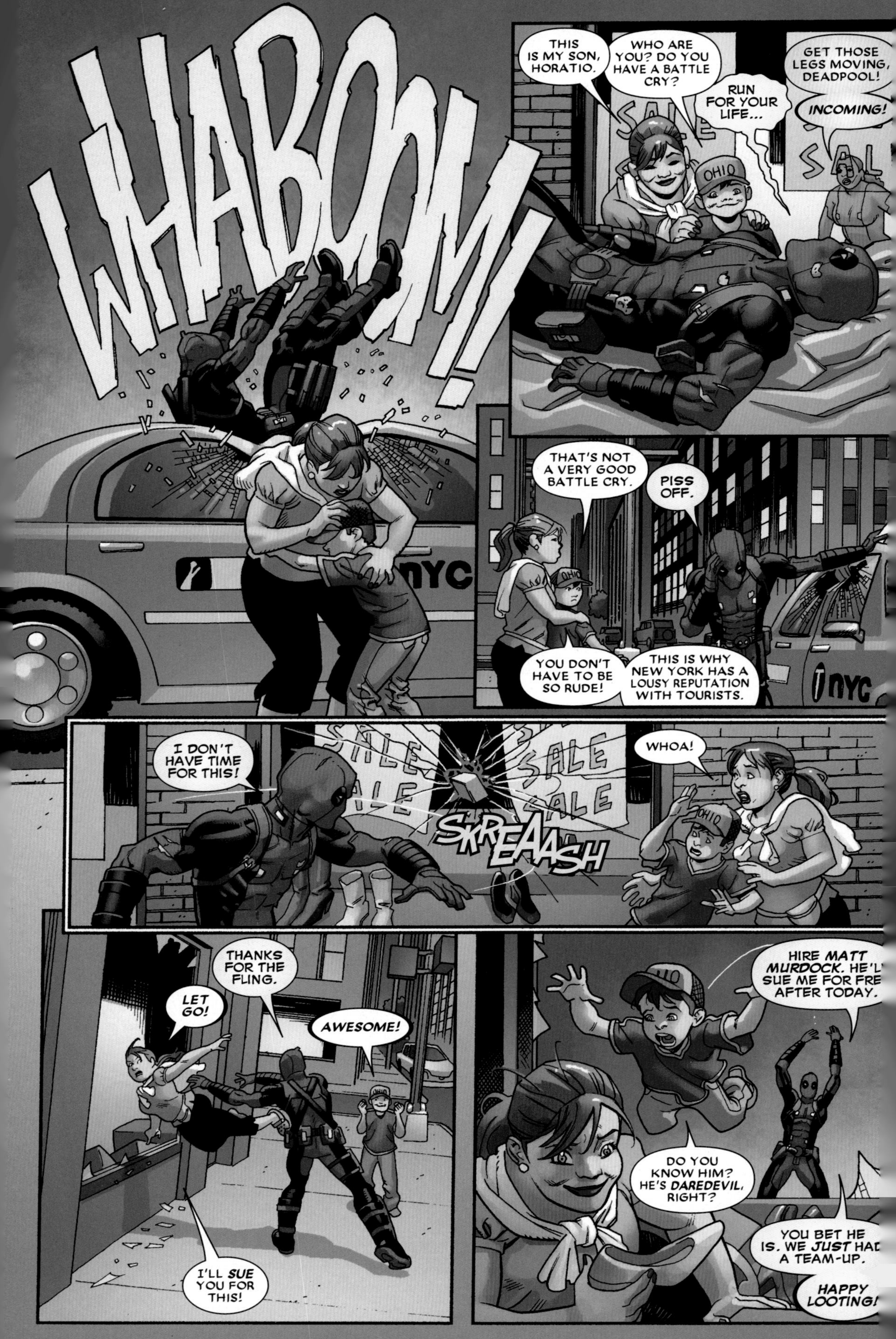
WHABOOM!
THIS IS MY SON, HORATIO.
WHO ARE YOU? DO YOU HAVE A BATTLE CRY?
RUN FOR YOUR LIFE...
GET THOSE LEGS MOVING, DEADPOOL!
INCOMING!
SALE
OHIO
THAT'S NOT A VERY GOOD BATTLE CRY.
PISS OFF.
YOU DON'T HAVE TO BE SO RUDE!
THIS IS WHY NEW YORK HAS A LOUSY REPUTATION WITH TOURISTS.
NYC
I DON'T HAVE TIME FOR THIS!
WHOA!
SKREEAASH
SALE
THANKS FOR THE FLING.
LET GO!
AWESOME!
I'LL SUE YOU FOR THIS!
HIRE MATT MURDOCK. HE'L SUE ME FOR FRE AFTER TODAY.
DO YOU KNOW HIM? HE'S DAREDEVIL, RIGHT?
YOU BET HE IS. WE JUST HAD A TEAM-UP.
HAPPY LOOTING!

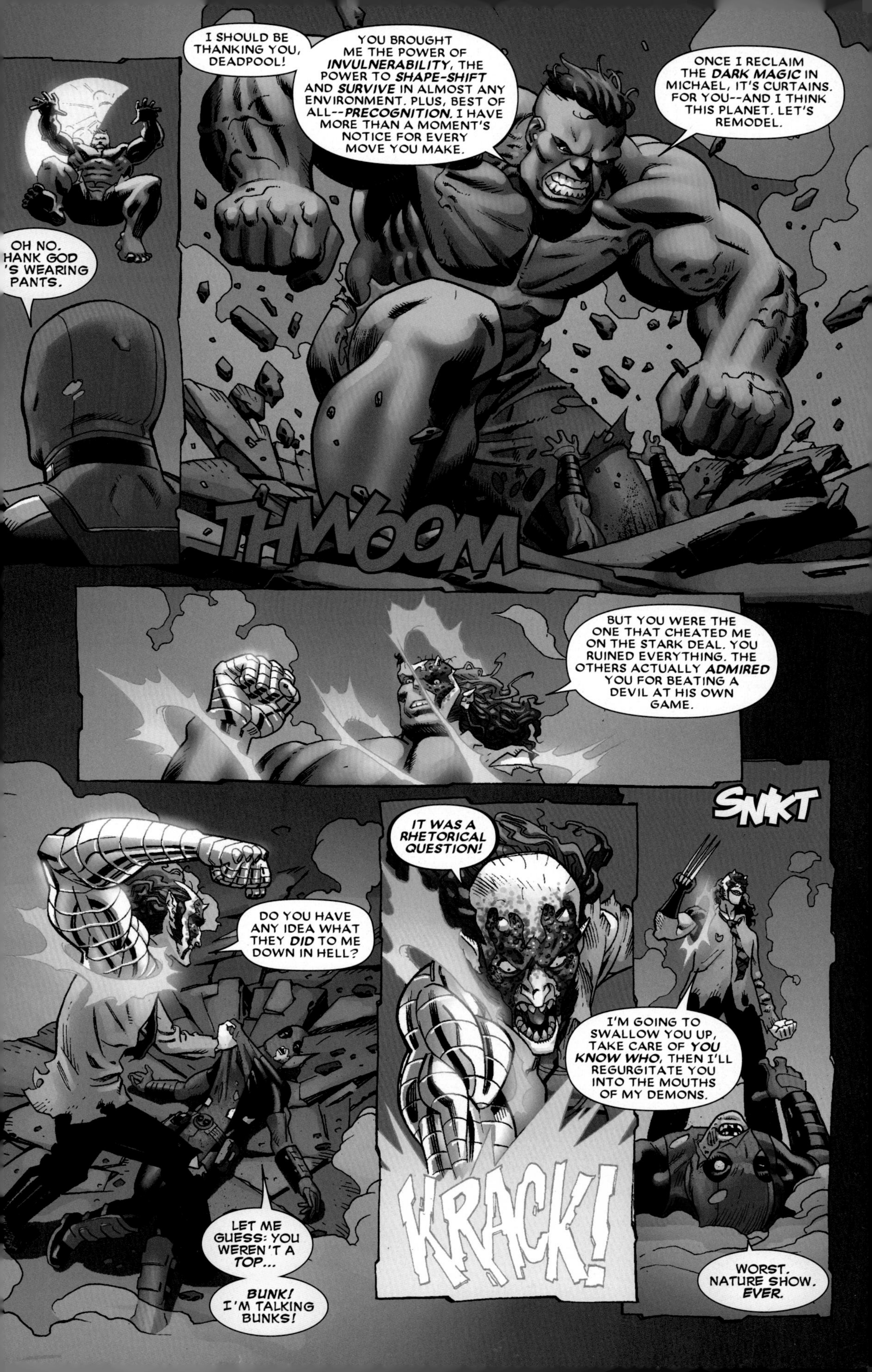

OH NO.
HANK GOD
'S WEARING
PANTS.
I SHOULD BE THANKING YOU, DEADPOOL!
YOU BROUGHT ME THE POWER OF INVULNERABILITY, THE POWER TO SHAPE-SHIFT AND SURVIVE IN ALMOST ANY ENVIRONMENT. PLUS, BEST OF ALL--PRECOGNITION. I HAVE MORE THAN A MOMENT'S NOTICE FOR EVERY MOVE YOU MAKE.
ONCE I RECLAIM THE DARK MAGIC IN MICHAEL, IT'S CURTAINS. FOR YOU--AND I THINK THIS PLANET. LET'S REMODEL.
THWOOM
BUT YOU WERE THE ONE THAT CHEATED ME ON THE STARK DEAL. YOU RUINED EVERYTHING. THE OTHERS ACTUALLY ADMIRED YOU FOR BEATING A DEVIL AT HIS OWN GAME.
DO YOU HAVE ANY IDEA WHAT THEY DID TO ME DOWN IN HELL?
LET ME GUESS: YOU WEREN'T A TOP...
BUNK! I'M TALKING BUNKS!
IT WAS A RHETORICAL QUESTION!
KRACK!
SNIKT
I'M GOING TO SWALLOW YOU UP, TAKE CARE OF YOU KNOW WHO, THEN I'LL REGURGITATE YOU INTO THE MOUTHS OF MY DEMONS.
WORST. NATURE SHOW. EVER.

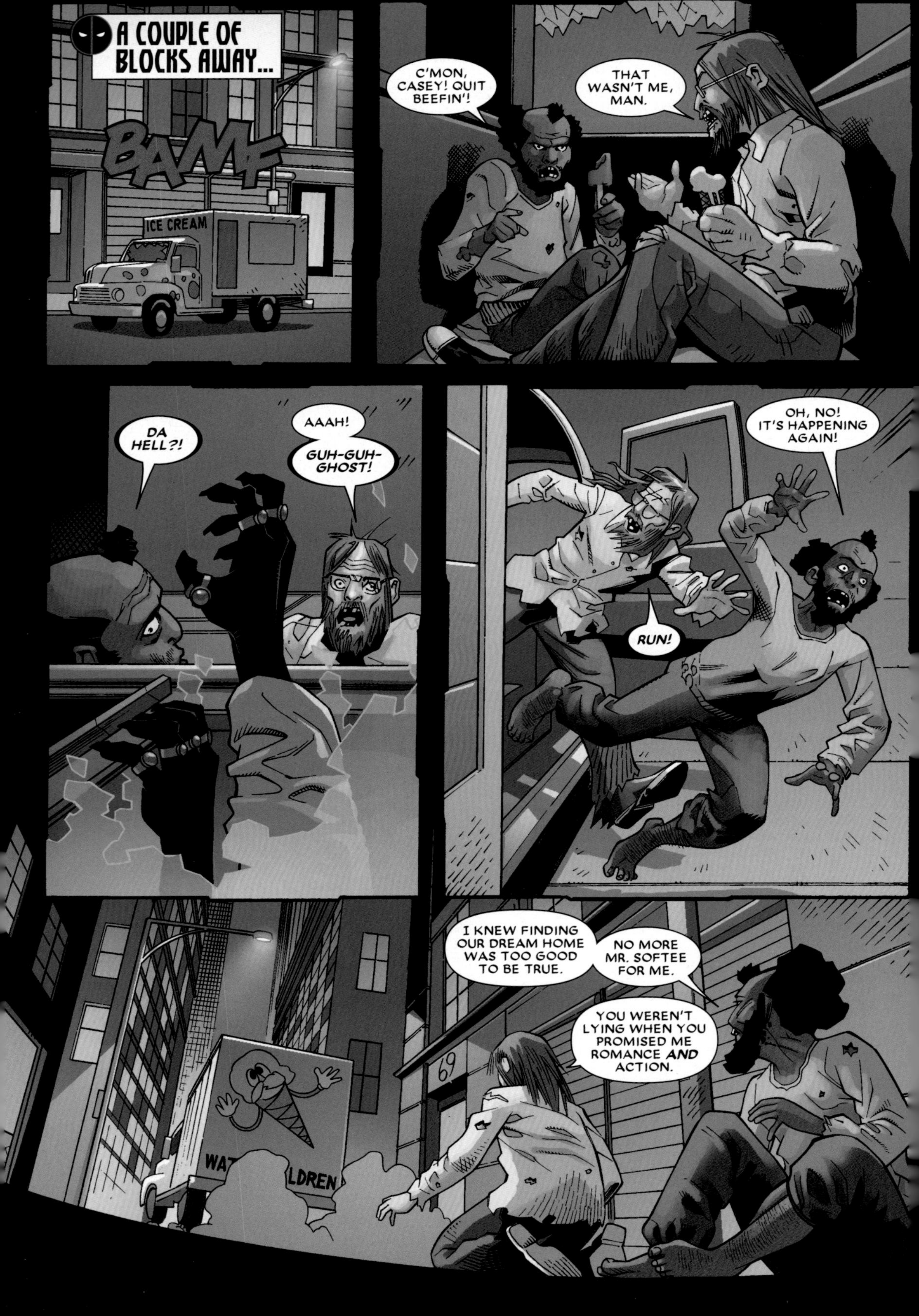
A COUPLE OF BLOCKS AWAY...
BAMF
ICE CREAM
C'MON, CASEY! QUIT BEEFIN'!
THAT WASN'T ME, MAN.
DA HELL?!
AAAH!
GUH-GUH-GHOST!
OH, NO! IT'S HAPPENING AGAIN!
RUN!
I KNEW FINDING OUR DREAM HOME WAS TOO GOOD TO BE TRUE.
NO MORE MR. SOFTEE FOR ME.
YOU WEREN'T LYING WHEN YOU PROMISED ME ROMANCE *AND* ACTION.
69

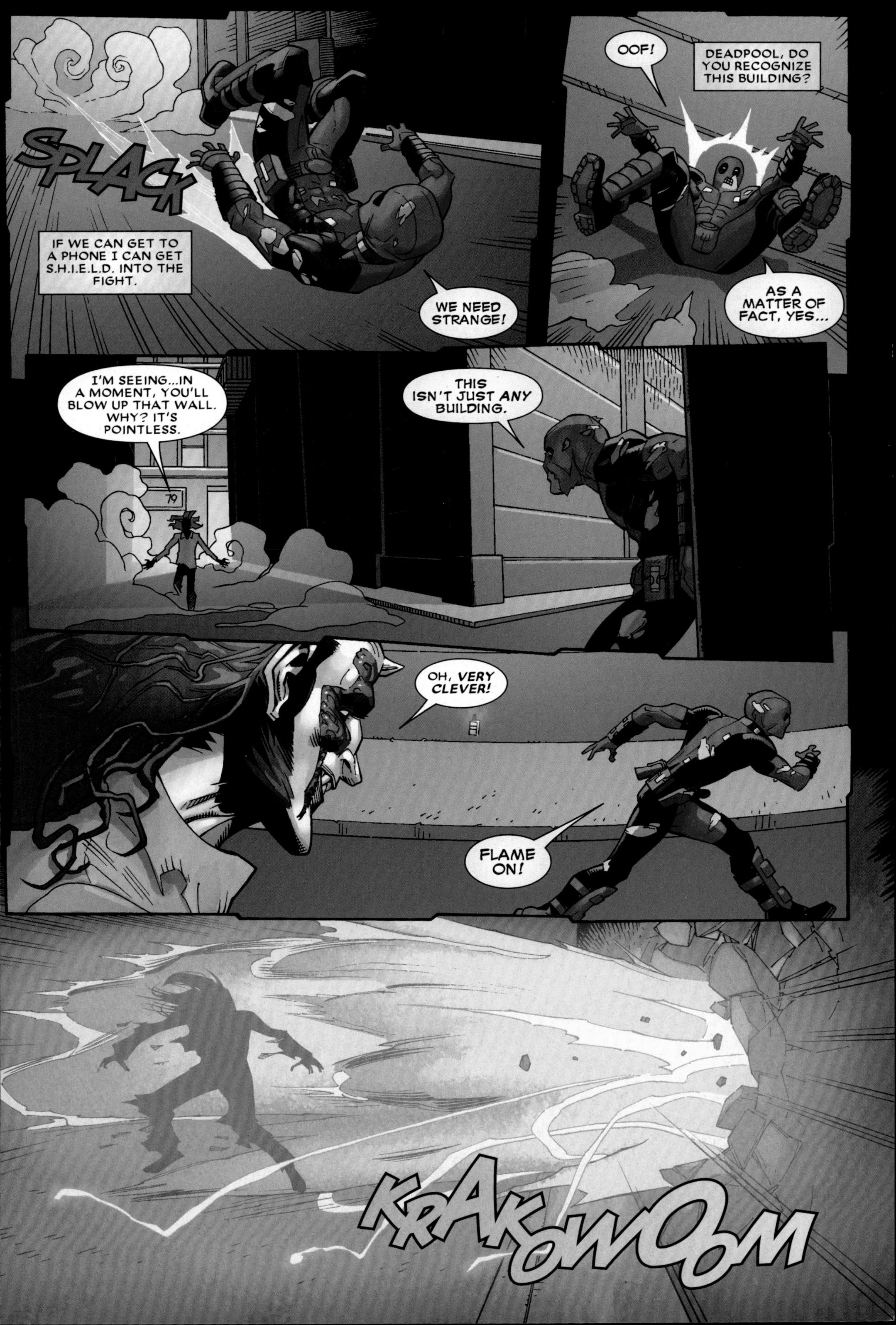
SPLACK
IF WE CAN GET TO A PHONE I CAN GET S.H.I.E.L.D. INTO THE FIGHT.
WE NEED STRANGE!
OOF!
DEADPOOL, DO YOU RECOGNIZE THIS BUILDING?
AS A MATTER OF FACT, YES...
I'M SEEING...IN A MOMENT, YOU'LL BLOW UP THAT WALL. WHY? IT'S POINTLESS.
79
THIS ISN'T JUST ANY BUILDING.
OH, VERY CLEVER!
FLAME ON!
KRAKOWOOM

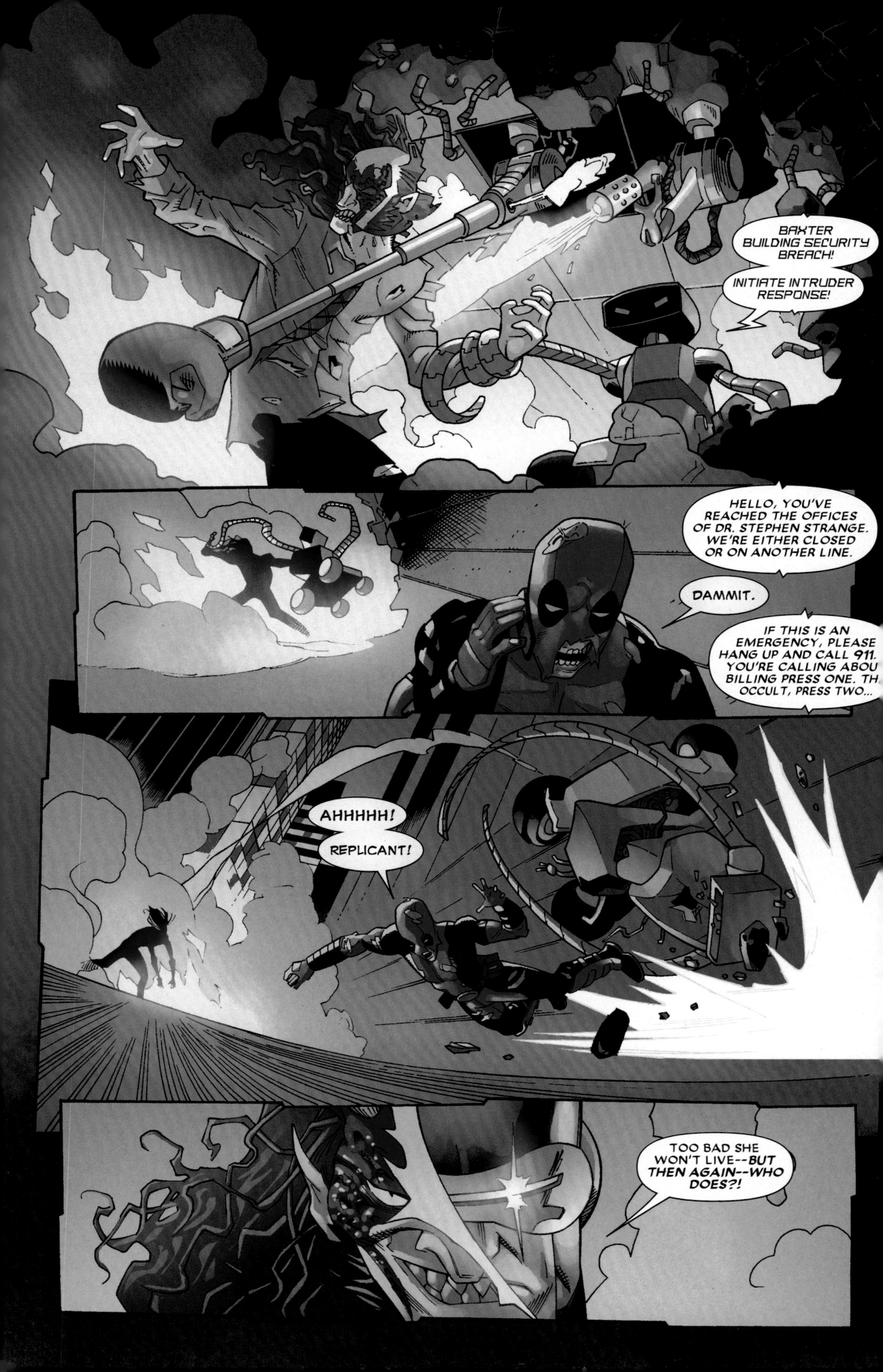
BAXTER BUILDING SECURITY BREACH!
INITIATE INTRUDER RESPONSE!
HELLO, YOU'VE REACHED THE OFFICES OF DR. STEPHEN STRANGE. WE'RE EITHER CLOSED OR ON ANOTHER LINE.
DAMMIT.
IF THIS IS AN EMERGENCY, PLEASE HANG UP AND CALL 911. YOU'RE CALLING ABOU BILLING PRESS ONE. TH OCCULT, PRESS TWO...
AHHHHH!
REPLICANT!
TOO BAD SHE WON'T LIVE--BUT THEN AGAIN--WHO DOES?!

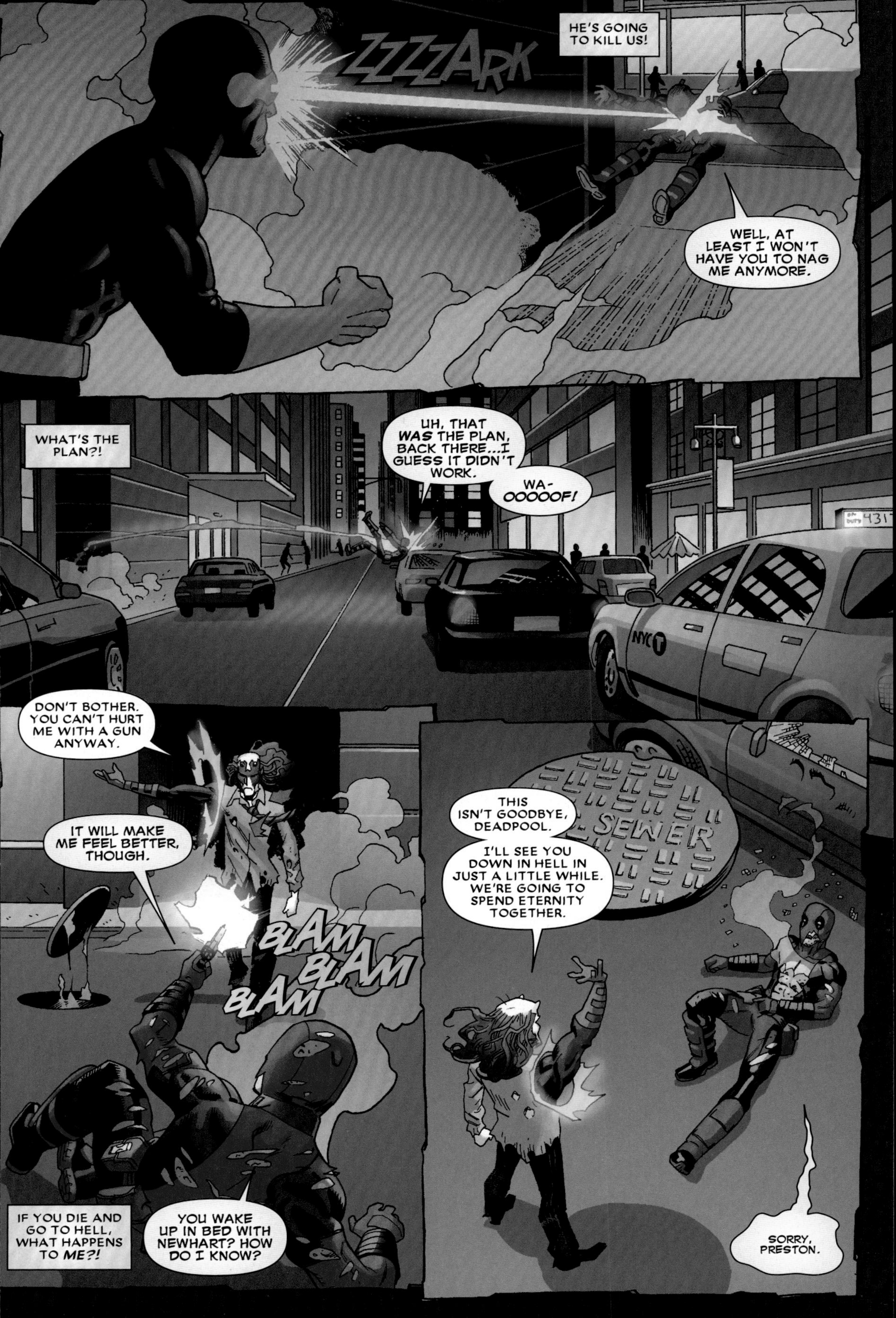
ZZZZARK
HE'S GOING TO KILL US!
WELL, AT LEAST I WON'T HAVE YOU TO NAG ME ANYMORE.
WHAT'S THE PLAN?!
UH, THAT WAS THE PLAN, BACK THERE...I GUESS IT DIDN'T WORK.
WA-OOOOOF!
DON'T BOTHER. YOU CAN'T HURT ME WITH A GUN ANYWAY.
IT WILL MAKE ME FEEL BETTER, THOUGH.
BLAM BLAM BLAM
IF YOU DIE AND GO TO HELL, WHAT HAPPENS TO ME?!
YOU WAKE UP IN BED WITH NEWHART? HOW DO I KNOW?
THIS ISN'T GOODBYE, DEADPOOL.
I'LL SEE YOU DOWN IN HELL IN JUST A LITTLE WHILE. WE'RE GOING TO SPEND ETERNITY TOGETHER.
SORRY, PRESTON.

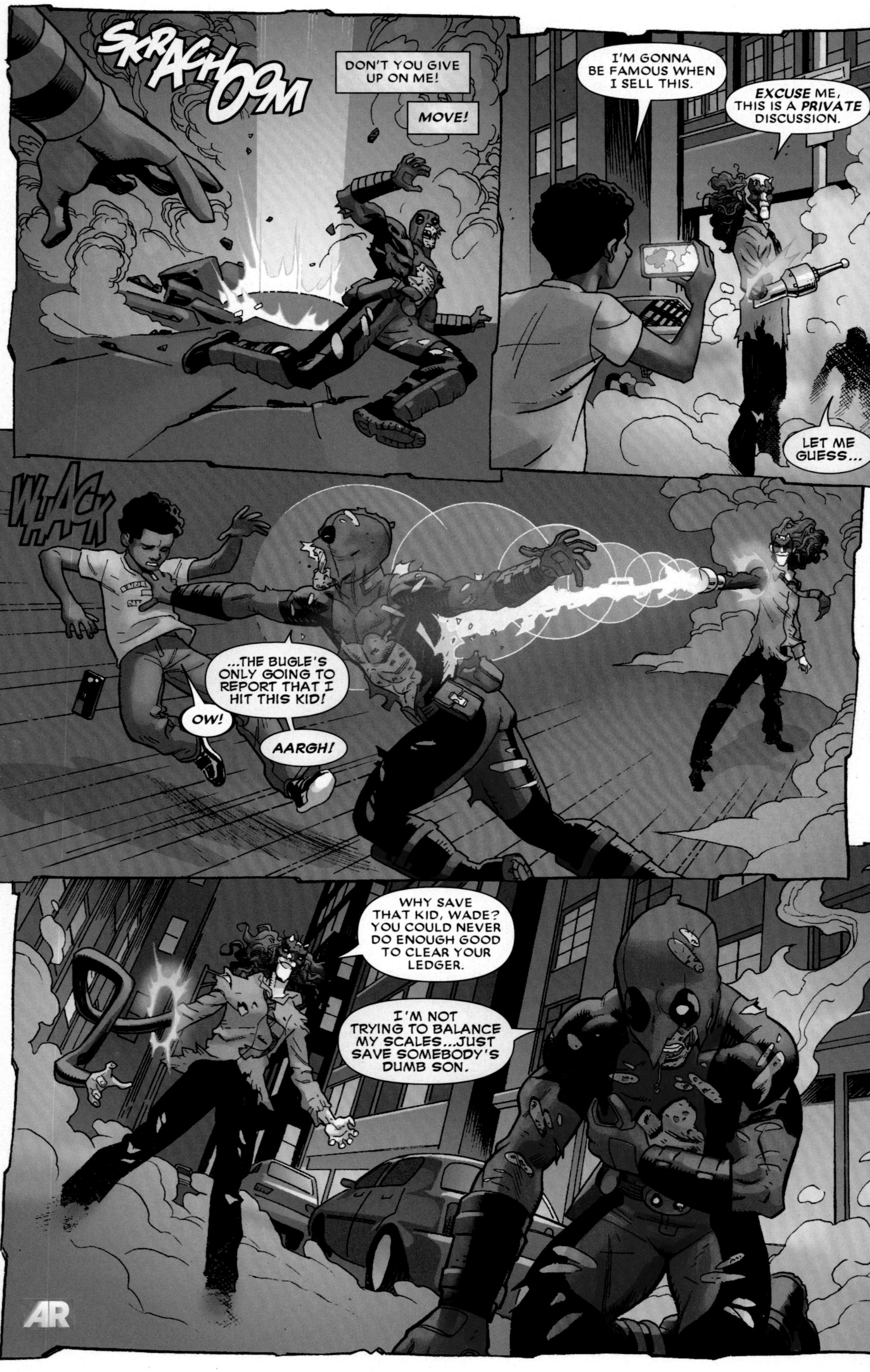

SKRACHOOM
DON'T YOU GIVE UP ON ME!
MOVE!
I'M GONNA BE FAMOUS WHEN I SELL THIS.
EXCUSE ME, THIS IS A PRIVATE DISCUSSION.
LET ME GUESS...
WHACK
...THE BUGLE'S ONLY GOING TO REPORT THAT I HIT THIS KID!
OW!
AARGH!
WHY SAVE THAT KID, WADE? YOU COULD NEVER DO ENOUGH GOOD TO CLEAR YOUR LEDGER.
I'M NOT TRYING TO BALANCE MY SCALES...JUST SAVE SOMEBODY'S DUMB SON.
AR

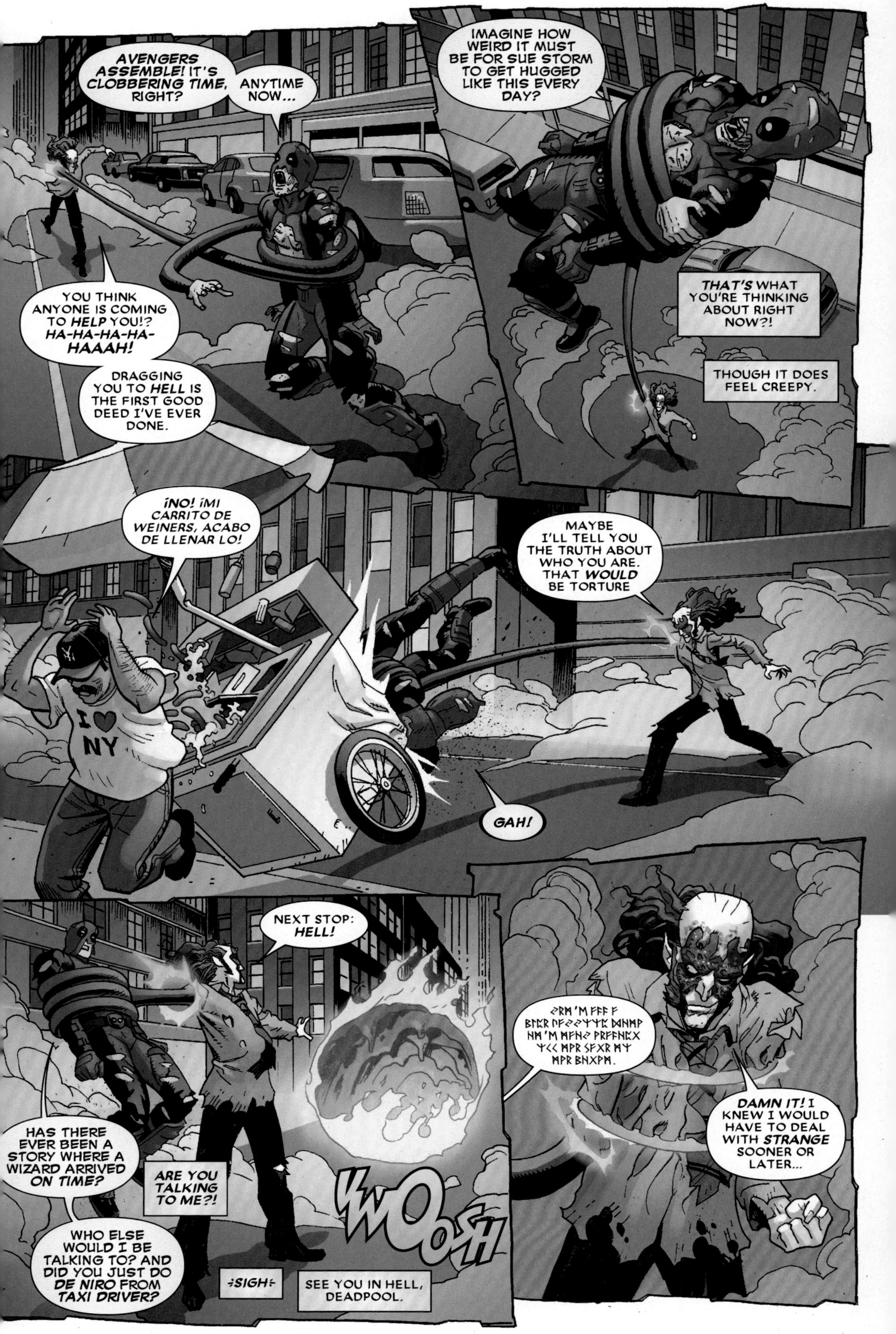
AVENGERS ASSEMBLE! IT'S CLOBBERING TIME, RIGHT?
ANYTIME NOW...
YOU THINK ANYONE IS COMING TO HELP YOU!? HA-HA-HA-HA-HAAAH!
DRAGGING YOU TO HELL IS THE FIRST GOOD DEED I'VE EVER DONE.
IMAGINE HOW WEIRD IT MUST BE FOR SUE STORM TO GET HUGGED LIKE THIS EVERY DAY?
THAT'S WHAT YOU'RE THINKING ABOUT RIGHT NOW?!
THOUGH IT DOES FEEL CREEPY.
¡NO! ¡MI CARRITO DE WEINERS, ACABO DE LLENAR LO!
MAYBE I'LL TELL YOU THE TRUTH ABOUT WHO YOU ARE. THAT WOULD BE TORTURE
GAH!
NEXT STOP: HELL!
HAS THERE EVER BEEN A STORY WHERE A WIZARD ARRIVED ON TIME?
ARE YOU TALKING TO ME?!
WHO ELSE WOULD I BE TALKING TO? AND DID YOU JUST DO DE NIRO FROM TAXI DRIVER?
*SIGH*
SEE YOU IN HELL, DEADPOOL.
WOOSH
DAMN IT! I KNEW I WOULD HAVE TO DEAL WITH STRANGE SOONER OR LATER...

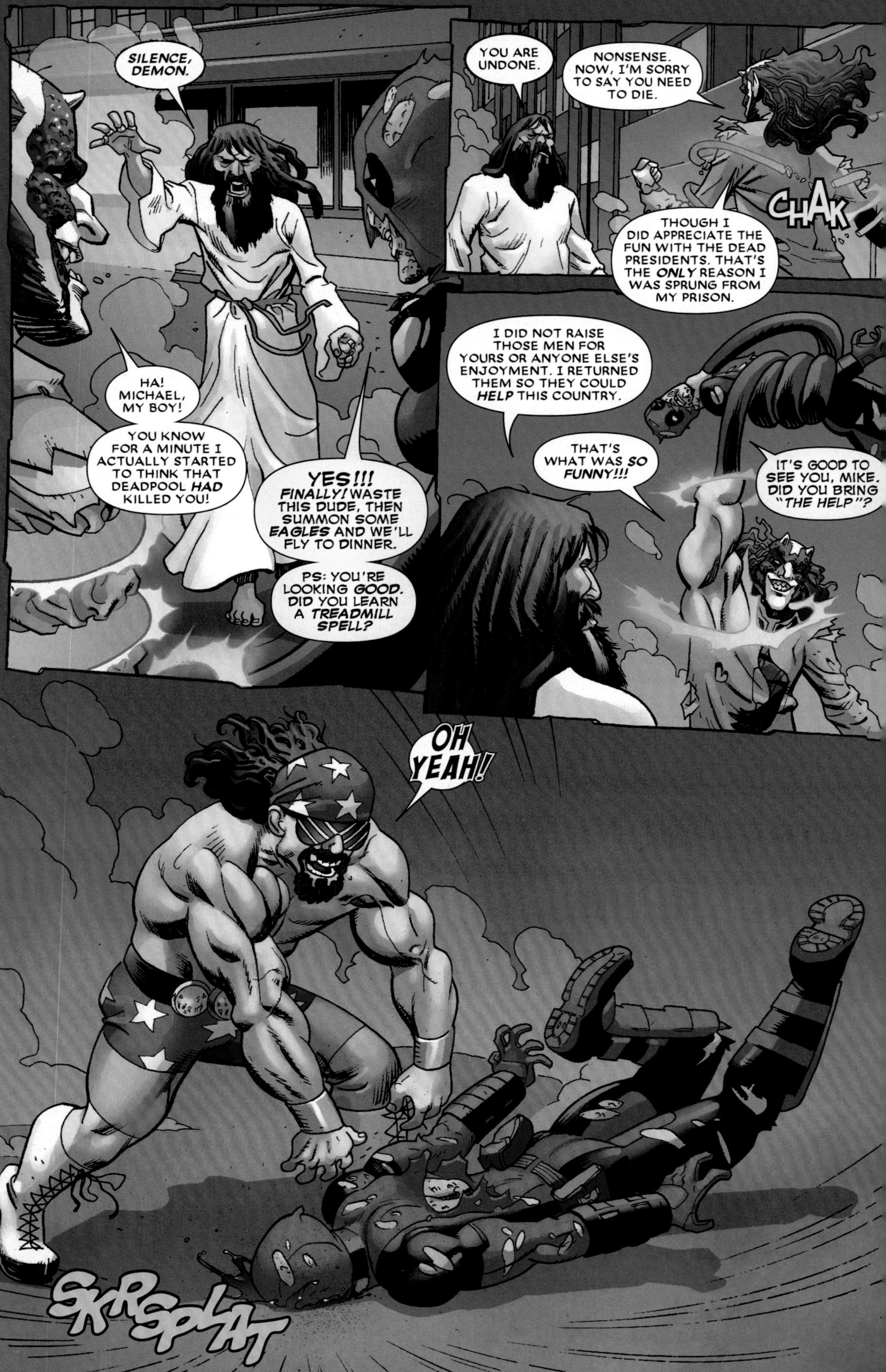
SILENCE, DEMON.
HA! MICHAEL, MY BOY!
YOU KNOW FOR A MINUTE I ACTUALLY STARTED TO THINK THAT DEADPOOL HAD KILLED YOU!
YES!!! FINALLY! WASTE THIS DUDE, THEN SUMMON SOME EAGLES AND WE'LL FLY TO DINNER.
PS: YOU'RE LOOKING GOOD. DID YOU LEARN A TREADMILL SPELL?
YOU ARE UNDONE.
NONSENSE. NOW, I'M SORRY TO SAY YOU NEED TO DIE.
CHAK
THOUGH I DID APPRECIATE THE FUN WITH THE DEAD PRESIDENTS. THAT'S THE ONLY REASON I WAS SPRUNG FROM MY PRISON.
I DID NOT RAISE THOSE MEN FOR YOURS OR ANYONE ELSE'S ENJOYMENT. I RETURNED THEM SO THEY COULD HELP THIS COUNTRY.
THAT'S WHAT WAS SO FUNNY!!!
IT'S GOOD TO SEE YOU, MIKE. DID YOU BRING "THE HELP"?
OH YEAH!
SKRSPLAT

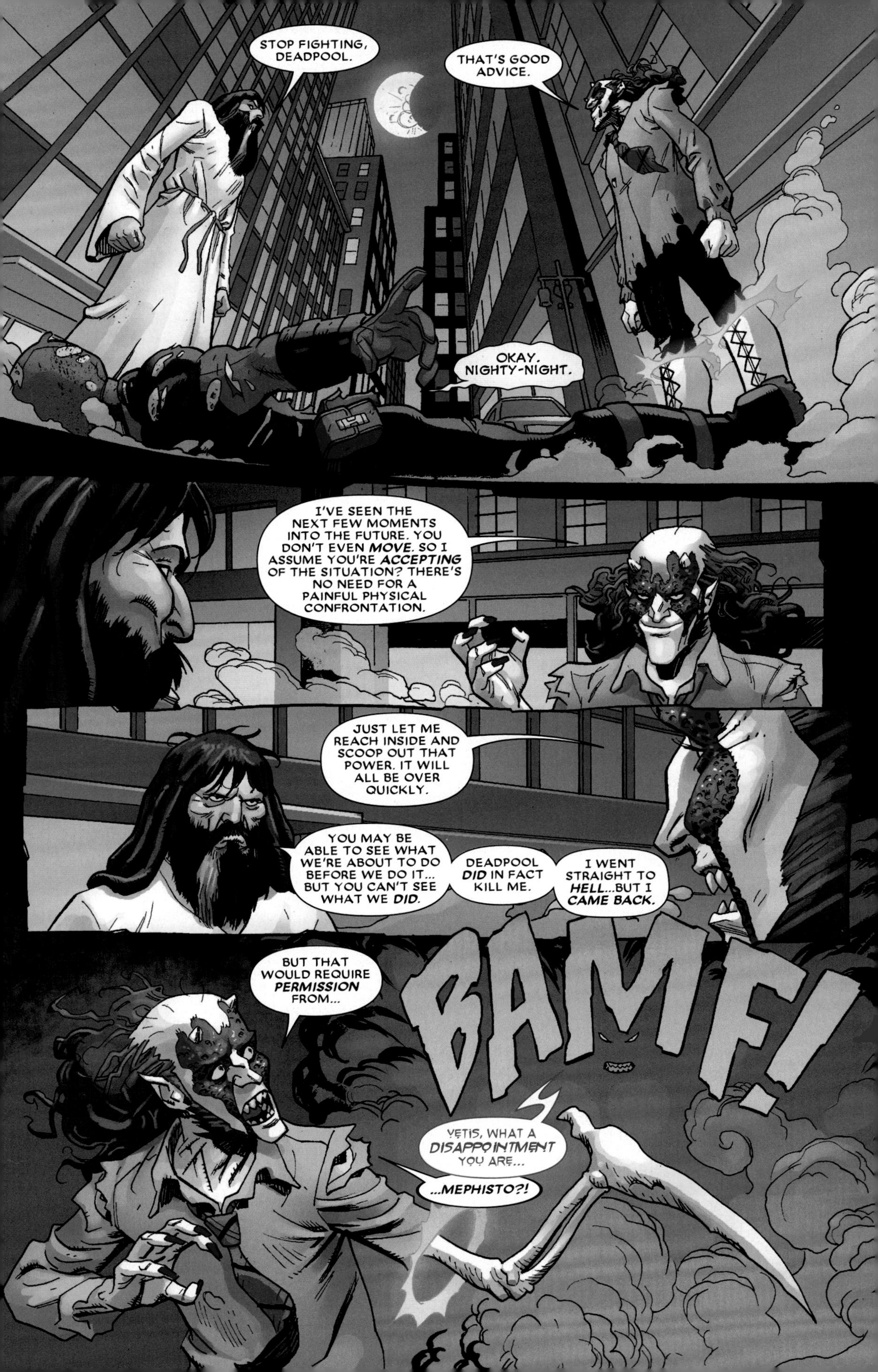
STOP FIGHTING, DEADPOOL.
THAT'S GOOD ADVICE.
OKAY. NIGHTY-NIGHT.
I'VE SEEN THE NEXT FEW MOMENTS INTO THE FUTURE. YOU DON'T EVEN MOVE. SO I ASSUME YOU'RE ACCEPTING OF THE SITUATION? THERE'S NO NEED FOR A PAINFUL PHYSICAL CONFRONTATION.
JUST LET ME REACH INSIDE AND SCOOP OUT THAT POWER. IT WILL ALL BE OVER QUICKLY.
YOU MAY BE ABLE TO SEE WHAT WE'RE ABOUT TO DO BEFORE WE DO IT... BUT YOU CAN'T SEE WHAT WE DID.
DEADPOOL DID IN FACT KILL ME.
I WENT STRAIGHT TO HELL...BUT I CAME BACK.
BUT THAT WOULD REQUIRE PERMISSION FROM...
BAMF!
VETIS, WHAT A DISAPPOINTMENT YOU ARE...
...MEPHISTO?!

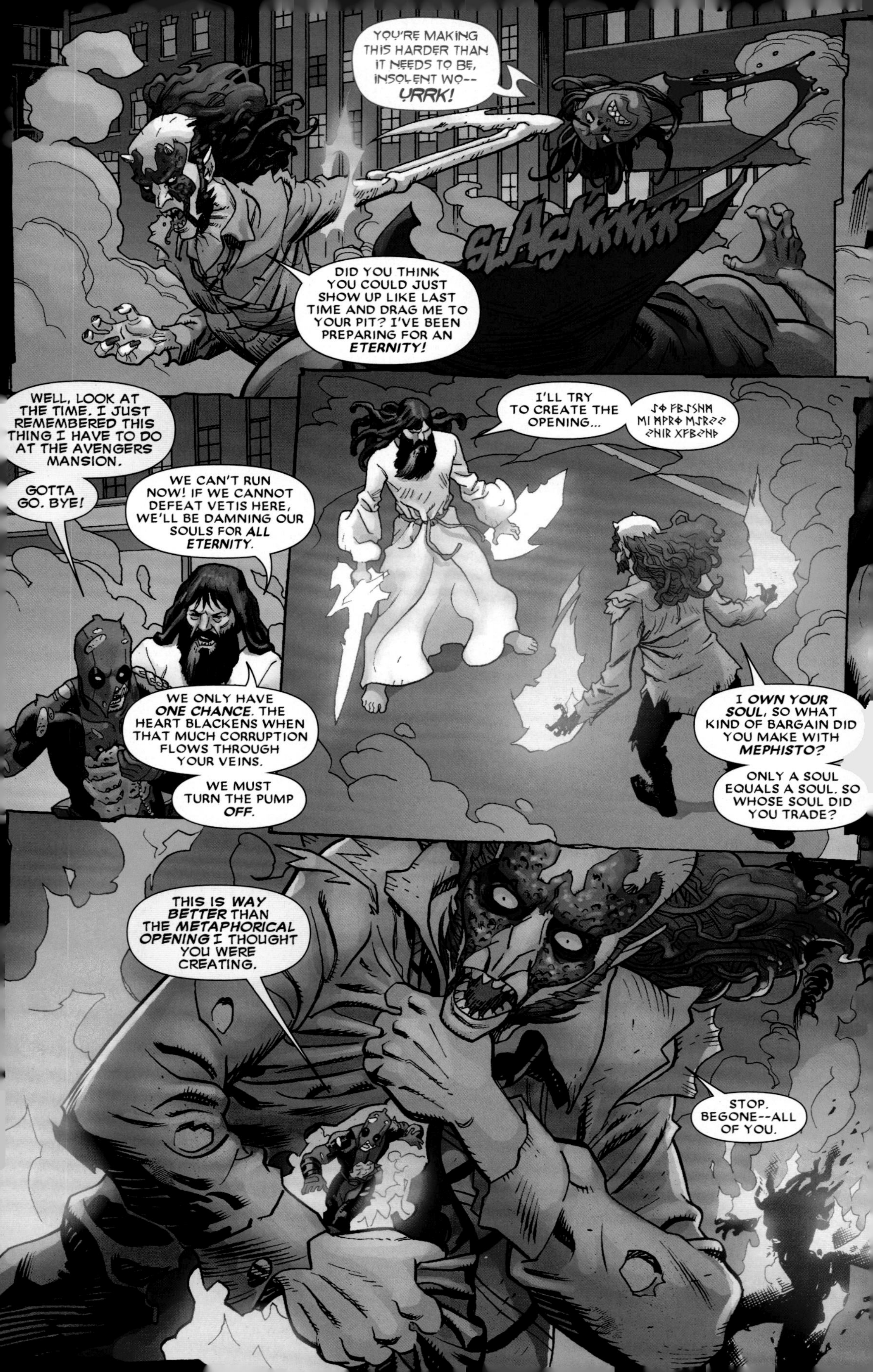
YOU'RE MAKING THIS HARDER THAN IT NEEDS TO BE, INSOLENT WO-- URRK!
SLASHKKKK
DID YOU THINK YOU COULD JUST SHOW UP LIKE LAST TIME AND DRAG ME TO YOUR PIT? I'VE BEEN PREPARING FOR AN ETERNITY!
WELL, LOOK AT THE TIME. I JUST REMEMBERED THIS THING I HAVE TO DO AT THE AVENGERS MANSION.
GOTTA GO. BYE!
WE CAN'T RUN NOW! IF WE CANNOT DEFEAT VETIS HERE, WE'LL BE DAMNING OUR SOULS FOR ALL ETERNITY.
WE ONLY HAVE ONE CHANCE. THE HEART BLACKENS WHEN THAT MUCH CORRUPTION FLOWS THROUGH YOUR VEINS.
WE MUST TURN THE PUMP OFF.
I'LL TRY TO CREATE THE OPENING...
I OWN YOUR SOUL, SO WHAT KIND OF BARGAIN DID YOU MAKE WITH MEPHISTO?
ONLY A SOUL EQUALS A SOUL. SO WHOSE SOUL DID YOU TRADE?
THIS IS WAY BETTER THAN THE METAPHORICAL OPENING I THOUGHT YOU WERE CREATING.
STOP. BEGONE--ALL OF YOU.

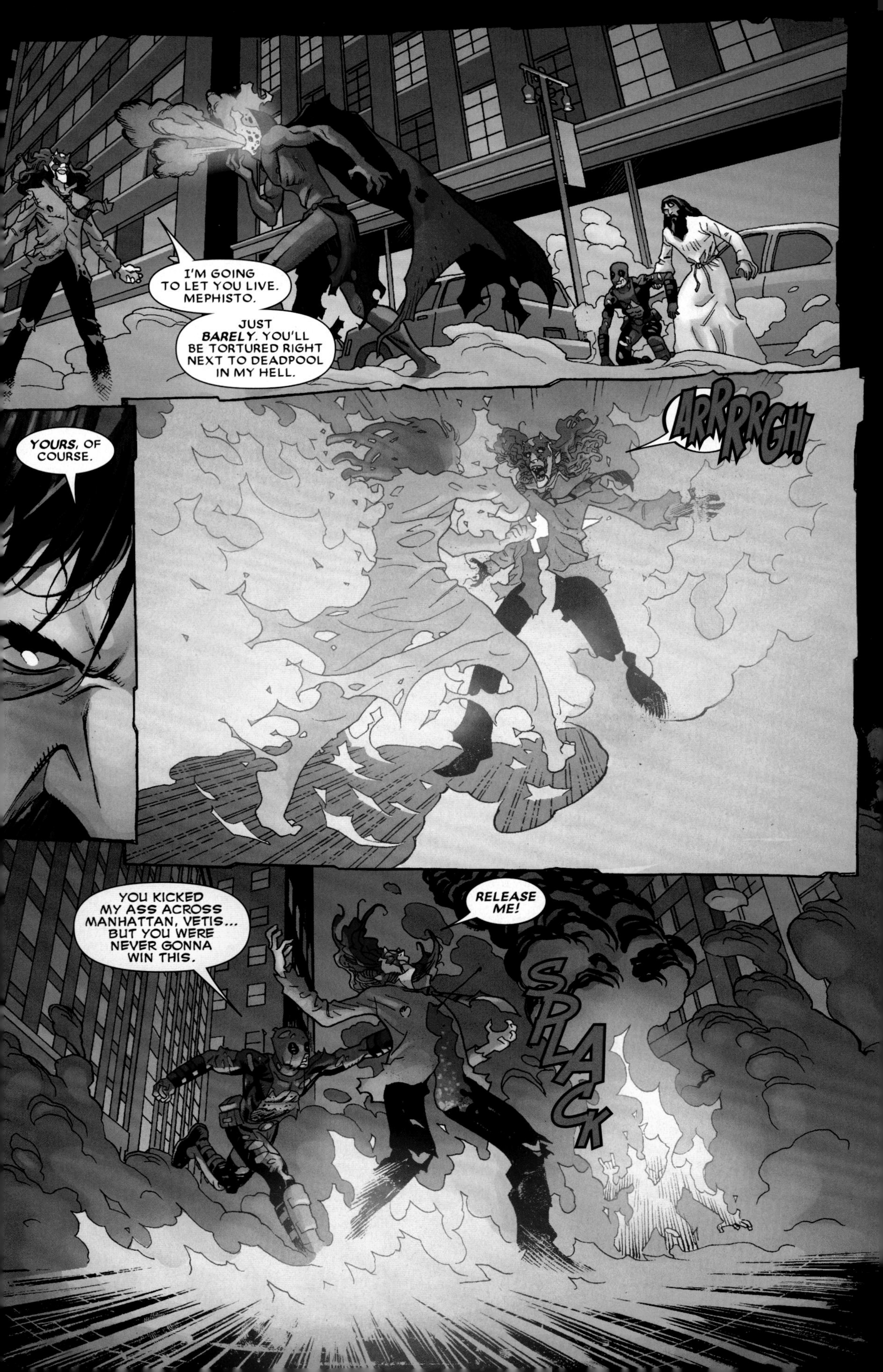

I'M GOING TO LET YOU LIVE. MEPHISTO.
JUST BARELY. YOU'LL BE TORTURED RIGHT NEXT TO DEADPOOL IN MY HELL.
YOURS, OF COURSE.
ARRRRGH!
YOU KICKED MY ASS ACROSS MANHATTAN, VETIS... BUT YOU WERE NEVER GONNA WIN THIS.
RELEASE ME!
SPLACK

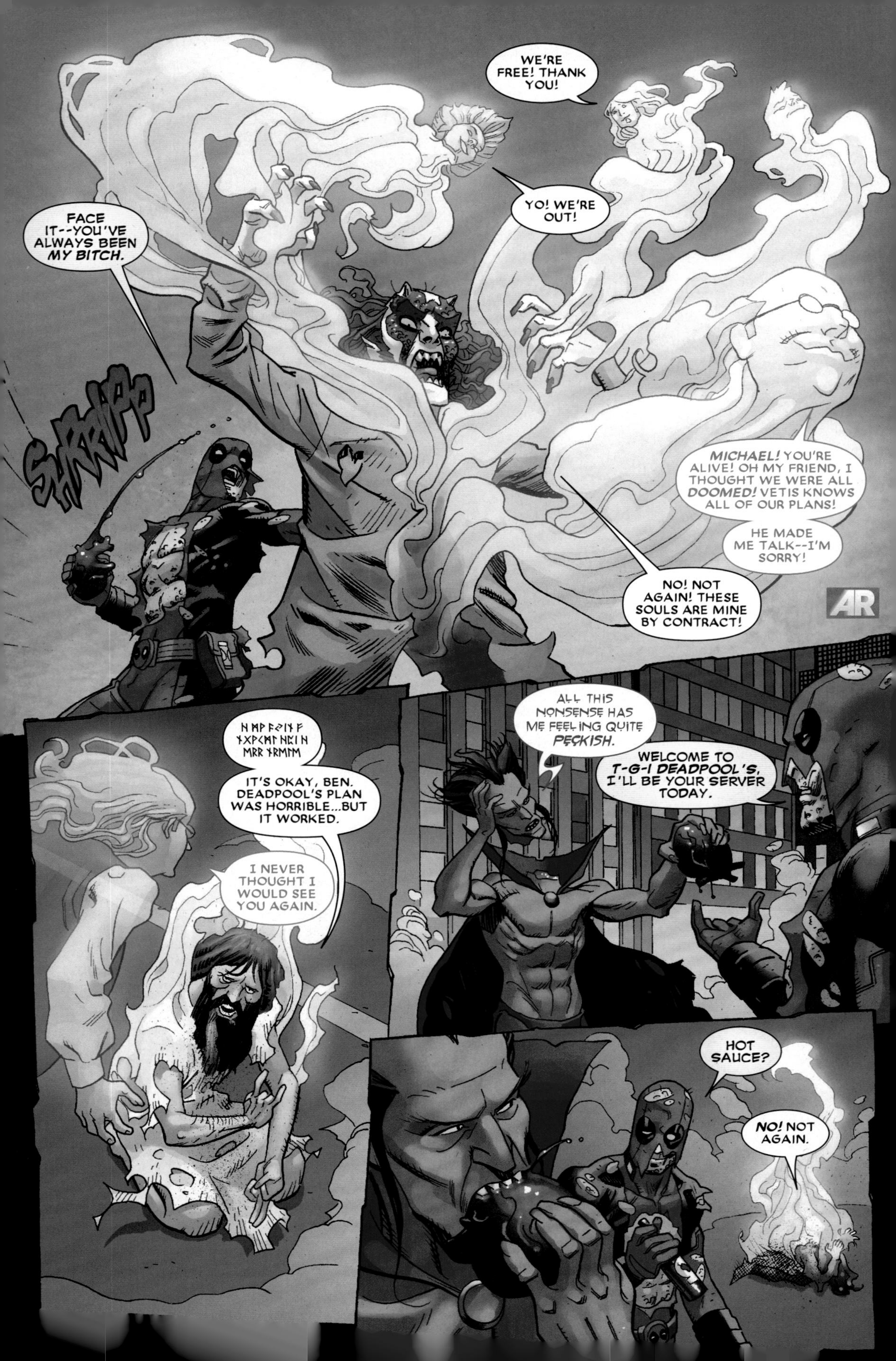

FACE IT--YOU'VE ALWAYS BEEN MY BITCH.
WE'RE FREE! THANK YOU!
YO! WE'RE OUT!
MICHAEL! YOU'RE ALIVE! OH MY FRIEND, I THOUGHT WE WERE ALL DOOMED! VETIS KNOWS ALL OF OUR PLANS!
HE MADE ME TALK--I'M SORRY!
NO! NOT AGAIN! THESE SOULS ARE MINE BY CONTRACT!
IT'S OKAY, BEN. DEADPOOL'S PLAN WAS HORRIBLE...BUT IT WORKED.
I NEVER THOUGHT I WOULD SEE YOU AGAIN.
ALL THIS NONSENSE HAS ME FEELING QUITE PECKISH.
WELCOME TO T-G-I DEADPOOL'S, I'LL BE YOUR SERVER TODAY.
HOT SAUCE?
NO! NOT AGAIN.

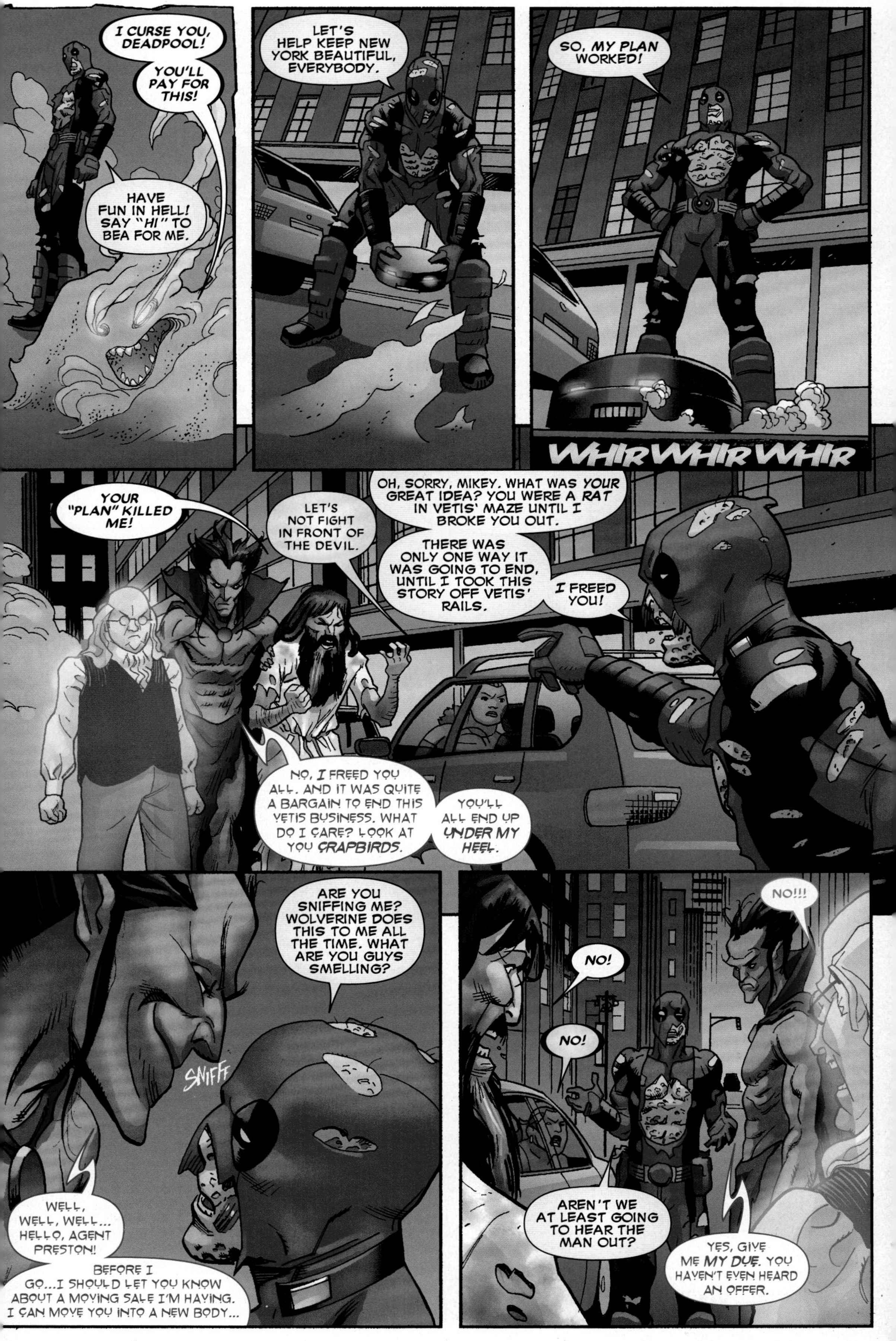
I CURSE YOU, DEADPOOL!
YOU'LL PAY FOR THIS!
HAVE FUN IN HELL! SAY "HI" TO BEA FOR ME.
LET'S HELP KEEP NEW YORK BEAUTIFUL, EVERYBODY.
SO, MY PLAN WORKED!
WHIR WHIR WHIR
YOUR "PLAN" KILLED ME!
LET'S NOT FIGHT IN FRONT OF THE DEVIL.
OH, SORRY, MIKEY. WHAT WAS YOUR GREAT IDEA? YOU WERE A RAT IN VETIS' MAZE UNTIL I BROKE YOU OUT.
THERE WAS ONLY ONE WAY IT WAS GOING TO END, UNTIL I TOOK THIS STORY OFF VETIS' RAILS.
I FREED YOU!
NO, I FREED YOU ALL. AND IT WAS QUITE A BARGAIN TO END THIS VETIS BUSINESS. WHAT DO I CARE? LOOK AT YOU CRAPBIRDS.
YOU'LL ALL END UP UNDER MY HEEL.
ARE YOU SNIFFING ME? WOLVERINE DOES THIS TO ME ALL THE TIME. WHAT ARE YOU GUYS SMELLING?
SNIFFF
WELL, WELL, WELL... HELLO, AGENT PRESTON!
BEFORE I GO...I SHOULD LET YOU KNOW ABOUT A MOVING SALE I'M HAVING. I CAN MOVE YOU INTO A NEW BODY...
NO!!!
NO!
NO!
AREN'T WE AT LEAST GOING TO HEAR THE MAN OUT?
YES, GIVE ME MY DUE. YOU HAVEN'T EVEN HEARD AN OFFER.

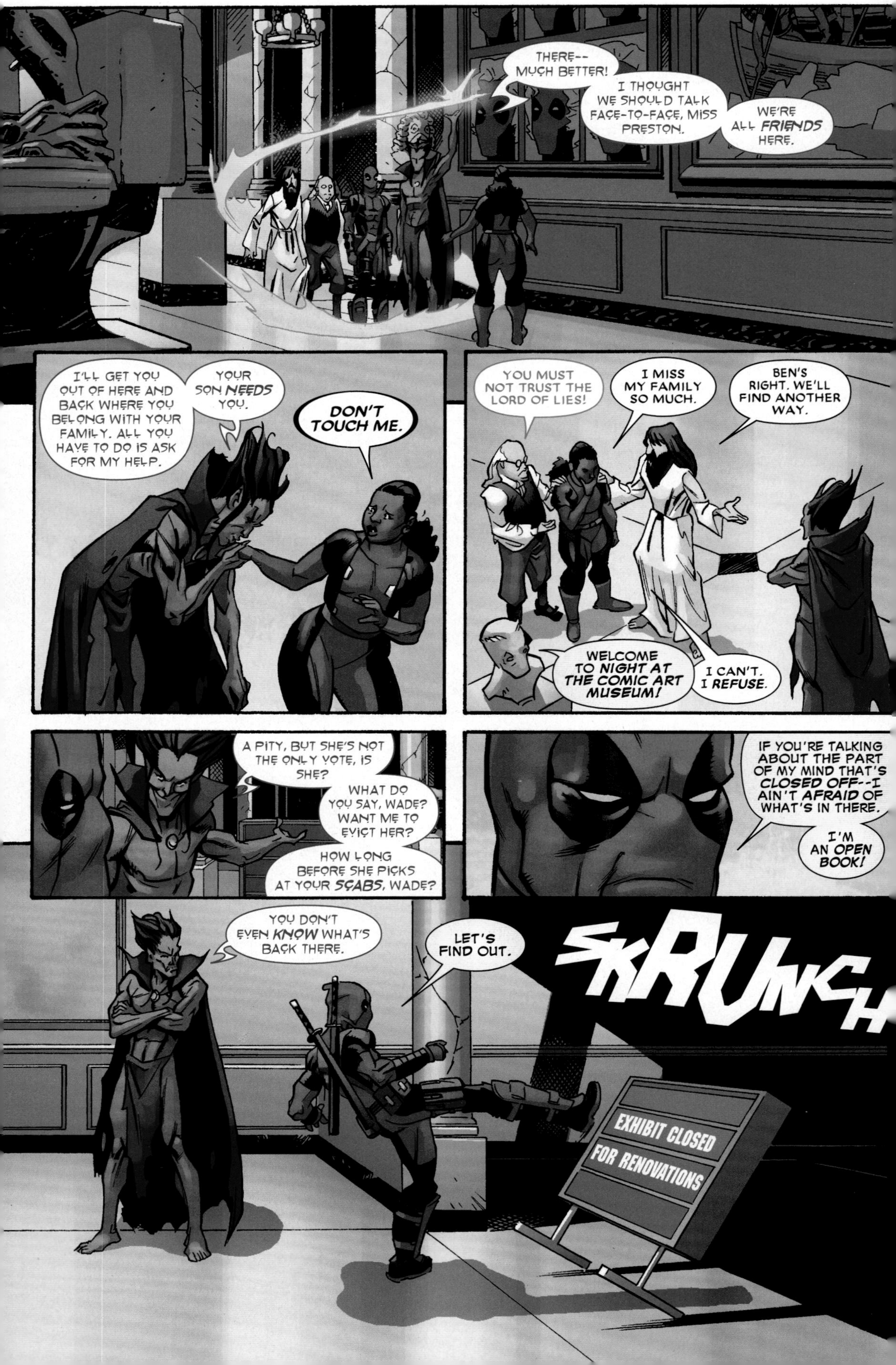
THERE-- MUCH BETTER!
I THOUGHT WE SHOULD TALK FACE-TO-FACE, MISS PRESTON.
WE'RE ALL FRIENDS HERE.
I'LL GET YOU OUT OF HERE AND BACK WHERE YOU BELONG WITH YOUR FAMILY. ALL YOU HAVE TO DO IS ASK FOR MY HELP.
YOUR SON NEEDS YOU.
DON'T TOUCH ME.
YOU MUST NOT TRUST THE LORD OF LIES!
I MISS MY FAMILY SO MUCH.
BEN'S RIGHT. WE'LL FIND ANOTHER WAY.
WELCOME TO NIGHT AT THE COMIC ART MUSEUM!
I CAN'T. I REFUSE.
A PITY, BUT SHE'S NOT THE ONLY VOTE, IS SHE?
WHAT DO YOU SAY, WADE? WANT ME TO EVICT HER?
HOW LONG BEFORE SHE PICKS AT YOUR SCABS, WADE?
IF YOU'RE TALKING ABOUT THE PART OF MY MIND THAT'S CLOSED OFF--I AIN'T AFRAID OF WHAT'S IN THERE.
I'M AN OPEN BOOK!
YOU DON'T EVEN KNOW WHAT'S BACK THERE.
LET'S FIND OUT.
SKRUNCH
EXHIBIT CLOSED
FOR RENOVATIONS

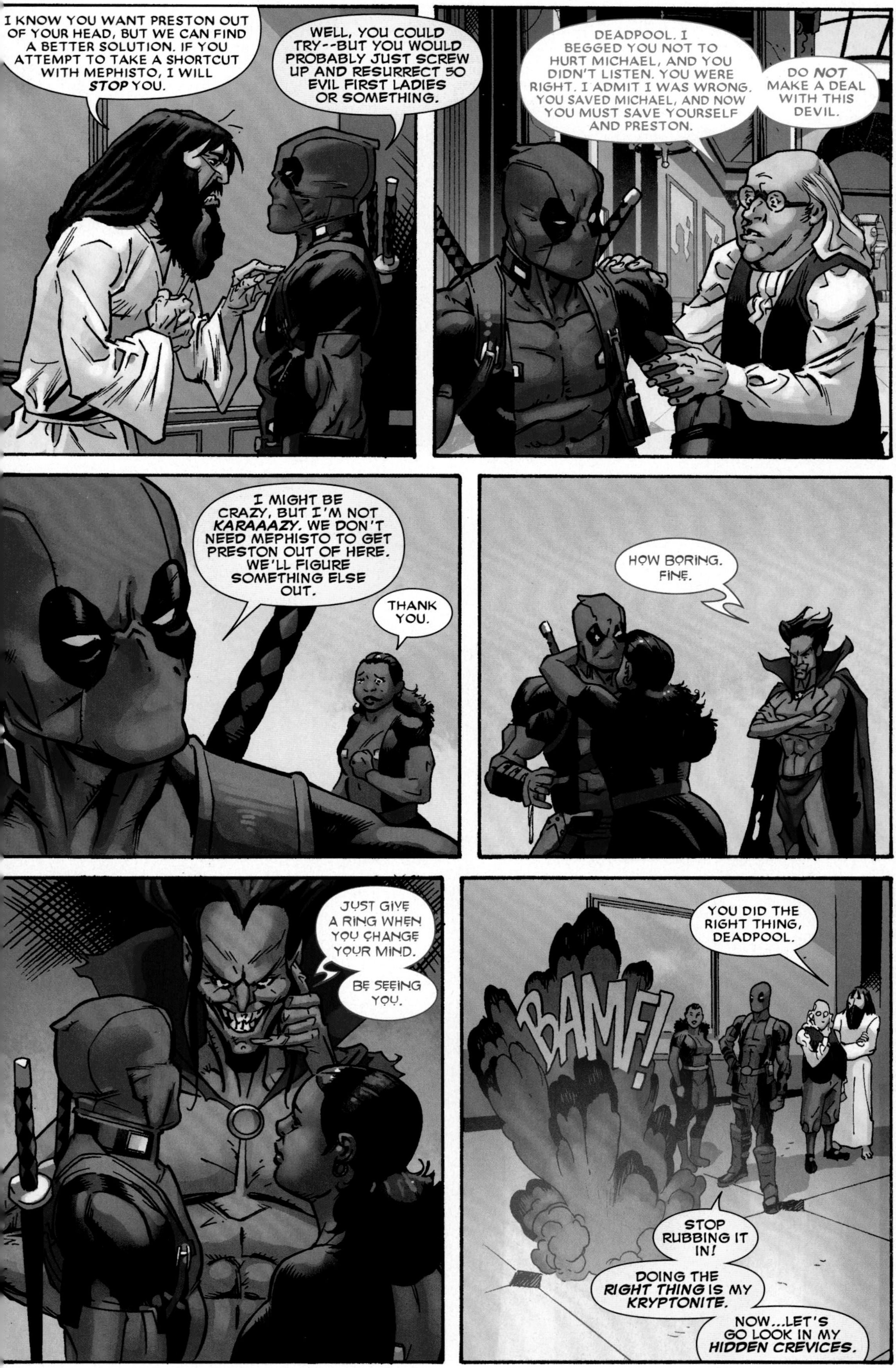
I KNOW YOU WANT PRESTON OUT OF YOUR HEAD, BUT WE CAN FIND A BETTER SOLUTION. IF YOU ATTEMPT TO TAKE A SHORTCUT WITH MEPHISTO, I WILL STOP YOU.
WELL, YOU COULD TRY--BUT YOU WOULD PROBABLY JUST SCREW UP AND RESURRECT 50 EVIL FIRST LADIES OR SOMETHING.
DEADPOOL. I BEGGED YOU NOT TO HURT MICHAEL, AND YOU DIDN'T LISTEN. YOU WERE RIGHT. I ADMIT I WAS WRONG. YOU SAVED MICHAEL, AND NOW YOU MUST SAVE YOURSELF AND PRESTON.
DO NOT MAKE A DEAL WITH THIS DEVIL.
I MIGHT BE CRAZY, BUT I'M NOT KARAAAZY. WE DON'T NEED MEPHISTO TO GET PRESTON OUT OF HERE. WE'LL FIGURE SOMETHING ELSE OUT.
THANK YOU.
HOW BORING. FINE.
JUST GIVE A RING WHEN YOU CHANGE YOUR MIND.
BE SEEING YOU.
YOU DID THE RIGHT THING, DEADPOOL.
BAMF!
STOP RUBBING IT IN!
DOING THE RIGHT THING IS MY KRYPTONITE.
NOW...LET'S GO LOOK IN MY HIDDEN CREVICES.

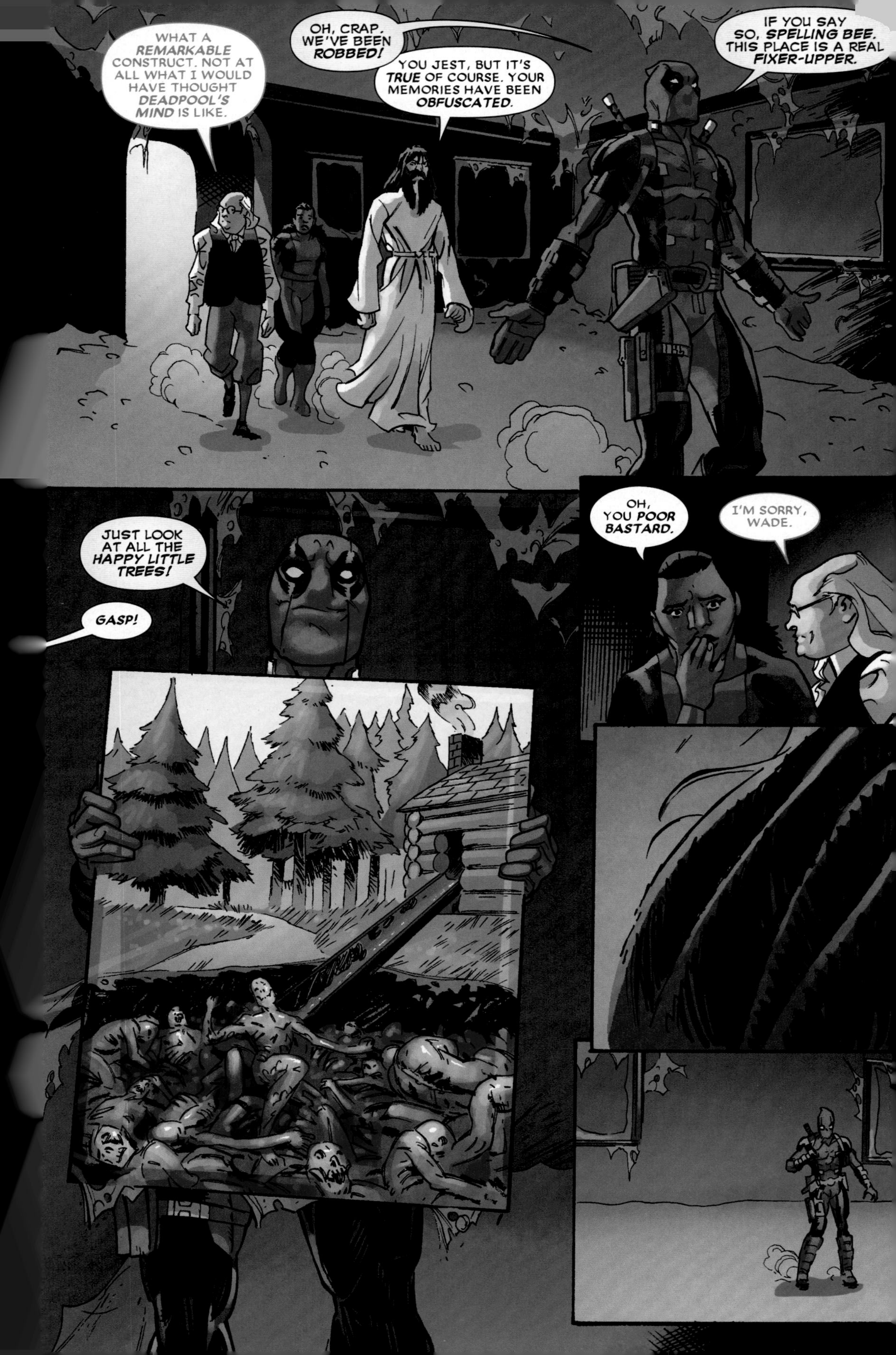
WHAT A REMARKABLE CONSTRUCT. NOT AT ALL WHAT I WOULD HAVE THOUGHT DEADPOOL'S MIND IS LIKE.
OH, CRAP. WE'VE BEEN ROBBED!
YOU JEST, BUT IT'S TRUE OF COURSE. YOUR MEMORIES HAVE BEEN OBFUSCATED.
IF YOU SAY SO, SPELLING BEE. THIS PLACE IS A REAL FIXER-UPPER.
JUST LOOK AT ALL THE HAPPY LITTLE TREES!
GASP!
OH, YOU POOR BASTARD.
I'M SORRY, WADE.

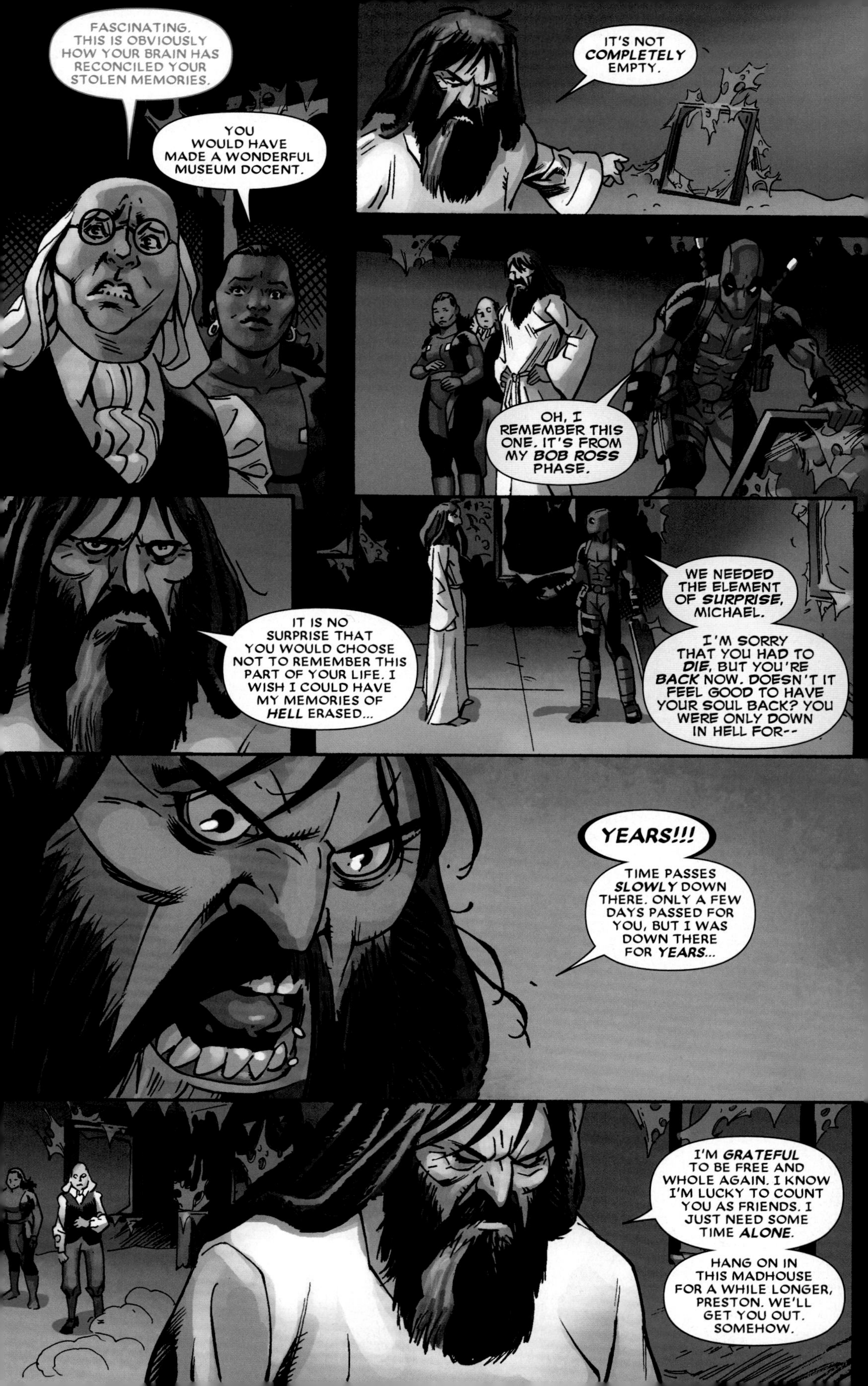
FASCINATING. THIS IS OBVIOUSLY HOW YOUR BRAIN HAS RECONCILED YOUR STOLEN MEMORIES.
YOU WOULD HAVE MADE A WONDERFUL MUSEUM DOCENT.
IT'S NOT COMPLETELY EMPTY.
OH, I REMEMBER THIS ONE. IT'S FROM MY BOB ROSS PHASE.
IT IS NO SURPRISE THAT YOU WOULD CHOOSE NOT TO REMEMBER THIS PART OF YOUR LIFE. I WISH I COULD HAVE MY MEMORIES OF HELL ERASED...
WE NEEDED THE ELEMENT OF SURPRISE, MICHAEL.
I'M SORRY THAT YOU HAD TO DIE, BUT YOU'RE BACK NOW. DOESN'T IT FEEL GOOD TO HAVE YOUR SOUL BACK? YOU WERE ONLY DOWN IN HELL FOR--
YEARS!!!
TIME PASSES SLOWLY DOWN THERE. ONLY A FEW DAYS PASSED FOR YOU, BUT I WAS DOWN THERE FOR YEARS...
I'M GRATEFUL TO BE FREE AND WHOLE AGAIN. I KNOW I'M LUCKY TO COUNT YOU AS FRIENDS. I JUST NEED SOME TIME ALONE.
HANG ON IN THIS MADHOUSE FOR A WHILE LONGER, PRESTON. WE'LL GET YOU OUT. SOMEHOW.

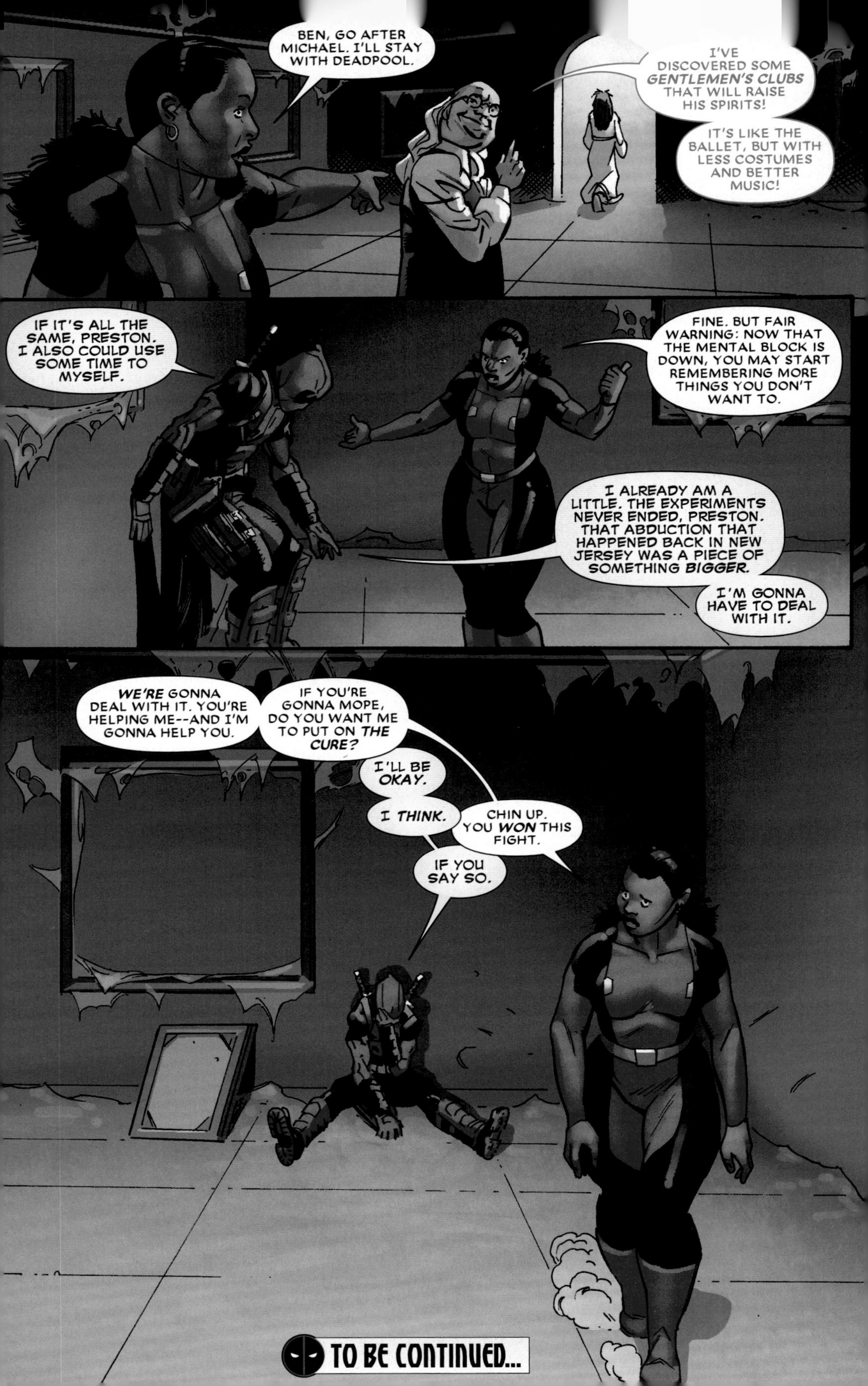
BEN, GO AFTER MICHAEL. I'LL STAY WITH DEADPOOL.
I'VE DISCOVERED SOME GENTLEMEN'S CLUBS THAT WILL RAISE HIS SPIRITS!
IT'S LIKE THE BALLET, BUT WITH LESS COSTUMES AND BETTER MUSIC!
IF IT'S ALL THE SAME, PRESTON. I ALSO COULD USE SOME TIME TO MYSELF.
FINE. BUT FAIR WARNING: NOW THAT THE MENTAL BLOCK IS DOWN, YOU MAY START REMEMBERING MORE THINGS YOU DON'T WANT TO.
I ALREADY AM A LITTLE. THE EXPERIMENTS NEVER ENDED, PRESTON. THAT ABDUCTION THAT HAPPENED BACK IN NEW JERSEY WAS A PIECE OF SOMETHING BIGGER.
I'M GONNA HAVE TO DEAL WITH IT.
WE'RE GONNA DEAL WITH IT. YOU'RE HELPING ME--AND I'M GONNA HELP YOU.
IF YOU'RE GONNA MOPE, DO YOU WANT ME TO PUT ON THE CURE?
I'LL BE OKAY.
I THINK.
CHIN UP. YOU WON THIS FIGHT.
IF YOU SAY SO.
TO BE CONTINUED...

# DEAR DEADPOOL

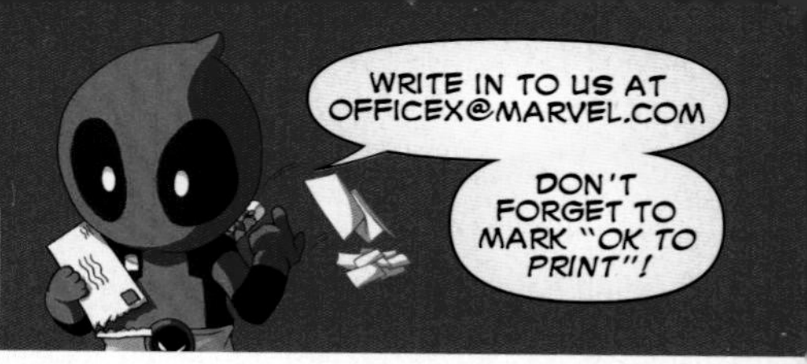
WRITE IN TO US AT OFFICEX@MARVEL.COM
DON'T FORGET TO MARK "OK TO PRINT"!

ear Deadpool,
I've read almost everything you've been in and I'm ssessed with you, in a non-creepy completely platonic ay. I have to say this new series is already looking e my new favorite. Love the changes to the outfit d the Big Lebowski reference. Tell Gerry and Brian ey're doing a great job, and I have a katana waiting anyone who says otherwise. I can't wait to keep ading, especially after that surprisingly dark ending to . Good luck with the rest of the series and with the underbolts, too!

Sincerely,
Kyle "City of" Compton

P.S. Will you sign my copy of Deadpool#1?

ll let those two idiots know that you don't hate my ventures in Marvel NOW! I will be happy to sign whatever u want me to. I'm usually dressed as Wolverine at comic nventions so people will leave me alone.

Sincerely,
DEAD "CITY OF" POOL

ar Deadpool,
Sorry! This is my second letter! I realized today that e previous one had some grammar errors and I was vastated when I found out! Please print this one! :D m loving your adventure to kill the reanimated dead esidents so far! Nobody could put them back in their ave better than you, that's for sure! And not in as any pieces as you either. I almost felt tears coming on most) when you were talking about how you don't get make many friends in issue #5! I can be your friend! d I got tons of chimichangas in my freezer so help urself! I leave the key under the mat so come on in any ne! ;) ....I'll be waiting.

Cameron Gable

Almost every sentence in your letter ended with exclamation point. Unnecessary! This seems odd someone that's concerned with using proper ammar. Here's an example of how to properly use an clamation point: STOP USING EXCLAMATION POINTS MUCH!!!

Gradepool

ar Deadpool,
I can't help but be offended by your face. Is there any y you can seal the mask to the outfit with unbreakable eads? It would save me having to go through all my ns while reading your comic adventures.

Daniel Bellay
"The Guy With the Golden Face"

Go read Iron Man if you want some pretty comic ok faces.

HurtPoole

ar Deadpool,
You can tell a lot about a man by the way he eats his ybeans, and zombie Reagan's apparent failure to even ew them is a no doubt a prime indicator of his evil bent. may also be evidence of a deep longing to be a pinata. ould you agree with this interpretation? I am unable to e a properly qualified analysis as I'm still in the middle of six month correspondence course in psychology.
It is also interesting to note that black jellybeans were rpo Marx's favourite treat as a kid. Other differences ween you and Harpo are that you speak more while u work, and he had more hair on his head. There is, I nk, a lesson there for all of us.

Just a little food for thought,
William Lane

Thanks for your note, I'm so glad you're enjoying my nic in the turn of the last century. Say hi to Harpo, d Polio for me.

Deadbored.

y Deadpool!
I noticed that whilst you were fighting Regan, you d you didn't have anyone to talk to. That made me feel da sad - no, I'm not feeling soppy and sorry for you or ything. I'm just reminded that your old voices are still ssing (good old white box and yellow box). Where did ey go? They were a laugh!
I'm enjoying your witty banter and your fourth-wall-areness, but surely, three Deadpools chatting is more ertaining (and insightful) than just one? :)

hvg3
Sydney, Australia

Speaking of walls--do Australians even have them? Don't you guys sleep in burned out cars and fight each other for gas and boomerangs?

Just walk away,
Roadpool

Dear Deadpool,
After all the attention from women around the world, the Fifty Shades of Grey book series is obviously a favorite to them. But that got me thinking, it is only because this new breed of women have not familiarized themselves with the Merc with a Mouth! So how about a Fifty Shades of Deadpool series? I know it may be too much for some women, but the payoff some of us fans get from our wives and girlfriends would put us in your debt!

Dan,
Reno, NV

Marvel will only let me penetrate lonely house wives with a sword, sorry.

Sexpool

HEY DEADPOOL!
Big fan, loving this undead president theme… gives me warm fuzzes inside. Anyways, as a fellow Canadian aspiring to become a super hero, I'm wondering if you have any tips for me. I've got a mask, looking for a name, and I'm looking for some actual villains…(I can see why you moved to America, with all their weird punks and goons). If you still have any connections with the super soldier people, I'd like to get in touch with them so I too can have ultimate healing powers.

Youdabest,
Griffin Pickel

P.S. I heard you like chimichangas, so I'd like to share a bite with a disgustingly awesome face like you sometime! Oh and, what does P.S. even mean?

Your name is Griffin Pickel? I should be asking you for advice. I'm glad the bullies didn't get you, Griffin Pickel. I'd like to tickle you, Griffin Pickel.

Your friend
PicklePool

Dead Dearpool,
I've watched you slay poltergeist presidents, barbecue an Innocent animal and chill out on the beach with your scabby body in a Deadpool Speedo (ew, gross). When do you find the time to chill out and watch the Boob Tube? Any particular shows or movies you enjoy? You strike me as a Leslie Nielsen fan.

Jeremy Hensley

I think Storage Wars is funny. Watching scumbags pick through the broken dreams of strangers always makes me laugh. People call me crazy, but I don't delude myself into thinking I can sell a heavily used toaster for 75 bucks. NOOOOOOOOOPPE!

Deady

Dear Deadpool,
Greetings from Germany!
I just finished reading issue 5 and I must say that the book is simply awesome. These past 5 issues are so much more fun than the last 30 issues of the last Deadpool book. The story is so simple and yet so much fun. Also it's nice to learn about some lesser known presidents (you don't really get to know about them over here, beside the usual suspects) and the supporting cast you created is original, yet it fits.
I personally liked the last pages of issue 5. This brief moment when you could see that Deadpool began to see Agent Preston as a friend and then she's killed. It's sad but defines Deadpool as something more rather than the fool he is mostly portrayed. I liked that.
Last but not least, I wanted to say that the AR stuff in your book is brilliant way better than in other books. I'm always looking forward what interesting videos I get to see next and the AR recaps are something I'm looking forward to as well.

Keep up the good work!
Nils Schlemonat
Oberhausen, Germany

Thanks, Nils Schlemonat. That's the nicest thing a German has ever written.

DADPÜÜL

Deadpool,
It brings me great pleasure to tell you that you are my first. My first series to collect and actually keep up with, that is. Thanks to you and MARVEL NOW! I've gotten into a few of the other books, like Thunderbolts. Thank you for breaking up the monotony in my routine every month(ish) and for giving me something new to draw (you mostly) in my notebook. Seeing your statuesque form overshadowing my Political Science notes really promotes my learning! OK, maybe not. Perhaps I should try and focus more to the lectures.

Your Easily Distracted Friend,
Stephanie Fehr

Stephanie, you don't even want to know what I used to draw in class when I was easily distracted. Rhymes with noobies and mutts.

Dudepool

Dear Deadpool,
I absolutely love what your team has been doing thus far and I'm glad you stuck it to the dead presidents. Having said that, all the Spider-Man jokes have run its course. Anyone who truly knows you knows that they were working on your costume/character in 1961, one year before Spider-Man came out. Unfortunately, Steve Ditko stole your costume idea and threw Spider-Man into a Marvel comic before Deadpool came out in 1962. I don't know why it took them so long to get you into a comic until 1991, but whatever. Anyway I just want to know why your team is stealing the idea from Superior Spider-Man. Preston's soul in Deadpool's body… Otto Octavius in Peter Parker's body… come on Deadpool, you're better than that. No worries though, I will never stop reading your monthly issue!!!

Sincerely,
Clark Diesel 63

P.S. I hope you defeat Ultron in "Age of Ultron" because everyone knows you're bad-ass enough to accomplish it!

Marvel won't let me appear in Age Of Ultron because then the story becomes unbelievable. There's no way I don't kill Marvel's C3-PO in a couple of pages. In fact, here's how I would do it: sync him to the cloud, and he'll immediately stop working. Boom.

Geniuspool

Dear Deadpool,
After you killed pretty much all the presidents, who are you going to fight now? Also, do you have a medical condition that makes you say jokes randomly at the wrong place, wrong time?

HYGYYour Fan,
Louis Sheid
(loo-E) (Shide)

P.S. Where do you stash all your guns? In your pants? I know you have that belt but all I see is 4 pistol pouches and ammo holders? What about your SMGs?!

P.S.S. When you curse, I have no clue what you're saying! To make it more funny, you should at least put the first letter of the word.

P.S.S.S. (sorry for the S's) If you could choose one Avenger to be your friend (or enemy) who would it be???

Loo-E,
What is this 60 Minutes???
My butt-wallet is huge, that's where the SMGs go, and is also the answer to all your other questions.

Pool

Dear Deadpool,
What do you think is the best way to get girls? And also, how do you cope with all of the girls throwing themselves at you?

Regards,
George Arveladze

Women don't even throw themselves at me out of burning buildings. You're probably thinking of that dancing cosplayer, D-Piddy.

Lonepool

Dear Deadpool,
Why don't you try chemotherapy or radiotherapy for the cancer? It's not like it can kill you (at least not permanently).

Caroline

P.S. You're hot.

P.P.S. Can we get married? I can cook Mexican food very well…

Hiiiiiiii, Caroline.
Let's do it. Let's get married. Come find me at

Comic-Con. I'm going as Deathstroke this year.

DP

Dear Deadpool,
1. Why are you playful when you have a bad look face?
2. Who is the hottest woman you've seen?
3. ARE YOU BAD GUY OR A GOOD GUY!?!
4. Get something so your face will look good. Because all the hot women will die if they see your face.
5. YOU ARE ONE OF THE COOLEST MEN IN MARVEL.

JUDE
AKA, YOUR #1 FAN

Why does writing you back after this note feel like John Lennon signing an autograph for the guy that shot him?

Giving peace a chance,
DokoPoolo

Dear Deadpool,
Will you go on a taco date with me? I'll bring the tacos, you bring the katanas.

xoxo,
Matt

P.S. You and Spider-Man would make a cute couple. Peter Parker Spider-Man, not Otto. That would just be weird.

You know the way to a man's heart, Matt. If the tacos don't work, then we'll katana him with hot sauce.

Del Deadbell

Hey Pooly D, my favorite Merc with a Mouth!
You don't seem to have very much going on in your head so far. I'm glad Preston will be there to keep you company now. When your new game comes out will that increase how much you play with yourself? The comic is dandy so far and I expect that level of quality to be upheld my good sir!

Love, Mary Watts

P.S. I miss Hydra Bob.

I miss Hydra Bob, too. I was poking through the filth on Jordan D.'s computer and I thought I saw something that had "Hydra Bob" on it. Or Hydra boob. Dunno, it was all a flash of ukulele music and mustache recipes.

D-Pol'

Dear Smelly Man,
As someone who finds you generally despicable, I'd like to ask a general question in hopes of creating some sort of interest in you as a super "hero." Who is cooler than Morbius? If you answered "nobody," congratulations, I semi-respect you. Also, why do you have to write to yourself pretending to be Patton Oswalt? That man is too respectable and far too busy to be socializing with the likes of your face.

Hail Morbius,
Daniel Bellay

Morbius isn't even the coolest guy to live under New York. First would be D-Man, then C.H.U.D.s.

D.P.O.O.L.

Dear Brian Posehn,
I've been a Marvel reader for a while now and I, have to say, this Deadpool series is my favorite on the current Marvel Now! roster. This is for a number of reasons. I understand all of your heavy metal humor since I've been playing guitar for 6 years and am influenced by bands like System of a Down, Pantera, Moore, Guns N' Roses, and Slipknot among others. I'm even in a fairly new metalcore band called A Fathom Farewell. Just, everything about your heavy metal humor completes me. Your "Metal By Numbers" video was one of the funniest things I have ever seen in my life. I can say the same about your stand-up and roasts. I am just an all around huge fan.
Spider-Man and Deadpool are two of my favorite Marvel characters due to their awkwardly timed sense of humor. Your personal touch on Deadpool's comedy just completes everything I love about the character and nobody has portrayed him better than you have. You have successfully combined three of my favorite things: Heavy Metal, Marvel Comics, and Comedy.
Another reason why I love this comic so much is because I am in Honors U.S. History in high school and we are learning about all of these presidents. I don't miss out on a single one of your references which makes these comics perfect. Keep up the incredible work and I will continue supporting you as I always have.

Love,
A HUGE Fan
Barkev Chaghlasian
Waltham, Massachusetts

P.S. Spidey Deadpool team-up PLEASE?

Uh…it makes me really uncomfortable that you sent me a super personal love letter to some other dude.

I feel like I should reply by going into intimate detail on how I feel about John Lithgow, and nobody wants to hear that. Even though Harry & the Hendersons LITERALLY CHANGED MY LIFE.
I've been told by the "writers" that Spidey shows up in issue 10 of my new comic. Good luck escaping Massachusetts someday.

DEAD

Dear Deadpool,
Can you edit this letter to make me sound as funny as you? Like say something good but pretend I'm the one who said it? Thanks.

Josh "Diarrhea Monkey" Richardson
Duluth, GA

Way to own the nickname, dude.

P.S. Did your brain get fixed? What happened to the yellow box? Oh well, I like that a somewhat sassy black woman is in your head, LOL. Is that permanent?

Yes!
NO!

Hey Deadpool, maybe you can help me out. My wife is really worried. Seems like for a while there those adorable kids from Power Pack were teaming up with just about everyone, now everything's been real quiet… TOO QUIET if you know what I mean!
She's thinking someone needs to go check up on them and make sure they aren't getting into any kind of trouble. Last time they got up to hijinks with Thor… who knows what could be happening if they're left unsupervised!
Just a little friendly adult supervision--you know--with swords! It would go a long way to making my wife stop worrying…Thanks!

Jordan Lund
Portland, Oregon

Tell your wife "Hi" for me.
LOLOLOLOLOLOLOLOLOLOLO

The "D"

Dear Deadpool,
Your new writers are the bomb diggity. Loving the art too. I am a lady, by the way. Do you ever think about settling down, like, with a lady? What is your type? I'm a skinny broad with long black hair, arm tattoos, and big knockers. I hope you like black heads (the hair, not the face nasty). I don't even mind that your skin looks like a scabby diarrhea anus, I still love you (I have low standards). Do you have any diseases, besides the cancer? xoxo!

Sincerely yours,
Sara Dixon
Nashville, TN

P.S. You must like cats or we can't be together.
P.P.S. I cosplay as Lady Deadpool, will you cosplay as me?!
P.P.P.S. If you print this, I'll get a Deadpool tattoo!

Sara Dixon,
I can't wait to be all over you. I'm thinking of a tasteful shot of me above your butt, or knuckle tats spelling out D-E-A-D & P-O-O-L. Be sure to put me on a piece of you that we can show the kids, and mark it OK TO PRINT!

Who's Your Deady?
DP

Dear Deadpool writers,
It has been a very long time since I enjoyed a Deadpool comic but issue 007…Oh! it was like the good old days!!!! A BIG 'THANK YOU' to you!!!!
The jokes were great, there wasn't an excessive amount of violence (yes, yes I know it's Deadpool we are talking about) and he was his usual clever and caring self: looking after Tony and outsmarting that demon. What more could a girl ask for? Maybe that you finally get him a nice lady that he deserves. Who would make chimichangas, polish his swords and tuck him in at night.
Thanks again:)
Love,
D

Thanks for your letter. It's the first one of yours I've enjoyed in a long time. And what fun ideas you have! Eating big meals, weapons maintenance & sleeping!

Dead

Dearest Deadpool,
YOU TOOK MY action hero comic VIRGINITY. Thank you for being so gentle. Your superhero comics are the first to have ever caught my interest enough to actually pick up a comic and read them. I'm proud to say you're my first! Because boy, do I enjoy a freakish man that can make me laugh. Keep it golden, Pooly boy.

Love,
Monica Mae

Monica,
I hope it was as good for you as it was for me, a[nd] above all else I hope you're not a miner. I do not li[ke] people who dig in the filthy ground.
We'll always have Marvel NOW!, Monica.

Wa[de]

To all the people on the Deadpool team (Poseh[n,] Duggan, Moore, Staples, and whoever else),
I am a really big fan and I love the new comics, I[']m new to comic books but I'm really hooked thanks [to] Deadpool. I like Deadpool so much that I decided to pai[nt] my motorcycle red and paint his symbol on the ta[nk] along with some airbrushed bullet holes. I hope that [it] comes out nice so I can send in a picture when I'm don[e.]

Sincere[ly]
Cody

P.S. I wasn't sure what to paint on the back fend[er] but then it hit me, I thought I could mail it to you gu[ys] and have all of you autograph it. I would really apprecia[te] it and it would make for a really kick ass bike. I would ju[st] need to know if/where I could send the fender.

Sure!
SEND IT TO JORDAN D. WHITE AT MARVEL!*

Let me know what your blood type is, and who yo[ur] next of kin are, and we'll make you a fun and function[al] motorcycle fender!

D-P[ool]

*Uh…Please, don't. He's kidding. (Right? Righ[t,] Wade?) - Jordan

Dear Deadpool,
I love you comics but I think it be great if you went [to] a bagel shop or fast food place to get food without yo[ur] mask on. I love other people's reactions. I don't kn[ow] how you could be confused for Spider-Man. You're wa[y] funnier and a thousand times cuter, in a gross, heav[ily] scarred, skin-cancerous way.

Much Lov[e]
Sanja Petrash[?]

Have you seen the people that eat at fast food joint[s?] I'm RYAN GOSLING when I go to one.

Pool

Hey,
Can I get my email in your dumb book, or are t[he] stupid writers' jerk comedian friends gonna hog up t[he] crappy page?

Thank[s]
Joe Ler[?]

We cut a letter from Paula Poundstone for this?

Dear Joe,
Whoa! Back off. I don't go to where you work a[nd] knock the Harvard Law Degree and fulfilling family l[ife] out of your mouth!

Mike Druck[?]

Suck it, Joe.

Deadpo[ol]

Dear Mr. Pool,
So, in issue 4 you recommended some Pantera [to] listen to in order to make our reading experiences th[at] much more metal. I have to say, it warms my soul [to] know that you have such good taste in music. Now w[ith] that said, I have to ask, do you listen to Rush? I fe[el] it's a given seeing as they're from Canada and so a[re] you. I can just imagine you air drumming away to so[me] "Tom Sawyer". Maybe even slappin' some bass. Do the[y] get your blood pumping when you have to prepare for [a] job? And if they don't, who does? Inquiring minds wa[nt] to know.

Keep on rockin' \m[/]
Brandon Krat[?]

Brandon,
The only thing Brian loves more than Pantera [is] Rush.
Good letter.
You sound like you need a haircut.

Deadpo[ol]

Dear Deadpool,
My class was playing hangman and when it was m[y] turn I used your name as the hidden word and no o[ne] could guess what it was and when I told them, none [of] them even knew who you were. So I'm going to base m[y] next class speech around you to inform everyone w[ho] you are.

Your beloved hero and champio[n]
Nathaniel Tow[?]

Keep up the good work, Nathaniel. I'm sorry to lea[rn] you were put in a class with a bunch of moronic stupid[s.] If I ever needed a squire, I would at least think about y[ou] (then pick Dinklage).

It Gets Better For Deadpool Fan[s]
Poo[l]

# MARVEL AUGMENTED REALITY (AR) ENHANCES AND CHANGES THE WAY YOU EXPERIENCE COMICS!

## TO ACCESS THE FREE MARVEL AR CONTENT IN THIS BOOK*

1. Locate the **AR** logo within the comic.
2. Go to Marvel.com/AR in your web browser.
3. Search by series title to find the corresponding AR.
4. Enjoy Marvel AR!

*All AR content that appears in this book has been archived and will be available only at Marvel.com/AR — no longer in the Marvel AR App. Content subject to change and availability.

# DEADPOOL

## AR INDEX

**Issue #7**
Anti-drinking PSA video ..................................................................... Page 10, Panel 1
1980s usenet version of Marvel AR .................................................. Page 18, Panel 4

**Issue #8**
Deadpool pizza parlor song ............................................................... Page 1, Panel 1
Deadpool *Yelp* review ...................................................................... Page 9, Panel 6

**Issue #9**
Scapie Says: the Ancient One............................................................ Page 9, Panel 4
Behind the scenes SFX explanation.................................................. Page 15, Panel 7

**Issue #10**
Behind the scenes SFX explanation.................................................. Page 6, Panel 5
Spidey & Deadpool post-date interview ........................................... Page 20, Panel 1

**Issue #11**
Review of Michael's magic act .......................................................... Page 4, Panel 1
Radar sense ...................................................................................... Page 12, Panel 2

**Issue #12**
Vetis wants your soul ........................................................................ Page 8, Panel 4
Scapie Says: What happened to the released souls?........................ Page 14, Panel 1